The Money Bible

The Spiritual Secrets of Attracting Prosperity and Abundance

A Metaphysical Compilation to Attracting Wealth
Through Laws, Principles & Science

Compiled and Edited
by
David Allen

10 Metaphysical and Spiritual Classics on Prosperity by:

Henry Harrison Brown (1903) Olive Estelle Robbins (1928), James Allen (1907), Edward Beals (1907), Robert Collier (1949), Orison Swett Marden (1922), Lillian DeWaters (1916), Maude Rockwell (1933), Harriet Hale Rix (1914) Wallace Wattles (1910)

Copyright © 2017

Copyright © 2017 by Shanon Allen / David Allen

All rights reserved. No part of this publication may be reproduced, distributed, or transmitted in any form or by any means, including photocopying, recording, or other electronic or mechanical methods, without the prior written permission of the publisher, except in the case of brief quotations embodied in critical reviews and certain other noncommercial uses permitted by copyright law.
Printed in the United States of America.

First Printing, December 2017

ISBN: 978-0-9995435-1-1

Visit Us At **NevilleGoddardBooks.com** for a complete listing of all our books and **1000's of Free Books to Read online and download.**

Published
by
Shanon Allen
Copyright © 2017

Table of Contents

Book 1 - Henry Harrison Brown - Dollars Want Me (1903) - **Page 5**

Book 2 - Olive Estelle Robbins - How to Demonstrate Prosperity (1928) - **Page 35**

Book 3 - James Allen - The Path of Prosperity - (1907) - **Page 65**

Book 4 - Edward Beals - The Law of Financial Success - (1907) - **Page 131**

Book 5 - Robert Collier - Be Rich! The Science of Getting What You Want (1949) - **Page 217**

Book 6 - Orison Swett Marden - Prosperity, How To Attract It (1922) - **Page 259**

Book 7 - Lillian DeWaters - How to Have Abundance (1916) - **Page 474**

Book 8 - Maude Rockwell - Riches Manifest (1933) - **Page 499**

Book 9 - Harriet Hale Rix - The Rich Mentality (1914) - **Page 552**

Book 10 - Wallace Wattles - The Science of Getting Rich (1910) - **Page 568**

Suggested Reading - **Page 658**

Metaphysical / Law of Attraction Books - **Page 659**

The Money Bible

The Spiritual Secrets of Attracting Prosperity and Abundance

Dollars Want Me

by

Henry Harrison Brown

Originally Published 1903

Supply

"He who dares assert the I, May calmly wait While hurrying fate meets his demands with sure supply." . . Helen Wilmans.

Harmony

There is neither health nor prosperity without harmony. There is no peace, no health, where there is want, be it want of material Supply, wisdom Supply or love Supply. Love, Truth and Dollars . . these are necessary to human well-being.

Mind, body and estate must be cared for. In order that there may be health, happiness and prosperity, there must be Harmony. This harmony is found in merely giving Self, the Soul, its way. Harmony is living in obedience to mental law. It is found in right thinking.

Bane of Poverty

Poverty is the main cause of the unrest, the disease (the unease) that afflicts mankind. Remove poverty by right thinking and all attendant evils will disappear. This right thinking means that there shall be on the part of the individual a change of attitude toward the Dollar.

Mental Attitude

The prevalent attitude is want for the Dollar, belief that Dollars are power. This must be outgrown and the attitude must be that ALL POWER IS IN MAN. Dollars are machines with power delegated to them by man. They are useless without man. Dollars want me! is to be the thought of the

"Coming man." A few so think now and have obtained mastery of Supply.

Demand and Supply

It is a legitimate demand on the part of each individual that he have enough. To supply human needs is the function of the universe. All is for man. The sun shines for him: the waters run for him: the flowers bloom for him: the grain ripens for him; and the earth teems with beauty for him. All would be useless, would be purposeless but for him. When he ceases to be, there is no use for the universe or anything in it. Without Man these are virtually nonexistent. Man alone gives a meaning, a use. a value, a purpose to the universe.

There is enough in the Universal One from which all things materialize, for each one to have enough to meet all desires without robbing any. Infinite Supply is all about us and yet there is want. Whose the fault? Not of The One. It is in ourselves. We have not known how to claim, nor have we claimed our own.

Law of Supply

The law is simple and it is laid down by the greatest political economist as well as the greatest Mental Scientist the world has in its historic records. He was not a theologian, neither did he deal with questions of a future life, as many seem to think: he was a sociologist and a socialist. He dealt with questions of "the life that now is." His name was Jesus. He gave the Law thus: "Seek first the Kingdom of God and his righteousness. and all things shall be added unto you."

Study the Law

Analyze the Law thus: . . "Kingdom of God?" Where? "Within you." "God is Spirit," he said. "The Kingdom of God'" is then in the Soul. It is the Ego or Soul of man. Know thyself as Soul: know thyself as Spirit . . this is the Law. Live rightly, is the meaning of "his righteousness." Live in accord with your sense of right: obey your own conscience. Then all things shall be yours. Things of whatever kind, of all kinds, are manifestations of the One Substance.

Things are, like yourself, manifestations of the One God. Dollars are things. Dollars are manifestations of the One God.

The Law is Simple

Plain directions, these: Live true to self; live spiritually; give the first place in your thought to the eternal, from which things come and then all things will come to you at need. "First?" Yes! Not things first, but that mental condition which controls things. Not Dollars first, but that mental attitude which attracts Dollars.

I Trust Myself

That mental condition is Faith in Self as a manifestation of Omnipotence, Faith in Self as a manifestation of the All-Good, Faith in the Universe as Justice, Faith in the Universal One as entirely Good, Faith in the Life yon are, to draw its necessary Supply of things demanded for its highest expression. Then let things come. This is all, but it is . . God. This is the "strait gate." Few there be that enter in, but all may.

Things are Second

Few place things "second." Dollars, position, influence, show, . . these, in common thought, come "first." But these are results of Power. First become one with the Power, become the Power, and these desired things will come. The ordinary process of business, the customary method of thinking, is to be reversed. Think from inward Power, think from Being.

Be Master

You will then be the Master and things will take their right place. Become "one with God" by recognizing Him as King in your Soul. Listen to Him in the edicts of your Soul. Say, as you thus become negative to the Higher in you, "Now, God, do your work your way! and it will be done satisfactorily to me." No one can fail when he assumes this attitude of Love and Trust. It would be an impotent God, and therefore no God, that did not work when these conditions are made.

Poverty: How Cured

Poverty is a mental condition. It can be cured only by the Affirmation of Power to cure: . . I AM part of the One and, in the One, possess all. I possess all! Affirm this and patiently wait for the manifestation. You have sown the thought-seed, now, like the rancher, wait for the sprouting and the harvest. It can never fail you when, like him, you trust.

Cure of Poverty

Repeat this Affirmation, no matter what the appearances. No matter if hungry, houseless and alone, affirm: . . God is my Supply. My Supply is Infinite. Dollars want me! Trust implicitly in the inviolable Law of Cause and Effect. You are

Cause: Supply is the Effect that must follow your Affirmation.

"As Ye Sow So Shall Ye Reap"

In the past, you have sown poverty seeds, and are now reaping the crop. You do not enjoy this harvest. Sow, amid these results of previous sowing, Plenty-seeds and Plenty will come. Supply is yours when you sow Supply-seeds. Sow, no matter how seemingly black the conditions. The seeds have God-in-them and cannot fail.

Affirmations for Use

MY SUPPLY IS INFINITE! For God is my Supply. Supply can never fail me. Make this your Affirmation and hold it. HOLD IT.

Supply is Sure

The Law of Supply is as sure as gravity. In this Affirmation, All is Mine! Dollars want me I you have repolarized your aura. You have changed your vibrations and you will draw, as the magnet draws the needle, all you can use. Try it! Never let go of your trust that Dollars, or that for which they stand, will come. Thy Kingdom, O Soul, has come and thy will is done for God and Soul are One.

"All is mine; 'tis but by asking: Ere I make my silent plea Life unlocks her richest treasures For my waiting eyes to see."

Opulence

You conquer fate by thought. If you think the fatal thought of men and institutions, you need never pull the trigger. The consequences of thinking inevitably follow. . . Carlyle.

The Dollar Side

Personal ideals, of necessity. must differ, yet, since money represents objective power, its consideration must enter as a factor into every ideal of success. Money represents Supply. It stands in our thought, for food, clothing and shelter; for books, pictures and companionship; for enjoyment, unfoldment and expression.

Material Supply is a necessity of Life. The Dollar is the concrete representative of this necessity. But the Dollar also means opportunity for the realization of high ideals.

The individual must be free and, until the necessities of life are assured, he is not free. Personal Liberty

Thus the Dollar stands for INDIVIDUAL LIBERTY. Personal liberty finds its basis in pecuniary independence. Financial independence and personal liberty bear very largely the relation of cause and effect. We can almost say that in the popular mind the Dollar confers liberty. In Soul Culture, a mental attitude of superiority to the Dollar results in personal liberty. There is no liberty to him who feels himself limited by the want of the Dollar.

Debt is one of the most tyrannical of masters. Mackay well says: . .

"The debtor is ever a shame faced dog With his creditor's name on his collar."

There can be no liberty to him who feels the slavery of debt.

Ideals of Success

Into your ideal of Success, therefore, there must be firmly builded this ideal of pecuniary independence.

This independence does not lie in freedom from debt, neither does it lie in large bank accounts nor the possession of property. Monetary success and personal liberty do not go hand in hand. Indeed the average man of wealth is the veriest slave, enslaved to the necessities that his monetary possessions involve, and a worse slave to his fears.

What is Success

Success lies in the mental ATTITUDE THAT ARISES FROM THAT SENSE OF PERSONAL POWER WHICH MEETS EVERY CONDITION WITHOUT ANXIETY.

That cannot be called success which results in ill health and unhappiness, unrest or fear. Eliminate these from your ideal and you have, as a necessary concomitant of success, financial ease.

The New Thought

In the old competitive thought men sought business and wanted the dollar. Under the New Thought, it is: "Seek first the kingdom of God and its right living and all things necessary to my happiness will be added to me." The Soul has only to exercise its drawing power. When the conscious mind lets itself be led or drawn, it will be drawn to what it desires. Desire is the magnet. Let it have its way. Trust in your own Love of Truth and Love of Goodness and never question. That you desire it, is enough. That you desire it, is evidence that it already exists for you on the Soul-side. Be passive to the desire and LET it manifest. This attitude is itself Success.

What to Think

Think positively: THINGS BELONG TO ME. I AM ALREADY POSSESSOR. They will come to me at NEED. Then LET them come. If they do not readily come, hold no anxious thought about them. Having accepted Truth that ALL is mine and that ALL DESIRED CONDITIONS OR THINGS WILL manifest, . . keep on working in an equable, confident frame of mind, and LET them come. Anxiety, doubt, mistrust show that you have not claimed them as realities but have held them as dreams or possibilities. Until you hold them as realities, they cannot come.

The Right Mental Attitude

Change your attitude toward business. Do not seek it. See IT mentally already yours and LET it come. Attend yourself to details as they come to the surface. Consider business a Principle that will run, as runs a mountain stream, when you remove your conscious will from it. All your concern is to be ready to use this business stream as the ranchman uses the water as it comes to his ditch.

There is but one Power and that is the Universal, the Infinite Power.

Business is Power

Business is a manifestation of the One Power. Use Power as does the telegrapher: LET it come and then direct it. The wisdom for the day comes with the day. LET it come by having faith in Self. Work each moment as if what you desire were here and it IS here.

Place of Money

As to money, regard it also as merely the power that keeps business going. Welcome its coming and rejoice at its going. It never does its work until, like water in the stream, it has passed under the wheel. The hoarded Dollar does not work and is of no real value to you. The Dollar you spend is the only one you really have, for by the experience of spending it you gain a growth, an enlargement, that is yours forever.

You are Power

Money has only delegated Power. You direct its expression. Change your attitude toward money. It is not "the almighty dollar." Almighty Power uses the dollar. Say to the dollar, "I do not need you. You need me. You are of no use until my brain and hand use you. You wish to be used. You come to me that you may be used. I do not need a dollar. Dollars need me." Assume this mental attitude and see what a change it makes for you. When you have changed your aura, dollars will be drawn. You need not think of their coming, for they will come to you through the opportunities which this new mental attitude will reveal to you. Think only of using them.

Mental Attitude towards Dollars

Change your attitude towards the dollars you have. Tell them they are of no use until they are expended. As you see them lying about, say to them: . . "Idle dollars, go to work. Go out and circulate. Each one of you go and pay a million in wages and debts. When I need you, come back again. You are useless and have no value until you go to work." Then LET them go to work, knowing that, when you send this thought with them, they or their fellows will come back to you to be set at work.

Spend the Dollars

Before you spend a dollar, the question comes. "Is it right?" Whether you have a single dollar, or whether behind the one you think of spending are a million, makes no difference. If it is right to spend the dollar in the proposed way, had you the million, it is right thus to spend this, the lone one. Therefore, when you feel it is right to spend a dollar for any purpose, spend it as royally as if you were a millionaire. From the Inner Life, this message was given to me years ago:

"Let a thought of use stand guard over your purse and then spend freely." Amend this by affirming: "A thought of the righteousness of the spending stands guard over my dollars and I send them forth with blessing."

Thoughts do the Work

These dollars, like every thought of good you send out, will return to bless. You do business with thoughts only; dollars are but materialized thoughts. Each dollar in any man's hand represents his thought in material form. Send out at all times with your dollars the thoughts you wish to return to you, for what you sow in your dollars, you reap in dollars that either do, or do not, come back to you. Put the thought of Success, Happiness and Health into every dollar that passes out and it will return so laden.

Poles of Having acquired the proper Thought mental attitude, there is something necessary for you to do to draw the Dollar. Your magnet of desire must have two poles. First, you must have something which the world needs and is willing to pay for. In this respect you must follow the law of supply and demand. You must honestly feel that you will give the Dollar's worth for every Dollar that you desire. Secondly, you must, in all sincerity, dedicate every Dollar that comes to you to noble service. You can then feel that Dollars want you; that through them you can give what you have of value to the world. Feel that Dollars wish you to use them for the accomplishment of your purpose to use them justly. With this ideal, you can conscientiously invite Dollars and they will come. They need your heart, brain and hand that they may benefit the world.

What are Dollars?

Dollars are manifestations of the One Infinite Substance as you are, but, unlike you, they are not Self-Conscious. They have no power till you give them power. Make them feel this through your thought-vibrations as you feel the importance of your work. They will then come to you to be used. They will not come, nor can you in this Thought draw them, to be hoarded. Use, Helpfulness and Happiness must be in your thought of Success. This held firmly, perseveringly, as your Affirmation, will turn the current of Dollars your way.

What to Think

Your thought should be: I possess that which the world wants. Dollars want me to use them in scattering that which I have to bless. Use these Affirmations persistently: . . DOLLARS LOVE ME. DOLLARS WANT ME. I AM READY TO USE DOLLARS AND THEY FREELY COME TO ME TO BE USED.

Make no limit as to the amount. Claim abundance. CLAIM ALL YOU CAN USE FOR GOOD, all that is needed to enable you to be useful and happy. ABUNDANT SUPPLY, be your demand.

Time A Factor

In all your Self-Culture, you are to remember that time is a necessary factor in unfoldment. It is not a measure of duration. This mistake of measuring time by the figures on a dial, will never do in this culture. Time is to be measured by growth. Some may grow more while the hands count twenty-four hours than others in ten times that. Take no thought of time. You have all there is. You are Spirit (or Mind, if you prefer the word) and have all eternity. Seeds require time to germinate, grow, leaf, bud, bloom, blossom and fruit. Each thought, each change in your ideal, is a seed. It will follow nature's line of evolution.

You will require time as you change your attitude! A period will be required to change your vibrations so that the Dollar will feel you and learn that it wants you. This period will vary according to your power of concentration and your fidelity to your ideal as couched in the Affirmation: Dollars want me. The thought-field is first to be cleared of the weeds of the old thought-sowing and the seeds of the new must germinate and bear fruit in the garden of Supply.

Forget the Past

Pay no attention to the old conditions. Keep at your Affirmation, knowing that it is the gate to the reservoir and every irrigating ditch will fill as soon as water can come down from the reservoir to it.

"I Want!"

The echo, "I want dollars," must become still before the real sound of Dollars want me can vibrate in your aura.

Know, as the merchant knows that he has that which the people want, that you have that which Dollars want. In your thought, in your hand, in your life, advertise your purpose to the Dollar. Tell it that it wants all these: that without you, it has no power; that, without you, it can do nothing. Tell it that all that it wants, you have: that it will come to you that it may accomplish its mission. Then like a patient merchant, wait for your customers. Dollars will soon flock, as do customers to a "bargain" counter. The "Want column" has attracted them. Use here only the same commonsense, perseverance and patience the successful business man uses and Dollars will find their wants supplied in you, and you will find Supply.

FUNDAMENTAL CONSIDERATIONS

Consciousness of Want

"God hid the whole world in thy heart," says Emerson. This fact man has been long in perceiving. From caveman to twentieth century millionaire the propelling force has been a consciousness of lack. "I want food," said primitive man. This drove him to activity and led to his unfoldment, for it awakened in him a consciousness of his ability to supply that want. It led him to recognize the fact that food already existed. He did not, however, reach our higher viewpoint.

Neither has the twentieth century millionaire reached it, for he still shares that primeval ignorance and says, "I want

Dollars." This little book is a call to him to leave that primeval attitude and come up onto this higher plane where he will hear the World's work calling to him . . "I want you."

Necessity the Spur to Unfoldment

In the development of man necessity has been a big incentive. Necessity has driven the wheels of progress. Animals also feel the spur of necessity. But there is in man a plus . . the imagination, a psychic quality, which has been a stronger factor in his development than has been animal necessity. This power of imagination differentiates him from the animal, lifts him above the animal plane and makes him man.

The Ideal

It was imagination that led caveman to paint his face and to carve pictures on bones. The Ideal, "The haunting dream of the Better," floating before him, has lured him on to thought and action. From the animal matrix the power of the Ideal drew forth the human. Necessity drives: the Ideal draws. As the Ideal develops so does its power to draw develop. When Man in his unfoldment shall have left the animal entirely behind, he will know no necessity, but will in all ways live from the ideal. Then there will be neither necessity nor want. Brutes want; Man has.

Human Possibility

The Human Soul possesses potentially all possible power. Like heat in coal, this Power in man waits for expression. Power in coal or steam waits for opportunity for expression, but Man makes his opportunity.

Power Needs Man

As fast as Man learns that the power in coal, electricity or radium waits for him to use it, he puts them to use, and learns that from all eternity they have waited for the Thought necessary to direct them in work for him.

All Things Await Man's Thought

All progress is but a change of mental attitude toward conditions that exist. "A weed is a plant man does not know the use of," says Emerson. So the condition, whatever it be, that is today untoward, when Man knows how to use it, will be found favorable. There are millions of weeds waiting for Man to learn their use. Weeds want man. They will tell their secret to the listening ear. "Weeds as well as roses live for our happiness."

The Ideal Leads to Discoveries

Desire for something new led man to find coloring matter in what were useless weeds; to find food in others and in others clothing and building material. Plants, minerals and unknown forces are still waiting for man to use them. Man is ever to think: "New Forces want me!"

Love of the Ideal

Love for the ideal leads to desire. Desire leads to action, action converts untoward conditions into the actual ideal. In the old thought Man was controlled by "want."

He was ignorant of his place and power in Nature. In this thought of want he labored. Aye, even in his religious life, he wrought in the want of heaven. But the fact is, heaven holds out rewards for man, because it wants him.

Want is Lack of Manhood

Want is born from the non-intelligence of the brute which Man has not yet outgrown. The individual, conscious of his power, does not want. He knows that whatever is needed for his health, happiness and unfoldment already is. All he needs to know is where and how to get it. The Psalmist said in a most matter-of-fact way:

"The Lord is my shepherd. I shall not want!" Why? Because the Power that called him into Being prepared conditions for him before he came. Jesus saw the same truth in the realization that he was an integral portion of the universe. He said: "I and my Father are one." "All things that the Father hath are mine!" And he had learned how to get them. He could not lack. He knew his power. "Even the wind and the sea obeyed him!" Nature's Demand

THINGS FOR MAN AND NOT MAN FOR THINGS! Whoever realizes this Truth cannot want. ALL NATURE WANTS HIM, is constantly bidding for him, and even lying in wait for him.

Opportunities are ever present for man to use. Power and things which represent power are at all times present for his unfolding into consciousness of himself as Being; as a child of Infinite wisdom. The constant enlargement of this consciousness causes a constant change of mental attitude, so that man learns to use opportunities and conditions instead of being used by them.

Worth of a Man

When once an individual has reached this consciousness of himself, he realizes the value of Emerson's admonition: . . "Let a man know his worth and keep things under his feet. Let him not peep or steal, or skulk up and down like a charity-boy, a bastard, or an interloper, in the world which exists for him." He will know that all that is, is for the unfolding into consciousness of the embryo god which he is.

Following the Ideal

He will follow in love his Ideal, and there will constantly open fields of activity that want him. There will constantly be more power asking him to harness it. In radium he is finding now only the promise of future knowledge, a vaster use. Power is an atmosphere that cannot be limited or lessened. In consciousness of himself as Power-to-use-power, man will not seek to possess things, but will learn to use things. Thus will the Law be fulfilled . . "Seek first the kingdom, then will things be added!"'

No Life Waste

This truth perceived, man will not waste life in hoarding and clinging to things. Each day he will use, in love, everything that is his to use and thus will develop his power to draw other things that want him to use them. He will gradually unfold the ability to see and improve the incessant opportunities that force themselves upon him. He will come to know that nature wants his thought and love to help her express her latent forces, which are merely waiting for the hand of man to loose for his use. Nothing has value save that which adds to man's health, happiness or usefulness. Said James Freeman Clarke, "Nature writes upon all her works 'Service to Man!' "

Inventions

The power of the inventions of Watt, Stephenson, Edison and Langly to revolutionize civilization is small compared with the transforming power flowing through the mental attitude expressed in the Thought: "Things want me!" "Dollars want me!" "Nature wants me. God wants me!"

Power of Truth

Every new perception of Truth causes changes in every line of thought and endeavor. Not an avenue of human expression but was changed by Copernicus, and by Darwin, Wallace and Spencer. The Truth that A Tan is WANTED will work a greater advancement in spiritual welfare than these perceptions of scientist and philosopher have wrought in material and intellectual good.

Universal Principle

THE PRINCIPLE IS UNIVERSAL. Man must entirely reverse his attitude toward Nature, himself, and things. He must recognize that, as the crowning expression of Infinite Power, he is to accept his place as the ruler and he is to exercise dominion over all things. He must affirm: "The world exists for me. It is for my use. It has no other use than to minister to me. Without me there is no purpose, no ultimate in Nature."

Social Change

There can never be a happy and equitable condition in society until the present attitude of "want" is changed. Whenever the race, shall affirm, 'Things want me!" then the millennium will be near. Man will then see that he is infinite in his possibilities: that time and things are simply the means by which he comes into consciousness of his own divinity and immortality. That change comes to each individual when he learns to affirm in Truth: "I possess!" in place of, as he now says: "I Want!"; "Dollars want me!" in place of "I want dollars!"

Great is This Change

This change is so great that when proposed to the average man he no more sees the Principle and its import than would the boy by Franklin's side have understood him, had Franklin said that the lightning which he was drawing from the sky would run streetcars and drive automobiles and airplanes. "Dollars want me" will work a no less marvelous change in the world's social life.

Criticism

I am aware that the principles of this little book are an easy mark for the humorous or satirical pen of the superficial critic. Plain as my point of view is, the blind critic can easily miss it. And the point of view is all important.

The Position of the Book

I affirm the infinite possibilities of the human soul. I have faith in man as power to overcome all limitations and to realize that he is able, through expressing his divinity, to have dominion over all nature. He will have this as fast as he learns his power. I affirm that there is but One Power, One Mind. All phenomena are but a manifestation of that One.

The Self-Conscious manifestation of that Mind . . Man . . because he is Self-Conscious, has power to command obedience from all that is not self-conscious, to command all that is not himself. Money, being a part of All and also being a creation of Human Thought, is subject to Human will. All this my critic may not accept, and consequently he will look from the Old Thought point of view. Having no Thought in common, he cannot agree with me.

Work and Practice

Do you wish to know the truth of these principles? Practice them and await results. The final test is always "By their fruits ye shall know them." Practice is necessary. No ideal can be reached without great effort. Your desire must be accompanied by earnest work. Indolence will never draw. The magnet works or it would not draw the needle. Thought is work. Concentration and will and effort are necessary.

Plan and Stick

Accept the Principle and then, as the architect plans and concentrates on his work till his house rises complete, for otherwise it would be a medley, so one must build an ideal of opulence and stick to it, no matter what comes, until he actualizes his Ideal in the objective. It is no easy task to develop the faith that moves dollars. But it is easier than to endure the poverty. Let one be as persistent in thinking and declaring "I AM rich!" as he has been in declaring "I am poor": let him with equal persistency say, "I have dollars!" as he has been saving: "I want dollars!" I will promise him that he will grow into that mental attitude of perception that will see and take advantage of opportunities to earn the dollars that lie all about him now unperceived. No man can do his best under the thought of poverty, under a thought of want. Knowing his ability, the workman does his best. Under fear, doubt, mistrust he can never do good work. "The poor workman quarrels with his tools!" The good workman knows he has the power and uses to best advantage his tools.

It is always the mental attitude that determines success. Let that attitude be: "Business wants me!"

An instance of Success

A gentleman in my class in Boston who furnished a noon luncheon to hundreds said: "Mr. Brown, I don't understand how dollars want me!" "Why did you select that location for your business?" I asked. "Because it was in the center of the business district and there was opportunity for me!" he answered. "Surely," said I. "You have answered my question. You went there because business called you. Business wanted you. You said, 'Men want dinners and I go to furnish them.' " He saw the point, applied it, and thinking thereafter, "Men want dinners!" drew men and increased his business. We radiate a mental atmosphere that is sensed and is potent. He who says, "I want your dollars!" repels you. he who says, "You want my goods and I am glad to serve you!" draws business.

Rockefeller

When you realize the power of Mind through concentration and right thinking you will see that the great financiers each unconsciously applied the Law which this book teaches. I have this instance from some "Reminiscences" which Mr. Rockefeller has published: . . "As our success began I seldom put my head upon the pillow at night without speaking a few words to myself in this wise, 'Now a little success; soon you will fall down; soon you will be overthrown. Because you think you are quite a merchant; look out, or you will lose your head . . go steady!' These intimate conversations with myself I am sure had a great influence in my life. I was afraid I could not stand prosperity and I tried to teach myself not to get puffed up with any foolish notions."

Talk to Yourself

Treat yourself as teacher and pupil; as doctor and patient. 'With constraining directness make your affirmations to yourself. Only thus can you open up the sources of infinite power that are within you. This talking is best done in formulas positively expressing 'I AM' AFFIRMATIONS FOR SUCCESS

The teachings of preceding pages have been necessary that you, my reader, may fully understand the Principle of Affirmation. Now I will give you some examples in the way of Affirmations that, if you will repeat them until it becomes a habit for you to think along their lines of thought as automatically and persistently as you have in the old lines, will so completely change your life expression that you will, in comparison with your past, seem like a new person.

What to Avoid

Avoid negative expression. Never use words that are not in line with your desire. Here are three imp expressions to avoid:

I cannot afford it!

It is common when one desires a thing and does not feel that he can expend the cash for it to say: "I cannot afford it!" For what are the dollars in your purse?

To spend. Can you afford to spend them? Is it not that for which you have them? You do not mean that you cannot afford. This thought makes you the servant of the dollar. What you really mean is: "I do not feel that this thing is the one I can best buy now. I prefer to use the dollar in other ways."

This is the proper attitude of mind. In it you continue to be the Master and the dollar is subject to your decision. This may seem like a very little thing. But it is the most important thought you can apply in your career for success. It is "Dollars want me!" thought, and not the thought, "I want dollars to tell me what I shall do with them!"

A gentleman once said to me, "I'd like to buy some of your books, but I cannot afford it!" "Excuse me," said I. "You smoke ten-cent cigars?" "Certainly," was his reply. "At least five a day?" "Sure," he said. "You can afford them?" "I do!"

"Then you will pardon me. You should have said, 'I can afford to buy some books if I decide, but I prefer to spend the dollar for cigars.' This is your privilege. Exercise your personal liberty and be master of your pocket book and say, I spend the dollar as I desire!'

I have spent so much!

This is the second imp expression. Have you spent or exchanged that which represented value for something of value which it stood for? You bought a suit of clothes. Twenty dollars exchanged for clothes. In taking an account of stock you only change twenty dollars from cash account to assets. Your account balances the same.

Investment

Another way to look at money expended is as an investment. Fifty dollars invested in mining stock and you look for dividends. So invest every dollar that passes out of your hands.

It is an investment in education, in health, in experience. Feel thus toward the dollars, as they go, and then your mental attitude will be so clear that you will see opportunities for other investments that will bring sure dividends. Regret, sorrow, fears, remorse, and all such attitudes of mind so cloud the judgment that other effects similar to those regretted will follow. Happy, peaceful, contented, trustful, self-respectful mental states keep the reason, conscience and judgment clear and proper investments will be made under them.

Always see a dividend coming in from every dollar that goes from your purse. The greatest of all dividends is Experience, for it is ever afterward a mental asset, that increases the value of every decision.

I've lost so much!

This, the third imp expression, is akin to the spending idea, but worse. Away with it. The lesson learned is worth all it cost. Nature always gives "measure for measure" So much experience for future guidance is always adequate recompense. All one gets out of life is the result of experience. Experience is the expression of life . . the pressing out of life into consciousness. All our present consciousness is the result of experience. The present is but adding, through experience, to the sum total of our consciousness. So is it true that we act with all our past, and think in the present. For this reason, no one has any cause to regret, or repent, or be sorry for any experience. One is today, in consciousness, all that he has expressed of the infinite possibilities of the Soul. Let him say: "I have always expressed as my reason, my desire and my will have determined. I have learned by experience what expression brings happiness and what misery. According to my power to choose, to decide and to persist have I used the experience. Because of my use of dollars I learn how to use them if I am wise. If I do not learn, then the want which I allow myself to feel for the dollar will be the cause of more suffering!" Once one has mastered that want by realizing the principles set down in this book he will feel no sorrow over lost dollars, for he will know that the dollar spent, or the dollar others call "lost," is his as experience forever.

Financial Freedom

Financial freedom is the real desire which actuates men in their labors for the dollar. That freedom will never come as long as one puts in the dollar any power to add to, or to detract from, his happiness. Until he realizes that it is his attitude toward the use of the dollar, that will bring satisfaction, there will always be the cry of "Want!"

AFFIRMATIONS

I therefore recommend that the following affirmations be used till the mental attitude they express becomes habitual:

I.

I desire a deep consciousness of financial freedom.

I desire that the flow of prosperity become equalized.

I desire a greater consciousness of my power to attract the dollar.

I desire a constant success in my business.

II.

When you have used this until you are conscious of a definiteness in your desire you may use the following::

I have a deeper consciousness of financial freedom.

I AM financially free. "Dollars want me."

The Indwelling Power cares for my purse.

I have whatever I desire.

I have no question of expenditure.

What I feel I need, that I purchase. I can afford to use dollars for my happiness.

I have clothes, food, books, entertainment and whatever I need for health., happiness, friendship, and service to others.

III.

Here is another which was developed with the assistance of a friend for myself in a time of my own weakness:

I MUST ALWAYS SAY TO MYSELF:

"I'm financially free."

I must see to it that the two men . . the material and the spiritual . . that I AM, shall blend, to the purpose of financial success.

I see myself in such a financial condition that the money is always there,

. . actually, vividly, there, . . to use, freely and in fullness.

I always have a good bank account. I actually see it.

My one idea of the Law is to use, use, USE.

I insist most rigidly upon using my Law most persistently, until I have my full demonstration.

I have strength of character, stamina, backbone, powerful purpose in accomplishing,

I demonstrate that I'll have my home, funds for business, for recreation, and for any improvement in myself.

I affirm:

Real emancipation.

Real freedom, . . to make the very best in my life.

An Editor's Opinion

O Hashnu Hara, editor of Wings of Truth, London, in the April, 1903, number of that journal has this to say of "The Law of Opulence":

'The February issue of NOW contained an article on 'Opulence.' I've read a good many articles on opulence, some have impressed me. some fell flat . . flat as a pancake . . this one didn't. First of all, it placed all my former theories in a wrong light: my idea was to say 'I WANT.' It is quite true that when I did this I generally got what I wanted sooner or later, but If. H. B. says that you must not say, I want, . . in effect, he says you. must affirm, 'I don't want dollars; dollars want me! "H. H. B. " is Right"

A very little consideration will show this is right; but consideration wasn't enough for me . . I put it to the test. The first five days, my receipts fell almost to zero, but I was determined to hang on. I felt it was right, that the drop in my business was due to the readjustment of the vibrations, for long experience has taught me that you cannot turn round from one method of thought to another very suddenly without disturbing the currents and these have to get readjusted to the new rate of vibration before you can work them. The sixth day my patience was amply rewarded: for every one order I had been in the habit of receiving, I got twenty and it has kept up ever since.

The Honey Pot

"Now I never weaken my position by affirming that I want anything. I say it wants me, and I know it will come. It is not any use making that statement, of course, if you doubt it. You must back up your statement with faith and feel it is already yours. It is rather on the principle of the honey pot and the swarm of summer flies; you are the pot of honey . . the dollars are the flies.

"Now the honey doesn't worry about the flies, it is content to be sweet, to give off a faint sweet smell and to stick, but the flies do want, they come from all quarters, they swarm into it, sip its sweetness, and buzz-zz-zz all, all around. The honey is a power . . irresistible power so far as flies go . . they want, it is a great center of attraction. "Now say you run some particular line of business . . you are the honey . . in the world there are many people who want what you have to give them, who will gladly pay cash for it, who cannot help being attracted to your honey, as the flies might be. Thought is Power

"Your thought is strong and potent beyond measure, but. when you assume the 'wanting' attitude, although you do most certainly attract, it is nothing like the powerful attraction formed by your quiet, confident attitude of absolute conviction that the thing wants you. The attitude of desire is strong, but the attitude of certainty . . of possession . . which this new thought makes possible is wonderful, and a veritable tower of strength: it has made things possible to me that were quite out of the question before."

How to Demonstrate Prosperity

by

Olive Estelle Robbins

Originally Published 1928

Foreword

The principles set forth in this book for the Demonstration of Prosperity, are so fundamental and exact that if earnestly and intelligently put into practice, SUCCESS, in a big way, is absolutely certain.

I have purposely refrained from going deeply into the matter of the Higher Powers which are ever available for our immediate use, because I know full well that many people, in their limited vision, entertain a feeling of resistance and antagonism toward anything which touches along these lines.

I wish this volume to be a great help to all, regardless of their prejudices and therefore have confined myself in this book to certain vital points which can be recognized by all.

To those of open mind, who are willing to investigate and understand the higher laws of Power and Dominion which God gave to the world when mankind was created, there is a vast treasure-house of rare jewels awaiting the claiming of them through the understanding of the powers of Mind, as set forth by various teachers of Practical Psychology, wherein a great, new world is opened up to those who are ready and willing to enter it.

In my Course of Lessons in Practical Psychology and Scientific Living, I go into this matter in such detail and in such a simple manner, that it can be readily understood by anyone desirous of learning.

Chapter I

Everybody in the world is in business of some sort. The Standard Dictionary defines business as "A pursuit or occupation that employs or requires energy, time and thought." From this definition we see that business does not necessarily have to do with the earning of money. Even the Society woman is in "business", though she would doubtless loudly disclaim such an assertion. But her pursuit of society and society's demands, occupying her time, energy and thought, which she gives in order to achieve certain results, is a form of business.

The housewife and mother is in business . . the business of keeping the home and raising the family; and by virtue of her position she receives, in return, a certain financial compensation, though it may seem indefinite. She has certain rights and certain privileges of her position and in return for the service she renders.

The woman of wealth may appear to be an exception to this rule; but, she, also, is giving a service in return for what she has, even though that service may be but the maintaining of a certain position and scale in society and in her home.

Even the child gives a certain return for what it receives, . . the return of filling a child's place in the family, the object upon which love can be bestowed, the comfort which can be derived from his presence in the family and his demand for unselfishness and attention from those around him which is an ennobling influence upon those who care for him.

I want you to begin to watch and see how every person in the world is giving some degree of service of some kind, if he amounts to anything in the world. And try to catch this deeper thought of Service.

The entire business world is founded upon the law of demand and supply. And business is the service of supplying the demands, the needs, of humanity. SERVICE is the keynote of Business.

Viewed in this light, business becomes something sublime, something to which one can give his heart and attention with enjoyment and pleasure, so that the very work of the business, the very doing of the things demanded by the business, becomes a delight, a pleasure, instead of a hardship.

Perhaps this sounds idealistic to you. Perhaps you think you are in business simply and solely for the money you can get out of your fellow man, and that therefore you are making him serve you. But, note this: Unless you are giving him service and good service, you will not long continue to get money out of him.

Money is only a medium of exchange. It is a symbol, a sign that you have rendered to the world a certain amount of service and that therefore you are entitled to a certain amount of service or goods in return.

In ancient times men traded service for goods, or service for service, or goods for goods, direct. When civilization became more complicated and people lived in larger and larger groups, this elemental way of conducting business became impractical and therefore money was devised as a medium of exchange to enable them to make the exchange more conveniently.

In a still higher sense, every man and every woman in business is simply the channel through which the Universal Intelligence (or God) supplies all humanity with that which it needs.

The Grocer is the channel through which the Infinite supplies or distributes the daily food. The Landlord is the channel through which the possibility is afforded of renting a home to those who are not in position to own one or in places where it is not convenient to own one. The Architect is the channel through which wisdom is supplied to properly build homes, business places, public buildings, etc.

And so on, without end. Each line of business is a line of divine provision for human needs through kindly service. The manifestly imperfect working out of this ideal is due to the false mental attitude of those who have not awakened to this sublime idea and ideal of business. And every man and every woman who does awaken to this beautiful concept of business and makes it the working plan of their daily work, is throwing a stronger weight and balance on the right side to help bring about this ideal as a generally accepted and recognized standard in the business world.

Even without this deeper understanding, this higher concept, the business world today is recognizing that SERVICE is the keynote of successful business. To give better and more service than anyone else in the same line, is the sure road to success.

There is a beautiful world of thought to be enjoyed in connection with the idea of business as the channel through which the Infinite supplies our wants, and also the Bible passage "Before they call, I will answer".

As you sit in your room in the quiet and silence of Meditation, let your mind dwell upon the furnishings, the furniture, carpets and draperies. Take one article at a time and ponder over it. For instance, take one of the chairs, let your mind rest completely upon it to the exclusion of everything else. Analyze it, go back in mind to the time when the wood was a mere tree growing in the forest. Trace it through its growth to maturity, picture the decision of the owner that it was time to fell the tree. His faith that there was a demand for it in the business world, a faith strong enough to justify cutting the tree down, taking it to market and disposing of it.

Then there was the faith of the lumber merchant who bought it, the confidence that there would be a market for it with some furniture manufacturer. Then the faith of the furniture manufacturer that when made up into a certain design it would meet someone's need and thus find a market. There was also the faith of the furniture merchant to buy it and trust to someone's wanting just that sort of a piece of furniture, and the faith of the salesman that he could find the person or place where it was wanted and place it there, and who gave his time and energy to do so.

Then picture the faith of the person who put in his time, energy and money to build the house, hotel or apartment house in which you are living. His faith, or confidence, that it would appeal to people and meet their need for that purpose.

Then analyze the process and the history of the manufacture of the carpet on the floor. Visualize the entire history and various processes from the time it was the wool on the sheep's back, until it was a finished article adorning your floor.

And so, with every article in the room. And see it all as the work of "Faith" and "Love" working together so that as you sit in that room you have the comfort which it brings you. That the entire process has also brought joy and happiness to many others, as well as yourself, makes it only the more beautiful lesson.

Try to sense deeply the "Faith" that was placed in every step of the way, and that "Faith" is the cornerstone upon which every business transaction rests. And I want you to realize that "Love" was the controlling motive behind it all. You probably think, upon first thought, that Love was not the controlling motive which actuated, but that every step of the way was accomplished because of the money that the person could make out of it, whether as a merchant, or as a laborer in its manufacture.

But, wait a moment! Why did that merchant want to make money out of the transaction? Was it not largely that he could supply the wants of his loved ones? Why did the laborer work so long and so intensely, but to earn the money for his family? Why are men and women in business, but to earn money to supply the needs of those they love, as well as their own needs.

I want you to get deeply and indelibly into your consciousness the fact that even though people do not realize it, and even though most men would scoff the idea, that nevertheless, in reality, business is composed of three great elements, viz: Service, Faith and Love. These are the three legs upon which all business rests.

Faith is the great rock foundation of every business in existence. What mountain was ever tunnelled without faith that it could be done and that when done it would meet a need of humanity? What chasm was ever bridged without

Faith in the undertaking? What building was ever built without Faith that it would meet a need, supply a want, and so bring its financial return? And what business was ever undertaken which did not rest on the same foundation? Not faith in some outside Being interfering in their behalf, but Faith in certain immutable laws.

When we come into this higher understanding of what business really means, it becomes something sublime and beautiful.

Now, another important fact is that every human being comes into this world endowed with certain capabilities which fit him for certain lines of service in the world's affairs. You have certain talents which have been entrusted to you, which fit you for a definite niche in life, and, when you find that niche, you will not only be happy in the very doing of the work, but you will be financially successful.

Just as Service is the law of business, so is there an absolute law that as we give the service we will receive in return for that service. The Law of Prosperity is, "Give and it shall be given to you again." Therefore, our first and only concern need be that we give and give the best in us, the best service in every way, and the return is as inevitable as night and day.

There are various ways of learning what is the right place for you in life. A Character Analyst may help you, but the Silence is your great Instructor, and your Great Desire is an indicator.

If you have had a great Ambition in life, that really almost seemed to devour you in its intensity of desire; if you have had a Dream of what life could mean to you; if you have loved to build a certain Air-Castle and dwell in it in your imagination; these are very fair indications of what you should do in life, . . what you should make your business.

Deep, intense Desire in the heart to accomplish a certain thing is the way the Infinite Intelligence, or Universal Mind, takes to call our attention to that particular work. And, the mere fact that it has possessed us to such a consuming degree, is proof positive that we have within us the power and the capability to make it a reality in our life. The business which you should engage in is the thing that you love most to do; for in that path will lie your greatest service to the world, and, in return, you will receive the greatest remuneration financially. It is your work in life. It is what you were sent here to do. And if you will definitely find out what it is that you love most to do, and will follow the instructions given by Practical Psychology teachers, you can ultimately bring your life to the point where you not only do that work and do it well, but do it remuneratively.

Anything which you really love to do can be perfected to the point of a successful business. But, there is one supreme test which business of any kind must meet in order to be successful, viz.: it must be absolutely legitimate business; and, the fundamental principle of business is that no business is legitimate unless every party to the transaction is benefited. For instance: If I want to sell you certain goods, your money is worth more to me than the goods, because I have more of the goods than I can use or they are not suited to my particular needs; but the goods should be worth more to you than the money, and so we make the exchange. I give you the goods and you are benefited; You give me the money and I am benefited.

The symbol of Justice is an inspired symbol. The scales, evenly balanced, exactly alike at the two ends, neither end heavier than the other. This is a beautiful symbol of true business. Both sides of the transaction equally benefited, though in different ways. Neither side should have any advantage over the other.

When we make our transactions conform to this standard, then the more Service we give, the more we can expect in return of money or other goods. Therefore the thing for us to give our entire attention to is to see that we give the finest service possible, and the most of it, in the most agreeable way, and we need have no anxiety about the return which we will receive. That will come automatically.

Having determined thoughtfully and carefully what it is you want most to do in life, make up your mind definitely, once for all, that you expect to do that work and make it your life work. And let nothing, no circumstance, no condition, no seeming obstacles, shake your absolute confidence that this will come about in the right way and at the right time. You may not be able to do it at once, but everything you do can be made a step toward it. Nothing can prevent you but your own doubt.

Obstacles will arise, of course, but obstacles are not to block our passage, they are simply stepping stones by which we are to climb.

What glory would there be in winning a race where the opponent gave nothing to overcome. What credit would there be in accomplishing anything where everything was in your favor and you exerted no skill or ability? We instinctively give our greatest round of cheers and admiration to the fellow who wins against great odds. For, it is the manhood, the womanhood, the skill, the accomplishment which wins the admiration of mankind.

If you have been a failure heretofore; if your Dreams have seemed elusive and disappointing; if your Air Castles have seemed to topple or have been but idle dreams to you; even if the whole wide world has gone to smash, apparently, and all your best laid plans have gone astray, I challenge you today in the name of the Infinite Creator of the Universe, shake yourself from your shackles of despair; throw off the weight of disappointment; take a new grip on yourself, clench your hand, throw back your head, and declare in unflinching terms, "In the name of the Infinite Creator of all, who gave me my Dominion, I will assert that Dominion and I do assert that Dominion now. I will win, yet!!! So help me God." And you can say this reverently, for God intended you to win, if your aim is legitimate and constructive.

God is no more proud of poor relations than we are, and He never intended us to be failures.

"Whatsoever things ye desire, when ye pray, believe that ye receive them and ye shall have them," said Jesus. And one of our modern authors has so beautifully expressed this wonderful thought "Prayer is the soul's sincere desire, unuttered or expressed."

Here we have the secret of the whole matter of demonstration, i. e., that we "believe that we receive it," and we are learning today that this is a scientific fact, capable of absolute demonstration. Not a faith in an outside Being or in an outside Power to give it to us, but science is proving beyond doubt today that the Expectant Thought is a veritable magnet which attracts to us the things which we Desire or Expect or Believe that we will have. Thought is a mold, or forms a mold, into which the Universal Substance flows and creates the thing which was expected.

Faith is nothing more nor less than positive expectancy, a firm belief that a certain thing is true and will come into manifestation.

Therefore, we see that the essential thing is to first definitely decide what it is we wish to accomplish, then to make up our mind definitely and beyond doubt that we will achieve it and circumstances and conditions will be brought about which will bring it to pass. We are to make our Ideal, our aim, our blueprint clear and big and grand. We are then to Expect it with absolute assurance, regardless of the seeming obstacles in the way, but we must not limit the law by attempting to dictate as to how it is to come about.

Recognize and Realize that "Life is just One Grand Opportunity after another." Sometimes the very thing which you consider as an adverse condition, is the very thing which will prove a shortcut to the thing which you desire.

When once you have begun to work with the Law, you can never tell just what moment your Desire will be coming toward you. It may be just around the corner, and nine times out of ten will come in an entirely different way than you expected it to.

If you try to dictate as to how it is to come, it will probably never come at all. This attempting to say How it is to come about is the cause of our failures to demonstrate.

At best, our knowledge is small compared to the Universal Intelligence, which sees and knows all. The Infinite Intelligence sees every angle of the whole situation. It knows where to go over all the world to gather together the persons and events which will combine to answer your demand.

We are, therefore, to make our plan and expect its fulfillment, but we are not to limit the Law as to how it shall come about.

For your Concentration Period take the thought presented in this chapter of the history of the furnishings of the room in which you sit. Let your mind go back step by step, way to the beginning of things and trace down through the various processes to where the article stands in your room a finished product to give you enjoyment. Visualize, as clearly and in as much detail as possible, every element entering into it. See the family of the workman, the wife rejoicing over the pay-envelope for the opportunity to provide necessities for the family. See the families of the different ones concerned in the manufacture of the articles. See the factories and visualize each step of the processes. See how clearly and in detail you can analyze and recognize the elements of Service, Faith and Love which entered into completing the entire room as you sit there. See the vast army of people who have given their labor to bring about the comfort which you now enjoy.

Then analyze the business in which you are engaged. See what your business really stands for in the way of Service, so that when you go to your daily work or business the next day you will see it through different eyes. Get the grander vision of the work you are doing, then put your whole soul into it.

If what you are doing now does not meet the requirements of your great Desire, recognize what you are now doing as a beautiful steppingstone to that Desire; and do the work of today absolutely faithfully and to the very best of your ability. Otherwise, the opportunity for your higher work will not present itself.

Do the thing nearest at hand, and do it faithfully, beautifully and lovingly to the very best of your ability, all the time holding the faith that at just the right time and in just the right way, the opportunity will arise to do the work your soul longs for. "Weld your link" today, and you will be ready for the next link tomorrow.

Chapter II

In the foregoing chapter I tried to inspire in you a conscious realization of the tremendous truth that there is a line of work, of service to the world, for which you are naturally fitted, and that it is a part of the great scheme of things that you should do that work for the world and that in the doing of it you will find happiness, joy and wealth.

The question which naturally arises after such a statement is: "Then, why do so few attain wealth or happiness in their work? Why do so few seem to find this wonderful place of world-service and realize the wealth which is promised as a return for that service?"

This is not only a very pertinent question, but it is a vital question to ask and to have answered, for until this is satisfactorily answered and understood, comparatively little progress can be made in acquiring the joy, happiness and prosperity which we are now discussing.

Inharmony of any kind, anywhere, at any time and in any place, is always due to failure to understand, apply and use great universal laws. In other words, it is caused by a failure to know the truth and apply it correctly. This is true of everything in existence and of every spot in the universe, no matter how near or how remote. Inharmony of any kind means failure to know, use and comply with great universal laws.

For instance, we know that all disease, or claim of disease, is the result of failure to comply with the laws of health. There is no one who will dispute this assertion, no matter how widely we may differ in our ideas as to what really constitutes the laws of health. The materialist will claim that these laws of health are purely material, physical laws, and will probably classify them under laws of food, laws of climate, laws of weather conditions, laws of contagion, etc., etc., etc.; while the Metaphysician will say that all disease has its rise in erroneous thought and erroneous concepts. But, both are agreed that disease is caused by breaking, infringing or disregarding some great law of life.

In Psychology we know that disease is not an entity of itself, but simply an apparent lack of health or harmonious action of the physical body, . . that disease is not a thing, but a lack of something. We know that in order to heal disease metaphysically, we have to erase from the mind the belief in the disease and put in its place the belief, the picture, or pattern, of health for the subconscious mind to work with as a pattern in rebuilding, reconstructing and renewing the body. When the perfect pattern obtains in the subconscious mind, the outer manifestation will also become perfect.

In HEALING THE POCKET BOOK, curing the Poverty Disease, and overcoming seeming lack and limitation on the financial plane, it is necessary that we do exactly the same thing, i. e., we must erase from the subconscious mind the erroneous thought and unsatisfactory pattern and put in its place the perfect pattern and the true thought. We must get rid of the false beliefs about money and moneymaking and come into a conscious realization of the Law of Abundance in such a way that we can demonstrate this law in our life as a vital, living fact.

All this has been talked about and written about so much that theoretically it is common knowledge, and many suggestions are given of methods whereby the thought of lack can thus be changed to the thought of affluence and the picture or pattern of abundance given to the subconscious mind, in order that the subconscious mind may reproduce them in the outer manifestation in our lives.

But, Reason and Experience are very strong factors in the Habit of Mind, and it is extremely difficult for the conscious mind to accept the thought of, and belief in, the Law of Abundance, as long as Reason and Experience stand as witnesses on the other side. A thought, to be successfully launched into the subconscious mind as a pattern and to bring forth results in the outer world, MUST BE ACCOMPANIED BY STRONG CONVICTION OF THE TRUTH of the thought so presented, M. Coue' to the contrary notwithstanding. "According to your Faith (or Belief) be it unto you." said Jesus. Following M. Coue's formula, it may be possible to automatically keep up a Gatling gun fire of affirmations to the subconscious mind so fast that a dissenting thought from the conscious mind cannot obtrude itself, just as it is possible to talk so fast and so continuously that another person cannot get a word in edgewise; but such a process is no more convincing to the conscious mind than it is to our auditor, who may give up the attempt to argue but is unconvinced just the same.

It is the thought which we believe, in our conscious mind, with all our power of reason or evidence of the senses, which sinks into the subconscious mind and produces the strongest impression there; and one great, engulfing, soul stirring realization of a great Truth can sink deeper into the subconscious mind than any amount of automatic surface affirmations we can make, if unaccompanied by strong conviction.

Therefore we are not to set aside our reason, but to reeducate our reason by throwing in a higher light, revealing a higher law and the unfoldment of a higher knowledge, and in the light of this the old false beliefs melt away, as ice melts and disappears under the warming influence of the sun's rays. And, as this higher Truth sinks into our subconscious mind, it finds good soil and brings forth good fruit in abundance.

Therefore, in our work of demonstrating the Law of Abundance in our life, overcoming the sense of poverty and lack and coming into the money-consciousness, it is of the utmost importance that we turn the searchlight of investigation upon the matter of money and money-making, and the laws underlying prosperity, and acquaint ourselves with the laws underlying this phase of existence, in order that we may intelligently cooperate with those laws and benefit by them.

When we come to understand the laws underlying prosperity we will find it very easy to visualize it, for we will see it as the great, natural order of things. We will have a reason for our belief in the great Law of Abundance and therefore it will be easier to "believe that we receive" and impress the subconscious mind with the correct pattern.

I want, now, to briefly consider and destroy several great, erroneous ideas regarding the matter of money and money-making. The world, in its mistaken ideas about this phase of life, has built up several great mythical Giants of Mistaken Belief, which have stood with a drawn sword preventing thousands from coming into true success. There are seven of these great misconceptions which I wish to consider here:

1. There has been a belief that the way to get rich is to "work hard and save our money."

2. The belief that when we get a dollar we take that dollar away from the rest of the world, and that the rest of the world is that much poorer.

3. The belief that our buying power lies in the dollar instead of in the great universal laws which underlie and are really a part of the great Law of Abundance.

4. The failure to understand that the Law of Growth applies to money, and to Prosperity, as well as to everything else.

5. The belief that the supply of money in the world is limited, and that hence our buying power is proportionately limited.

6. Ignorance of the great universal or spiritual laws which lie back of finance.

7. Ignorance of the difference between the earning power of money and the rental power of money.

Of course, a large book could be written upon the subject matter suggested in this chapter. Obviously, all we can do here is to briefly consider each one of the fallacies mentioned and see wherein the error lies, in order that we may come to the truth of the subject and so straighten out our own thought in the matter.

First: let us consider the fallacious belief that "the way to get rich is to work hard and save our money."

This is the fundamental error peculiar to a large part of mankind. I leave it to any mechanic if I am not right when I say that a machine which is "working hard" is doing poor work and tearing itself to pieces. A machine which is working smoothly, efficiently, is not "working hard," but working easily, without friction, without strain. The same is true of us. When we are "working hard" we are not working in the line of work for which we were intended, and we are not working smoothly nor efficiently. When we are in the work we love, the work for which we were intended by the Universal Mind, we may work long hours, we may work continuously and intensely, but we work joyously, lovingly, happily and successfully, and we will never do our best work nor our most successful work nor get the largest return financially for our work until we are in the work we love to do so well that we hate to stop working. Then we can make money.

Again, the way to get rich is not to "save our money" but to intelligently invest it. The rental power of money, which the bank gives us as interest for the use of our money, usually a mere 4% or 5%, is too small to ever do very much toward making us rich, but a very few hundred dollars properly invested, can make more for us than a man constantly employed at daily wages.

Someone has said:

"I can't make much, working with my hands alone;

I can't make much, working with my head alone;

I can't make such an awful lot working with both my hands and my head;

But, when I get my money working for me, then I can make money worthwhile." But, it is of the most tremendous importance that we learn how to Intelligently invest the money, because until we do know exactly the ground on which we stand and understand which investments are absolutely sound and safe and which are mere gambles, we had better far keep our money in the bank.

But, to the man or woman who will learn scientifically how to safely invest his or her money and know intelligently how to put his money to working for him, there is a great law of compensation and earning power undreamed by many. But, there are innumerable pitfalls for the man or woman who has not so learned to distinguish the natural and safe investment from the wildcat schemes which are being constantly offered to the public and in which such vast amounts of money are lost. We must KNOW the difference between the safe investment and the promotion schemes which are such a dangerous temptation to the average man or woman without the proper knowledge and understanding of how these schemes are carried through.

It is not "saving our money" which makes us rich, but wisely investing it. But, note, I say "wisely" investing it, and in order to wisely invest our money we must make a careful and comprehensive study of the matter of investment.

Second: When we make a dollar, we have not taken that dollar from the rest of the world nor made the world poorer. On the contrary we have made the world richer. Have you ever stopped to consider that every time a dollar changes hands it multiplies its buying power? A dollar may change hands a dozen times, and each time the person to whom it comes gets a dollar's worth of buying power. Therefore, if that dollar changes hands a dozen times, it has had twelve dollars of buying power. If it changes hands a hundred times, it has had a hundred dollars of buying power. It is when money is circulating freely that we have prosperous times. When we begin to fear hard times, fear to spend the dollars we have, we take those dollars out of circulation; and the result of this, if carried very far, is that we have a money panic and hard times.

In our large cities the average amount which goes through the Bank Clearing House each day is more than fifty times as much as the actual money in the city. That is, each dollar of actual money has a buying power of at least fifty dollars, by the fact of its changing hands fifty times and each person having a dollar of buying power out of it. If it changes hands but three or four times, it has but three or four dollars of buying power and only three or four people have had the benefit of it, whereas at least fifty people should have been benefitted by each having the use of its buying power of one dollar for every person into whose hands it came, as it would if it had been kept in circulation.

Here we see the great Law of Prosperity: "Give, and it shall be given to you again; good measure, pressed down and running over, shall men give into your bosom." Again, "There is that scattereth and yet increaseth, and there is that withholdeth more than is mete, yet tendeth to poverty."

Third: The true road to wealth is to find some service which the world needs, either a new service not heretofore rendered, or else a new and better way of giving an old service, which will cause the people to gladly give you their dollars in return for that service, which will, in other words, cause the dollars to change hands once more. Then, when we have the dollars, invest them again, send them on their way to bless the world, taking in return the service which we want from others, and again rendering the service which continually keeps the dollars coming our way and continually sending them on their way to multiply and grow and return to us.

Many of us are familiar with the old chain pump. We know that there was an endless chain, and every few inches on this chain there were little discs which caught the water and drew it up through the wooden pipe, so that a continual stream was kept flowing into the trough; and as fast as the disc emptied its load of water it returned to the well for a new supply. This is a fine illustration of the money-consciousness. Continually drawing from the great Universal Supply through our disc of Service rendered, and continually carrying it to the top of the well to discharge its load and send it on its way, knowing that there is an abundant supply for all our needs in the well.

Fourth: The Law of Growth applies to money as well as to everything else in the Universe. The physical body grows by constantly throwing off the old cells and making room for the new cells, building new cells to take the place of the old cells, the law of Biology, dividing in order to multiply. When a thing ceases to be active, to move on, to grow, it stagnates and decays and wastes away, and money does the same thing when it ceases to flow on its journey of usefulness.

Fifth: If money multiplies its buying power every time it changes hands, then the only limit there is to money, or to the buying power of money, is the limit we set by not causing it to change hands in accordance with the great Law of Life which is, service rendered, service received; more service rendered, more service received. The river which stops flowing becomes stagnant and a menace to the community. Money, hoarded, becomes a curse to the possessor by reason of his failure to cooperate with this great universal law, and it works loss to others by its inability to circulate.

Money is limited as to the amount of its buying power at one turnover, but there is no limit to the number of times it can turn over and every time it turns over it multiplies its buying power, or more people have the benefit of its buying power. This is the secret of Capitalists making money. The secret of the poor man's poverty is that he hangs onto his money instead of sending it on its errand of buying in intelligent investment.

Sixth: When we come to understand these great, stupendous, universal laws which lie back of the law of prosperity, we will see that the only way to prosper is to come into conscious cooperation with these great laws.

Seventh: It is up to us to learn the difference between the rental power of money and the earning power of money. We need to study the laws back of Finance. It is strange, when people the world over are giving their lives to the struggle of earning money, that so very few give any time or attention to the study of the laws which govern in finance and the handling of their money after it is so earned. So much time and work are devoted to earning our money and so little thought or attention to learning how to make our money work for us in safe channels.

In the next chapter I shall try to show the relation between these great, natural, universal laws of prosperity, and the Psychological laws of Visualization and Affirmation.

Chapter III

It might seem, at first glance, that the two previous chapters on Demonstrating Prosperity were contradictory. They are not contradictory, but rather two sides of the same thing. Let us see if we cannot weave them together in such a way that we will see that they are but the warp and the woof of the same great plan of achievement.

First, we are to recognize fully and clearly that all business, of every kind and nature, is service of some kind and that there is a line of work, of service for the world, which we are, individually, especially fitted to give, and that in the giving of it we not only meet the need of mankind, but reap a return for ourself of joy, happiness and prosperity. This recognition is the first great step in our demonstration of Prosperity.

When we become firmly convinced of this fact, believe it to the very depths of our being and accept it as a great fact of life, we will naturally begin to seek to know what that particular work is in our own life, what particular service we are qualified to give to the world, which will yield us such wonderful returns. This seeking to know what is our own particular work is the next great step for us to take.

The first step is the realization of the fact that there must be one particular work for which we are especially fitted. The second step is the seeking to know and finding out what that particular work is for which we are best fitted. This step may require years to fully develop, again it may be reached very quickly. Sometimes we will think we have found it and will later discover that it was in reality not the ultimate goal but just a preliminary step leading to the great discovery we are seeking. But this seeking is the second great step.

The first chapter showed how to go about the seeking and the finding of our own individual life work. When we know we have come into this realization, this understanding, we will know we have safely climbed the second step, and then we are ready to begin on the third step.

The third step is the launching of ourself into this chosen life work, and here we have sometimes a very difficult step to climb. Perhaps the chosen line of work requires an education which we have not been fortunate enough to obtain.

Sometimes it requires quite an expenditure of capital which we have no apparent means of securing.

Sometimes duties in other directions or in the care and help of others, seem to make it necessary for us to continue in an uncongenial line of work because thereby we can have the ready money to meet those demands, while the chosen line of work may offer no prospect of such immediate returns.

Sometimes other members of our family oppose our wish and it seems that if we wish peace and harmony we must give up the dear dream of what we wished to do.

In all such cases, there is one great beautiful truth to remember which will help greatly in adjusting our mind and straightening out the seeming perplexity. That truth is this: "The Real is One". The great plan of the universe takes into consideration every part of the universe. Every person has his or her own rightful place and work in the world, and each person who becomes properly placed makes it just that much easier for every other person to become properly placed in his own rightful place and environment; just as in our old picture puzzles which we played with as a child.

You remember there was a large picture or map pasted upon cardboard or thin wood, and cut into strange shapes, and the puzzle was to fit each piece into its proper place. Every piece that we fitted properly into its place made it easier for all the other pieces to be properly placed; but, if we tried to crowd a piece into some place in which it did not exactly fit, we made it still more difficult to properly place the other pieces.

So long as we consider the whole game of life as helter skelter chance, we will believe that everybody's interests are conflicting with every other person's interests. But when we get the right perspective and know and realize that what is right for one helps to bring about the right for everyone else, then that great spectre of conflicting interests disappears forever.

So, put away from your mind, once and for all, the idea that your duty to others prevents your following out the great dream of your life. It may postpone it, apparently, but if so, it is because you, also, needed just that lesson, just that development which you are getting during the postponement. And you will be led into just such experiences, just such lessons, just such development as you need to fit you for this great work which you were sent to this earth plane to do.

If you have not the necessary education required for the chosen work, then get busy and get that education. I don't care how old you are, there is abundant opportunity for you to get all the education you need along this line.

In this day of Correspondence Courses, Free Libraries and Evening Classes, any man or woman who has a backbone instead of a wishbone, has no excuse but his own laziness or indifference for not acquiring the necessary education along any line which he needs for his best self-expression.

If it is necessary capital which seems to prevent the accomplishment of your great work, then work at the next best thing while you have to, and in the mean time save and accumulate toward the time when you will have enough to take up your chosen work. But, we are not to limit the Law by trying to outline how the necessary capital will come.

Right here comes a beautiful part of the demonstration. We are not to feel that we have to accomplish this great undertaking by ourself. We must realize that the great Universal Mind is desiring this thing through us, and that it is the will of the Infinite that we shall do this great work, and then KNOW, with all the fervor of our being, that some way will open whereby it will be accomplished.

We will save, Yes, but we will also trust and KNOW in our deepest consciousness, that the way will open for us. And, in the meantime, we are preparing ourself in every way for this great work. We will be acquiring the education we need along this line. We will be reading books that throw light upon it. We will be living in thought in the great purpose we hold and fitting ourself so that when the opportunity opens, as it surely will if we hold the thought and belief as we should, then we will be ready to step right into it.

You remember that it is said that Lincoln, when a boy, studying and delving by the firelight said, "I will study and get ready, and maybe the chance will come." Why, of course, it came. It could not help but come with that way of going about it. But, from a material point of view, what possible reason was there for him to dream that he would ever be President of the United States? But, he fitted himself for the position and then the position sought him. We do not have to seek the positions of life. If we are big enough and fitted for them, the positions will seek us.

By following the rules herein outlined, it is possible for anyone to demonstrate an opening for himself in his chosen line of work in life. It may take time, but during that time he is growing bigger and better qualified to fill the position, so that he won't "rattle" in the position, as Ralph Parlette expressed it. Be willing and glad to take a small opening and fill it so full it will become a Great Opportunity. Let the Law of Growth operate in its beautiful exactness.

Now, right along with this, apply the points which were brought out in the last chapter. These are very practical points; and the application of them will not only assist us in a practical application of our principles in a practical, everyday world, but the better understanding of them will give us new ground for confidence and faith in our ultimate success.

When we analyze the great Dream of our life work we will find that it is some form of great world service, and then we can picture in our mind the eagerness with which the world will desire that service and the cheerfulness with which they will pay for it. We will also realize that in the giving of this service and in reaping the dollars from it, we have not impoverished the world but made it richer and everyone is better off for our service.

We will apply the Law of Growth both to our desire and to the business as it begins to develop, and to the earning power of the dollars which we receive from it.

We will study to know the true laws of investment, so as to make our money work for us in absolutely safe channels, with good returns of profit.

And as we come to understand these various points, we will see that the whole thing fits into one great, beautiful plan, and that nothing can prevent its ultimate maturing except our own laziness, indifference or disbelief.

This gives us a new, great, joyous hope and sense of power. We will go forth to achieve and every day will mark a new step in the achievement, and every night we should be able to see where we have progressed at least a few feet nearer to our great Desire and Dream, to our great Joy, Happiness and Prosperity.

"And Nothing shall be impossible to you"

The Path of Prosperity

By

James Allen

Originally Published 1907

Contents

Foreword

Chapter 1 - The Lesson of Evil

Chapter 2 - The World . . A Reflex of Mental States

Chapter 3 - The Way out of Undesirable Conditions

Chapter 4 - The Silent Power of Thought:
Controlling and Directing One's Forces

Chapter 5 - The Secret of Health, Success and Power

Chapter 6 - The Secret of Abounding Happiness

Chapter 7 - The Realization of Prosperity

Foreword

I looked around upon the world, and saw that it was shadowed by sorrow and scorched by the fierce fires of suffering. And I looked for the cause. I looked around, but could not find it; I looked in books, but could not find it; I looked within, and found there both the cause and the self made nature of that cause. I looked again, and deeper, and found the remedy.

I found one Law, the Law of Love; one Life, the Life of adjustment to that Law; one Truth, the truth of a conquered mind and a quiet and obedient heart. And I dreamed of writing a book which should help men and women, whether rich or poor, learned or unlearned, worldly or unworldly, to find within themselves the source of all success, all happiness, all accomplishment, all truth. And the dream remained with me, and at last became substantial; and now I send it forth into the world on its mission of healing and blessedness, knowing that it cannot fail to reach the homes and hearts of those who are waiting and ready to receive it.

James Allen

Chapter 1

The Lesson of Evil

Unrest and pain and sorrow are the shadows of life. There is no heart in all the world that has not felt the sting of pain, no mind has not been tossed upon the dark waters of trouble, no eye that has not wept the hot blinding tears of unspeakable anguish. There is no household where the Great Destroyers, disease and death, have not entered, severing heart from heart, and casting over all the dark pall of sorrow.

In the strong, and apparently indestructible meshes of evil all are more or less fast caught, and pain, unhappiness, and misfortune wait upon mankind.

With the object of escaping, or in some way mitigating this overshadowing gloom, men and women rush blindly into innumerable devices, pathways by which they fondly hope to enter into a happiness which will not pass away.

Such are the drunkard and the harlot, who revel in sensual excitements; such is the exclusive aesthete, who shuts himself out from the sorrows of the world, and surrounds himself with enervating luxuries; such is he who thirsts for wealth or fame, and subordinates all things to the achievement of that object; and such are they who seek consolation in the performance of religious rites.

And to all the happiness sought seems to come, and the soul, for a time, is lulled into a sweet security, and an intoxicating forgetfulness of the existence of evil; but the day of disease comes at last, or some great sorrow, temptation, or misfortune breaks suddenly in on the unfortified soul, and the fabric of its fancied happiness is torn to shreds.

So over the head of every personal joy hangs the Damocletian sword of pain, ready, at any moment, to fall and crush the soul of him who is unprotected by knowledge.

The child cries to be a man or woman; the man and woman sigh for the lost felicity of childhood. The poor man chafes under the chains of poverty by which he is bound, and the rich man often lives in fear of poverty, or scours the world in search of an elusive shadow he calls happiness.

Sometimes the soul feels that it has found a secure peace and happiness in adopting a certain religion, in embracing an intellectual philosophy, or in building up an intellectual or artistic ideal; but some overpowering temptation proves the religion to be inadequate or insufficient; the theoretical philosophy is found to be a useless prop; or in a moment, the idealistic statue upon which the devotee has for years been laboring, is shattered into fragments at his feet.

Is there, then, no way of escape from pain and sorrow? Are there no means by which bonds of evil may be broken? Is permanent happiness, secure prosperity, and abiding peace a foolish dream?

No, there is a way, and I speak it with gladness, by which evil can be slain for ever; there is a process by which disease, poverty, or any adverse condition or circumstance can be put on one side never to return; there is a method by which a permanent prosperity can be secured, free from all fear of the return of adversity, and there is a practice by which unbroken and unending peace and bliss can be partaken of and realized.

And the beginning of the way which leads to this glorious realization is the acquirement of a right understanding of the nature of evil.

It is not sufficient to deny or ignore evil; it must be understood. It is not enough to pray to God to remove the evil; you must find out why it is there, and what lesson it has for you. It is of no avail to fret and fume and chafe at the chains which bind you; you must know why and how you are bound. Therefore, reader, you must get outside yourself, and must begin to examine and understand yourself.

You must cease to be a disobedient child in the school of experience and must begin to learn, with humility and patience, the lessons that are set for your edification and ultimate perfection; for evil, when rightly understood, is found to be, not an unlimited power or principle in the universe, but a passing phase of human experience, and it therefore becomes a teacher to those who are willing to learn.

Evil is not an abstract something outside yourself; it is an experience in your own heart, and by patiently examining and rectifying your heart you will be gradually led into the discovery of the origin and nature of evil, which will necessarily be followed by its complete eradication.

All evil is corrective and remedial, and is therefore not permanent. It is rooted in ignorance, ignorance of the true nature and relation of things, and so long as we remain in that state of ignorance, we remain subject to evil.

There is no evil in the universe which is not the result of ignorance, and which would not, if we were ready and willing to learn its lesson, lead us to higher wisdom, and then vanish away. But men remain in evil, and it does not pass away because men are not willing or prepared to learn the lesson which it came to teach them.

I knew a child who, every night when its mother took it to bed, cried to be allowed to play with the candle; and one night, when the mother was off guard for a moment, the child took hold of the candle; the inevitable result followed, and the child never wished to play with the candle again.

By its one foolish act it learned, and learned perfectly the lesson of obedience, and entered into the knowledge that fire burns. And, this incident is a complete illustration of the nature, meaning, and ultimate result of all sin and evil.

As the child suffered through its own ignorance of the real nature of fire, so older children suffer through their ignorance of the real nature of the things which they weep for and strive after, and which harm them when they are secured; the only difference being that in the latter case the ignorance and evil are more deeply rooted and obscure.

Evil has always been symbolized by darkness, and Good by light, and hidden within the symbol is contained the perfect interpretation, the reality; for, just as light always floods the universe, and darkness is only a mere speck or shadow cast by a small body intercepting a few rays of the illimitable light, so the Light of the Supreme Good is the positive and life giving power which floods the universe, and evil the insignificant shadow cast by the self that intercepts and shuts off the illuminating rays which strive for entrance.

When night folds the world in its black impenetrable mantle, no matter how dense the darkness, it covers but the small space of half our little planet, while the whole universe is ablaze with living light, and every soul knows that it will awake in the light in the morning.

Know, then, that when the dark night of sorrow, pain, or misfortune settles down upon your soul, and you stumble along with weary and uncertain steps, that you are merely intercepting your own personal desires between yourself and the boundless light of joy and bliss, and the dark shadow that covers you is cast by none and nothing but yourself. And just as the darkness without is but a negative shadow, an unreality which comes from nowhere, goes to nowhere, and has no abiding dwelling place, so the darkness within is equally a negative shadow passing over the evolving and Light-born soul.

"But," I fancy I hear someone say, "why pass through the darkness of evil at all?" Because, by ignorance, you have chosen to do so, and because, by doing so, you may understand both good and evil, and may the more appreciate the light by having passed through the darkness.

As evil is the direct outcome of ignorance, so, when the lessons of evil are fully learned, ignorance passes away, and wisdom takes its place. But as a disobedient child refuses to learn its lessons at school, so it is possible to refuse to learn the lessons of experience, and thus to remain in continual darkness, and to suffer continually recurring punishments in the form of disease, disappointment, and sorrow.

He, therefore, who would shake himself free of the evil which encompasses him, must be willing and ready to learn, and must be prepared to undergo that disciplinary process without which no grain of wisdom or abiding happiness and peace can be secured. A man may shut himself up in a dark room, and deny that the light exists, but it is everywhere without, and darkness exists only in his own little room.

So you may shut out the light of Truth, or you may begin to pull down the walls of prejudice, self-seeking and error which you have built around yourself, and so let in the glorious and omnipresent Light.

By earnest self-examination strive to realize, and not merely hold as a theory, that evil is a passing phase, a self-created shadow; that all your pains, sorrows and misfortunes have come to you by a process of undeviating and absolutely perfect law; have come to you because you deserve and require them, and that by first enduring, and then understanding them, you may be made stronger, wiser, nobler.

When you have fully entered into this realization, you will be in a position to mold your own circumstances, to transmute all evil into good and to weave, with a master hand, the fabric of your destiny.

> What of the night, O Watchman! see'st thou yet
> The glimmering dawn upon the mountain heights,
> The golden Herald of the Light of lights,
> Are his fair feet upon the hilltops set?
> Cometh he yet to chase away the gloom,
>
> And with it all the demons of the Night?
> Strike yet his darting rays upon thy sight?
> Hear'st thou his voice, the sound of error's doom?
> The Morning cometh, lover of the Light;
>
> Even now He gilds with gold the mountain's brow,
> Dimly I see the path whereon even now
> His shining feet are set toward the Night.
> Darkness shall pass away, and all the things
> That love the darkness, and that hate the Light
> Shall disappear for ever with the Night:
> Rejoice! for thus the speeding Herald sings.

Chapter 2

The World .. A Reflex of Mental States

What you are, so is your world. Everything in the universe is resolved into your own inward experience. It matters little what is without, for it is all a reflection of your own state of consciousness.

It matters everything what you are within, for everything without will be mirrored and colored accordingly.

All that you positively know is contained in your own experience; all that you ever will know must pass through the gateway of experience, and so become part of yourself.

Your own thoughts, desires, and aspirations comprise your world, and, to you, all that there is in the universe of beauty and joy and bliss, or of ugliness and sorrow and pain, is contained within yourself.

By your own thoughts you make or mar your life, your world, your universe, As you build within by the power of thought, so will your outward life and circumstances shape themselves accordingly.

Whatsoever you harbor in the inmost chambers of your heart will, sooner or later by the inevitable law of reaction, shape itself in your outward life.

The soul that is impure, sordid and selfish, is gravitating with unerring precision toward misfortune and catastrophe; the soul that is pure, unselfish, and noble is gravitating with equal precision toward happiness and prosperity.

Every soul attracts its own, and nothing can possibly come to it that does not belong to it. To realize this is to recognize the universality of Divine Law.

The incidents of every human life, which both make and mar, are drawn to it by the quality and power of its own inner thought-life. Every soul is a complex combination of gathered experiences and thoughts, and the body is but an improvised vehicle for its manifestation. What, therefore, your thoughts are, that is your real self; and the world around, both animate and inanimate, wears the aspect with which your thoughts clothe it.

All that we are is the result of what we have thought.

It is founded on our thoughts; it is made up of our thoughts." Thus said Buddha, and it therefore follows that if a man is happy, it is because he dwells in happy thoughts; if miserable, because he dwells in despondent and debilitating thoughts,

Whether one be fearful or fearless, foolish or wise, troubled or serene, within that soul lies the cause of its own state or states, and never without. And now I seem to hear a chorus of voices exclaim, "But do you really mean to say that outward circumstances do not affect our minds?" I do not say that, but I say this, and know it to be an infallible truth, that circumstances can only affect you in so far as you allow them to do so.

You are swayed by circumstances because you have not a right understanding of the nature, use, and power of thought.

You believe (and upon this little word belief hang all our sorrows and joys) that outward things have the power to make or mar your life; by so doing you submit to those outward things, confess that you are their slave, and they your unconditional master; by so doing, you invest them with a power which they do not, of themselves, possess, and you succumb, in reality, not to the mere circumstances, but to the gloom or gladness, the fear or hope, the strength or weakness, which your thought-sphere has thrown around them.

I knew two men who, at an early age, lost the hard earned savings of years. One was very deeply troubled, and gave way to chagrin, worry, and despondency.

The other, on reading in his morning paper that the bank in which his money was deposited had hopelessly failed, and that he had lost all, quietly and firmly remarked, "Well, it's gone, and trouble and worry won't bring it back, but hard work will."

He went to work with renewed vigor, and rapidly became prosperous, while the former man, continuing to mourn the loss of his money, and to grumble at his "bad luck," remained the sport and tool of adverse circumstances, in reality of his own weak and slavish thoughts. The loss of money was a curse to the one because he clothed the event with dark and dreary thoughts; it was a blessing to the other, because he threw around it thoughts of strength, of hope, and renewed endeavor.

If circumstances had the power to bless or harm, they would bless and harm all men alike, but the fact that the same circumstances will be alike good and bad to different souls proves that the good or bad is not in the circumstance, but only in the mind of him that encounters it.

When you begin to realize this you will begin to control your thoughts, to regulate and discipline your mind, and to rebuild the inward temple of your soul, eliminating all useless and superfluous material, and incorporating into your being thoughts alone of joy and serenity, of strength and life, of compassion and love, of beauty and immortality; and as you do this you will become joyful and serene, strong and healthy, compassionate and loving, and beautiful with the beauty of immortality.

And as we clothe events with the drapery of our own thoughts, so likewise do we clothe the objects of the visible world around us, and where one sees harmony and beauty, another sees revolting ugliness.

An enthusiastic naturalist was one day roaming the country lanes in pursuit of his hobby, and during his rambles came upon a pool of brackish water near a farmyard.

As he proceeded to fill a small bottle with the water for the purpose of examination under the microscope, he dilated, with more enthusiasm than discretion, to an uncultivated son of the plough who stood close by, upon the hidden and innumerable wonders contained in the pool, and concluded by saying, "Yes, my friend, within this pool is contained a hundred, nay, a million universes, had we but the sense or the instrument by which we could apprehend them." And the unsophisticated one ponderously remarked, " I know the water be full o' tadpoles, but they be easy to catch."

Where the naturalist, his mind stored with the knowledge of natural facts, saw beauty, harmony, and hidden glory, the mind unenlightened upon those things saw only an offensive mud puddle.

The wild flower which the casual wayfarer thoughtlessly tramples upon is, to the spiritual eye of the poet, an angelic messenger from the invisible.

To the many, the ocean is but a dreary expanse of water on which ships sail and are sometimes wrecked; to the soul of the musician it is a living thing, and he hears, in all its changing moods, divine harmonies.

Where the ordinary mind sees disaster and confusion, the mind of the philosopher sees the most perfect sequence of cause and effect, and where the materialist sees nothing but endless death, the mystic sees pulsating and eternal life.

And as we clothe both events and objects with our own thoughts, so likewise do we clothe the souls of others in the garments of our thoughts.

The suspicious believe everybody to be suspicious; the Liar feels secure in the thought that he is not so foolish as to believe that there is such a phenomenon as a strictly truthful person; the envious see envy in every soul; the miser thinks everybody is eager to get his money; he who has subordinated conscience in the making of his wealth, sleeps with a revolver under his pillow, wrapped in the delusion that the world is full of conscienceless people who are eager to rob him, and the abandoned sensualist looks upon the saint as a hypocrite.

On the other hand, those who dwell in loving thoughts, see that in all which calls forth their love and sympathy; the trusting and honest are not troubled by suspicions; the good natured and charitable who rejoice at the good fortune of others, scarcely know what envy means; and he who has realized the Divine within himself recognizes it in all beings, even in the beasts.

And men and women are confirmed in their mental outlook because of the fact that, by the law of cause and effect, they attract to themselves that which they send forth, and so come in contact with people similar to themselves.

The old adage, "Birds of a feather flock together," has a deeper significance than is generally attached to it, for in the thought world as in the world of matter, each clings to its kind.

Do you wish for kindness? Be kind.
Do you ask for truth? Be true.
What you give of yourself you find;
Your world is a reflex of you.

If you are one of those who are praying for, and looking forward to, a happier world beyond the grave, here is a message of gladness for you, you may enter into and realize that happy world now; it fills the whole universe, and it is within you, waiting for you to find, acknowledge, and possess. Said one who knew the inner laws of Being,"

When men shall say Io here, or Io there, go not after them; the kingdom of God is within you."

What you have to do is to believe this, simply believe it with a mind unshadowed by doubt, and then meditate upon it till you understand it.

You will then begin to purify and to build your inner world, and as you proceed, passing from revelation to revelation, from realization to realization, you will discover the utter powerlessness of outward things beside the magic potency of a self-governed soul.

If thou would'st right the world,
And banish all its evils and its woes,
Make its wild places bloom,
And its drear deserts blossom as the rose,
Then right thyself.

If thou would'st turn the world
From its long, lone captivity in sin,
Restore all broken hearts,
Slay grief, and let sweet consolation in,
Turn thou thyself.

If thou would'st cure the world
Of its long sickness,
end its grief and pain;
Bring in all-healing joy,
And give to the afflicted rest again,
Then cure thyself.

If thou would'st wake the world
Out of its dream of death and dark'ning strife,
Bring it to Love and Peace,
And Light and brightness of immortal Life,
Wake thou thyself.

Chapter 3

The Way out of Undesirable Conditions

Having seen and realized that evil is but a passing shadow thrown, by the intercepting self, across the transcendent Form of the Eternal Good, and that the world is a mirror in which each sees a reflection of himself, we now ascend, by firm and easy steps, to that plane of perception whereon is seen and realized the Vision of the Law.

With this realization comes the knowledge that everything is included in a ceaseless interaction of cause and effect, and that nothing can possibly be divorced from law. From the most trivial thought, word, or act of man, up to the groupings of the celestial bodies, law reigns supreme. No arbitrary condition can, even for one moment, exist, for such a condition would be a denial and an annihilation of law.

Every condition of life is, therefore, bound up in an orderly and harmonious sequence, and the secret and cause of every condition is contained within itself, The law, "Whatsoever a man sows that shall he also reap," is inscribed in flaming letters upon the portal of Eternity, and none can deny it, none can cheat it, none can escape it.

He who puts his hand in the fire must suffer the burning until such time as it has worked itself out, and neither curses nor prayers can avail to alter it. And precisely the same law governs the realm of mind. Hatred, anger, jealousy, envy, lust, covetousness, all these are fires which burn, and whoever even so much as touches them must suffer the torments of burning.

All these conditions of mind are rightly called "evil," for they are the efforts of the soul to subvert, in its ignorance, the law, and they, therefore, lead to chaos and confusion within, and are sooner or later actualized in the outward circumstances as disease, failure, and misfortune, coupled with grief, pain, and despair.

Whereas love, gentleness, goodwill, purity, are cooling airs which breathe peace upon the soul that woes them, and, being in harmony with the Eternal Law, they become actualized in the form of health, peaceful surroundings, and undeviating success and good fortune. A thorough understanding of this Great Law which permeates the universe leads to the acquirement of that state of mind known as obedience.

To know that justice, harmony, and love are supreme in the universe is likewise to know that all adverse and painful conditions are the result of our own disobedience to that Law. Such knowledge leads to strength and power, and it is upon such knowledge alone that a true life and an enduring success and happiness can be built.

To be patient under all circumstances, and to accept all conditions as necessary factors in your training, is to rise superior to all painful conditions, and to overcome them with an overcoming which is sure, and which leaves no fear of their return, for by the power of obedience to law they are utterly slain.

Such an obedient one is working in harmony with the law, has in fact, identified himself with the law, and whatsoever he conquers he conquers forever, whatsoever he builds can never be destroyed.

The cause of all power, as of all weakness, is within; the secret of all happiness as of all misery is likewise within.

There is no progress apart from unfoldment within, and no sure foothold of prosperity or peace except by orderly advancement in knowledge.

You say you are chained by circumstances; you cry out for better opportunities, for a wider scope, for improved physical conditions, and perhaps you inwardly curse the fate that binds you hand and foot.

It is for you that I write; it is to you that I speak. Listen, and let my words burn themselves into your heart, for that which I say to you is truth:

You may bring about that improved condition in your outward life which you desire, if you will unswervingly resolve to improve your inner life.

I know this pathway looks barren at its commencement (truth always does, it is only error and delusion which are at first inviting and fascinating,) but if you undertake to walk it; if you perseveringly discipline your mind, eradicating your weaknesses, and allowing your soul-forces and spiritual powers to unfold themselves, you will be astonished at the magical changes which will be brought about in your outward life.

As you proceed, golden opportunities will be strewn across your path, and the power and judgment to properly utilize them will spring up within you. Genial friends will come unbidden to you; sympathetic souls will be drawn to you as the needle is to the magnet; and books and all outward aids that you require will come to you unsought.

Perhaps the chains of poverty hang heavily upon you, and you are friendless and alone, and you long with an intense longing that your load may be lightened; but the load continues, and you seem to be enveloped in an ever-increasing darkness. Perhaps you complain, you bewail your lot; you blame your birth, your parents, your employer, or the unjust Powers who have bestowed upon you so undeservedly poverty and hardship, and upon another affluence and ease. Cease your complaining and fretting; none of these things which you blame are the cause of your poverty; the cause is within yourself, and where the cause is, there is the remedy. The very fact that you are a complainer, shows that you deserve your lot; shows that you lack that faith which is the ground of all effort and progress.

There is no room for a complainer in a universe of law, and worry is soul-suicide. By your very attitude of mind you are strengthening the chains which bind you, and are drawing about you the darkness by which you are enveloped, Alter your outlook upon life, and your outward life will alter.

Build yourself up in the faith and knowledge, and make yourself worthy of better surroundings and wider opportunities. Be sure, first of all, that you are making the best of what you have.

Do not delude yourself into supposing that you can step into greater advantages whilst overlooking smaller ones, for if you could, the advantage would be impermanent and you would quickly fall back again in order to learn the lesson which you had neglected. As the child at school must master one standard before passing onto the next, so, before you can have that greater good which you so desire, must you faithfully employ that which you already possess.

The parable of the talents is a beautiful story illustrative of this truth, for does it not plainly show that if we misuse, neglect, or degrade that which we possess, be it ever so mean and insignificant, even that little will be taken from us, for, by our conduct we show that we are unworthy of it.

Perhaps you are living in a small cottage, and are surrounded by unhealthy and vicious influences.

You desire a larger and more sanitary residence. Then you must fit yourself for such a residence by first of all making your cottage as far as possible a little paradise. Keep it spotlessly clean. Make it look as pretty and sweet as your limited means will allow. Cook your plain food with all care, and arrange your humble table as tastefully as you possibly can.

If you cannot afford a carpet, let your rooms be carpeted with smiles and welcomes, fastened down with the nails of kind words driven in with the hammer of patience. Such a carpet will not fade in the sun, and constant use will never wear it away.

By so ennobling your present surroundings you will rise above them, and above the need of them, and at the right time you will pass on into the better house and surroundings which have all along been waiting for you, and which you have fitted yourself to occupy. Perhaps you desire more time for thought and effort, and feel that your hours of labor are too hard and long. Then see to it that you are utilizing to the fullest possible extent what little spare time you have.

It is useless to desire more time, if you are already wasting what little you have; for you would only grow more indolent and indifferent.

Even poverty and lack of time and leisure are not the evils that you imagine they are, and if they hinder you in your progress, it is because you have clothed them in your own weaknesses, and the evil that you see in them is really in yourself.

Endeavor to fully and completely realize that in so far as you shape and mold your mind, you are the maker of your destiny, and as, by the transmuting power of self-discipline you realize this more and more, you will come to see that these so-called evils may be converted into blessings.

You will then utilize your poverty for the cultivation of patience, hope and courage; and your lack of time in the gaining of promptness of action and decision of mind, by seizing the precious moments as they present themselves for your acceptance.

As in the rankest soil the most beautiful flowers are grown, so in the dark soil of poverty the choicest flowers of humanity have developed and bloomed.

Where there are difficulties to cope with, and unsatisfactory conditions to overcome, there virtue most flourishes and manifests its glory.

It may be that you are in the employ of a tyrannous master or mistress, and you feel that you are harshly treated. Look upon this also as necessary to your training. Return your employer's unkindness with gentleness and forgiveness.

Practice unceasingly patience and self-control. Turn the disadvantage to account by utilizing it for the gaining of mental and spiritual strength, and by your silent example and influence you will thus be teaching your employer, will be helping him to grow ashamed of his conduct, and will, at the same time, be lifting yourself up to that height of spiritual attainment by which you will be enabled to step into new and more congenial surroundings at the time when they are presented to you.

Do not complain that you are a slave, but lift yourself up, by noble conduct, above the plane of slavery. Before complaining that you are a slave to another, be sure that you are not a slave to self. Look within; look searchingly, and have no mercy upon yourself. You will find there, perchance, slavish thoughts, slavish desires, and in your daily life and conduct slavish habits. Conquer these; cease to be a slave to self, and no man will have the power to enslave you. As you overcome self, you will overcome all adverse conditions, and every difficulty will fall before you.

Do not complain that you are oppressed by the rich. Are you sure that if you gained riches you would not be an oppressor yourself?

Remember that there is the Eternal Law which is absolutely just, and that he who oppresses today must himself be oppressed tomorrow; and from this there is no way of escape. And perhaps you, yesterday (in some former existence) were rich and an oppressor, and that you are now merely paying off the debt which you owe to the Great Law. Practice, therefore, fortitude and faith.

Dwell constantly in mind upon the Eternal justice, the Eternal Good. Endeavor to lift yourself above the personal and the transitory into the impersonal and permanent.

Shake off the delusion that you are being injured or oppressed by another, and try to realize, by a profounder comprehension of your inner life, and the laws which govern that life, that you are only really injured by what is within you. There is no practice more degrading, debasing, and soul-destroying than that of self-pity.

Cast it out from you. While such a canker is feeding upon your heart you can never expect to grow into a fuller life.

Cease from the condemnation of others, and begin to condemn yourself. Condone none of your acts, desires or thoughts that will not bear comparison with spotless purity, or endure the light of sinless good.

By so doing you will be building your house upon the rock of the Eternal, and all that is required for your happiness and well-being will come to you in its own time.

There is positively no way of permanently rising above poverty, or any undesirable condition, except by eradicating those selfish and negative conditions within, of which these are the reflection, and by virtue of which they continue.

The way to true riches is to enrich the soul by the acquisition of virtue. Outside of real heart-virtue there is neither prosperity nor power, but only the appearances of these. I am aware that men make money who have acquired no measure of virtue, and have little desire to do so; but such money does not constitute true riches, and its possession is transitory and feverish.

Here is David's testimony: For I was envious at the foolish when I saw the prosperity of the wicked. Their eyes stand out with fatness; they have more than heart could wish . . Verily I have cleansed my heart in vain, and washed my hands in innocence. When I thought to know this it was too painful for me; until I went into the sanctuary of God, then understood I their end."

The prosperity of the wicked was a great trial to David until he went into the sanctuary of God, and then he knew their end.

breathes upon neighbor and stranger, friend and enemy alike the breath of blessedness.

As the effect is related to the cause, so is prosperity and power related to the inward good and poverty and weakness to the inward evil.

Money does not constitute true wealth, nor position, nor power, and to rely upon it alone is to stand upon a slippery place.

Your true wealth is your stock of virtue, and your true power the uses to which you put it. Rectify your heart, and you will rectify your life. Lust, hatred, anger, vanity, pride, covetousness, self-indulgence, self-seeking, obstinacy, all these are poverty and weakness; whereas love, purity, gentleness, meekness, compassion, generosity, self-forgetfulness, and self-renunciation, all these are wealth and power.

As the elements of poverty and weakness are overcome, an irresistible and all-conquering power is evolved from within, and he who succeeds in establishing himself in the highest virtue, brings the whole world to his feet.

But the rich, as well as the poor, have their undesirable conditions, and are frequently farther removed from happiness than the poor. And here we see how happiness depends, not upon outward aids or possessions, but upon the inward life.

Perhaps you are an employer, and you have endless trouble with those whom you employ, and when you do get good and faithful servants they quickly leave you.

As a result you are beginning to lose, or have completely lost, your faith in human nature. You try to remedy matters by giving better wages, and by allowing certain liberties, yet matters remain unaltered. Let me advise you.

The secret of all your trouble is not in your servants, it is in yourself; and if you look within, with a humble and sincere desire to discover and eradicate your error, you will, sooner or later, find the origin of all your unhappiness.

It may be some selfish desire, or lurking suspicion, or unkind attitude of mind which sends out its poison upon those about you, and reacts upon yourself, even though you may not show it in your manner or speech.

Think of your servants with kindness, consider of them that extremity of service which you yourself would not care to perform were you in their place.

Rare and beautiful is that humility of soul by which a servant entirely forgets himself in his master's good; but far rarer, and beautiful with a divine beauty, is that nobility of soul by which a man, forgetting his own happiness, seeks the happiness of those who are under his authority, and who depend upon him for their bodily sustenance.

And such a man's happiness is increased tenfold, nor does he need to complain of those whom he employs. Said a well known and extensive employer of labor, who never needs to dismiss an employee: "I have always had the happiest relations with my workpeople.

If you ask me how it is to be accounted for, I can only say that it has been my aim from the first to do to them as I would wish to be done by." Herein lies the secret by which all desirable conditions are secured, and all that are undesirable are overcome.

Do you say that you are lonely and unloved, and have "not a friend in the world"? Then, I pray you, for the sake of your own happiness, blame nobody but yourself.

Be friendly towards others, and friends will soon flock round you. Make yourself pure and lovable, and you will be loved by all.

Whatever conditions are rendering your life burdensome, you may pass out of and beyond them by developing and utilizing within you the transforming power of self-purification and self-conquest.

Be it the poverty which galls (and remember that the poverty upon which I have been dilating is that poverty which is a source of misery, and not that voluntary poverty which is the glory of emancipated souls), or the riches which burden, or the many misfortunes, griefs, and annoyances which form the dark background in the web of life, you may overcome them by overcoming the selfish elements within which give them life.

It matters not that by the unfailing Law, there are past thoughts and acts to work out and to atone for, as, by the same law, we are setting in motion, during every moment of our life, fresh thoughts and acts, and we have the power to make them good or ill.

Nor does it follow that if a man (reaping what he has sown) must lose money or forfeit position, that he must also lose his fortitude or forfeit his uprightness, and it is in these that his wealth and power and happiness are to be found.

He who clings to self is his own enemy and is surrounded by enemies.

He who relinquishes self is his own savior, and is surrounded by friends like a protecting belt. Before the divine radiance of a pure heart all darkness vanishes and all clouds melt away, and he who has conquered self has conquered the universe.

Come, then, out of your poverty; come out of your pain; come out of your troubles, and sighings, and complainings, and heartaches, and loneliness by coming out of yourself. Let the old tattered garment of your petty selfishness fall from you, and put on the new garment of universal Love. You will then realize the inward heaven, and it will be reflected in all your outward life.

He who sets his foot firmly upon the path of self-conquest, who walks, aided by the staff of Faith, the highway of self-sacrifice, will assuredly achieve the highest prosperity, and will reap abounding and enduring joy and bliss.

> To them that seek the highest good
> All things subserve the wisest ends;
> Nought comes as ill, and wisdom lends
> Wings to all shapes of evil brood.
>
> The dark'ning sorrow veils a Star
> That waits to shine with gladsome light;
> Hell waits on heaven; and after night
> Comes golden glory from afar.
>
> Defeats are steps by which we climb
> With purer aim to nobler ends;
> Loss leads to gain, and joy attends
> True footsteps up the hills of time.

James Allen - The Path of Prosperity

Pain leads to paths of holy bliss,
To thoughts and words and deeds divine,
And clouds that gloom and rays that shine,
Along life's upward highway kiss.

Misfortune does but cloud the way
Whose end and summit in the sky
Of bright success, sunkiss'd and high,
Awaits our seeking and our stay.

The heavy pall of doubts and fears
That clouds the Valley of our hopes,
The shades with which the spirit copes,
The bitter harvesting of tears,

The heartaches, miseries, and griefs,
The bruisings born of broken ties,
All these are steps by which we rise
To living ways of sound beliefs.

Love, pitying, watchful, runs to meet
The Pilgrim from the Land of Fate;
All glory and all good await
The coming of obedient feet.

Chapter 4

The Silent Power of Thought:

Controlling and Directing One's Forces

The most powerful forces in the universe are the silent forces; and in accordance with the intensity of its power does a force become beneficent when rightly directed, and destructive when wrongly employed.

This is a common knowledge in regard to the mechanical forces, such as steam, electricity, etc., but few have yet learned to apply this knowledge to the realm of mind, where the thought-forces (most powerful of all) are continually being generated and sent forth as currents of salvation or destruction.

At this stage of his evolution, man has entered into the possession of these forces, and the whole trend of his present advancement is their complete subjugation. All the wisdom possible to man on this material earth is to be found only in complete self-mastery, and the command, "Love your enemies," resolves itself into an exhortation to enter here and now, into the possession of that sublime wisdom by taking hold of, mastering and transmuting, those mind forces to which man is now slavishly subject, and by which he is helplessly borne, like a straw on the stream, upon the currents of selfishness.

The Hebrew prophets, with their perfect knowledge of the Supreme Law, always related outward events to inward thought, and associated national disaster or success with the thoughts and desires that dominated the nation at the time.

The knowledge of the causal power of thought is the basis of all their prophecies, as it is the basis of all real wisdom and power. National events are simply the working out of the psychic forces of the nation.

Wars, plagues, and famines are the meeting and clashing of wrongly-directed thought-forces, the culminating points at which destruction steps in as the agent of the Law. It is foolish to ascribe war to the influence of one man, or to one body of men. It is the crowning horror of national selfishness. It is the silent and conquering thought-forces which bring all things into manifestation.

The universe grew out of thought. Matter in its last analysis is found to be merely objectified thought. All men's accomplishments were first wrought out in thought, and then objectified.

The author, the inventor, the architect, first builds up his work in thought, and having perfected it in all its parts as a complete and harmonious whole upon the thought-plane. he then commences to materialize it, to bring it down to the material or sense-plane. When the thought-forces are directed in harmony with the over-ruling Law, they are up-building and preservative, but when subverted they become disintegrating and self-destructive.

To adjust all your thoughts to a perfect and unswerving faith in the omnipotence and supremacy of Good, is to cooperate with that Good, and to realize within yourself the solution and destruction of all evil. Believe and ye shall live.

And here we have the true meaning of salvation; salvation from the darkness and negation of evil, by entering into, and realizing the living light of the Eternal Good.

Where there is fear, worry, anxiety, doubt, trouble, chagrin, or disappointment, there is ignorance and lack of faith.

All these conditions of mind are the direct outcome of selfishness, and are based upon an inherent belief in the power and supremacy of evil; they therefore constitute practical atheism; and to live in, and become subject to, these negative and soul-destroying conditions of mind is the only real atheism.

It is salvation from such conditions that the race needs, and let no man boast of salvation whilst he is their helpless and obedient slave.

To fear or to worry is as sinful as to curse, for how can one fear or worry if he intrinsically believes in the Eternal justice, the Omnipotent Good, the Boundless Love? To fear, to worry, to doubt, is to deny, to disbelieve.

It is from such states of mind that all weakness and failure proceed, for they represent the annulling and disintegrating of the positive thought-forces which would otherwise speed to their object with power, and bring about their own beneficent results.

To overcome these negative conditions is to enter into a life of power, is to cease to be a slave, and to become a master, and there is only one way by which they can be overcome, and that is by steady and persistent growth in inward knowledge.

To mentally deny evil is not sufficient; it must, by daily practice, be risen above and understood. To mentally affirm the good is inadequate; it must, by unswerving endeavor, be entered into and comprehended.

The intelligent practice of self-control, quickly leads to a knowledge of one's interior thought-forces, and, later on, to the acquisition of that power by which they are rightly employed and directed.

In the measure that you master self, that you control your mental forces instead of being controlled by them, in just such measure will you master affairs and outward circumstances.

Show me a man under whose touch everything crumbles away, and who cannot retain success even when it is placed in his hands, and I will show you a man who dwells continually in those conditions of mind which are the very negation of power.

To be forever wallowing in the bogs of doubt, to be drawn continually into the quicksands of fear, or blown ceaselessly about by the winds of anxiety, is to be a slave, and to live the life of a slave, even though success and influence be forever knocking at your door seeking for admittance.

Such a man, being without faith and without self-government, is incapable of the right government of his affairs, and is a slave to circumstances; in reality a slave to himself. Such are taught by affliction, and ultimately pass from weakness to strength by the stress of bitter experience. Faith and purpose constitute the motive-power of life.

There is nothing that a strong faith and an unflinching purpose may not accomplish. By the daily exercise of silent faith, the thought-forces are gathered together, and by the daily strengthening of silent purpose, those forces are directed toward the object of accomplishment.

Whatever your position in life may be, before you can hope to enter into any measure of success, usefulness, and power, you must learn how to focus your thought-forces by cultivating calmness and repose. It may be that you are a business man, and you are suddenly confronted with some overwhelming difficulty or probable disaster. You grow fearful and anxious, and are at your wit's end.

To persist in such a state of mind would be fatal, for when anxiety steps in, correct judgment passes out. Now if you will take advantage of a quiet hour or two in the early morning or at night, and go away to some solitary spot, or to some room in your house where you know you will be absolutely free from intrusion, and, having seated yourself in an easy attitude, you forcibly direct your mind right away from the object of anxiety by dwelling upon something in your life that is pleasing and blissgiving, a calm, reposeful strength will gradually steal into your mind, and your anxiety will pass away.

Upon the instant that you find your mind reverting to the lower plane of worry bring it back again, and reestablish it on the plane of peace and strength.

When this is fully accomplished, you may then concentrate your whole mind upon the solution of your difficulty, and what was intricate and insurmountable to you in your hour of anxiety will be made plain and easy, and you will see, with that clear vision and perfect judgment which belong only to a calm and untroubled mind, the right course to pursue and the proper end to be brought about.

It may be that you will have to try day after day before you will be able to perfectly calm your mind, but if you persevere you will certainly accomplish it. And the course which is presented to you in that hour of calmness must be carried out.

Doubtless when you are again involved in the business of the day, and worries again creep in and begin to dominate you, you will begin to think that the course is a wrong or foolish one, but do not heed such suggestions.

Be guided absolutely and entirely by the vision of calmness, and not by the shadows of anxiety. The hour of calmness is the hour of illumination and correct judgment.

By such a course of mental discipline the scattered thought-forces are reunited, and directed, like the rays of the searchlight, upon the problem at issue, with the result that it gives way before them.

There is no difficulty, however great, but will yield before a calm and powerful concentration of thought, and no legitimate object but may be speedily actualized by the intelligent use and direction of one's soul-forces.

Not until you have gone deeply and searchingly into your inner nature, and have overcome many enemies that lurk there, can you have any approximate conception of the subtle power of thought, of its inseparable relation to outward and material things, or of its magical potency, when rightly poised and directed, in readjusting and transforming the life-conditions.

Every thought you think is a force sent out, and in accordance with its nature and intensity will it go out to seek a lodgment in minds receptive to it, and will react upon yourself for good or evil. There is ceaseless reciprocity between mind and mind, and a continual interchange of thought-forces.

Selfish and disturbing thoughts are so many malignant and destructive forces, messengers of evil, sent out to stimulate and augment the evil in other minds, which in turn send them back upon you with added power.

While thoughts that are calm, pure, and unselfish are so many angelic messengers sent out into the world with health, healing, and blessedness upon their wings, counteracting the evil forces; pouring the oil of joy upon the troubled waters of anxiety and sorrow, and restoring to broken hearts their heritage of immortality.

Think good thoughts, and they will quickly become actualized in your outward life in the form of good conditions. Control your soul-forces, and you will be able to shape your outward life as you will.

The difference between a savior and a sinner is this, that the one has a perfect control of all the forces within him; the other is dominated and controlled by them.

There is absolutely no other way to true power and abiding peace, but by self-control, self-government, self-purification. To be at the mercy of your disposition is to be impotent, unhappy, and of little real use in the world.

The conquest of your petty likes and dislikes, your capricious loves and hates, your fits of anger, suspicion, jealousy, and all the changing moods to which you are more or less helplessly subject, this is the task you have before you if you would weave into the web of life the golden threads of happiness and prosperity.

In so far as you are enslaved by the changing moods within you, will you need to depend upon others and upon outward aids as you walk through life.

If you would walk firmly and securely, and would accomplish any achievement, you must learn to rise above and control all such disturbing and retarding vibrations.

You must daily practice the habit of putting your mind at rest, "going into the silence," as it is commonly called. This is a method of replacing a troubled thought with one of peace, a thought of weakness with one of strength.

Until you succeed in doing this you cannot hope to direct your mental forces upon the problems and pursuits of life with any appreciable measure of success. It is a process of diverting one's scattered forces into one powerful channel.

Just as a useless marsh may be converted into a field of golden corn or a fruitful garden by draining and directing the scattered and harmful streams into one well-cut channel, so, he who acquires calmness, and subdues and directs the thought-currents within himself, saves his soul, and fructifies his heart and life.

As you succeed in gaining mastery over your impulses and thoughts you will begin to feel, growing up within you, a new and silent power, and a settled feeling of composure and strength will remain with you.

Your latent powers will begin to unfold themselves, and whereas formerly your efforts were weak and ineffectual, you will now be able to work with that calm confidence which commands success.

And along with this new power and strength, there will be awakened within you that interior Illumination known as "intuition," and you will walk no longer in darkness and speculation, but in light and certainty.

With the development of this soul-vision, judgment and mental penetration will be incalculably increased, and there will evolve within you that prophetic vision by the aid of which you will be able to sense coming events, and to forecast, with remarkable accuracy, the result of your efforts.

And in just the measure that you alter from within will your outlook upon life alter; and as you alter your mental attitude towards others they will alter in their attitude and conduct toward you.

As you rise above the lower, debilitating, and destructive thought-forces, you will come in contact with the positive, strengthening, and up-building currents generated by strong, pure, and noble minds, your happiness will be immeasurably intensified, and you will begin to realize the joy, strength, and power, which are born only of self-mastery.

And this joy, strength, and power will be continually radiating from you, and without any effort on your part, nay, though you are utterly unconscious of it, strong people will be drawn toward you, influence will be put into your hands, and in accordance with your altered thought-world will outward events shape themselves.

"A man's foes are they of his own household," and he who would be useful, strong, and happy, must cease to be a passive receptacle for the negative, beggarly, and impure streams of thought; and as a wise householder commands his servants and invites his guests, so must he learn to command his desires, and to say, with authority, what thoughts he shall admit into the mansion of his soul.

Even a very partial success in self-mastery adds greatly to one's power, and he who succeeds in perfecting this divine accomplishment, enters into possession of undreamed of wisdom and inward strength and peace, and realizes that all the forces of the universe aid and protect his footsteps who is master of his soul.

> Would you scale the highest heaven,
> Would you pierce the lowest hell,
> Live in dreams of constant beauty,
> Or in basest thinkings dwell.
>
> For your thoughts are heaven above you,
> And your thoughts are hell below,
> Bliss is not, except in thinking,
> Torment nought but thought can know.
>
> Worlds would vanish but for thinking;
> Glory is not but in dreams;
> And the Drama of the ages
> From the Thought Eternal streams.
>
> Dignity and shame and sorrow,
> Pain and anguish, love and hate
> Are but maskings of the mighty
> Pulsing Thought that governs Fate.
>
> As the colors of the rainbow
> Makes the one uncolored beam,
> So the universal changes
> Make the One Eternal Dream.
>
> And the Dream is all within you,
> And the Dreamer waiteth long
> For the Morning to awake him
> To the living thought and strong.
>
> That shall make the ideal real,
> Make to vanish dreams of hell

In the highest, holiest heaven
Where the pure and perfect dwell.

Evil is the thought that thinks it;
Good, the thought that makes it so
Light and darkness, sin and pureness
 Likewise out of thinking grow.

Dwell in thought upon the
Grandest, And the Grandest you shall see;
Fix your mind upon the Highest,
And the Highest you shall be.

Chapter 5

The Secret of Health, Success and Power

We all remember with what intense delight, as children, we listened to the never-tiring fairytale. How eagerly we followed the fluctuating fortunes of the good boy or girl, ever protected, in the hour of crisis, from the evil machinations of the scheming witch, the cruel giant, or the wicked king.

And our little hearts never faltered for the fate of the hero or heroine, nor did we doubt their ultimate triumph over all their enemies, for we knew that the fairies were infallible, and that they would never desert those who had consecrated themselves to the good and the true. And what unspeakable joy pulsated within us when the Fairy-Queen, bringing all her magic to bear at the critical moment, scattered all the darkness and trouble, and granted them the complete satisfaction of all their hopes, and they were "happy ever after."

With the accumulating years, and an ever-increasing intimacy with the so-called "realities" of life, our beautiful fairy-world became obliterated, and its wonderful inhabitants were relegated, in the archives of memory, to the shadowy and unreal.

And we thought we were wise and strong in thus leaving forever the land of childish dreams, but as we re-become little children in the wondrous world of wisdom, we shall return again to the inspiring dreams of childhood and find that they are, after all, realities. The fairy-folk, so small and nearly always invisible, yet possessed of an all-conquering and magical power, who bestow upon the good, health, wealth, and happiness, along with all the gifts of nature in lavish profusion, start again into reality and become immortalized in the soul-realm of him who, by growth in wisdom, has entered into a knowledge of the power of thought, and the laws which govern the inner world of being.

To him the fairies live again as thought-people, thought-messengers, thought-powers working in harmony with the over-ruling Good. And they who, day by day, endeavor to harmonize their hearts with the heart of the Supreme Good, do in reality acquire true health, wealth, and happiness.

There is no protection to compare with goodness, and by "goodness" I do not mean a mere outward conformity to the rules of morality; I mean pure thought, noble aspiration, unselfish love, and freedom from vainglory.

To dwell continually in good thoughts, is to throw around oneself a psychic atmosphere of sweetness and power which leaves its impress upon all who come in contact with it. As the rising sun puts to rout the helpless shadows, so are all the impotent forces of evil put to flight by the searching rays of positive thought which shine forth from a heart made strong in purity and faith.

Where there is sterling faith and uncompromising purity there is health, there is success, there is power. In such a one, disease, failure, and disaster can find no lodgment, for there is nothing on which they can feed.

Even physical conditions are largely determined by mental states, and to this truth the scientific world is rapidly being drawn.

The old, materialistic belief that a man is what his body makes him, is rapidly passing away, and is being replaced by the inspiring belief that man is superior to his body, and that his body is what he makes it by the power of thought.

Men everywhere are ceasing to believe that a man is despairing because he is dyspeptic, and are coming to understand that he is dyspeptic because he is despairing, and in the near future, the fact that all disease has its origin in the mind will become common knowledge.

There is no evil in the universe but has its root and origin in the mind, and sin, sickness, sorrow, and affliction do not, in reality, belong to the universal order, are not inherent in the nature of things, but are the direct outcome of our ignorance of the right relations of things.

According to tradition, there once lived, in India, a school of philosophers who led a life of such absolute purity and simplicity that they commonly reached the age of one hundred and fifty years, and to fall sick was looked upon by them as an unpardonable disgrace, for it was considered to indicate a violation of law.

The sooner we realize and acknowledge that sickness, far from being the arbitrary visitation of an offended God, or the test of an unwise Providence, is the result of our own error or sin, the sooner shall we enter upon the highway of health.

Disease comes to those who attract it, to those whose minds and bodies are receptive to it, and flees from those whose strong, pure, and positive thought-sphere generates healing and life-giving currents.

If you are given to anger, worry, jealousy, greed, or any other inharmonious state of mind, and expect perfect physical health, you are expecting the impossible, for you are continually sowing the seeds of disease in your mind.

Such conditions of mind are carefully shunned by the wise man, for he knows them to be far more dangerous than a bad drain or an infected house.

If you would be free from all physical aches and pains, and would enjoy perfect physical harmony, then put your mind in order, and harmonize your thoughts. Think joyful thoughts; think loving thoughts; let the elixir of goodwill course through your veins, and you will need no other medicine. Put away your jealousies, your suspicions, your worries, your hatreds, your selfish indulgences, and you will put away your dyspepsia, your biliousness, your nervousness and aching joints.

If you will persist in clinging to these debilitating and demoralizing habits of mind, then do not complain when your body is laid low with sickness. The following story illustrates the close relation that exists between habits of mind and bodily conditions.

A certain man was afflicted with a painful disease, and he tried one physician after another, but all to no purpose. He then visited towns which were famous for their curative waters, and after having bathed in them all, his disease was more painful than ever.

One night he dreamed that a Presence came to him and said, "Brother, hast thou tried all the means of cure?" and he replied, "I have tried all." "Nay," said the Presence, "Come with me, and I will show thee a healing bath which has escaped thy notice."

The afflicted man followed, and the Presence led him to a clear pool of water, and said, "Plunge thyself in this water and thou shalt surely recover," and thereupon vanished. The man plunged into the water, and on coming out, lo! his disease had left him, and at the same moment he saw written above the pool the word "Renounce." Upon waking, the fall meaning of his dream flashed across his mind, and looking within he discovered that he had, all along, been a victim to a sinful indulgence, and he vowed that he would renounce it forever.

He carried out his vow, and from that day his affliction began to leave him, and in a short time he was completely restored to health. Many people complain that they have broken down through over-work. In the majority of such cases the breakdown is more frequently the result of foolishly wasted energy.

If you would secure health you must learn to work without friction. To become anxious or excited, or to worry over needless details is to invite a breakdown.

Work, whether of brain or body, is beneficial and health-giving, and the man who can work with a steady and calm persistency, freed from all anxiety and worry, and with his mind utterly oblivious to all but the work he has in hand, will not only accomplish far more than the man who is always hurried and anxious, but he will retain his health, a boon which the other quickly forfeits.

True health and true success go together, for they are inseparably intertwined in the thought-realm. As mental harmony produces bodily health, so it also leads to a harmonious sequence in the actual working out of one's plans.

Order your thoughts and you will order your life. Pour the oil of tranquility upon the turbulent waters of the passions and prejudices, and the tempests of misfortune, howsoever they may threaten, will be powerless to wreck the barque of your soul, as it threads its way across the ocean of life.

And if that barque be piloted by a cheerful and never-failing faith its course will be doubly sure, and many perils will pass it by which would otherwise attack it.

By the power of faith every enduring work is accomplished. Faith in the Supreme; faith in the over-ruling Law; faith in your work, and in your power to accomplish that work, here is the rock upon which you must build if you would achieve, if you would stand and not fall.

To follow, under all circumstances, the highest promptings within you; to be always true to the divine self; to rely upon the inward Light, the inward Voice, and to pursue your purpose with a fearless and restful heart, believing that the future will yield unto you the meed of every thought and effort; knowing that the laws of the universe can never fail, and that your own will come back to you with mathematical exactitude, this is faith and the living of faith. By the power of such a faith the dark waters of uncertainty are divided, every mountain of difficulty crumbles away, and the believing soul passes on unharmed.

Strive, O reader! to acquire, above everything, the priceless possession of this dauntless faith, for it is the talisman of happiness, of success, of peace, of power, of all that makes life great and superior to suffering.

Build upon such a faith, and you build upon the Rock of the Eternal, and with the materials of the Eternal, and the structure that you erect will never be dissolved, for it will transcend all the accumulations of material luxuries and riches, the end of which is dust.

Whether you are hurled into the depths of sorrow or lifted upon the heights of joy, ever retain your hold upon this faith, ever return to it as your rock of refuge, and keep your feet firmly planted upon its immortal and immovable base.

Centered in such a faith, you will become possessed of such a spiritual strength as will shatter, like so many toys of glass, all the forces of evil that are hurled against you, and you will achieve a success such as the mere striver after worldly gain can never know or even dream of. "If ye have faith, and doubt not, ye shall not only do this, . . . but if ye shall say unto this mountain, be thou removed and be thou cast into the sea, it shall be done."

There are those today, men and women tabernacled in flesh and blood, who have realized this faith, who live in it and by it day by day, and who, having put it to the uttermost test, have entered into the possession of its glory and peace.

Such have sent out the word of command, and the mountains of sorrow and disappointment, of mental weariness and physical pain have passed from them, and have been cast into the sea of oblivion.

If you will become possessed of this faith you will not need to trouble about your success or failure, and success will come.

You will not need to become anxious about results, but will work joyfully and peacefully, knowing that right thoughts and right efforts will inevitably bring about right results.

I know a lady who has entered into many blissful satisfactions, and recently a friend remarked to her, "Oh, how fortunate you are! You only have to wish for a thing, and it comes to you."

And it did, indeed, appear so on the surface; but in reality all the blessedness that has entered into this woman's life is the direct outcome of the inward state of blessedness which she has, throughout life, been cultivating and training toward perfection.

Mere wishing brings nothing but disappointment; it is living that tells.

The foolish wish and grumble; the wise, work and wait. And this woman had worked; worked without and within, but especially within upon heart and soul; and with the invisible hands of the spirit she had built up, with the precious stones of faith, hope, joy, devotion, and love, a fair temple of light, whose glorifying radiance was ever round about her. It beamed in her eye; it shone through her countenance; it vibrated in her voice; and all who came into her presence felt its captivating spell.

And as with her, so with you. Your success, your failure, your influence, your whole life you carry about with you, for your dominant trends of thought are the determining factors in your destiny.

Send forth loving, stainless, and happy thoughts, and blessings will fall into your hands, and your table will be spread with the cloth of peace.

Send forth hateful, impure, and unhappy thoughts, and curses will rain down upon you, and fear and unrest will wait upon your pillow. You are the unconditional maker of your fate, be that fate what it may. Every moment you are sending forth from you the influences which will make or mar your life.

Let your heart grow large and loving and unselfish, and great and lasting will be your influence and success, even though you make little money.

Confine it within the narrow limits of self-interest, and even though you become a millionaire your influence and success, at the final reckoning will be found to be utterly insignificant. Cultivate, then, this pure and unselfish spirit, and combine with purity and faith, singleness of purpose, and you are evolving from within the elements, not only of abounding health and enduring success, but of greatness and power.

If your present position is distasteful to you, and your heart is not in your work, nevertheless perform your duties with scrupulous diligence, and whilst resting your mind in the idea that the better position and greater opportunities are waiting for you, ever keep an active mental outlook for budding possibilities, so that when the critical moment arrives, and the new channel presents itself, you will step into it with your mind fully prepared for the undertaking, and with that intelligence and foresight which is born of mental discipline.

Whatever your task may be, concentrate your whole mind upon it, throw into it all the energy of which you are capable. The faultless completion of small tasks leads inevitably to larger tasks. See to it that you rise by steady climbing, and you will never fall. And herein lies the secret of true power.

Learn, by constant practice, how to husband your resources, and to concentrate them, at any moment, upon a given point. The foolish waste all their mental and spiritual energy in frivolity, foolish chatter, or selfish argument, not to mention wasteful physical excesses.

If you would acquire overcoming power you must cultivate poise and passivity. You must be able to stand alone. All power is associated with immovability. The mountain, the massive rock, the storm-tried oak, all speak to us of power, because of their combined solitary grandeur and defiant fixity; while the shifting sand, the yielding twig, and the waving reed speak to us of weakness, because they are movable and non-resistant, and are utterly useless when detached from their fellows.

He is the man of power who, when all his fellows are swayed by some emotion or passion, remains calm and unmoved. He only is fitted to command and control who has succeeded in commanding and controlling himself.

The hysterical, the fearful, the thoughtless and frivolous, let such seek company, or they will fall for lack of support; but the calm, the fearless, the thoughtful, and let such seek the solitude of the forest, the desert, and the mountain top, and to their power more power will be added, and they will more and more successfully stem the psychic currents and whirlpools which engulf mankind.

Passion is not power; it is the abuse of power, the dispersion of power. Passion is like a furious storm which beats fiercely and wildly upon the embattled rock whilst power is like the rock itself, which remains silent and unmoved through it all.

That was a manifestation of true power when Martin Luther, wearied with the persuasions of his fearful friends, who were doubtful as to his safety should he go to Worms, replied, "If there were as many devils in Worms as there are tiles on the housetops I would go." And when Benjamin Disraeli broke down in his first Parliamentary speech, and brought upon himself the derision of the House, that was an exhibition of germinal power when he exclaimed, "The day will come when you will consider it an honor to listen to me."

When that young man, whom I knew, passing through continual reverses and misfortunes, was mocked by his friends and told to desist from further effort, and he replied, "The time is not far distant when you will marvel at my good fortune and success," he showed that he was possessed of that silent and irresistible power which has taken him over innumerable difficulties, and crowned his life with success.

If you have not this power, you may acquire it by practice, and the beginning of power is likewise the beginning of wisdom. You must commence by overcoming those purposeless trivialities to which you have hitherto been a willing victim.

Boisterous and uncontrolled laughter, slander and idle talk, and joking merely to raise a laugh, all these things must be put on one side as so much waste of valuable energy. St. Paul never showed his wonderful insight into the hidden laws of human progress to greater advantage than when he warned the Ephesians against "Foolish talking and jesting which is not convenient," for to dwell habitually in such practices is to destroy all spiritual power and life.

As you succeed in rendering yourself impervious to such mental dissipations you will begin to understand what true power is, and you will then commence to grapple with the more powerful desires and appetites which hold your soul in bondage, and bar the way to power, and your further progress will then be made clear.

Above all be of single aim; have a legitimate and useful purpose, and devote yourself unreservedly to it. Let nothing draw you aside; remember that the double-minded man is unstable in all his ways.

Be eager to learn, but slow to beg. Have a thorough understanding of your work, and let it be your own; and as you proceed, ever following the inward Guide, the infallible Voice, you will pass on from victory to victory, and will rise step by step to higher resting places, and your ever broadening outlook will gradually reveal to you the essential beauty and purpose of life.

Self-purified, health will be yours; faith-protected, success will be yours; self-governed, power will be yours, and all that you do will prosper, for, ceasing to be a disjointed unit, self-enslaved, you will be in harmony with the Great Law, working no longer against, but with, the Universal Life, the Eternal Good.

And what health you gain it will remain with you; what success you achieve will be beyond all human computation, and will never pass away; and what influence and power you wield will continue to increase throughout the ages, for it will be a part of that unchangeable Principle which supports the universe.

This, then, is the secret of health, a pure heart and a well-ordered mind; this is the secret of success, an unfaltering faith, and a wisely-directed purpose; and to rein in, with unfaltering will, the dark steed of desire, this is the secret of power.

> All ways are waiting for my feet to tread,
> The light and dark, the living and the dead,
> The broad and narrow way, the high and low,
> The good and bad, and with quick step or slow,
> I now may enter any way I will,

James Allen - The Path of Prosperity

And find, by walking, which is good, which ill.

And all good things my wandering feet await,
If I but come, with vow inviolate,
Unto the narrow, high and holy way
Of heart-born purity, and therein stay;
Walking, secure from him who taunts and scorns,
To flowery meads, across the path of thorns.

And I may stand where health, success, and power
Await my coming, if, each fleeting hour,
 I cling to love and patience; and abide
With stainlessness; and never step aside
From high integrity; so shall I see
At last the land of immortality.

And I may seek and find; I may achieve,
I may not claim, but, losing, may retrieve.
The law bends not for me, but I must bend
Unto the law, if I would reach the end
Of my afflictions, if I would restore
My soul to Light and Life, and weep no more.

Not mine the arrogant and selfish claim
To all good things; be mine the lowly aim
To seek and find, to know and comprehend,
And wisdom-ward all holy footsteps wend,
Nothing is mine to claim or to command,
But all is mine to know and understand.

Chapter 6

The Secret of Abounding Happiness

Great is the thirst for happiness, and equally great is the lack of happiness. The majority of the poor long for riches, believing that their possession would bring them supreme and lasting happiness.

Many who are rich, having gratified every desire and whim, suffer from ennui and repletion, and are farther from the possession of happiness even than the very poor.

If we reflect upon this state of things it will ultimately lead us to a knowledge of the all important truth that happiness is not derived from mere outward possessions, nor misery from the lack of them; for if this were so, we should find the poor always miserable, and the rich always happy, whereas the reverse is frequently the case.

Some of the most wretched people whom I have known were those who were surrounded with riches and luxury, whilst some of the brightest and happiest people I have met were possessed of only the barest necessities of life.

Many men who have accumulated riches have confessed that the selfish gratification which followed the acquisition of riches has robbed life of its sweetness, and that they were never so happy as when they were poor.

What, then, is happiness, and how is it to be secured? Is it a figment, a delusion, and is suffering alone perennial? We shall find, after earnest observation and reflection, that all, except those who have entered the way of wisdom, believe that happiness is only to be obtained by the gratification of desire.

It is this belief, rooted in the soil of ignorance, and continually watered by selfish cravings, that is the cause of all the misery in the world.

And I do not limit the word desire to the grosser animal cravings; it extends to the higher psychic realm, where far more powerful, subtle, and insidious cravings hold in bondage the intellectual and refined, depriving them of all that beauty, harmony, and purity of soul whose expression is happiness.

Most people will admit that selfishness is the cause of all the unhappiness in the world, but they fall under the soul-destroying delusion that it is somebody else's selfishness, and not their own.

When you are willing to admit that all your unhappiness is the result of your own selfishness you will not be far from the gates of Paradise; but so long as you are convinced that it is the selfishness of others that is robbing you of joy, so long will you remain a prisoner in your self-created purgatory.

Happiness is that inward state of perfect satisfaction which is joy and peace, and from which all desire is eliminated. The satisfaction which results from gratified desire is brief and illusionary, and is always followed by an increased demand for gratification.

Desire is as insatiable as the ocean, and clamors louder and louder as its demands are attended to.

It claims ever-increasing service from its deluded devotees, until at last they are struck down with physical or mental anguish, and are hurled into the purifying fires of suffering. Desire is the region of hell, and all torments are centered there.

The giving up of desire is the realization of heaven, and all delights await the pilgrim there,

> I sent my soul through the invisible,
> Some letter of that after life to spell,
> And by-and-by my soul returned to me,
> And whispered, I myself am heaven and hell,"

Heaven and hell are inward states. Sink into self and all its gratifications, and you sink into hell; rise above self into that state of consciousness which is the utter denial and forgetfulness of self, and you enter heaven.

Self is blind, without judgment, not possessed of true knowledge, and always leads to suffering. Correct perception, unbiased judgment, and true knowledge belong only to the divine state, and only in so far as you realize this divine consciousness can you know what real happiness is.

So long as you persist in selfishly seeking for your own personal happiness, so long will happiness elude you, and you will be sowing the seeds of wretchedness.

In so far as you succeed in losing yourself in the service of others, in that measure will happiness come to you, and you will reap a harvest of bliss.

> It is in loving, not in being loved,
> The heart is blessed;
> It is in giving, not in seeking gifts,
> We find our quest.

Whatever be thy longing or thy need,

That do thou give;
So shall thy soul be fed, and thou indeed
Shalt truly live.

Cling to self, and you cling to sorrow, relinquish self, and you enter into peace. To seek selfishly is not only to lose happiness, but even that which we believe to be the source of happiness.

See how the glutton is continually looking about for a new delicacy wherewith to stimulate his deadened appetite; and how, bloated, burdened, and diseased, scarcely any food at last is eaten with pleasure.

Whereas, he who has mastered his appetite, and not only does not seek, but never thinks of gustatory pleasure, finds delight in the most frugal meal. The angel-form of happiness, which men, looking through the eyes of self, imagine they see in gratified desire, when clasped is always found to be the skeleton of misery. Truly, "He that seeketh his life shall lose it, and he that loseth his life shall find it."

Abiding happiness will come to you when, ceasing to selfishly cling, you are willing to give up. When you are willing to lose, unreservedly, that impermanent thing which is so dear to you, and which, whether you cling to it or not, will one day be snatched from you, then you will find that that which seemed to you like a painful loss, turns out to be a supreme gain. To give up in order to gain, than this there is no greater delusion, nor no more prolific source of misery; but to be willing to yield up and to suffer loss, this is indeed the Way of Life. How is it possible to find real happiness by centering ourselves in those things which, by their very nature, must pass away? Abiding and real happiness can only be found by centering ourselves in that which is permanent.

Rise, therefore, above the clinging to and the craving for impermanent things, and you will then enter into a consciousness of the Eternal, and as, rising above self, and by growing more and more into the spirit of purity, self-sacrifice and universal Love, you become centered in that consciousness, you will realize that happiness which has no reaction, and which can never be taken from you.

The heart that has reached utter self-forgetfulness in its love for others has not only become possessed of the highest happiness but has entered into immortality, for it has realized the Divine.

Look back upon your life, and you will find that the moments of supremest happiness were those in which you uttered some word, or performed some act, of compassion or self-denying love. Spiritually, happiness and harmony are, synonymous.

Harmony is one phase of the Great Law whose spiritual expression is love. All selfishness is discord, and to be selfish is to be out of harmony with the Divine order.

As we realize that all-embracing love which is the negation of self, we put ourselves in harmony with the divine music, the universal song, and that ineffable melody which is true happiness becomes our own.

Men and women are rushing hither and thither in the blind search for happiness, and cannot find it; nor ever will until they recognize that happiness is already within them and round about them, filling the universe, and that they, in their selfish searching are shutting themselves out from it.

James Allen - The Path of Prosperity

I followed happiness to make her mine,
Past towering oak and swinging ivy vine.
She fled, I chased, o'er slanting hill and dale,
O'er fields and meadows, in the purpling vale;

Pursuing rapidly o'er dashing stream.
I scaled the dizzy cliffs where eagles scream;
I traversed swiftly every land and M.
But always happiness eluded me.

Exhausted, fainting, I pursued no more,
But sank to rest upon a barren shore.
One came and asked for food, and one for alms
I placed the bread and gold in bony palms.

One came for sympathy, and one for rest;
I shared with every needy one my best;
When, lo! sweet Happiness, with form divine,
Stood by me, whispering softly, 'I AM thine'.

These beautiful lines of Burleigh's express the secret of all abounding happiness. Sacrifice the personal and transient, and you rise at once into the impersonal and permanent.

Give up that narrow cramped self that seeks to render all things subservient to its own petty interests, and you will enter into the company of the angels, into the very heart and essence of universal Love.

Forget yourself entirely in the sorrows of others and in ministering to others, and divine happiness will emancipate you from all sorrow and suffering.

"Taking the first step with a good thought, the second with a good word, and the third with a good deed, I entered Paradise." And you also may enter into Paradise by pursuing the same course. It is not beyond, it is here. It is realized only by the unselfish.

It is known in its fullness only to the pure in heart. If you have not realized this unbounded happiness you may begin to actualize it by ever holding before you the lofty ideal of unselfish love, and aspiring towards it.

Aspiration or prayer is desire turned upward. It is the soul turning toward its Divine source, where alone permanent satisfaction can be found. By aspiration the destructive forces of desire are transmuted into divine and all-preserving energy.

To aspire is to make an effort to shake off the trammels of desire; it is the prodigal made wise by loneliness and suffering, returning to his Father's Mansion.

As you rise above the sordid self; as you break, one after another, the chains that bind you, will you realize the joy of giving, as distinguished from the misery of grasping . . giving of your substance; giving of your intellect; giving of the love and light that is growing within you. You will then understand that it is indeed "more blessed to give than to receive."

But the giving must be of the heart without any taint of self, without desire for reward. The gift of pure love is always attended with bliss. If, after you have given, you are wounded because you are not thanked or flattered, or your name put in the paper, know then that your gift was prompted by vanity and not by love, and you were merely giving in order to get; were not really giving, but grasping.

Lose yourself in the welfare of others; forget yourself in all that you do; this is the secret of abounding happiness.

Ever be on the watch to guard against selfishness, and learn faithfully the divine lessons of inward sacrifice; so shall you climb the highest heights of happiness, and shall remain in the never-clouded sunshine of universal joy, clothed in the shining garment of immortality.

Are you searching for the happiness that does not fade away?

Are you looking for the joy that lives, and leaves no grievous day?

Are you panting for the water-brooks of Love, and Life, and Peace?

Then let all dark desires depart, and selfish seeking cease.

Are you ling'ring in the paths of pain, grief-haunted, stricken sore?

Are you wand'ring in the ways that wound your weary feet the more?

Are you sighing for the Resting-Place where tears and sorrows cease?

Then sacrifice your selfish heart and find the Heart of Peace.

Chapter 7

The Realization of Prosperity

It is granted only to the heart that abounds with integrity, trust, generosity and love to realize true prosperity. The heart that is not possessed of these qualities cannot know prosperity, for prosperity, like happiness, is not an outward possession, but an inward realization. The greedy man may become a millionaire, but he will always be wretched, and mean, and poor, and will even consider himself outwardly poor so long as there is a man in the world who is richer than himself, whilst the upright, the open-handed and loving will realize a full and rich prosperity, even though their outward possessions may be small.

He is poor who is dissatisfied; he is rich who is contented with what he has, and he is richer who is generous with what he has.

When we contemplate the fact that the universe is abounding in all good things, material as well as spiritual, and compare it with man's blind eagerness to secure a few gold coins, or a few acres of dirt, it is then that we realize how dark and ignorant selfishness is; it is then that we know that self-seeking is self-destruction.

Nature gives all, without reservation, and loses nothing; man, grasping all, loses everything. If you would realize true prosperity do not settle down, as many have done, into the belief that if you do right everything will go wrong. Do not allow the word "competition" to shake your faith in the supremacy of righteousness.

I care not what men may say about the "laws of competition," for do I not know the unchangeable Law, which shall one day put them all to rout, and which puts them to rout even now in the heart and life of the righteous man?

And knowing this Law I can contemplate all dishonesty with undisturbed repose, for I know where certain destruction awaits it. Under all circumstances do that which you believe to be right, and trust the Law; trust the Divine Power that is imminent in the universe, and it will never desert you, and you will always be protected.

By such a trust all your losses will be converted into gains, and all curses which threaten will be transmuted into blessings. Never let go of integrity, generosity, and love, for these, coupled with energy, will lift you into the truly prosperous state.

Do not believe the world when it tells you that you must always attend to "number one" first, and to others afterwards. To do this is not to think of others at all, but only of one's own comforts.

To those who practice this the day will come when they will be deserted by all, and when they cry out in their loneliness and anguish there will be no one to hear and help them. To consider one's self before all others is to cramp and warp and hinder every noble and divine impulse.

Let your soul expand, let your heart reach out to others in loving and generous warmth, and great and lasting will be your joy, and all prosperity will come to you. Those who have wandered from the highway of righteousness guard themselves against competition; those who always pursue the right need not to trouble about such defense.

This is no empty statement, There are men today who, by the power of integrity and faith, have defied all competition, and who, without swerving in the least from their methods, when competed with, have risen steadily into prosperity, whilst those who tried to undermine them have fallen back defeated.

To possess those inward qualities which constitute goodness is to be armored against all the powers of evil, and to be doubly protected in every time of trial; and to build' oneself up in those qualities is to build up a success which cannot be shaken, and to enter into a prosperity which will endure forever.

> The White Robe of the Heart Invisible
> Is stained with sin and sorrow, grief and pain,
> And all repentant pools and springs of prayer
> Shall not avail to wash it white again.
>
> While in the path of ignorance I walk,
> The stains of error will not cease to cling
> Defilements mark the crooked path of self,
> Where anguish lurks and disappointments sting.
>
> Knowledge and wisdom only can avail
> To purify and make my garment clean,
> For therein lie love's waters; therein rests
> Peace undisturbed, eternal, and serene.
>
> Sin and repentance is the path of pain,
> Knowledge and wisdom is the path of Peace
> By the near way of practice I will find
> Where bliss begins, how pains and sorrows cease.
>
> Self shall depart, and Truth shall take its place
> The Changeless One, the Indivisible
> Shall take up His abode in me, and cleanse
> The White Robe of the Heart Invisible.

The Law of Financial Success

By

Edward Beals

Originally Published 1907

Contents

Introduction

Chapter I - Money
Chapter II - Mental Attitude
Chapter III - Fear and Worry
Chapter IV - Faith
Chapter V - Latent Powers
Chapter VI - Ambition
Chapter VII - Desire
Chapter VIII - Will Power
Chapter IX - Auto-Suggestion
Chapter X - Harmony
Chapter XI - Creation
Chapter XII - Concentration
Chapter XIII - Persistence
Chapter XIV - Habit
Chapter XV - Claiming Your Own
Chapter XVI - Making Money

Introduction

The LAW of Financial Success

To some this title may appear presumptuous, and indicative of an overweening vanity on the part of a writer who wishes to impress upon the world the belief that his ideas and opinions regarding the subject of Financial Success are of such transcendent value as to be worthy of the appellation of "The LAW." Patience, patience, good friends, the author has no such bumptious conceit . . no such vainglory. He is not attempting to frame a law; nor seeking to impose upon the world a set code of conduct, emanating from his finite mind, and claiming for it the authority of a LAW. Nay, nay, he has learned to smile at such exhibitions of folly on the part of some so-called thinkers of our times, and begs to be absolved from the suspicion of such childish desire or intent.

He does not wish to pose as the formulator, discoverer, or enunciator of a new Law. He knows that any Law. to be really a LAW, must rest upon the eternal foundations of Reality, and cannot be created, made, or formed by the finite mind of man. And, so, good friends, he does not claim to have *made, created or formed* this great Universal Law to the consideration of which this little book is devoted. It is not his mental offspring, but a great, eternal, universal Law of Life, which springs from the source of all Laws of Life. In fact, it is an integral part and portion of the ONE GREAT LAW underlying all Life, and fits into those other Natural Laws, which, when combined in an Universal Harmony, form the outward manifestation of the GREAT LAW underlying, inherent in, and manifesting in all that we call Life.

"But," you may ask, "is there then really a fundamental LAW underlying that which we call Financial Success? Is there a LAW which if once discovered, understood and practiced, will enable one to accomplish that for which this great modern world is so strenuously striving, toiling and desiring? Is there a LAW, which, when operated will make one the master of Financial Success, instead of a mere blind groper after its fruits? Indeed. Financial Success is the result of the operations of a LAW, instead of the operation of mere luck, chance, or accident."

Ah, yes, good friends, all this that you seek comes only from the application and operation of a great LAW, which the successful men and women of the world make use of either consciously or unconsciously. And this great LAW is as well defined as is any other Natural Law, and when grasped and understood may be practiced and operated just as may any of its related Laws on other planes of universal activity.

There is no such thing in Nature as blind chance, accident, or uncaused luck. Everything in Nature operates in accordance with LAW. LAW underlies everything. You may doubt this, but stop a moment and try to think of anything in our finite world that is not the effect of some cause. A great stone is dislodged and rolls down the mountain side, striking a tree which it uproots and sends rolling down into a stream which is dammed up, causing a flood that sweeps away a fertile field, and so on, and on, effect succeeding effect. Was all this mere blind chance? Not at all. The stone was dislodged in response to the operation of causes that had been at work for centuries disintegrating the stone, and which caused the boulder to become dislodged exactly at the moment when the inherent power of the Cause reached that particular stage. There was no more chance in the dislodgment of the stone than there was in the striking of a clock that had been wound up a day. or a week, or a year before. It was all the result of invariable and consistent LAW.

And so was the direction of the stone's fall; and all the succeeding incidents.

But mark you this, had some Man been able to discover and understand the LAW in operation in that latent power inherent in the stone, he would have been able to prevent the stone striking the tree and causing all the resulting damage; and he might, and would, have been able to divert the stone from its path of damage, and turn it into some place in which it would have done no harm, and in which he could have broken it into bits at his leisure, and thus secured building stone for the foundation of his cottage, or the material from which a hard roadbed could have been made. The LAW behind the stone was always there, and was consistent in its operation, and yet Man, by the power of his mind could have turned the LAW into his own channels and converted it to his use. He could have made a servant and a slave of this Universal Law, instead of allowing it to master him, and become his tyrant; for in this way has man mastered the forces of Gravitation, Steam, Hydraulics and Electricity, *which once mastered him.*

Thus has Man risen from savagery and barbarism into what he is today. And thus will he advance from what he is today into what he will become in the days to come . . a creature as much superior to Man of today as the latter is superior to the barbarian. The story of Man's Attainment may be expressed in these words: "The subjugation and mastery of Nature's forces." And so it will ever be. Man first is mastered and operated upon by Nature's forces. Then he discovers the LAW underlying these forces. Then he harnesses the force, and makes it work his will. As the great English scientist Ray Lankester has recently declared in his works: "Man is held to be a part of Nature, a product of the definite and orderly evolution which is universal; a being resulting from and driven by the one great nexus of mechanism which we call Nature. He stands alone, face to face with the relentless mechanism. It is his destiny to understand and control it."

"But," you may object, "this is all very well, and undoubtedly true of the physical forces of Nature. but Financial Success cannot be classed with these forces. Why, it is purely a latter-day development, and cannot be identified with the great Natural forces of which you have spoken."

Patience, again, good friends! As we proceed you shall see that the Law of Financial Success is a part and parcel of the Great Law of Use and Nourishment which is in operation all through animal and vegetable life. It is the same LAW that manifests in the form of the securing of food by the animal, the securing of nourishment by the plant. Nay. more, it is the same LAW by and through which Nature operates when it causes the atom of oxygen to attract to itself the two atoms of hydrogen in order to form the molecule of water. Water all over the world is composed of just these two substances, combined in just this proportion. The atom of oxygen has the power to operate the great Law of Attraction and Use, upon the two atoms of hydrogen, and when it draws them to itself, the tiny globule of water results.

The oxygen needs the hydrogen to accomplish *its* life mission; the plant needs the drop of water to accomplish *its* life mission; and the animal needs the plant to accomplish *its* life mission. And modern man needs Financial Success to accomplish *his* life's mission. And each one draws to itself that which it needs in proportion to its use of the LAW. The same LAW in its various forms is in operation everywhere in the same way.

But in the chemical, mineral, vegetable and animal worlds, the desire which prompts the attraction, and the will which manifests the desire, are unconsciously exerted. With man, it is different. He has developed consciousness, and to live his full life, and to accomplish his manifest destiny he must use that consciousness in discovering, understanding and availing himself of the natural forces inherent in the LAW.

And this is why this little book has been written.

To point out; first, the existence of the Law of Financial Success; second, to lead you to an understanding of it; and third, to give you the result of the experience of successful men in the direction of operating the LAW. And now, to "sum up" this introduction, as our legal friends would say, the writer asks you to consider the following propositions:

All progress, whether physical, mental, moral, spiritual or *financial,* is based upon LAW. And he who wins success in any line does so because he has followed the LAW or LAWS pertaining to his business, whether he does it consciously or unconsciously.

Some of our great "Captains of Industry," who have won marvelous successes in financial affairs (though they may have failed as moral or spiritual beings), have won their great success along this line because they, consciously or unconsciously, have discovered the underlying LAW, and by concentrating upon it alone, to the exclusion of everything else in life, have manifested the operation of the LAW to an almost abnormal degree.

What most of us want is "all "round" success, but what we must remember is that no one can be an "all "round" success without Financial Independence. No matter how much good a person may want to do, he is handicapped by a lack of money. All the air-castles that he has built; all the beautiful plans that he has created; all the cherished desires to do good . . all go unfulfilled because there is no money with which to complete them. Before these air-castles can become real buildings; before these plans can become realities; before these great desires can be fulfilled; before any of these great things can be manifested into living realities . . the LAW must be seen, understood, and put into conscious operation. And the purpose of this little book is to tell you HOW TO DO IT!

For several years the writer has seen the need, among advanced thought circles, of a book filling this want. In his own life he has found that Financial Success is not a matter of grind, and rush, and fight and struggle. It is a matter of getting into harmony with the LAW, and then following that LAW to its logical conclusion. In this little book he will place this information and the result of his experience. In it he will state the LAW . . how to get in harmony with it . . and what to do to keep in the closest touch with it.

This book is no magic potion to be swallowed with wonderful results . . it is. instead, a plain statement of the LAW, so that all who run may read, and then act. And he who acts will win success, because he is following the LAW that has been laid down from time immemorial. Whether rich or poor, successful or unsuccessful . . it matters not . . this book will be of great value to you. If you are a natural money-maker, you must have been using this LAW unconsciously, and in such case this book will enable you to do *consciously* that which you have been partly doing unconsciously. If you are unsuccessful, and money seems not to be attracted by or to you. this book will guide your thought and actions into proper channels where you will be able to manifest the LAW and thus get the highest possible results.

And, now that you have been told of the feast of good things ahead of you, draw up your chairs to the table and partake of what nourishing food has been provided in the following pages. After all, you know, "the proof of the pudding lies in the eating thereof," and so fall to and taste that which has been gathered together for your mental, physical and financial wellbeing. And now. while you are filling your plates, the writer proposes the opening toast, to be drunk in Nature's sparkling fluid: "Here's to you . . may you live long and prosper by following the Law of Financial Success!"

EDWARD E. BEALS. Chicago. August 1. 1907.

Chapter I

Money

THERE is no idea that seems so much misunderstood as this idea of "Money." On the one hand we find many people engaged in a mad chase after "money for money's sake," and on the other hand, many others who are decrying money as the root of all evil, and severely criticizing the tendency of the age to seek money actively. Both of these classes of people are wrong . . they are occupying the opposite sides of the road of reason, whereas truth is found here, as always, "in the middle of the road."

The man who seeks money as a thing of value in itself . . the man who worships money as a very god . . such a man is a fool, for he is mistaking the symbol for the reality. And, likewise, the man who decries the pursuit and desire for money as a foul, evil thing . . he who would make of money a devil . . this man is likewise a fool. The wise man is he who sees money as a symbol of something else behind, and who is not deluded by mistaking the shadow for the substance, either for good or evil. The wise man makes neither a god nor a devil of money . . he sees it as a symbol of almost everything that man may obtain from the outside world, and he respects it as such. He sees, while it is true that avarice and greed are detestable and hurtful qualities of mind, still the lack of the proper desire for, and striving after, money, makes of man a creature devoid of all that makes life worth the living.

When the sane man desires money, he really desires the many things that money will purchase. Money is the symbol of nearly everything that is necessary for man's well-being and happiness. With it he opens the door to all sorts of opportunities, and without it he can accomplish practically nothing. Money is the tool with which man may carve many beautiful things, and without the aid of which he is helpless. Money is but the concentrated essence of things desired, created and established by society in its present stage of development. There have been times in which there was no money . . there may be times coming in which the race will have passed beyond the need of money as the symbol of exchange and possession . . but, be this as it may, the fact remains that now, right here in the beginning of the Twentieth Century, there is nothing that is so necessary for man's well-being and content as this much-abused money.

Remember this, first, last and all the time, that when I say, "man needs money," I mean that he needs *the many things that money will purchase for him.* And for one to decry the desire for money is for him to decry the desire for nearly all the good and desirable things of life. As a recent writer has said: "Unless a man acquires money, then shall he not eat; nor be clothed; nor have shelter; nor books; nor music; nor anything else that makes life worth living for one who thinks and feels."

The people who decry the desire for money are generally those who have found themselves lacking in the qualities that tend to attract money; or else those who are in possession of money that has been inherited, or is otherwise acquired without the labor, excitement or satisfaction of having been made by themselves. With the first mentioned class it is a case of "sour grapes"; with the second it is financial dyspepsia, which has left the victim devoid of a normal appetite.

In spite of the loud cries and protests of our longhaired brothers and short-haired sisters . . so-called "reformers" . . money is still necessary in order that man may have the necessities of life, as well as a few luxuries. We cannot live on beautiful theories, but must have bread and butter, and potatoes, and sometimes a piece of cake or pie . . *and it takes money to get them.* Money means freedom, independence, liberty, and the ability to do great good, as well as great evil. It means the opportunity to carry out great plans and to fulfill great ideals. It means the filling in of those mental pictures that we have sketched out in our minds. It means the chance of materializing those airy "Castles in Spain" that we have dwelt upon in moments of hopeful ecstasy. Ah, yes, money is the wizard, able and willing to work wonders. It is, indeed, the genie who can and will do its master's bidding.

I hold that in the present stage of evolution of man, money is to mankind what air, water, sunshine and mother-earth are to the plant . . it is *nourishment.* And, as in the plant, the desire for nourishment is a natural and worthy instinct, so is the desire for this financial nourishment in man a perfectly natural and worthy instinct . . it is the working of the same natural law. And, mark you this, that as the desire of the plant is a natural indication of the existence of the nourishment-need, so is this desire in the breast of man a certain indication of the possibility of its satisfaction and attainment, if natural laws are but followed. Nature is no mocker . . it causes no desire to spring up in a living thing, unless it also endows that living thing with the faculties and powers to attain that which it craves. A realization of this great natural law will do many of my readers much good just now.

But note this, also. Nature does not encourage the hoarding up of anything for the mere sake of acquisition. It punishes this error severely. The Law of Use underlies all of nature's instinctive cravings. It desires that the living thing shall draw to itself the nourishment and material it needs, in order to use it. And this desire for money on the part of man is governed by this same law . . the Law of Use. Nature wishes you to desire money . . to attract it to you . . to possess and acquire it . . and lastly, and most important of all, *to use it.* By using money, and keeping it working and in action, you will fall in line with the workings of this great Law of Use. By falling in with this Law, you work in harmony with the great natural forces and purposes. You bring yourself into harmony with the Cosmic Plan, instead of opposing it, and when man so brings himself into harmony with the natural forces around him, he reduces friction and receives the reward that comes to all living things that work with, instead of against, the LAW.

So, friends, in closing this chapter, I would say to you: Be not afraid, but assert the desirability of the possession and use of money; recognize that it is your natural right to possess it, just as it is the natural right of the plant to sunshine, light and air. And do more than this . . it belongs to you . . *demand it* of the LAW, just as does the plant.

Cease all this talk of the beauty of poverty, and the joy of the humble . . you know that in the bottom of your heart you do not mean a word of it. You know that you are just laying these things because you are afraid that you cannot have that which you want. Throw off this mask of hypocrisy, and self-deception, and stand out in the open like a man, throwing your head up and looking the world in the face, saying, "Yes, I *do* desire Money; I *want* it and I want it *earnestly,* and through the LAW I *demand* it as my rightful inheritance . . and I'm going to *get it,* beginning right now!"

Throw off the shackles of the slave, and assert your freedom. Assert your own mastery of that which is your own. Don't be afraid to assert what you want, and to see it clearly ahead of you . . then march straight onward to the mark, without turning to the right, or to the left, without fear or favor, without flinching or fouling . . straight to the mark which is called Financial Success! For in that goal, alone, may you find that for which you seek . . that which your heart desires.

Chapter II

Mental Attitude

YOU remember the saying of the sacred writer: As a man thinketh in his heart, so is he." A truer statement never was uttered. For every man or woman is what he or she is, by reason of what he or she has thought. We have thought ourselves into what we are. One's place in life is largely determined by his Mental Attitude.

Mental Attitude is the result of the current of one's thoughts, ideas, ideals, feelings, and beliefs. You are constantly at work building up a Mental Attitude, which is not only making your character but which is also having its influence upon the outside world, both in the direction of your effect upon other people, as well as your quality of attracting toward yourself that which is in harmony with the prevailing mental state held by you. Is it not most important, then, that this building should be done with the best possible materials . . according to the best plan . . with the best tools?

The keynote of this chapter is: "A Positive Mental Attitude Wins Financial Success." Before going any further, let us define the word "Positive" and its opposite, "Negative," and then see how the former wins success and the latter attracts failure. In the sense in which I use the terms, "Positive" means Confident Expectation, Self-Confidence, Courage, Initiative, Energy, Optimism, Expectation of Good, not Evil . . of Wealth, not Poverty . . Belief in Oneself and in the LAW, etc., etc.; "Negative" means Fear, Worry, Expectation of Undesirable Things, Lack of Confidence in Oneself and the LAW, etc., etc.

In the first place Mental Attitude tends towards success by its power in the direction of "making us over" into individuals possessing qualities conducive to success. Many people go through the world bemoaning their lack of the faculties, qualities or temperament that they instinctively recognize are active factors in the attainment of success. They see others possessing these desirable qualities moving steadily forward to their goal, and they also feel if they themselves were but possessed of these same qualities they, too, might attain the same desirable results. Now, so far, their reasoning is all right . . but they do not go far enough. They fail here because they imagine that since they have not the desired qualities at the moment, they can never expect to possess them. They regard their minds as something that once fixed and built can never be improved upon, repaired, rebuilt, or enlarged. Right here is where the majority of people "fall down," to use the expressive although slangy words of the day.

As a matter of fact, the great scientific authorities of the present time distinctly teach that a man by diligent care and practice may completely change his character, temperament, and habits. He may kill out undesirable traits of character, and replace them by new and desirable traits, qualities and faculties. The brain is now known to be but the instrument and tool of something called Mind, which uses the brain as its instrument of expression.

And the brain is also now known to be composed of millions of tiny cells, the majority of which are not in use. It is also known that if one turns his attention and interest in certain directions, the unused cells in the area of his brain which is the center of such subject, will be stimulated into action and will begin to manifest actively. Not only this, but the stimulated sections of cells will begin also to actively manifest their reproductive qualities, and *new brain cells* will be evolved, grown and developed in order to furnish proper mental tools with which to manifest the new desires, qualities and feelings pressing forward for expression.

Scientific Character Building is not a mere idle theory, but a live, vital, actual, practical fact, being put into operation in the psychological laboratories of the country, and by thousands of private individuals all over the world who are rapidly "making themselves over" by this method. *And the prevailing Menial Attitude is the pattern upon which the brain cells build.* If you can but grasp this truth you have the key to success in your hands.

Now, let us consider the second phase of the action of Mental Attitude toward Financial Success. I allude to the effect upon others of one's Mental Attitude. Did you ever stop long enough to think that we are constantly giving other people suggestive impressions of ourselves and qualities? Do you not know that, if you go about with the Mental Attitude of Discouragement, Fear, Lack of Self-Confidence, and all the other Negative qualities of mind, other people are sure to catch the impression and govern themselves toward you accordingly?

Let a man come into your presence for the purpose of doing business with you and if he lack confidence in himself and in the things he wishes to sell you, you will at once catch his spirit and will feel that you have no confidence in him or the things he is offering. You will catch his mental atmosphere at once, and he will suffer thereby. But let this same man fill himself up with thoughts, feelings, and ideals of Enthusiasm, Success, Self-Confidence, Confidence in his proposition, etc., and he will fairly radiate success toward you, and you will unconsciously "take stock" in him and interest in his goods, and the chances are that you will be willing and glad to do business with him.

Do you not know men who radiate Failure, Discouragement and "I Can't"? Are you not affected by their manifested Mental Attitude to their hurt? And, on the other hand, do you not know men who are so filled with Confidence, Courage, Enthusiasm, Fearlessness, and Energy, that the moment you come into their presence, or they into yours, you at once catch their spirit, and respond thereto? I contend that there is an actual atmosphere surrounding each of these men . . which if you are sensitive enough you can feel . . one of repulsion, and the other of attraction. And further, that these atmospheres are the result of the constant daily thought of these men or the Mental Attitude of each toward life. Think over this a bit, and you will see at once just how the LAW works.

The third phase of the action of Mental Attitude towards Financial Success may be called the working of the Law of Attraction. Now, without attempting to advance any wild theories, I still must assert that all thinking, observing men have noticed the operation of a mental Law of Attraction, whereby "like attracts like."

Avoiding all theories on the subject, I state the general principle that a man's Mental Attitude acts as a *magnet*, attracting to him the things, objects, circumstances, environments, and people in harmony with that Mental Attitude. If we think Success firmly and hold it properly before us, it tends to build up a constant Mental Attitude which invariably attracts to us the things conducive to its attainment and materialization. If we hold the ideal of Financial Success . . in short, Money . . our Mental Attitude will gradually form and crystallize the MONEY ideal. And the things pertaining to Money . . people calculated to help us win Money . . circumstances tending to bring us Money . . opportunities for making Money . . in fact, all sorts of Money things . . will be attracted toward us.

You think this visionary talk, do you? Well, then, just make a careful study of any man who has attained Financial Success and see whether or not his prevailing attitude is not that of *expectation of money.* He holds this Mental Attitude as an ideal, and he is constantly realizing that ideal.

Fix your mind firmly upon anything, good or bad, in the world, and you attract it to you or are attracted to it in obedience to the LAW. You attract to you the things you expect, think about and hold in your Mental Attitude.

This is no superstitious idea, but a firmly established, scientific, psychological fact.

To further illustrate the workings of the above LAW. "like attracts like." and "birds of a feather flock together," I might here present the theory which of late has been the subject of much discussion among noted psychologists, i. e., that there are thought currents in the mental realm just as there are air currents in the atmosphere, and ocean currents in the seas. For instance, there are thought currents of vice and others of virtue; thought currents of fear and others of courage; thought currents of hate and others of love; thought currents of poverty and others of wealth. And, further than this, the person who thinks and talks and expects poverty is drawn into the poverty thought currents of the world and attracts to himself others who think and talk along the same lines; and vice versa: the person who thinks, talks and expects wealth and prosperity attracts, or is attracted to, people of wealth and comes, in time, to share their prosperity with them.

I am not trying to champion this theory, but if it should be true it behooves each one of us to watch our thought and talk, getting rid of the poverty thought, and in its place substituting the wealth and prosperity thought.

Sweep out from the chambers of your mind all these miserable negative thoughts like "I can't," "That's just my luck," "I knew I'd do it," "Poor me," etc., and then fill up the mind with the positive, invigorating, helpful, forceful, compelling ideals of Success, Confidence, and expectation of that which you desire; and just as the steel filings fly to the attraction of the magnet, so will that which you need fly to you in response to this great natural principle of mental action . . the Law of Attraction. Begin this very moment and build up a new ideal . . that of Financial Success . . see it mentally . . expect it . . demand it! This is the way to create it in your Mental Attitude.

Chapter III

Fear and Worry

THE great negative note in the lives of most people is Fear. Fear is the mother of all the negative emotions, and her brood is found clustering very closely around her. Worry, Lack of Confidence, Bashfulness, Irresolution, Timidity, Depression, and all the rest of the negative brood of feelings and emotions are the progeny of Fear. Without Fear none of these minor emotions or feelings would exist. By killing off the parent of this possible brood of mental vampires, you escape the entire coming generations of negative thoughts, and thus keep your Mental Attitude garden free from these pests and nuisances.

Fear and the emotions that come from its being do more to paralyze useful effort, good work, and finely thought out plans, than aught else known to man. It is the great hobgoblin of the race. It has ruined the lives of thousands of people. It has destroyed the finely budding characters of men and women, and made negative individuals of them in the place of strong, reliant, courageous doers of useful things.

Worry is the oldest child of Fear. It settles down upon one's mind, and crowds out all of the developing good things to be found there. Like the cuckoo in the sparrow's nest, it destroys the rightful occupants of the mind. Laid there as an egg by its parent, Fear, Worry soon hatches out and begins to make trouble. In place of the cheerful and positive "I Can and I Will" harmony. Worry begins to rasp out in raucous tones: "Supposing," "What if," "But," "I can't,""I'm unlucky," "I never could do things right," "Things never turn out right with me," and so on until all the minor notes have been sounded. It makes one sick bodily, and inert mentally. It retards one's progress, and is a constant stumbling block in our path upward.

The worst thing about Fear and Worry is that while they exhaust a great part of the energy of the average person, they give nothing good in return. Nobody ever accomplished a single thing by reason of Fear and Worry. Fear and Worry never helped one along a single inch on the road to Success. And *they* never *will,* because their whole tendency is to retard progress, and not to advance it The majority of things that we fear and worry about never *come to* pass *at all,* and the few that do actually materialize are never as bad as we feared they would be. It is not the cares, trials and troubles of today that unnerve us and break us down . . it is the troubles that we fear may come sometime in the future. Everyone is able to bear the burdens of today, but when he heaps on the burdens of tomorrow, the next day, and the day after that, he is doing his mind an injustice, and it is no wonder that after a bit he heaps on the last straw that breaks the back of the mental camel.

The energy, work, activity and thought that we expend on these imaginary "maybe" troubles of the future would enable us to roaster and conquer the troubles of each day as they arise. Nature gives each of us a reserve supply of strength and energy upon which to draw and oppose unexpected troubles and problems as they come upon us each day. But we poor, silly mortals draw upon this reserve force and dissipate it in combating the imaginary troubles of next week, or next year, the majority of which never really put in an appearance . . and when we have need of the force to oppose some real trouble of the day we find ourselves bankrupt of power and energy, and are apt to go down in defeat, or else be compelled to beat an inglorious retreat.

I tell you, friends, that if you once learn the secret of killing off this vampire of Fear, and thus prevent the rearing of her hateful brood of reptile emotions, life will seem a different thing to you. You will begin to realize what it is to live. You will learn what it is to have a mind cleared of weeds, and fresh to grow healthy thoughts, feelings, emotions and ambitions.

And you will find that with Fear killed out, you will cease to give out to others the suggestions of incompetence, lack of reliance on yourself, and the other impressions that hurt one's chances. You will find that when you are rid of Fear you will radiate hope, and confidence, and ability, and will impress all those with whom you come in contact.

And you will find also that the eradication of Fear will work wonders in your Mental Attitude, and the operation of it through the Law of Attraction. When one fears a thing *he really attracts it to him,* just as if he desired it. The reason is this . . when one desires or fears a thing (in either case the principle is the same) he creates a mental picture of the thing, which mental picture has a tendency toward materialization.

With this mental picture in his mind . . if he holds to it long enough . . he draws the things or conditions to him, and thus "thought takes form in action and being." The majority of our fears and worries are silly little things that take our thought for a moment, and then are gone. They are great wasters of energy, but we do not concentrate on any one of them long enough to put into operation the Law of Attraction.

And so you see, that unless you get rid of Fear, it will tend to draw toward you the thing you fear, or else force you toward the thing itself. Fear makes of the feared object a flame around which you circle and flutter, like the moth, until at last you make a plunge right into the heat of the flame and are consumed. Kill out Fear, by all means.

"But, how may I kill it out?" you cry. Very easily! This is the method: Suppose you had a roomful of darkness. Would you start to shovel or sweep out the darkness? Or would you not throw open the windows and admit the light? When the light pours in, the darkness disappears. And so with the darkness of Fear . . throw open the windows, and "let a little sunshine in." Let the thoughts, feelings, and ideals of Courage, Confidence and Fearlessness pour into your mind, and Fear will vanish. Whenever Fear shows itself in your mind, administer the antidote of Fearlessness immediately. Say to yourself: "I AM Fearless; I Fear Nothing; I AM Courageous." Let the sunshine pour in.

Chapter IV

Faith

"FAITH" *is* a word that has been often misused, misapplied and misunderstood. To many it means simply that attitude of mind which will accept anything that is told it, merely because someone else has said it . . credulity, in fact. But those who have penetrated within the shell of the word know that it means something far more real than this . . something imbedded deep down in the Heart of Things. To those who understand the LAW, Faith is the trolley pole which one raises to meet the Great Forces of Life and Nature, and by means of which one receives the inflow of the Power which is behind, and in all things, and is enabled to apply that Power to the running of his own affairs.

To some, it may seem a far cry from Faith to Financial Success, but to those who have demonstrated the truths enunciated in this little book, the two are closely interwoven. For one to attain Financial Success he must first have Faith in Himself; second, Faith in his Fellowman; and third, Faith in the LAW.

Faith in oneself is of primary importance, for unless one has it he can never accomplish anything; can never influence any other person's opinion of him; can never attract to himself the things, persons and circumstances necessary for his welfare. A man must first learn to believe in himself before he will be able to make others believe in him. People are prone to take a person at his own estimate. If one is weak, negative and lacking in self-confidence, he surrounds himself with an atmosphere of negativity which unfavorably impresses those with whom he comes in contact If one be strong, confident and positive, he radiates like qualities, and those coming in contact with him receive an impression of these qualities. The world believes in those who believe in themselves. And so you see it is of the utmost importance to you that you cultivate this Faith in yourself.

And not only does Faith in yourself operate in the direction of influencing others with whom you come in contact, but it also has a most positive bearing upon your own mental status and thoughts. If you deaden your mind with a negative attitude toward yourself, you stifle budding ideas, thoughts and plans . . you choke the budding plants of your mentality. But, if you let pour forth a full, abiding, confident Faith in yourself . . your abilities, your qualities, your latent powers, your desires, your plans . . your Success, in short . . you will find that the whole mental garden responds to the stimulating influence; and ideas, thoughts, plans and other mental flowers will spring up rapidly. There is nothing so stimulating as a strong, positive "I Can and I Will" attitude toward oneself.

And you remember what has been said about the Law of Attraction . . you remember how "like attracts like," and how one's Mental Attitude tends to draw toward him the things in harmony with his thoughts. Well, this being so, can you not see that a Mental Attitude of Faith or Confidence in Oneself is calculated to attract to you that which fits in with such Faith . . that will tend to materialize your ideal?

"Confidence is the basis of all trade"; so says one of our recent business philosophers, and this statement is true; for if we did not have Confidence or Faith in our Fellowman, all trade, all business, all commerce would come to a standstill. The wholesale merchant ships yearly hundreds of thousands of dollars' worth of goods to dealers in his territory. He has Faith that in thirty, sixty or ninety days those dealers will pay their bills and he will reap his profits. You go to the retail dealer and buy a suit, or dress, or hat, or groceries, having the same charged to your account. Your dealer has

Confidence or Faith enough in you to let you have these goods, expecting that you will pay your bill when it falls due. This same rule holds good in almost every transaction in life. You must have confidence in a man before you care to deal with him.

Some people seem to be of a naturally suspicious frame of mind, always of the opinion that somebody else is trying to "do" them. Others are gullible and swallow everything . . bait, hook and line. Neither is the wisest frame of mind. It is much better to maintain the thought of goodwill, fellowship, and confidence towards one's fellowman, weighing all things impartially from an unprejudiced standpoint, and then render your decision after due thought from the facts in the case. But, by all means, have faith in your Fellowman.

But, this Faith in Oneself, and Faith in your Fellowman, important though they be, are not the only kinds of Faith that one needs in order to attain Financial Success. There is that which may be called Faith in the LAW. This may seem a little strange to you, but when you consider it for a moment, you will see just how it operates.

You will note that nearly all successful men have a deep-rooted belief in Something Outside that helps them along. They do not know just what this Something is . . some call it "Luck"; some call it "their Destiny"; some call it their "Star"; and why not? But under all of these names there is an instinctive belief in, and faith in a Something Friendly that helps them along, and carries them over the hard places, and rounds the sharp corners of business life. Watch any successful man, and you will see that even when he is not able to reason out the means whereby he is going to get over, or around, or under a set of difficulties, still he exhibits a hopeful faith and belief that he is "going to get through it somehow." And he does, if he holds on to his Faith.

Something is there at work tending to "pull him through." Ask any successful business man if this is not so. And this Something, that successful men instinctively trust in, is nothing but this great LAW that underlies all of the affairs of Life. The nearer that one can feel in contact with this LAW, the more power does he receive from it. And thus Faith is the underlying channel by which the Power of the LAW is transmitted to you.

Why should you Fear? You seat yourself in a train or streetcar, and read your paper, having Faith that the engineer or motorman will take you to your destination. You manifest this Faith in everyday business life. Without Faith in the Whole Thing, business would be impossible. You manifest Faith at every turn of the road. And this being so, why should you not manifest Faith in the underlying LAW which is manifesting in things? Do you suppose for an instant that this whole Cosmic Machinery is run by Chance? There is no such thing as Chance! Everything is run under some great LAW! And the Law of Financial Success is just as much a part of that great system of LAW as is the Law of Gravitation.

You study the Laws of physical life, and find them invariable, and therefore worthy of bestowing Faith upon. Why should you not recognize the great Mental Laws operative in business life, and acquaint yourself with their workings? Why should you not have Faith in them? There is no better plan of bringing yourself into harmony with the Law of Financial Success, than to recognize and have Faith in it. Consider the careers of successful business men of your acquaintance and see if this is not so. By doing so you will receive a new light on a heretofore dark subject.

Chapter V

Latent Powers

IN beginning this chapter, I am reminded of the words of Lovell "There are infinite powers lying dormant in man, here, now . . powers which, could he but catch a glimpse of, would endow his life on this planet with greater splendor, and impart to it a redoubled interest."

The man who regards himself as a creature built on a certain mental plan, and incapable of any material change beyond an improvement of the faculties already being expressed, sees but a small portion of the truth regarding himself and his possibilities. Very few men express or manifest more than a small part of their latent power. They live long lives and go down to their graves without suspecting that within their mental kingdom there had reposed dormant faculties, and latent powers which, if expressed, would have enabled them to have lived far wider, broader, fuller lives.

Nearly every man who has attained success along any of the varied lines of human endeavor will tell you that at some period of his life he was called upon to assume certain responsibilities . . . undertake some unaccustomed task . . play some unfamiliar part on life's stage . . and then much to his surprise found that he had within him the power, capability, and qualifications for a successful accomplishment of the strange task. The crucial point was when he was brought face to face with the new undertaking. If, as is the case with the majority of men, he lacked nerve enough to say "I Can and I Will," the story was ended. But if he had that Something within him which enabled him to assert his determination to face the thing manfully and at least to go down with his flags flying rather than to run away, he would find much to his surprise that there was within him a power which responded to the needs of the hour and which enabled him to master the undertaking.

These experiences are not exceptional or unusual . . they are part of the common experience of nearly all successful men. And successful men get to realize that they have within them, hidden in some of the many recesses of the mind, latent powers, unsuspected talents, and dormant faculties which are awaiting calmly the hour of their call to action. The human mind is far from being the simple everyday thing that man regards it.

There are hidden chambers, and unexplored regions. Science is just beginning to learn some of these heretofore unsuspected truths about the mind, and the result is dazzling the observer whose eyes are suddenly seeing the brilliant truths. There seem to be within every man possibilities of which he has never even dreamed. There seem to be capabilities, the extent of which has never entered into even his wildest imagination. Some sudden call, some new responsibility, some new turn of fortune's tide, and the man is called upon to demand of his mentality all that it is holding in store for him . . and he is seldom disappointed, providing he has the nerve and courage to make the demand. Aye, but there's the rub . . few have that courage and nerve. Have YOU?

I know personally a man whose life up to the age of thirty-eight had been spent in active business and professional life. The thought of writing for the public had never occurred to him. AH of a sudden, by one of those strange upheavals that come into the lives of men, all was carried away from him. His health was shattered, his accumulations were swept away, he was apparently lifted up and placed in a new, strange and seemingly unpromising environment. He had his family to support . . he had practically nothing left with which to do it. His health was broken, and it was impossible for him to reengage in his accustomed occupation. While building up his health, he helped a new friend to get the mechanical part of a monthly magazine in shape.

At the last moment his friend discovered that they were short several pages of matter, and the printers were impatiently asking for their full supply. The friend was too busily occupied to write the additional matter, and so in desperation, he turned to my friend and said, "Did you ever write anything for publication?" "No," was the answer. "Well, somebody has got to write something, and mighty quick, too. Have you nerve enough to try it?" "Yes," was the reply. "I'm like the boy digging for woodchuck, who was asked whether he expected to catch it, and who replied, 'You bet I do . . we've got the preacher for dinner, and no meat in the house . . I've *just got to* catch that woodchuck.' And so like the boy. I've just *got to,* and I Can and I Will!" And he *did.*

He sat down to write to fill that space, although he had never written a line for publication before. He made a mighty effort of his Will, urged on by an imperative Desire, and almost in a daze he found his hand at work writing, easily and rapidly. Before long the article was turned out . . *arid it was good.* This success led to others, and that man has been writing books, editing magazines, and doing other work of that kind for the past seven years, and he has been successful all along the line. Within six months after the incident noted above, he had completed a book that has since run through over twenty editions. And since then he has written and had published over a dozen other books on various subjects, none of which has failed to reach his public and all of which have run through a number of editions. Inside of two years after the above incident, he was editing a magazine, built up by his writings, and which attained a circulation of over one hundred thousand per month.

And yet this man had never written a line up to that time. An apparent chance opportunity caused him to face the question, "Can You?" And instead of saying, "Oh, no, I've never done that kind of work . . it is impossible," he answered like the boy after the woodchuck: "I've just *got to* . . I Can and I Will." He met the crucial test . . had nerve enough to tackle the seemingly impossible proposition, and then found within himself unsuspected power, strength and ability . . and *won out*.

Is this merely a lesson in facing difficulties, and cultivating nerve and self-confidence? Not entirely . . it teaches these things and also teaches the still greater truth that every man has within himself wonderful powers, lying dormant and unsuspected, which are merely awaiting the word of the master Will, impelled by a burning, eager, ardent desire, to spring at once into being, full armed and equipped for the fray. And these powers and capabilities come under the LAW . . they are a part of that great Something behind, underneath, and within us all. The recognition of the existence of such powers is the first step toward their, development and unfoldment

You think that you have not ability for Financial Success, simply because you do not realize the existence of these latent powers within you. If you were brought suddenly face to face with the necessity of awakening these powers into action, and could muster up enough courage to say "I Can and I Will," you would find the ready response from within, and the steady flow of knowledge, wisdom, power and ability with which to accomplish the task set before you for completion.

And so my parting words in this chapter are: Do not hesitate to accept any new responsibility, whether the same is forced upon you, or whether you reach out for it yourself. Say to yourself over and over again. "I can and I will accomplish this task. It never would have been put before me unless I were able." And you will be surprised and delighted at the new and wonderful powers that will spring forth from your subconscious self to aid you in your undertaking.

These are not mere idle words, designed to make pleasant reading. They are the words of truths that have become apparent to every successful man or woman. Talk with the successful people of the world, and they will tell you that they have had this experience over and over again . . new opportunities and new necessities brought to them new faculties, and new powers, heretofore undreamed of. The demand always brings the supply, if we will but open ourselves to the inflow from the great Source of Supply . . the Universal Power House.

Chapter VI

Ambition

AMBITION . . what a glorious word! How the very sound of it stirs one's energies, and makes one feel the inspiration to be up and at work doing things, succeeding, creating, accomplishing!

And what does Ambition really mean, pray? It means more than a mere eagerness for things. It means the deep-seated desire to materialize certain ideals which exist in the mind as mental pictures. Before one can accomplish things he must be possessed of Ambition. And before he can feel Ambition he must have the preceding hunger which causes him to manifest Ambition with which to satisfy it. And so it follows, anything that will stimulate that mental hunger, will arouse Ambition, and thus create that eagerness for action and attainment. And how may that mental hunger be produced?

There is a psychological law underlying this mental hunger that manifests as Ambition. And that law is : . *that in order for that mental hunger to be manifested it must have ideals presented to the mind's eye.* Just as the gastric juices of the stomach may be stimulated and caused to flow by the sight, smell, or thought of food, so is this mental hunger produced by the sight, thought or idea of the things needed for its satisfaction. If you are contented with your present life, and want nothing better, it is chiefly because you *know nothing better* . . have seen nothing better . . have heard of nothing better, or else you are mentally and physically lazy.

The ignorant savage seeking to till his land by means of a sharpened stick, cannot desire a steel plow or other agricultural implements if he does not know of them. He simply keeps right at work in his old way . . the way of his forefathers . . and feels no desire for a better implement. But by-and-by some man comes along with a steel plow, and our savage opens his eyes in wide surprise at the wonderful thing. If he be a savage of discernment he begins to get up an interest in the new thing. He watches it at work, and sees how much better it accomplishes the task than does his rude pointed stick. If he be a progressive savage, he begins to wish he had one of the strange new implements, and *if he wants it hard enough* he begins to experience a new, strange feeling of mental hunger for the thing, which if sufficiently strong, causes his Ambition to bud.

And this is the critical point. Up to this time he has felt the strong Desire preceding Ambition. But now with the dawn of Ambition comes the arousing of the Will. And this is what Ambition is, *A Strong Will Aroused by a Strong Desire.*

Without these two elements there can be no Ambition. Desire without Will is not Ambition. One may want a thing very hard, but if he does not arouse his Will strongly enough to actively cooperate with the Desire, his Ambition will "die a-borning." And though one's Will be as strong as steel, yet if mere be not a strong Desire animating and inspiring it, it will not manifest as Ambition.

To manifest Ambition fully, one must first eagerly *desire* the thing . . not a mere "wanting" or "wishing" for it. but a fierce, eager, consuming hunger which demands satisfaction. And then one must have a Will aroused sufficiently strong to go out and get that which Desire is demanding. These two elements constitute the activity of Ambition.

Look around you at the successful men of the world in any line of human effort and endeavor, and you will see that they all have Ambition strongly developed. They have the fierce craving of Desire for things, and the firm Will which will brook no interference with the satisfaction of the Desire. Study the lives of Caesar, Napoleon, and their modern counterparts, the Twentieth Century Captains of Industry, and you will see the glare of this fierce Ambition burning brightly and hotly within them.

The trouble with the majority of the people is that they have been taught that one should take what was given him and be content But this is not Nature's way. Nature implants in each living being a *strong desire* for that which is necessary for its well-being and nourishment, and a *strong will* to gratify that natural desire. On all sides in Nature, you may see this law in effect. The plant and the animal obey it, and are not afraid. But Man, as he ascended the scale of evolution, while seeing the necessity and advantage of curbing and restraining certain tendencies and desires, which if freely gratified would work harm on himself and upon society, has swung to the other extreme. In cutting off the dead branches of Desire, he has lopped off some live ones at the same time . . that is, the majority of men have . . the few who haven't reach out and gather to themselves (he good things of life, throwing the "cores" and leavings to the rest.

There is no earthly reason why a man should not earnestly desire the good things of life . . no reason why he should not stimulate that fierce hunger for attainment by painting mental pictures of what he needs . . by looking upon the good things in the world in the possession of others, so that he can see what he wants. "But does this not arouse covetousness?" you may ask. Not at all . . you are not *coveting* the things the others have, but are merely desiring *other things like them.* You are willing that these other people should retain their things, *but are demanding similar good things for yourself.* This is not covetousness, but laudable Ambition.

And laudable Ambition is all right. There is enough of the good things of life in this world for all of us, if we demand them, and reach out for them. Demand causes supply, in and under the LAW, so be not afraid. Arouse your Ambition . . it is a good thing and not something of which to be ashamed. Urge it on . . feed it . . stimulate its growth. It is not a foul weed, but a strong, vigorous, healthy plant in the garden of life, bearing more fruit than any other growing thing there.

Do not let the argument that men have used Ambition to accomplish evil ends disconcert you. Every natural law is capable of being used for good or evil. Because any law has been used for evil, it is no reason why those who desire to do good should avoid it, and refrain from using it for right purposes. To do so would be like the Angels of Light running away and leaving the powers of darkness in possession of all the good things of the world. The best way is to grasp the weapon and turn it against the enemy.

The LAW is there awaiting man's use. If you prefer to leave it for the evil disposed persons, very well, that is your own loss. But the wise, the sane., the strong men of the day are now reaching out for the use of the LAW and are accomplishing great things by reason of it. When the Many use the LAW, the Few will cease to be the sole possessors of the good things of life, which alas! so many of them have misused. When the secret is generally known, the evil will be eradicated and good will supersede it.

Therefore, be not afraid to stand boldly out, crying: "I want this, and I am going to have it! It is my rightful heritage, and I demand it of the LAW!" Be ambitious to attain Financial Success because that is the goal for which you are striving.

Chapter VII

Desire

IN some of the previous chapters I have spoken of the operation of Desire and Will in the manifestation and expression of personal power under the LAW. Now, while there have been many writers who have discoursed ably regarding the mighty power of me Will, there have been but few who have given to the subject of Desire the attention that it deserves, and the consideration it merits. Many persons seem afraid to speak of Desire, for they have gotten the term and idea mixed up with desires of an unworthy and detrimental nature. They have overlooked the fact that Desire must underlie all human action . . must be the causing power back of and underneath Will itself.

We might compare Desire with the fire that burns brightly beneath the receptacle containing water, which latter represents the mind. Unless the fire of Desire burns brightly and imparts its heat to the water, or mind, there will be nothing but water. But let the fire manifest its ardent energy and heat, and lo! the water is converted into steam which turns mighty wheels, and drives powerful machinery, and in fact "makes things go." We are apt to forget the causes that have operated in order that the steam be produced, in our wonder, amazement and admiration of the power and effect of the manifested steam. But, in order to get the right idea of the matter fixed in our mind we must take into consideration the water of the mind, and the fire of Desire.

The mind is well represented by water, for it is unstable, changeable, in motion, having eddies, storms, ripples and calms. And Desire is well represented by fire, for it is ardent, hot, strong and burning, and when manifested properly invariably acts upon the water-mind and produces the will-steam which may be turned to the accomplishment of any task, and the moving of the material necessary for our plans. By all means keep the fire of Desire brightly burning under your mental boilers, and you will be sure to manifest the proper amount and degree of the steam of Will which may then be applied to the accomplishing of your life tasks.

If you will keep the figure of speech before your mind . . this idea of the fire of desire, the water of the mind, and the steam of will . . you will find it easier to put into operation these great mental forces, and to be known as the man or woman of the "Strong Will." But if you allow the fires of Desire to burn low, or to become clogged with the ashes of dead and gone things, long since exhausted and useless, you will find that there will be little or no steam of will produced, and you will be in the position of the majority of people who are like tea kettles simmering over a faint fire, and accomplishing nothing.

Unless you want a thing "the worst way," and manifest that Desire in the shape of a strong impelling force, you will have no will with which to accomplish anything. You must not only "want" to do a thing, or to possess a thing, but you must "want to hard."

You must want it as the hungry man wants bread as the smothering man wants air. And if you will but arouse in yourself this fierce, ardent, insatiate Desire, you will set in operation one of Nature's most potent mental forces.

What is that great impelling force that you have felt within yourself whenever you have made a mighty effort to accomplish something? Is it not that surging, restless, impelling force of your being that you know as Desire? Did you do the thing simply because you thought it best, or because you felt within yourself a strong feeling that you WANTED to do the thing,, or to possess the thing, in the strongest possible way? Did you not feel this strong force of Desire rising within you and impelling you to deed, and action?

Desire is the great moving power of the Mind . . that which excites into action the will and powers of the individual. It is at the bottom of all action, feeling, emotion or expression. Before we reach out to do a thing, or to possess a thing, we must first "want to," and in the degree that that "want to" is felt, so will be our response thereto. Before we love, hate, like or dislike, there must be a Desire of some kind. Before we can arouse ambition there must be a strong Desire. Before we can manifest energy, there must be a strong impelling Desire.

Did you ever stop to think that the difference between the strong of the race, and the weak, is largely a matter of Desire? The degree of Desire manifests in the different degrees of strength and weakness. The strong men of the race are filled with strong desires to do this thing, or to possess that. They are filled with that strong creative Desire that makes them want to build up, create, modify, change, and shift around. It is not alone the fruits of their labor that urge them on, but that insistent urge of the creative Desire that drives them on.

Do not be afraid to allow your Desire for Financial Success to burn brightly. Keep the ashes of past failures, disappointments, and discouragements well cleared away so that you may have a good draught. Keep the fire of Desire burning brightly, ardently and constantly. Do not be sidetracked by outside things, for remember, concentrated Desire is that which produces the greatest steam producing power. Keep your mind fixed on that which you want, and keep on demanding that which belongs to you, for it is your own. The Universal Supply is adequate for all needs of everyone, but it responds only to the insistent demand and the earnest Desire. Learn to Desire things in earnest, and rest not content with a mere wanting and wishing.

Desire creates Mental Attitude . . develops Faith . . nourishes Ambition . . unfolds Latent Powers . . and tends directly and surely toward Success. Let the strong, dominant desire for Financial Independence possess you from the tips of your toes to the roots of your hair, . . feel it surging through every part of your body . . and then don't stop until you reach your goal.

Chapter VIII

Will Power

O WELL for him whose Will is strong!," writes Tennyson, and the poets of all nations and times have sung the same song. Tennyson well voices this human regard and admiration for the power of the Will. He tells us again: "O living Will, thou shalt endure, when all that seems shall suffer shock."

The Will of man is a strange, subtle, intangible, and yet very real thing that is closely connected with the inmost essence of his "I." When the "I" acts, it acts through the Will. The Will is the immediate expression of the Ego, or "I" in Man, which rests at the very seat of his being. This Ego, or "I" within each of us . . that inmost self of each one of us . . expresses itself in two ways. It first asserts "I AM," by which it expresses its existence and reality; then it asserts "I *Will*" by which it expresses its desire to act, and its determination to do so. The "I Will" comes right from the center of your being, and is the strongest expression of the Great Life Force within you. And in the degree that you cultivate and express it, is the degree of positivity that you manifest. The person of weak Will is a negative, cringing weakling, while he of strong Will is the positive, courageous, masterful individual in whom Nature delights and whom she rewards.

The human Will is an actual living force. It is just as much an active force of Nature as is Electricity, Magnetism, or any other form of natural force. Will is as real an Energy as is gravitation. From atom to man. desire and Will are in evidence . . first comes the desire to do a thing, and then comes the Will that does it. It is an invariable law pervading all natural forms, shapes, degrees of things . . animate and inanimate.

Nothing is impossible to the man who can Will . . providing he can Will sufficiently strong. And as Will depends so very much upon one's belief in his ability, it may be said that all action depends upon belief. One does not Will unless he believes that he has a Will. And many a man of inherent strong Will does not express it or exert it, simply because he does not realize that he possesses it It is only when the necessity arises from some new unexpected demand for the exercise of the Will, that many men realize that they really possess such a Will. To many, alas, such a necessity never comes.

In speaking about the Will, I do not mean stubbornness. You will find plenty of people who are as stubborn as mules and their friends and neighbors will say that "they are strong-willed," meaning by this that when they decide a thing "is so, it's so, and you can't make me believe it isn't." This is the mulish attitude of mind coming from prejudice or ignorance and has nothing to do with the Will. The man with the strong Will knows when to recede from his position as well as when to go forward; he never stands still. When the occasion warrants it, he steps back, but only for the purpose of getting a better start, for he always has a definite goal in view. When the command from within calls him to go forward, he drives right ahead like the mighty ocean steamer, majestic in his power and stopping for nothing. This frame of mind is best illustrated by the following quotation written of Howard the philanthropist:

"The energy of his determination was so great, that if instead of being habitual, it had been shown only for a short time on particular occasions, it would have appeared a vehement impetuosity; but, by being unintermitted, it had an equability of manner which scarcely appeared to exceed the tone of a calm constancy, it was so totally the reverse of anything like turbulence or agitation. It was the calmness of an intensity, kept uniform by the nature of the human mind forbidding it to be more, and by the character of the individual forbidding it to be less."

The subject of the development of the Will is too large for a single chapter of any book. It is the study of a lifetime. Several fine books have been written covering the subject fairly well, but the best so far, are two recent books by Haddock, "Power of Will" and "Power for Success" which contain the essence of about everything ever written on the subject that is of value to one who desires development along these lines. Buy and study these books by all means.

The writer believes that the basis of all personal power resides in the Will and that if one intends to accomplish anything in this world he must acquire a powerful Will. The best way to do this is to first recognize your lack, and then by constant affirmations of "I can and I will accomplish this thing," and by the repetition of selections on the Will, taken from the best literature, build up within yourself, little by little, an invincible power and energy that will overcome every temptation to sidetrack you from your life purpose. At the end of this chapter I have appended some excellent selections and others you will find scattered throughout the book. These selections can be memorized and then repeated in times of trial and discouragement and they will prove invigorating tonic for the depressed mind.

The proper attitude of the student of the Law of Financial Success is that mental attitude which may best be expressed as the "I CAN AND I WILL" state of mind. In this mental attitude there are combined the two primary elements of the accomplishment of things. First there comes that belief in one's ability, powers, and force which begets confidence, and which causes one to make a clear mental channel over which the Will flows. Then, second, comes the assertion of the Will itself .. the "I WILL" part of it. When a man says "I WILL" with all the force and energy and determination of his character being poured into it, then does his Will become a very Dynamic Force which sweeps away obstacles before it in its mighty onrush.

Not only does this expression of the Will stir into activity the latent powers and dormant energies of the man's mind, bringing to the accomplishment of the task all his reserve force, power and strength, but it does much more. It impresses those around him with a mighty psychical power which compels attention to his words and demands recognition for himself. In all conflicts between men, the strongest Will wins the day. The struggle may be short, or it may be long, but the end is the same always .. the man of the strongest Will wins.

And not only does the awakened Will do this, but it also acts in the direction of affecting those at a distance from the person. It sets in motion certain natural laws which tend to compel things toward the center occupied by a mighty Will. Look around you, and you will see that the men of giant Wills set up a strong center of influence, which extends on all sides in all directions, affecting this one and that one, and drawing and compelling others to fall in with the movements instigated by that Will. There are men who set up great whirlpools or whirlwinds of Will, which are felt by persons far and near. And, in fact all persons who exert Will at all, do this to a greater or lesser extent, depending upon the degree of Will expressed. - Read, study, and absorb the following selections:

"The education of the Will is the object of our existence."

* * *

"They can who think they can. Character is a perfectly educated Will."

* * *

"Nothing can resist the Will of a man who knows what is true and wills what is good."

* * *

"To will evil is to will death. A perverse Will is the beginning of suicide."

* * *

"In all difficulties advance and Will, for within you is a Power, a living Force which, the more you trust and learn *to* use, will annihilate the opposition of matter."

* * *

"The star of die unconquered Will,
He rises in my breast,
Serene and resolute and still.
And calm and self-possessed."

* * *

"So nigh is grandeur to our dust.
So near is God to man.
When Duty whispers low, 'Thou must!'
The youth replies, 'I can"

* * *

Edward Beals - The Law of Financial Success

"I will to will with energy and decision! I will to persist in willing! I will to will intelligently and for a goal! I will to exercise the will in accordance with the dictates of reason and of morals."

* * *

"The human will, that force unseen.
The offspring of a deathless soul,
Can hew a way to any goal.
Though walls of granite intervene!

* * *

"You will be what you will to be.
Let failure find its false content
In that poor word environment,
But spirit scorns it and is free.
"It masters time, it conquers space.
It cows that boastful trickster, chance,
And bids the tyrant circumstance
Uncrown and fill a servant's place."

* * *

"There is no chance, no destiny, no fate.
Can circumvent, or hinder, or control
The firm resolve of a determined soul.
Gifts count for nothing, will alone is great;
AH things give way before it soon or late.
What obstacle can stay the mighty force
Of the sea-seeking river in its course.
Or cause the ascending orb of day to wait?
Each well-born soul must win what it deserves,
Let the fools prate of luck. The fortunate
r he whose earnest purpose never swerves.

Whose slightest action, or inaction
Serves the one great aim. Why, even Death itself
Stands still and waits an hour sometimes
For such a will."

Chapter IX

Auto Suggestion

You will have noticed that in the preceding chapters I have begun a serious campaign in the direction of having you "make yourself over" mentally, in order to bring you under the operation of the Law of Financial Success. You will remember that **first** I tried to get you to regard Money in a new light . . as a natural supply akin to the nourishment of the plant, and coming under the same general law of Natural Supply and Demand.

Second . . I urged upon you to build up the proper Mental Attitude, showing you how by so doing you would cultivate in yourself the faculties, qualities and powers conducive to success; the qualities likely to attract and influence people with whom you come in contact; and the mental state which would set into operation the beneficent phases of the Law of Attraction.

Third . . I proceeded to get Fear and Worry out of your mental system.

Fourth . . I went on to cultivate the quality of Faith in you.

Fifth . . came the consideration of the Latent Powers and the rules for their unfoldment.

Sixth . . came the explanation of the nature of Ambition, and the urge to cultivate and develop it.

Seventh . . came the explanation of the wonderful effect and office of Desire, and the advice to cultivate Desire as a means of cultivating Will.

Eighth . . I gave you instruction for the development of a powerful Will, the acquirement of which means so much to you.

Now. if you will stop a moment, you will see that the practical application of the instruction given and the precepts laid down for your guidance require a certain "making over" of yourself, on your part.

This being so the question arises: "How may I best accomplish the 'making-over' process?" And to answer this question, I shall now devote several chapters, for in the answering lies much of the essence of this instruction that I am desirous of imparting to you. And so this is the reason that we now take up the subject of "Auto Suggestion," a subject of the greatest importance to you, and which has engaged the minds of scientific men for the past few years. Let us hasten to a consideration of the subject.

In the first place the term "Suggestion," as used by psychologists means "an *impression* made upon the mind of another." And an "auto suggestion" is an *impression* made upon one's own mind in a manner similar to that used in impressing the mind of another. You will see this a little clearer in a moment. The whole essence of Suggestion lies in the idea of *"impression."* Think of the mind as a wax substance, and the Suggestion as a die making an *impression* on the wax,, and there you have it.

If you can manage to get in a strong Suggestion on the mind of a person, you really *impress* your notion or idea upon his mental wax, so to speak. Suggestion is *not a matter of argumentative effort,* but a process of saying a thing so positively, earnestly and convincingly that the other person takes up the idea *without argument.* We may be impressed by a man's earnestness, his manner, his attitude, his dress, and in many other ways, but the principle is the same . . if we are *impressed* by something about him, we have taken the Suggestion. Do you see what I mean?

Well, one may turn this Suggestive die upon the wax of his own mind and by repeated *impressions* may fix certain ideas, qualities, and characteristics upon it so that he will have really made himself over to that extent. It is a case of "sez I to myself, sez I" . . often repeated until "I" believes what "I sez." You know how a man may get to actually believe some old lie that he has been telling for some time. A man may act out a certain assumed character, until he actually becomes like the character. There are plenty of old chaps strutting around today with these assumed characters, which not only fool the people with whom they come in contact, but also actually fool the men themselves. Now if this be true about things of this kind, how important does the principle become when applied to the creation of new characteristics and qualities in oneself that are conducive to success. You all know just about the ones you need, and now here is the way to go about getting them.

To many people Auto Suggestion means simply the repeating of certain words to themselves, like "I AM Energetic . . I AM Ambitious," etc., etc. Now this plan is all very well, for a constant impression of this kind will undoubtedly tend to develop the suggested qualities in one. But there is a far more scientific plan known to psychologists, and that is the one I am going to urge upon your consideration. It is that not only should one "say" things to himself, but that he should also create Mental Images of the desired thing, and should also act out the part he wishes to play, in a sort of extended preliminary rehearsal.

All this may seem odd to you unless you have studied the psychological principles underlying it, which I have not time to go into here. The thing to remember is that constant thinking of a desired quality of mind, accompanied with the indulgence in the Mental Picture of yourself as actually possessed of the quality itself, and also accompanied by an "acting out" of the part you would like to play, will in due time so impress and mold your mind that you will *actually possess* the quality itself. Here is a great psychological law I have expressed. Read it again, study it, and make it your own.

For instance, let us suppose that you lack Ambition. Well, the first thing is to rouse the Desire to become Ambitious. Then start in the plan of "sez I to myself, sez I," and make constant affirmation of the fact that: "I AM *Ambitious . . very Ambitious . . my Ambition grows every day,"* and so on. Then picture yourself in your imagination as being Ambitious . . see yourself as moving around in the world possessed of an insatiable Ambition which is leading you to strenuous action and wonderful accomplishments. Then begin to act out the part of the Ambitious man . . study some Ambitious man until you catch his feelings and then begin to *look* Ambitious; *talk* in the tones of a man possessing Ambition; walk like an Ambitious man . . in short act out the part to the smallest details.

Now remember I do not mean to copy the mannerisms of the man you have taken for your model . . this is not the thing at all. Simply study him until you can get his *feelings* . . until you can recognize the Ambitious emotion and Mental Attitude animating him, and then go to work to *feel* the same inward feeling yourself, and to act out the feeling. If you can once get the *feeling,* then all you've got to do is to act it out right

You will find that this plan of mental discipline and exercise may be used for the acquirement of any and every one of the positive qualities you may desire to acquire and possess. This is no mere theory, but is a scientific fact known to and taught by some of the leading authorities on the subject in the world. It has been the basis of the making over of thousands of people, some of whom have paid enormous fees to teachers for just this plain advice, elaborated and padded out into long series of personal lectures and lessons. I offer you something here that is well "worthwhile." Now it is for you to take it and use it.

Chapter X

Harmony

ALL through Nature, and Nature's manifestations, there exists rhythm and Harmony. Everything in the Universe is in unceasing action. There is a universal vibratory movement apparent everywhere. From the atoms, and the particles composing the atoms, up through all the material combinations and groupings there is constant, incessant vibration and motion. And from this constant motion, and running through its entire manifestation, there is apparent a constant and invariable law of rhythm. Just as there is a rhythm apparent in all that we call music, so is there a rhythm in the music of Nature. And from that rhythm proceeds that which we call Harmony.

The planets as they swing in regular orbits around the sun . . yes, the suns as they swing around still greater suns . . and so on until the mind fails to grasp the wonder of it all . . all manifest rhythm. The sea in its manifestation of the rise and fall of the tides, exhibits rhythm. The heart of man breathes in rhythmic measure. In the great waves of light traveling to us from the sun and stars, millions upon millions of miles away, there exists a rhythmic measure registered upon the delicate instruments of science.

You have heard of the wonderful force latent in the rhythmic measure of music. You have read of instances in which mighty bridges have been shattered by the note of the violin constantly sounded in an uninterrupted rhythm. It seems almost incredible, but it is true that the soft note of a tiny violin, constantly sounded in regular rhythm can become powerful enough to make the bridge first tremble, and then shudder, and then sway to and fro until it finally collapses. Science teaches us that even the mighty steel skyscrapers of our great cities could be brought to the ground in a mass of twisted steel rods, if one were but to ascertain the keynote of the entire building, and then manage to start into motion the vibrations of a strong musical instrument, constantly sounding that one keynote, over and over again, for hour after hour, until the great giant structure would "catch the motion" and begin to tremble.

"To catch the motion," that is it. If we could but "catch me motion" of Nature's great rhythmic harmony we could accomplish anything. And this is not such a wild dream as might be supposed at first glance. There is a great rhythmic harmony inherent in the mind of man. Just as the bridge has its keynote, so has the mind of each man, and the great mind of the race of men. And if we will but withdraw ourselves from the incidents and distractions of the outer life and retire for a moment or so within the inner regions of ourselves, we may catch the faint echo of that great Universal Harmony of the mind, sounding clear and well denned. If we can do this, we have but to take up the mental keynote and sound it until we make our influence felt.

Men of the busy world . . the "practical" men of our day . . are beginning to realize this fact, and we hear strange stories of such men closing their private office doors for a few moments during the day, and communing with themselves, withdrawing their attention from the distracting thoughts and scenes of the outside world. This is no mere transcendental idea, but a fact that many shrewd business men of the day are turning to good account.

Remember, that "in quietness there is strength." Every person who is ambitious and has a definite object in life should take a few minutes off each day, and sit alone, giving himself a chance to think, meditate, and allow the great rhythmic harmony of Nature to flow through his cleared mind, and thus gain renewed strength and energy. It is in these quiet moments, when the outer mind is relaxed and resting, that the inner mind flashes to us that which is best for us to do. We should cultivate this habit in moments of meditation, when we may escape from the people and crowd, and thus be able to listen to the voice that sounds from within. By doing this we place ourselves in harmony with the great Universal Power from which all original ideas spring into our mental organism ready for use a few moments later when we reemerge into the world of action and of men.

Here are a few directions for entering into harmony with the Universal Rhythm of Nature: First, your mental attitude must be right. You must have gained control of your thoughts and words, so that your mind is open and receptive to the great good of the world. There must be no hate there, no discouragement, no pessimism, no negative, cringing, worm-of-the-dust or poverty thought . . your frame of mind must be that of goodwill, encouragement, optimism, with positive thoughts expectant of wealth, prosperity, and all the good things that man, heir of the universe, is entitled to by right of his sonship. This latter mental attitude will surround you with a personal thought atmosphere which repels from you the negative or evil things and attracts to you the positive or good things of life.

When you are satisfied that your personal atmosphere is right, then each day, preferably between twelve and one o'clock, or if that time is not convenient, early in the morning just after your bath, close the doors of your room, shutting out everybody and everything for a few moments. Take precautions that you shall not be disturbed, and then put away from your mind the fear of interruption and disturbance. Take a position of restful and peaceful calm. Relax every muscle, and take the tension off of every nerve. Take a few deep restful breaths, which will seem like great sighs, and will tend to relax your body and mind. Then detach your thoughts from the outer world, and things, and turn the mind inward upon yourself.

Shut out all the material cares, worries and problems of the day and sink into a mental state of peaceful calm. Think "*I open myself to the inflow of the Universal Rhythmic Harmony,*" and you will soon begin to feel a sense of relationship with that Harmony coming into you, filling your mind and body with a feeling of rest and peace, and latent power. Then shortly after will come to you a sense of new strength and energy, and a desire to once more emerge upon the scene of your duties. This is the time for you to close the meditation. Do not seek to prolong it, but go forth with your new energy, filled with the vibrations of the Universal, and you will see how refreshed and vigorous you are, and how your mind leaps eagerly and enthusiastically to the tasks before it.

Oh yes! all this does belong to the subject of Financial Success as you will find out if you will practice a little and discover the secret of the silence as given above. If you doubt it and smile with a quizzical, know-it-all smile then you are the one who needs it most Just remember that this is not written by some wild theorist soaring in the clouds of hazy metaphysics, but by a business man . . part of it during business hours amidst the cares, duties, and exactions of a strenuous business life . . who has applied these principles and knows whereof he speaks.

I shall now tell you a secret known only to a few. From this time on it is yours. See that you use it. Here it is: A few moments spent with your inner self and the Great Universal Power each day, as described above, if practiced assiduously, will establish within you the Creative Mind . . that wonderful thing which marks the difference between the Italian ditch digger, who plods along from day to day with never a new idea for his own or humanity's betterment, and the man "at the top" who "does things"; the constructive man who builds railroads, steamships, large mercantile establishments, and who furnishes funds to carry the great work of the world along. Both of these men are needed, but it feels better to be near the top.

The more you practice, the more you will open up that great subconscious reservoir of yours which is overflowing with original ideas. In time you will gain the power to get in touch with your inner self and tap that reservoir wherever you may be . . the street car . . out for a walk . . while you are shaving . . and there will flash through to your conscious mind, in vivid outlines, ideas that when worked out will mean for you Money and Financial Independence.

Chapter XI

Creation

THE title of this chapter may appear strange to some of those who find it in a book entitled "The Law of Financial Success," and such people may wonder what in the world "Creation" has to do with the subject of Financial Success. I ask such persons to wait patiently until the chapter is finished, and I promise to do my best to convince these doubters that Creation has *very much* to do with the attainment of Financial Success, and that, in fact, there can be little or no Financial Success without the operation of the creative energy of the mind.

Did you ever stop to think that in the case of some of the mighty bridges spanning the rivers surrounding New York City, each span, each strand of steel, each support, each bit of construction . . and the whole bridge in its entirety . . existed and was created in the mind of the designer before it was manifested or materialized?

Did you ever think that die great buildings which rear their imposing forms and shapes along our business streets were created in the minds of their architects, and actually existed in their minds before the buildings could be erected?

Did you ever think that the delicate mechanism of the watch you are carrying in your pocket existed in the mind of its designer long before the material watch was evolved from the parts? The watch would not be, and could not be, unless the designer had seen it all in his mind's eye, down to the smallest detail, before he materialized it.

The above statements are more or less commonplace, but the majority of people overlook these important facts in the contemplation of material things. They ignore the fact that anything and everything that has ever been created in material form must of necessity have been created in mental form previously. There is no exception to this rule. Everything that is materialized must have existed previously in the mind of the person creating it The house, the bridge, the watch, die suit of clothes, the hat, the penknife, the shoes, the buttons on the clothes . . everything that you can see, or think of, *that has been made,* has first been created mentally, in its every part and as a whole.

When we materialize a thing by creating or building it, we simply build the material around the mental picture of the thing that we have first created. *The primal building is in the mind.* And this is true of Financial Success just as it is true of everything else. Some build little by little, seeing only just a little in advance of their building, and thus do their mental creation by piecemeal. Others see the whole thing in general outlines, and then fill in the details as they go along. The principle is the same in both cases.

It is told of Thomas Lawson, of Boston . . he of "Frenzied Finance" fame . . that when he was a youth he painted a mental picture of a large estate on which there was the finest breed of horses, and the choicest cattle in the world; a beautiful home furnished and filled with objects of artistic value; and everything else necessary for the completion of his conception of an ideal home. He has said that his successive steps toward the acquirement of that home . . the gaining of the wealth necessary for its purchase, was like the filling in of the details of the picture, the image of which never faded away from his mind.

And so it is with Financial Success. You must form a mental picture of what you want, and then bend every effort to fill in the picture. Every person should have a purpose in life. To win anything one should have a definite goal for which to strive. We should have a picture in our mind of what we want to own or attain. If we want money, we should create a mental picture of money . . see ourselves using it, handling it, spending it, acquiring more, and in short going through all the motions of the man of money. One should paint a great mental picture of wealth, and then start to work to fill in the picture, and to materialize it.

What do you suppose would happen if the architect of the bridge, or building, or the designer of the watch should fail to see in his mind that which he was about to create? Can you not see that there would be no building worthwhile, and that the result of the attempt to build watch, bridge, or skyscraper in this way would result in a mere throwing together of material, without regard to beauty, stability or proper use?

And so it is with the majority of people . . they sit down and say "Oh, I want money . . I want money," and that is all there is to it They do not use their imaginations sufficiently to *mentally create money,* and then proceed to materialize it They are like a man who would sit down crying out: "Oh, I want a wood pile, high and big with good wood." The man who gets the wood pile, glances around the place where he wants the pile, and then he forms a mental picture of how that wood pile will look when completed . . just about how high and broad it should be, and then he starts to work to fill in the picture with the wood, working away sawing and piling until at last his picture is materialized.

Oh, I tell you friends, you must first know *just what you want,* before you will be able to materialize it. Unless you *know what you want,* you will never get anything. The great successful men of the world have used their imaginations, instead of despising them. They think *ahead* and create their mental picture, and then go to work materializing that picture in all its details, filling in here, adding a little there, altering this a bit and that a bit, but steadily building . . steadily building.

If you would attain Financial Success, you must become a mental creator and designer of that which you long for as well as a material builder. The two go hand in hand and work for Financial Success.

Chapter XII

Concentration

EVERY person who reads this chapter has heard the word "Concentration" used frequently; has seen it in print often; and has used it repeatedly in conversation. But how few really know just what it means . . or are able to form a mental picture of Concentration. Let us consider the term a moment, for until you are able to form a clear mental picture of it, you will not be able to apply it advantageously.

What is "Concentration"? Well, the dictionaries tell us that the word means the act or process of bringing or directing things toward a common center, and thereby condensing and intensifying the force of the thing. And that is the keynote of the word . . that is the mental picture of it . . this *bringing forces to a common center.*

One can best form a mental picture of the idea expressed in the word by thinking of a sunglass which so concentrates the rays of the sun to a focus, or common center, that their powers are intensified upon the spot so that they easily burn a hole through anything placed on the spot.

We can never expect to win out in anything unless we firmly concentrate our minds upon the thing we seek. We have got to make our mental picture of what we want, and then start in to desire it as hard as we are able to, and by so doing we will concentrate our attention and will upon that thing until "something happens." We must learn to concentrate our powers and will upon the desired object, just as the sunglass concentrates the rays of the sun upon the common focus. We must learn to focus our energies upon the thing we want, and then to keep the focus steady from day to day, never allowing ourselves to be sidetracked or swerved from our main object of desire, interest and will.

The majority of people have little or no concentration, and they resemble the puppy dog whose attention is attracted by first one thing and then another, and who runs from this thing to that, to and fro, not knowing what he wants long enough to get it, but continually wasting his energy in chasing things that have attracted the attention of the moment.

One should begin by practicing concentration on little things, until he masters them, and then he may move on to the consideration and contemplation of larger things. It is quite an art to be able to do one thing at a time, to the exclusion of distracting thoughts and objects. The best workmen along any line of human effort are those who are able to concentrate on their work, and practically lose themselves in their tasks for the time being.

The first step in acquiring Concentration begins, of course, in the control of the attention. Master the attention and you have acquired the art of Concentration. By holding your attention upon a thing, you direct to it your mental forces, and new ideas, plans and combinations spring into your mind and fly to a common center. Besides this you put into operation the Law of Attraction and direct its forces to that same common center. Without concentrated attention you scatter and dissipate your mental forces and accomplish nothing at all.

I urge upon all who read this book the importance of beginning to cultivate concentration. Begin by acquiring the habit of attending to one thing at a time, concentrating the attention upon it, and then completing it and passing on to another thing. Avoid the baneful practice of thinking of one thing while doing another. Think of and work upon the thing before you, and hold your attention there until it is completed. The thinking and action should pull together, instead of in opposite directions.

An eminent authority tells us that: "It is a matter of no small importance that we acquire the habit of doing only one thing at a time, by which I mean that while attending to any one object, our thoughts ought not to wander to another." Another authority adds: "A frequent cause of failure in the faculty of attention, is striving to think of more than one thing at a time." Another says: "She did things easily because she attended to them in the doing. When she made bread, she thought of bread, and not of the fashion of her next dress, or of her partner at the last dance." The celebrated Lord Chesterfield said: "There is time enough for everything in the course of a day. if you do but one thing at a time; but there is not time enough in a year if you try to do two things at a time."

If there is any secret of concentration, it is contained in the following sentence: *You can concentrate on anything you are intensely interested in, or dearly love.* For instance, if you are a young man engaged to a beautiful young lady, the ideal woman to make your life complete, you have no trouble in thinking about her and how happy you will be after the knot is tied. In fact, most of your time . . when you are not thinking of your work . . is given over to thoughts of *that girl,* and your future together. Sometimes even her face pops up before you and you think of her when you should be devoting your time and thought to the work you are paid for.

If you are the proud father of a new baby girl or boy you have no trouble in thinking about that dear little bit of humanity. If you are a mother whose son is forging to the front in business or one of the professions, your thought goes as naturally to that boy as a duck takes to water. And so we might go down the whole gamut of humanity and find some one thing which each person is *interested in* or *loves,* and we would soon see that it is not a hard task for a person to think about or concentrate on that which is most dear to him or her.

Just at the present time the thing closest to your heart, next, of course, to that which you actually love, is or should be Financial Independence. For with money at your disposal you can give that girl everything she needs to make her happy; you can insure that child's future and make sure that it has the education which it deserves; you can establish that boy in business and give him a chance to express his full ability; you can complete those plans you have had in mind so long and you can do many things which are now impossible.

It certainly ought not to be hard for you to concentrate on Financial Independence when it means so much to you, ought it? Well, go to work now, and when your mind is not occupied with your regular duties, when your thought is roaming around here and there accomplishing nothing, when you find yourself thinking of something foolish or vicious, exert your will, draw back your thought, use your imagination to picture an ideal of what Financial Independence will mean to you, and then concentrate your whole thought on that ideal to bring it into materialization. Now is the time to begin, friend; do not leave it until tomorrow.

Chapter XIII

Persistence

IN the last chapter we considered the subject of "Concentration," and I tried to show you what an important part it played in the workings of the Law of Financial Success. But, if you concentrate on one thing this minute, and another thing the next moment, and so on, flitting from one flower to another like the butterfly, you will accomplish very little. What is needed is a steady, determined, persistent application to the one object upon which you have set your mind. Having found the object of your desire and knowing how to concentrate upon it, you should then learn how to be Persistent in your concentration, aim, and purpose.

There is nothing like sticking to a thing. Many men are brilliant, resourceful, and industrious, but they fail to reach the goal by reason of their lack of "stick-to-it-iveness." One should acquire the tenacity of the bulldog, and refuse to be shaken off of a thing once he has fixed his attention and desire upon it. You remember the old Western hunter who when once he had gazed upon an animal and said "You're my meat," would never leave the trail or pursuit of that animal if he had to track it for weeks, losing his meat in the meantime. Such a man would in time acquire such a faculty of Persistence that the animals would feel like Davy Crockett's coon who cried out. "Don't shoot, mister. I'll come down without it."

You know the dogged persistence inherent in some men that strikes us as an irresistible force when we meet them and come into conflict with their persistent determination. We are apt to call this the "Will," but it is our old friend Persistence . . that faculty of holding the Will firmly up against objects, just as the workman holds the chisel against the object on the wheel, never taking off the pressure of the tool until the desired result is obtained.

No matter how strong a Will a man may have, if he has not learned the art of persistent application of it he fails to obtain the best results. One must learn to acquire that constant, unvarying, unrelenting application to the object of his Desire that will enable him to hold his Will firmly against the object until it is shaped according to his wishes. Not only today and tomorrow, but every day until the end.

Buxton has said: "The longer I live, the more certain I am that the great difference between men, between the feeble and the powerful, the great and the insignificant, is Energy . . Invincible Determination . . a purpose once fixed, and then Death or Victory. That quality will do anything that can be done in this world . . and no talents, no circumstances, no opportunities, will make a two-legged creature a man without it."

Donald G. Mitchell said: "Resolve is what makes a man manifest; not puny resolve; not crude determinations; not errant purpose . . but that strong and indefatigable Will which treads down difficulties and danger, as a boy treads down the heaving frost-lands of winter, which kindles his eye and brain with a proud pulse-beat toward the unattainable. Will makes men giants."

Disraeli said: "I have brought myself by long meditation to the conviction that a human being with a settled purpose must accomplish it, and that nothing can resist a Will which will stake even existence upon its fulfillment."

Sir John Simpson said: "A passionate desire and an unwearied Will can perform impossibilities, or what may seem to be such to the cold and feeble."

And John Foster adds his testimony, when he says: "It is wonderful how even the casualties of life seem to bow to a spirit that will not bow to them, and yield to subserve a design which they may, in their first apparent tendency, threaten to frustrate. When a firm decisive spirit is recognized, it is curious to see how the space clears around a man and leaves him room and freedom."

Abraham Lincoln said of General Grant: "The great thing about him is cool persistency of purpose. He is not easily excited, and he has got the grip of a bulldog. When he once gets his teeth in, nothing can shake him off."

Now, you may object that the above quotations relate to the Will, rather than to Persistence. But if you stop to consider a moment you will see that they relate to the PERSISTENT Will, and that the Will without Persistence could accomplish none of these things claimed for it. The Will is the hard chisel, but Persistence is the mechanism that holds the chisel in its place, firmly pressing it up against the object to be shaped, and keeping it from slipping or relaxing its pressure. You cannot closely read the above quotations from 'these great authorities without feeling a tightness of your lips, and a setting of your jaw, the outward marks of the Persistent Dogged Will.

If you lack Persistence, you should begin to train yourself in the direction of acquiring the habit of sticking to things. This practice will establish a new habit of the mind, and will also tend to cause the appropriate brain cells to develop and thus give to you as a permanent characteristic the desired quality that you are seeking to develop. Fix your mind upon your daily tasks, studies, occupation or hobbies, and hold your attention firmly upon them by Concentration, until you find yourself getting into the habit of resisting "side-tracking" or distracting influences. It is all a matter of practice and habit. Carry in your mind the idea of the chisel held firmly against the object it is shaping, as given in this chapter . . it will help you very much. And read this chapter over and over again, every day or so, until your mind will take up the idea and make it its own. By so doing you will tend to arouse the desire for Persistence and the rest will follow naturally, as the fruit follows the budding and flowering of the tree.

Chapter XIV

Habit

HABIT is a force which is generally recognized by the average thinking person, but which is commonly viewed in its adverse aspect to the exclusion of its favorable phase. It has been well said that all men are "The creatures of habit," and that "Habit is a cable; we weave a thread of it each day, and it becomes so strong that we cannot break it." But the above quotations only serve to emphasize that side of the question in which men are shown as the slaves of habit, suffering from its confining bonds. There is another side to the question, and that side shall be considered in this chapter.

If it be true that Habit becomes a cruel tyrant ruling and compelling men against their will, desire, and inclination . . and this is true in many cases, the question naturally arises in the thinking mind whether this mighty force cannot be harnessed and controlled in the service of man, just as have other forces of Nature. If this result can be accomplished, then man may master Habit and set it to work, instead of being a slave to it and serving it faithfully though complainingly. And the modern psychologists tell us in no uncertain tones that Habit may certainly be thus mastered, harnessed and set to work, instead of being allowed to dominate one's actions and character. And thousands of people have applied this new knowledge and have turned the force of Habit into new channels, and have compelled it to work their machinery of action, instead of being allowed to run to waste, or else permitted to sweep away the structures that men have erected with care and expense, or to destroy fertile mental fields.

A habit is a "mental path" over which our actions have traveled for some time, each passing making the path a little deeper and a little wider. If you have to walk over a field or through a forest, you know how natural it is for you to choose the clearest path in preference to the less worn ones, and greatly in preference to stepping out across the field or through the woods and making a new path. And the line of mental action is precisely the same. It is movement along the lines of the least resistance . . passage over the well-worn path.

Habits are created by repetition and are formed in accordance to a natural law, observable in all animate things and some would say in inanimate things as well. As an instance of the latter, it is pointed out that a piece of paper once folded in a certain manner will fold along the same lines the next time. And all users of sewing machines, or other delicate pieces of mechanism, know that as a machine or instrument is once "broken in" so will it tend to run thereafter. The same law is also observable in the case of musical instruments. Clothing or gloves form into creases according to the person using them, and these creases once formed will always be in effect, notwithstanding repeated pressings. Rivers and streams of water cut their courses through the land, and thereafter flow along die habit-course. The law is in operation everywhere.

The above illustrations will help you to form the idea of the nature of habit, and will aid you in forming new mental paths . . new mental creases. And. remember this always . . the best (and one might say the only) way in which old habits may be removed is to *form new habits* to counteract and replace the old undesirable ones. Form new mental paths over which to travel, and the old ones will soon become less distinct and in time will practically fill up from disuse. Every time you travel over the path of the desirable mental habit, you make the path deeper and wider, and make it so much easier to travel it thereafter. This mental path-making is a very important thing, and I cannot urge upon you too strongly the injunction to start to work making the desirable mental paths over which you wish to travel. Practice, practice, practice . . be a good path-maker.

The following rules will help you in your work in forming new habits:

1. At the beginning of the formation of a new habit, put *force* into your expression of the action, thought, or characteristic. Remember that you are taking the first steps toward making the new mental path, and it is much harder at the first than it will be afterwards. Make the path as clear and deep as you can, at the start, so that you can see it readily the next time you wish to travel it.

2. Keep your attention firmly concentrated on the new path building, and keep your eyes and thoughts away from the old paths, lest you incline toward them. Forget all about the old paths, and concern yourself only with the new one that you are building.

3. Travel over your newly made path as often as possible. Make opportunities for doing so, without waiting for them to arise. The oftener you go over the new path, the sooner will it become an old, well-worn, easily traveled one. Think out plans for passing over it and using it, at the start.

4. Resist the temptation to travel over the older, easier paths that you have been using in the past. Every time you resist a temptation, the stronger do you become, and the easier will it be for you to do so the next time. But every time you yield to the temptation, the easier does it become to yield again, and the more difficult does it become to resist the next time. You will have a fight on at the start, and this is the critical time. Prove your determination, persistency, and Will power now, right here at the start.

5. Be sure that you have mapped out the proper path . . plan it out well, and see where it will lead you to . . then go ahead without fear and without allowing yourself to doubt. "Place your hand upon the plow, and look not backward." Your goal is Financial Success . . then make a good, deep, wide mental path leading straight to it.

Chapter XV

Claiming Your Own

THERE has grown up in the minds of many people the delusion that there is some real merit in taking the mental position that desirable things are "too good for me," and denying that they have any merit whatsoever in them. So prevalent has become this idea that it has developed a race of hypocrites and Pharisees, who go about proclaiming their humble goodness, and their meek humility, until one gets tired of hearing their talk . . and *talk is* all there is to it, for these same people slyly manage to reach out for the good things in sight, even while decrying the value of the aforesaid good things, and denying their worthiness to receive anything at all.

I take quite the other position. I believe that there is nothing too good for the men and women who assert their right to live and to partake of the good things of earth. I am reminded of the French soldier who carried a dispatch to Napoleon, and whose horse dropped dead from fatigue as he sprang from it and handed the Emperor the dispatch which he had carried from miles away. Napoleon wrote an answer, and dismounting from his horse handed the bridle to the soldier, saying. "Take this horse and ride back, comrade." "Nay," cried the soldier as he gazed at the blooded horse and his trappings, "it is too magnificent and grand for me, a common soldier." "Take it!" cried Napoleon, *"There is nothing too grand and magnificent for a soldier of France!"* And these words, rapidly repeated through the ranks and columns of his army, gave to his tired troops a new and fresh inspiration and energy. "Nothing too grand and magnificent for a soldier of France," they said, and the thought that they were such worthy individuals inspired them to the almost miraculous deeds that followed.

Napoleon understood human nature, and the laws of psychology. Tell a man that he is A worm of the dust, and deserving of nothing but kicks and punishment, and if he believes you he will sink to the mental level of the worm and will cringe and crawl and eat dirt But let him know that he has within him the divine spark, and that there is nothing too good for him; nothing that he has not a right to aspire to; no heights which are not his own if he but climb to them . . tell him these things, I say, and he will become a transfigured creature, ready and willing to attempt great things, and do mighty deeds. "As a man thinketh in his heart, so is he."

And that is why I am trying to tell you that you have a right to all the good things there are . . that you are a worthy human being and not a crawling thing of the dust. That is why I tell you to raise up your head and look the world in the eyes, affirming your relationship with the Divine Cause that brought you into being, and asserting your right to partake of your heritage from that Power.

Does not all Nature seem to come to the aid and assistance of the strong individuals who assert their right to live, and prosper? Does not Nature seem to try in every way to build up strong, confident, self-reliant, self-respecting individuals? Does it not seem to reserve the prizes of life for the strong hand that has courage to reach out and take them, instead of to those cringing, shrinking personalities that cower and shiver back in the corner, afraid to call their souls their own? There is nothing in Nature that gives any encouragement whatsoever to this false teaching of mock humility, and self-abasement of which we hear so much. The very persons who hold up this weak, negative ideal to their followers, are not especially noted for their meekness or humility . . they are apt to be arrogant, selfish and grasping all the good things in sight, even while decrying and denying them.

They are all words, words, words, with their can't phrases and negative admonitions. Away with such destructive and hurtful teachings. Make way for the new teaching that the good things of earth have been placed here for man's use, and for his development and happiness. There is nothing too good for Men or Women, for they are the rightful inheritors and heirs of their Divine Causer. Does not Nature seem to strive to produce strong plants, strong animals, strong individuals? Does she not seem to delight in producing an individual, in either of the great kingdoms of life, who has the desire, energy, ambition and power to draw to itself the nourishment and nutriment which will enable it to express its life fully . . which will enable it to become a proper, efficient and worthy channel through which may flow the great Stream of Life that has its source in the Divine Cause which is behind and back of all things? Is life but an effort to produce weak, miserable, unhappy beings . . or is it an urge that seeks to develop strong, happy, noble individual forms? And how can one be happy, strong, and noble if the source of supply is denied him? What would the plant become if its nourishment were withdrawn?

And yet in spite of all these apparent facts of Nature, there are those who would have us refuse the full supply which the Divine Power has placed at our hand and bidden us partake thereof. These people would even deny the supply. Oh, I say to you, friends, the Power that called us into being has placed in this world of ours all that is necessary to our well-being, and has implanted in our breasts the natural hunger for nourishment, physical, mental and spiritual. This very hunger is Nature's promise that there exists that which is intended to satisfy it. And then, what folly to decry the hunger, or to deny the supply.

That which you need and for which you are hungry, exists for you. It is yours, and you are not robbing others when you seek for it and draw it to you.

Claim Your Own, friends. Claim Your Own! Deny it not . . decry it not . . but cry aloud "It is Mine Own . . I Demand It . . I attract it to Me!" Claim Your Own!

Chapter XVI

Making Money

"The possession of money gives confidence,
the lack it self-consciousness."

IN the preceding chapters of this book we have discussed "The Law of Financial Success," and suggested methods and given instruction for the development of the various positive qualities necessary to the one who desires to get into harmony with the LAW.

But our exposition of the LAW is not yet complete. Like everything else in Nature, it has two sides: for instance, we have male and female, heat and cold, light and darkness, sunshine and rain, and one is just as necessary to the whole as is the other.

We have said very little as to the handling of money. What has gone before was extremely practical and all very necessary, because we must "know" before we "do" . . we must "possess" before we "use." If you have read carefully and studied with a purpose that which has preceded, and have decided to take advantage of the suggestions given, you are now ready for this final chapter, "Making Money," toward which all the others have been leading you.

A person might possess every one of the positive qualities, but if he were in the back woods or the Desert of Sahara, where there is no money in circulation, he never could become financially independent, for the second part of the LAW could not be brought into action. And again, on the other hand, a person might be left a mint of money and if he did not know how to take care of it, or if he did not possess the necessary positive qualities by means of which he might make more money, he would lose it all in a few years, and he himself become a tramp of the worst type. This is not an uncommon occurrence, and may be verified at any shelter house or Salvation Army Barracks in our larger cities.

An illustration from real life, showing how the LAW worked in one instance will here be given. The writer is acquainted with a gentleman of middle age now occupying an enviable position in financial circles, and who, because of the development of the positive qualities, will before he dies become much more prominent and leave his mark on the world. This man was born "with a gold spoon in his mouth," and all during his youthful days had everything and anything a young man could want, as well as many things he did not need. In time reverses came, and these, combined with extravagance, swept away the fortune that had been bequeathed to him.

Here was a young man about twenty years of age left without a dollar, and with absolutely no training in the direction of earning a living. After a few years of the hardest kind of knocks, he made his way to the far West. There he obtained an inside position where he worked for a time, until it began to tell on his health. One day while at work in the office, and wondering what was going to become of him, a great truth dawned on his mind. It was this: *I can never amount to anything or become very wealthy like my father by merely working with my hands. The only way to make money is to compel money to work for me.*

With a definite object in view, he gave up his inside "position" and took a "job" on the railroad grade as a teamster. In less than six months, by depriving himself of every luxury, he had accumulated enough money to partly pay for one pair of mules. These he hired out, acting himself as driver. After a while he bought a second pair on credit, giving a mortgage on both pairs for payment, and hired a man to drive the second pair. When that pair was paid for he bought two more pairs, again mortgaging all he had to pay for the second two pairs. When they were paid for he bought four more pairs, and then he went to work, not as a hired man, but as a contractor on his own account in a small way, and thus made money. The capital invested in these mules worked for him, and step by step in a few years he was in a position of affluence and power.

This man, just like every other man, had the germs of the positive qualities in him. All they needed was developing. This development was obtained by the knocks he received, both before and after that great truth dawned upon him.

Let me again express that truth in a little different language so that it may be impressed upon the mind of every one of my readers: *No man ever became very wealthy working with his hands alone; this applies to the brain worker also. The only way to obtain much money is to make money Work for you.*

Jay Gould, the noted financier, once said: "One hundred dollars invested in the right place at the right time will earn as much as one man steadily employed." This is a great truth too. In financial matters, that we must let sink deeply into our consciousness.

But the question right now with many is, "How shall we acquire the first one hundred dollars so as to invest it?" And the only answer is, by saving it. There is no person, who, if he can earn wages, but can in time, by sacrificing some luxury, or by rigid economy, lay aside one, two or three hundred dollars. And the best way to do this is by putting in some good savings bank a stated sum each week, no matter how small that sum may be. One of the best aids to this is the metal bank in which you can drop your odd change, such as are loaned to their customers by up-to-date savings institutions. If you keep this up long enough, you are bound to acquire your first hundred dollars. By doing this you have acquired at the same time two valuable habits . . economy and patience.

It is now necessary to place or invest this money, and more to be obtained in like manner, where it will bring back to you the largest possible returns and yet be perfectly safe. And the question conies to one at this point, "Shall I go into business for myself, as the young man did, or shall I work for another and invest my savings and watch them grow?"

That depends. If you have developed the qualities of courage, initiative, self-confidence and grit to a remarkable degree, and the opportunity presents itself, go into business for yourself and you will win. ° If not, hold onto your present position, but be always on the lookout to better yourself, and increase your salary, and in the meantime invest your surplus money in some good security.

When making an investment do not be blinded either by your own prejudice or the prejudice or craftiness of some stock, bond, mortgage or banking house salesman. Remember this . . and in doing so realize that it is a frailty of human nature and the instinct of self-preservation that makes it so . . that whatever a man or firm is offering for sale at the time you approach them is the best thing for you to buy. Other investments offered by other firms *may be good* . . but, this is best for you. Realize this frailty, use your own judgment, don't knock the other fellow, and invest in what seems best to you after hearing the stories of all of them.

The writer can command no language strong enough in which to express his contempt for the social parasite who obtains the money of people under false pretenses or by making glittering promises of great wealth on short notice without ever intending or expecting to make any returns. It matters not whether he be an absconding cashier or president of a bank, the president or representative of a noted stock or bond house, who has knowingly sold the stocks or bonds of a corporation that is watered beyond all limits, or a "fake" mining promoter. These men all belong in the same class, they are rascals and their place is behind the prison bars.

I shall now present, as concisely as possible, the various methods of investing money, and in an unprejudiced manner give the advantages and disadvantages of each.

At the head of all investments, as regards safety of capital, stand government bonds. They are in no way attractive to the small investor, because of the low rate of interest. Their principal demand is by National Banks, which are compelled to buy and deposit these bonds with the United States Treasurer, to protect their issue of bank bills. State bonds are considered almost as safe as government bonds (though some states have repudiated their obligations), but also pay a low rate of interest.

Savings banks pay their depositors three and sometimes four per cent. Placing money in a savings bank may be regarded as an investment, since the depositor loans his money to the banker, and he in turn uses that money to earn money for the stockholders of the bank. It would take a great many years for a man to acquire a competence or to become financially independent by merely keeping his money in a savings bank.

Municipal bonds, including county, city, town, school, water, city hall, sewer and special assessment bonds pay from four to five per cent. The best ones are in large demand, at these low rates of interest, by large estates and trustees for the investment of trust funds, the investing of which is restricted by law to securities of this character. Some municipal bonds are safer than others, depending upon the standing and character of the municipality issuing them. All depend upon some form of taxation for the payment of interest, as well as principal. The best way to purchase municipal bonds is to get in touch with some reputable bond house making a specialty of them, ant) buy under the instruction of some man whom you can trust to tell the truth.

Steam and electric railway bonds and public service corporation bonds may all be classed together for convenience sake. They pay from four to seven per cent. In buying them it is best to consult an authority, as some are very much safer than others.

Real estate mortgages pay from four to eight per cent, depending upon locality and the character of security, and are in large demand by a class of investors who have sums varying from $5,000 and upwards, and who depend upon this class of investment for an income. In buying real estate mortgages, know the people who are placing the mortgages . . their ability to make the interest payments, and whether mere is any chance of default. There is a moral as well as a financial obligation involved here.

Real estate pays anywhere from five to ten per cent, depending upon its location. While there are opportunities for large profits in the appreciation of real estate in some localities, there is always the risk of great depreciation. One thing should be remembered in buying real estate for a permanent investment and that is die danger of booms, with their enthusiasm, lack of judgment, inflated prices and general lack of conservatism. Remember that the yield should be adequate to the risk . . see to it that the uncertainty of an income is reduced to a minimum.

Industrial stocks pay from five to twenty per cent, and are dependent largely upon the commercial conditions of the country, the nature of the business, the amount of competition, and the character of the management. The utmost caution should be exercised in investing your savings in stocks of this character, and you must know absolutely that you are dealing with reliable, capable and honest people.

The stocks of legitimate mining companies pay from six to many hundred per cent on the par value, and are dependent upon the character and location of the property, and the reliability of the men in control. There is always great danger to the small investor in putting his money into mining stocks, as he is not in a position to determine, as a rule, the intrinsic value of same. He must depend wholly upon the character and reliability of the men who are responsible for the intelligent and conscientious use of his money in the operation of a mining property. More fortunes have been made in mining man in any other of the many industries in the United States. There have also been many a poor man's and woman's hard earned savings lost by turning over their little all to some glib-tongued promoter while there was not at any time even a remote possibility of ever getting any returns.

The all-important question, when investing your money, is to know those with whom you are doing business. There are many meritorious propositions being handled by honest, capable men, which offer great opportunities to the small investor, and if he can but use careful judgment and discretion in determining the right persons to do business with, there is no reason why the most humble cannot acquire a competency by careful and intelligent investing.

The reader may know of or learn about lots of other ways of investing money, besides those presented above. If so, and they "look good to you," after putting the facts in each case through the mill of Reason and Judgment, take advantage of the opportunity. If you lose, do not be a "namby-pamby" and cry over spilt milk; "get busy" and begin again.

And even if great reverses come and everything you possess is swept away, don't sink back in despair and give up the ship. Rest a while and then go at it again harder than ever, but this time follow the LAW. It is no sin to go broke or even to be bankrupt. The dishonor lies in remaining so. As Josh Billings said: "Sukccs don't konsist in never makin' mistakes, but in never makin' the same one twict." And Ella Wheeler Wilcox writes:

> "Tis easy enough to be pleasant
> When life flows by like a song.
> But the man worthwhile
> Is the man with a smile
> When everything goes dead wrong."

In judging any investment it is always wise to know a few inside facts in regard to the proposition offered. The only way to find out anything is by asking questions either of yourself, while you are reading the "prospectus," or else of the officers of the company, if you do not find these questions answered somewhere in the literature.

Robert Collier

Be Rich! The Science of Getting What You Want

Originally Published 1949

Being "The Law of Increase"
As Used by the Prophets of Old.

Here is a secret of riches and success that has been buried 1,900 years deep. Since time began, mankind has been searching for this secret. It has been found and lost again . . a score of times. The Ancients of all races have had some inkling of it, as is proven by the folk tales and legends that have come down to us, like the story of Aladdin and his wonderful lamp, or Ali Baba and his "Open Sesame" to the treasure trove.

Every nation has such legends. Every nation has had its Wise Men, its men of genius and vision who glimpsed the truth that is buried in these old folk tales and who understood at least something of how it works.

But it remained for Jesus to rediscover this secret in its entirety and then to show us clearly, step by step, how we might use it to bring us anything of good we might desire.

For make no mistake about this: The miracles of Jesus were not something super-natural that could be performed only by Him, else how could He have picked seventy disciples . . ordinary men, uneducated, untaught, fishermen, farmers, tax-gatherers and the like and sent them out two by two to perform miracles and wonders second only to His own, so that they returned to Him with joy, saying, "Lord, even the devils are subject to us through Thy name." How could He have assured us "The thing that I do shall ye do also, and greater things than these shall ye do."?

The miracles of Jesus were divinely NATURAL. Instead of being departures from natural law, they were demonstrations of what the law will do for you if you understand how to use it! God does not deal in exceptions. As St. Augustine put it

"Miracles are not contrary to Nature, but only contrary to what we know about, Nature."

Every force in Nature works along definite, logical lines, in accord with certain principles. These forces will work for anyone who possesses the key to their use, just as Aladdin's fabled Genie would respond to the call of anyone who rubbed the magic lamp.

They can be neglected and allowed to lie idle, they can be used for good or evil, but the laws themselves do not change. It is merely the methods of using them that change. An airplane or an automobile would have seemed as great a miracle to the people of Jesus' day as the curing of a leper. Sending sound waves through the ether, to be picked up by a little box called a radio, would have been as wonderful to our fathers as is the sending of our voice over a beam of light to us today. Yet there is nothing super-natural about either of these.

The forces of Nature have always been there, ready for our use. It is our understanding of them that has changed, our knowledge of how to USE them.

Man in ancient times looked upon the lightning as the wrath of God, just as many deeply religious people look upon poverty and sickness and calamities today in the same way, as visitations of God. Yet man has learned to harness the lightning and make it serve him. The laws governing electricity were there all the time, waiting only for the understanding of someone wise enough to show us how to put them to good use. Just so the power to BE and HAVE what you want is right here, needing only for you to learn how it works.

Nineteen hundred years ago, there came to this earth a Son of Man who proclaimed that His mission was "That ye might have LIFE, and have it more ABUNDANTLY."

NOT, mind you, that you might learn how to die, thus reach Heaven and a life of comfort, but that you might have LIFE here and now. Over and over again He told us "What things soever ye desire ye shall have them." And lest you might think that this referred to some future state, He assured us "If two of you shall agree ON EARTH as touching anything they shall ask, it shall be done for them."

Furthermore, He gave exact instructions as to how to go about getting the things you desire. When you want more of the good things of life, when happiness or success or riches seem to elude you, there is a definite formula for you to use. "Seek ye first the Kingdom of Heaven," Jesus directed, "and all these things shall be added unto you."

"Ah ha!" you say. "There it is. You do have to die and go to Heaven in order to get the good you want." But Jesus must have anticipated that you might think just that, for He pointed out specifically that the Kingdom of Heaven is not afar off, in the clouds or in the next world. "The Kingdom of Heaven cometh not with observation," He said. "Neither shall they say 'Lo here, lo there!' For behold, the Kingdom of Heaven is within you."

What is "Heaven"?

That word "Heaven" is perhaps the most misunderstood word in the Bible. In the original Greek text, the word used for it is OURANOS which, translated literally, means EXPANSION. And what is expansion? It is increasing, spreading out, multiplying, is it not? "Seek ye first the Kingdom of EXPANSION, and all these things shall be added unto you." Seek a place or a state of being where you can expand, grow, increase, multiply, bring forth fruit.

This idea is further strengthened by Jesus' own description of what the Kingdom of Heaven is like. "The Kingdom of Heaven is like a grain of mustard seed, which a man took, and sowed in his field; which indeed is the least of all seeds, but when it is grown, it is the greatest among herbs, and becometh a tree, so that the birds of the air come and lodge in the branches thereof." "The Kingdom of Heaven is like unto leaven, which a woman took and hid in three measures of meal, until the whole was leavened."

What is the property of a mustard seed? It spreads a single seed will grow into a tree, a single tree will produce enough seed to plant a great field. And what is the property of leaven or yeast? It expands in a single night it can expand a hundred times in size.

Go back over any of the miracles of increase in the Bible and see if they are not all miracles of EXPANSION. How did Elijah make the oil and meal last, so that one measure of oil and a little meal fed him and the widow and her soon for an indefinite period? How did Elisha increase the pot of oil for that other widow who came to him to save her son from bondage, so that she had enough to fill all the vessels she could borrow from her neighbors? By EXPANDING them, did they not? And how can you expand things? We know of only two methods :

1 By PRESSURE from within.
2 By HEAT.

If you want to expand something elastic, you can blow air or liquid into it and thus force it up under pressure, or you can push it out with your hands. But that sort of expansion lasts only as long as the pressure is applied.

To produce INCREASE, expansion must come from within the object itself, just as it comes from within every seed that grows. Such expansion comes only from HEAT. To expand water, for instance, you heat it until it becomes steam, and from that expanded vapor, you can get power to do greater work that thousands of men or hundreds of horses could do. If you want to expand metal, you bring it to a white heat, and while in that state, you can make of it anything your skill can contrive.

If you want to expand coal, and draw from it the rich gases and coal tar and dyes and other derivatives hidden under its hard exterior, you have only to heat it. If you want to expand a seed of corn or wheat or any fruit or vegetable, and have it grow and bring forth fruit and multiply, you must plant and water it so it will heat and burst its shell and send its shoots upward. In short, the one prerequisite to the expansion of almost any element from within seems to be HEAT.

But how can we use heat to expand our riches? Should we then throw everything into the fire and hope to get our increase from the flames? By no means. Certainly that was not the way Jesus did it. Nor the Prophets.

They used heat, but it was a different kind of heat. It was the heat of LOVE, of PRAISE and BLESSING, fanned by the breath of FAITH. Take the time, for instance, when the multitudes had followed Jesus out of the cities into a desert place. In front of Him stood 5,000 hungry people. To feed them, Jesus had only five loaves and two small fishes. What did He do? He first BLESSED the bread and the fishes. He PRAISED them. He THANKED God for them.

You who have worked with people especially with children or simple-minded folk know the effects of praise. Children expand under it. They do things they would otherwise find impossible. It seems to increase their energy. Certainly it taps well-springs that are ordinarily closed to them. The same is true in the handling of animal or people.

A famous Sales Manager was having difficulty with his men. Their sales had slumped, and all his "prep" talks, his urgings, his threats, had failed to bring them up again. He put up a large electric sign in the main corridor of his building, where everyone who came through would see it: "The salesman whose work has been most outstanding this week is . . " Immediately the sales jumped, and from that week on he never had to worry about a slump again.

How does this apply to inanimate things? The answer is that there are no inanimate things. Science today shows us that everything is full of life. Inside the apparently inert lump of lead or iron are tiny atoms of whirling energy, dashing here and there, bounding and rebounding and circling around like miniature solar systems, with a rapidity to which the speed of an airplane is as nothing. The mass as a mass may be quiet, but inside is boundless energy. Where there is ceaseless energy, there is Life. Where movement is orderly and seemingly in accord with a well-laid plan, there is bound to be Intelligence. And where there is Intelligence, there must be RESPONSIVENESS.

It is this Responsiveness on the part of everything in life that makes it possible for you to prove the truth of the Scriptural promise that man should have DOMINION over the earth and over everything upon or under the earth.

How can you exercise that domination? Not by force. Not even by prayer. But by PRAISE! As Charles Fillmore puts it

"There is an inherent law of mind that we INCREASE whatever we PRAISE. The whole of creation responds to praise, and is glad. Animal trainers pet and reward their charges with delicacies for acts of obedience; children glow with joy and gladness when they are praised. Even vegetation grows better for those who love it. We can praise our own ability, and the very brain cells will expand and increase in capacity and intelligence, when we speak words of encouragement and appreciation to them."

God gave you dominion over the earth. Everything is your servant, but remember it is said in the Scriptures that God brought every beast and fowl to Adam, to see what he would call them. You are like Adam in this, that you can give to everything and everybody you come in contact with the name you like. You can call them good or bad. And whatever you call them, that is what they will be to you good servants or evil ones. You can praise or curse them, and as you do, so will they be to you.

The Law of Increase

There is one unfailing Law of Increase "Whatever is praised and blessed, MULTIPLIES." Count your blessings and they increase. If you are in need of supply, start in now to praise every small piece of money that come to you, blessing it is a symbol of God's abundance and love. You will be surprised how soon that small piece will increase to many pieces. Take God into your business. Bless your store, your cash register, every one that works for you, each customer that comes in.

If you are working for someone else and want a better job or more pay, start by BLESSING and being THANKFUL for what you have. Bless the work you are doing, be thankful for every opportunity it gives you to acquire greater skill or ability or to serve others. Bless the money you earn, no matter how little it may be. Be so thankful to God for it that you can give a small "Thank offering" from it to someone in greater need than yourself. Suppose the Boss does seem unappreciative and hard. Bless him just the same. Be thankful, for the opportunity to SERVE faithfully, no matter how small the immediate reward may seem to be. Give your best, give it cheerfully, gladly, thankfully, and you will be amazed how quickly the INCREASE will come to you not necessarily from your immediate boss, but from the Big Boss over all.

I remember reading a letter from a woman in the drought belt in which she said that they, unlike most of their neighbors, had an abundant supply of water, and excellent crops. "When my husband plows a field," she writes, "I ask God to bless each furrow. Each seed that goes into the seeder is blessed, and the realization held that it will produce abundantly according to His righteous law. Our neighbors marveled at the abundance of hay that we cut this year. The hay was sold before the third cutting was put up."

"Each day, in silence, I put the ranch 'Lovingly in the hands of the Father.' I ask God to bless everybody that comes in contact with the ranch."

Few realize the power of praise and blessing. Praise may be called the great liberator. You remember the story of Paul and Silas. They lay in jail bound with chains, but they did not despair. They rejoiced and sang hymns of praise, and lo the very walls were shaken down and they were set free. "What are the Servants of the Lord," asked one of the Saints of old, "but His Minstrels?"

Praise always magnifies. When we praise God and then look about us and praise His invisible presence in all that we see, we find that the good is so magnified that much becomes evident that we ordinarily fail to see. Running through all of Jesus Christ's acts as well as His teachings we find the glowing element of praise. When he looked at five loaves and two small fishes and realized that He had a multitude to feed, His first thought was a thought of praise. "And looking up to heaven, he blessed."

Go back over the Old Testament and see how often you are adjured to "Praise the Lord and be thankful, that THEN shall the earth yield be increased." Probably no life chronicled in the Scriptures was more beset with trials and danger than that of King David. And what was his remedy? What brought him through all tribulations to power and riches? Just read the Psalm of David and you will see.

"Jehovah reigneth; let the earth rejoice;
Let the multitude of ides be gad.
Bless Jehovah, O my soul;
And all that is within me, bless his holy name.
Who forgiveth all thine iniquities;
Who healeth all thy diseases."

"If anyone could tell you the shortest, surest way to all happiness and all perfection," wrote William Law, "he must tell you to make it a rule to yourself to thank and praise God for everything that happens to you. For it is certain that whatever seeming calamity happens to you, if you thank and praise God for it, you turn it into a blessing. Could you therefore work miracles, you could not do more for yourself than by this thankful spirit; for it turns all that it touches into happiness."

How then can YOU increase your supply? How can you get more of riches and happiness and every good thing of life? In the same way as the Wise Men and the Prophets of old. In the same way that Jesus fed the multitudes. In the same way that He filled the disciples' nets to over flowing with fish, after they had labored all night and caught nothing. By EXPANDING what you have! And the way to expand is through love, through praise and thanksgiving.

Throughout the Bible we are told . . "In everything by prayer and supplication WITH THANKSGIVING let your request be made known unto God." Again and again the root of inspiration and attainment is stressed: Rejoice, be glad, praise, give thanks!

"Prove me now herewith saith the Lord of Hosts, if I will not open you the windows of heaven and pour you out a blessing, that there shall not be room enough to receive it." One of the startling facts of modern science is that this universe is not a finished product. Creation is going on all around us . . new worlds being formed, cosmic energy taking shape in a million different molds.

But a far more startling fact to most of us is that WE ARE CREATORS, and that we can form today the world we personally shall be living tomorrow.

People blame their environment, their education, their opportunities, their luck, for their condition. They are wrong. There is one person to blame . . and only one . . THEMSELVES. They are today the result of their thoughts of yesterday and the many yesterdays that preceded it. They are forming today the mold for what they will be in the years to come.

For there is no such thing as failure. Whether you are poor or sickly, or rich and strong, you have succeeded in one thing. You have compressed the cosmic energy about you into the mold that you held before the mind's eye of your inner self. You have named the forces that worked with you "good" or "bad," and as you named them, so have they been to you as servant . . Good or Evil.

But there is a happy ending. You don't need to leave things as they are. If you don't like the present results, you can rename those servants. You can bless and praise the good, no matter how tiny it may seem, and by your praise and blessing, you can expand it a thousand-fold.

Perhaps this may be easier to believe if you remember that it is the way all of Nature works. Take the mineral kingdom: A group of cells shows "cohesion" or the ability to stick together. Why? Because all are of the same kind, the electronic life in them revolving at the same rate. In like manner, they possess the ability to repel any other kind of cell that attempt to join the group, because the rate of motion in those other cells is different.

In the vegetable kingdom, the process of selection is greater. Each group of cells attracts to itself from its immediate environment all those cells that are exactly like those forming that particular plan, and it repels all other. Thus tomatoes and potatoes and beans and a dozen other vegetables can all grow side by side, yet remain entirely separate and distinct in their organisms. No part of the potato will be attracted by or absorbed into the tomato, or vice versa. Each uses its selective properties to remain true to type.

Like Attracts Like

It all goes back to the electrons and protons of which each individual cell whether mineral, animal or vegetable is made. Everything in Nature starts with this. A single electron is touched in just the right way to start it revolving on its axis. Its awakening affects other particles of a like nature, drawing them to it, setting them in motion likewise. Each electron is a small universe in itself, with revolving particles turning about a common center with the same motion and at the same relative distances that the earth and planets revolve around the sun.

It is the RATE of movement that variation occurs. Those groups that have higher rate of movement produce the higher forms of life. The moment that the rate of movement changes, form and color are changed, and in the case of complicated organisms like the human body, the change in the rate of movement of any part of the body may readily affect the harmony of the whole, for with differences in rotation, the faster units have a tendency to break away from and throw off the slower.

Something of this kind is going on in the body all the time. Older cells slow down, break away and are thrown out. That is how a dog follows the scent of its master by the trail of old, discarded cells that he is continually throwing off. It is only when we fail to throw off the inharmonious cells that disease gets a foothold and we sicken or die.

Remember this: Starting with the individual cell, we attract to us only those elements that are identical in quality and character with ourselves, and that are revolving at the same rate of speed. Our selective ability is such that we are able to pick such material as will preserve our quality and identity. This is true of our bodies, of our circumstances, of our environment. Like attracts like. If we are not satisfied with ourselves as we are, if we want a healthier body, more attractive friends, greater riches, and success, we must start at the core within ourselves!

And that core lies in our thoughts. Thought can speed up or slow down the rate of motion of the whole body. Thought can retard certain organs, and thus cause inharmony throughout the whole body. Thoughts of anger, fear, worry, envy, hatred or discouragement can create such inharmony as to bring about cancerous growths in the body as well as disaster in one's affairs. You can cut out such growths with a surgeon's knife, and thus help the body organism to throw off the inharmonious elements, but an easier way, a better way, is to bring the body back into harmony, bring the entire organism into tune.

In Tune With the Infinite

The first essential to putting yourself in harmony with the Infinite Good about you is to relax, to take off the brakes. For what is worry or fear or discouragement but a brake on your thinking and the proper functioning of your organs, a slowing down of your entire rate of activity?

It is said that the Devil once held a sale of all the tools of his trade. Everything was displayed . . his keen-edged daggers of jealousy, his sledgehammer of anger, his bow of greed, his arrows of lust and covetousness, his weapons of vanity and fear and envy and pride. And under each was its price.

But in the place of honor, framed and set apart from all the rest was a small wedge, dented and marked with use. The name of this wedge was "Discouragement," and the price set upon it was higher than all the other tools combined.

Asked the reason for this amazing difference, the Devil explained . . "it is because this is the one tool I can use when all others fail. Let me get that little wedge into a man's consciousness, and it opens the way for everything else. That wedge has opened more doors to me than all my other weapons combined."

Few things will slow down your rate of activity as much as Discouragement. Few offer greater resistance to the good that is trying to manifest through you.

You remember Ohm's Law in electricity C = E divided by R. C is the amount of electrical energy to be delivered at the point of use. E is the amount available from the power house. R represents the resistance offered by all the things through which the current must flow. If there were no resistance, the full amount of current generated by E would be delivered. But there is always some resistance. Even the best conductor offers a little, and you can't deliver current without a conductor. So the amount actually delivered depends upon the power available, divided by the resistance.

All the energy of the universe is around you. You can have anything of good you desire. But it must first go through you . . and you won't let it. You put up more resistance to good than all the non-conductors that ever interfered with an electrical circuit.

You can't believe that good is so easily available. You feel that it can come to you only after hard struggle, and disappointments and pain. You insist upon putting these non-conductors in its path. You add worries and fears and hates and envies, so that by the time the good reaches you, its current is so weak that there is little left.

Like attracts like. Hate brings hate, and all the ills that follow in its wake. Envy and fear and worry attract discord and disease. If you want health, happiness, in your life, it you are seeking riches and success, attune your thoughts to these. BLESS the circumstances that surround you. Bless and praise those who come in contact with you. Bless even the difficulties you meet, for by blessing them, you can change them from discordant conditions to favorable ones, you can speed up their rate of activity to where they will bring you good instead of evil.

It is only lack of RESPONSIVENESS to good that produces the lacks in your life. Good works on the plane of EXPANSION. Good revolves at a high rate of activity. You can key your activity to the same rate by an expectant confident state of mind. You can bring all your surroundings and circumstances up to that same level by BLESSING them, PRAISING the good in them.

Remember, the basic magnet lies in your own thoughts. Upon the quality and activity of that magnet depend the good or evil that will be drawn to you. You are the Master of your fate. You are the architect who determines the materials that are to be used in making your life and your circumstances. You have the power of SELECTIVITY.

How, then, shall we order our lives, to the end that we may have the good things we seek . . riches and happiness, health and success?

"Seek ye first the Kingdom of EXPANSION. . . and all things else shall be added unto you."

The Nucleus

Remember, everything in this universe must start with a nucleus. A single electron is touched in the right way to start revolving on its axis. The magnetism engendered by it draws to it other particles of a like nature, setting them in motion likewise. With that as a nucleus, it can grow and multiply indefinitely, as long as its rate of motion continues. It is only when something slows it down that it disintegrates and dies.

How can you start such a nucleus? With an IDEA, backed by earnest desire and faith. Suppose you want to build a business of your own, for instance. I'll tell you how one man of my acquaintance did it.

When Bruce Haughton decided to start an automotive business in Jacksonville, FL., he had only $23.00 to his name. With $14.40 of his capital, he bought some tools. Then he rented the 2-car garage in the back yard of the house where he had secured a room and set up his sign!

He did not depend upon the sign, however, to bring in business. He figured that he was the only one who could do that. So he called upon a number of professional men and told them of the personal service he could give their cars, which they could not get elsewhere. In odd moments during the next few weeks, he continued those calls. Thereafter he used letters and postcards to tell more people about his distinctive service.

At the end of the first thirty days, he had a net return from his investment of money, work and brains of $476.80, with an overhead expense of only $50.00.

That was in the spring. By June, he found that he needed bigger quarters, for 591 regular customers were already coming to his "Back Yard Garage" for service they could not buy elsewhere.

In February of the following year, he had to move again this time to a corner in one of the best parts of the city. A year later, he moved a third time closer by five blocks to the business section, within easy reach of the big office building where the larger part of his clientele was located . . and ten times as big as his last place!

Not only that, but he started a Motor Club that soon had fifty branches all over Florida and Georgia. In these garages, his products were sold, his name became known, his service was talked about.

And all on a capital of $23.00! On that, and an idea, and work, and a thorough belief in his ability to render a better service than anyone else could give!

But perhaps you will say . . "He had special skill. He was a good auto mechanic. I have no particular skill or ability. What am I to do?"

Find some way of serving people better or more economically than it is now being done. Then learn HOW to do it, even though it means putting off the carrying out of your idea for months or years. With all the free night schools and public libraries of today, there is no excuse for not being able to learn anything you want to know.

Here is the way a friend of mine got out of the $25.00 a week class and into a highly profitable business. He had an idea that women's clothes cost entirely too much, that if he could bring down the price a third, he could get the trade of many girls working in offices and stores, girls who must look well dressed but have not too much money to spend on clothes.

So what did he do? He took a low-paid job as assistant to a resident buyer; really not much more than a messenger boy. But it took him into all the manufactures' workshops. It made him acquainted with everyone who made the kind of dresses he was interested in. It gave him an insight into wholesale prices and methods of buying. When he was ready, he raised a little money through family and friends and opened a small upstairs office.

Then he made daily rounds of the manufactures, picking up a discontinued model here, a job lot there, a few specials somewhere else . . all at prices far below the usual wholesale figures.

As soon as he felt that he had enough to start with, he sent letters to lists of women working in nearby offices and shops, telling them of the unusual bargains he was able to offer and the reason for them. The result? Before the year was out, he had a profitable, growing business.

First the nucleus, the idea. Then something to start it into action, to make it revolve and draw to itself everything it needs for growth.

What is it YOU want . . a home, a job, a business, money or health? You can get any or all of them, if you have the initiative to start something, the faith to carry on in the face of all obstacles.

For don't forget this: No matter how good your start, your nucleus will not carry on by itself. It needs faith to keep it moving. It needs the urge of BELIEF to speed it up and give it the magnetic power to draw to itself the elements it needs for growth and strength, when obstacles get in its way and threaten to slow it down or stop it.

Why is it that few businesses outlast their founder? Because only he had the necessary faith and determination to keep the nucleus whirling. Faith is the motive power without which no business can run, without which any nucleus will speedily slow down and lose all its magnetic force.

You want a home, let us say, but you lack the money to buy the kind you would like. Forget money for the moment. That is not the most important part. Instead, picture on paper the exact type of home you are longing for. Cut from magazines illustrations showing just what you want in a home . . the type of architecture, the construction, the grounds, the different rooms, even the furnishings. Put your Dream House on paper.

That is your nucleus. Now start it whirling. Now give it life. How? By doing something towards bringing that home into materialization.

One woman got a board and nails, and started to make a kitchen shelf. Another went to the 5 & 10 store each day and bought some item for the kitchen.

Do something to show your faith. Do something to start your nucleus into action, and continue to do little things. Not only that, but every time you look upon the picture of your Dream Home, admire it, be thankful for it and BELIEVE in it. "As your faith is, so shall it be unto you," for it is your faith that provides the propelling force to your nucleus and gives it power to draw to it every element needed for its growth and fruition. As Lord Bulwer-Lytton put it "Nothing can defeat the resolute mind of even a peasant who believes."

Suppose you want to sell something. Perhaps it is an idea you have for improving the business and you want to convince the boss of its value. Perhaps it is a car or an insurance policy or some other product that you feel some particular prospect should buy. Perhaps you want to sell some girl the idea that you would make her the ideal husband. How shall you go about it?

By selling YOURSELF first! Every sale, of whatever kind, must be made in your own mind first. Stand in front of a mirror and talk to the image reflected there. Sell him! Give him every argument you would give your prospect. Then look him in the eye and ask him "Do you believe this?" If he does not, depend upon it, your prospect will not. But if you can truly convince that man in the mirror, if you can look him in the eye and talk to him honestly, sincerely, convincingly, and have him nod in agreement with you, then believe me, you can sell anyone.

You have put life into your nucleus. You have started it whirling. You can call on your prospect, whoever he is, with the confident assurance that your sale is made. It may not be accomplished on the first visit. It may not be done on the second. Your nucleus may have to draw to itself other elements to complete the transaction, but if you can hold the faith, if you can keep the man in the mirror sold, your success is assured.

Napoleon Hill wrote "There is only one unfailing law of success in business it is BELIEF!" But how about health? What if you are ailing, weak, run down, and sickly?

More than 2,000 years ago, the Prophet Joel answered that question "Let the weak say, I AM strong!" Shakespeare told us much the same when he said "Assume a virtue if you have it not."

What is sickness? A slowing down of the vital processes, is it not? Every cell in your body is just a whirling bit of energy. Any that slow down are thrown off, excreted. But when the whole system slows down, you don't throw off the waste matter, you don't get rid of the poisons. The result? Aches and pains and a general feeling of lassitude and illness.

What better remedy could there be than speeding up your rate of motion, reenergizing all your cells and helping them to throw off all the elements that tend to slow you down. You CAN do it. You know that martial music will reanimate soldiers ready to drop with fatigue. You know that fragrant perfumes brighten you, that a sunshiny morning gives you more life and pep.

Why is it that inmates of insane asylums are more easily controlled if given plenty of sunshine? Why are children better behaved, why do YOU feel better, think better, act better when you have the benefit of the sun's rays? Why is there so much truth in the old Italian proverb "Where the sun goes, the doctor goes not?"

Because sunshine not only speeds up the rate of motion of your cells, but as one authority puts it . . "Sunlight is actually a food to the human body, stimulates growth, promotes the healthy functioning of blood and nerves."

Cheerful affirmations, convincingly given, have the same stimulating effect.

Thirty years ago, Emile Coue electrified the world with his cures of all manner of disease. "Nobody ought to be sick!" he proclaimed, and proceeded to prove it by curing hundreds who came to him after doctors had failed to relieve them. Not only that, but he showed how the same methods could be used to cure one's affairs, to bring riches instead of debts, success instead of drudgery.

What was back of his success? A law as old as the hills, a law that has been known to psychologists for years . . the law that the subconscious mind accepts as TRUE anything that is repeated to it convincingly and often. And once it has accepted such a statement as true, it proceeds to do everything in its power to MAKE IT TRUE!

You ask a friend how he is, and he carelessly answers . . "I am sick, I am poor, I am unlucky," never stopping to think that by those very words he is fastening misfortune upon himself, suggesting to his subconscious mind that it proceed on the assumption that he IS sick or poor or weak or unfortunate.

"Therefore I say unto you, what things soever ye desire when ye pray, believe that ye receive them, and ye shall HAVE them!"

That was the advice of the Master Psychologist of all time, the Great Healer, the Worker of Miracles. Again and again He assured those He cured that it was their FAITH that made them whole. And where such faith was lacking, as when He went back to the home of his childhood in Nazareth, it is written that . . "There He did no might works!"

But how, you may ask, can you work up such faith? There are two ways. The first is through affirmations . . CLAIMING the thing you want, telling your subconscious that you HAVE it, and keep on telling it in such convincing tones that it finally accepts the statement as fact and proceeds to bring it into being.

That was Coue's way. His "Every day in every way I AM getting better and better" or "richer and richer" helped many people. But if you want the best results, add this second factor: Stand in front of your mirror, look your reflection in the eye and talk to it as you would if you were a salesman, and upon you selling the man in the mirror depended everything important in your life. For it does!

If it is health you want, use some such affirmation as this:

"I AM energy. I AM strength. I AM power. I AM filled and thrilled with omnipotent life. The vitality of God permeates every fiber of my being. I AM well and whole in every part of my body. The grace and poise of our Lord Jesus Christ enfolds me. O Living Father, this is thy holy temple. Thou are making it a perfect dwelling place from which shall radiate thy healing love and wisdom to all mankind. Father, thou art glorifying me that I also may glorify thee." Tell him that and BELIEVE it! When you can convince him that you do believe it, you will be well.

Here is another potent affirmation:

"Life abundant quickens me now. Love all powerful heals me. God's strong, pure life is now active in and through every cell in my body. His perfect image of my every organ is now vitalized in me in perfect form. By the power and authority of Jesus Christ, every cell in my body is vitalized and restored. I have come to Him and I AM healed."

Money, success, happiness, can all be won in the same way. They all start with a nucleus, an idea, an ambition, a desire. They all require you to DO something to start that nucleus revolving on its axis and drawing to itself the elements necessary for its growth and successful completion. They all need faith to speed up the rate of motion and keep the nucleus growing.

Faith is the great impelling force. "If thou canst believe, all things are possible unto you."

There Is Magic In Believing

Professor William James of Harvard, the greatest psychologist America has known, declared that belief is oftentimes the only thing that can assure the successful conclusion of doubtful undertaking. Man's faith acts upon all the forces about him to bring into being the results that he images and believes in.

You can readily understand that when you realize that it is only faith that can keep the nucleus of an idea or a business going, if obstacles beset its path. You must hold to your image of the completed undertaking. You must see it successful in your mind's eye. You must BELIEVE in it.

How did God create the heavens and the earth and everything that in them is? You read in the Scriptures that God made "Every plant of the field before it was on the earth, and every herb of the field before it grew!"

How did he do it? In the same way that He made man. "In his image created He Him." He "Imaged" man in His mind. As the Psalmist put it . . "In Thy book, all members were written, when as yet there were none of them."

You read in St. John: "In the beginning was the word." What is a word? A mental image, is it not? "In the beginning was the mental image." That is the way everything in it is created right down to this day, from the building of a house to the laying of a transcontinental railway.

Do you remember the story of Jacob? He agreed to serve his Uncle Laban seven years to win the hand of Laban's daughter Rachel in marriage, but through the guile of Laban, Jacob had to serve a second seven years.

Even then, Laban begged him to tarry longer, and agreed to pay him as wages "all the speckled and spotted cattle, and all the brown cattle among the sheep, and the speckled and the spotted among the goats."

Since Laban first removed from the herds all cattle of this kind, the chances of Jacob's getting rich on the speckled offspring of solid-colored cattle seemed poor indeed. But Jacob evidently knew the power of "imaging," of visualization, for what did he do? "And Jacob took him rods which he had piled before the flocks in the gutters of the watering troughs when the flocks came to drink, that they should conceive when they came to drink." "And the flocks conceived before the rods, and brought forth ring-staked, speckled and spotted."

"And Jacob did separate the lambs, and set the faces of the flocks toward the ring-staked and all the brown in the flock of Laban; and he put his own flocks by themselves, and put their not unto Laban's cattle."

"And it came to pass, whensoever the strong cattle did conceive, that Jacob laid the rods before the eyes of the cattle in the gutters that they might conceive among the rods." "But when the cattle were feeble, he put them not in; so the feeble were Laban's and the stronger Jacob's."

"And the man increased exceedingly, and had much cattle, and maidservants and menservants and camels and asses."

In everything God created, the "Word" or mental image came first then the material form. And that is the way it is with you. Get the right image in your mind, put your faith in it and you can bring it into being.

You control your destiny, your fortune, your happiness, to the exact extent to which you can think them out, visualize them, see them as already yours allow no vagrant thought of fear or worry to mar their completion and beauty. The quality of your thought is the measure of your power.

"The source and center of all man's creative power," writes Glenn Clark, "the power that above all others lifts him above the level of brute creation and that gives him dominion, is his power of making images, or the power of the imagination."

There is a very real law of cause and effect which makes the dream of the dreamer come true. It is the law of visualization and belief . . the law that calls into being in this outer world everything that we truly believe to be real in the inner world.

Imagination pictures the thing you desire. Action starts your nucleus whirling and growing. Belief gives magnetic power to it, enabling it to attract to itself every element it needs to bring it into reality. It reaches beyond the thing that is, into the conception of what can be. Imagination gives you the picture. Belief gives you the power to make that picture your own. Make your mental image clear enough . . picture it vividly enough . . give it action and belief and all the powers of the universe will join to help you bring it into being.

That law holds true of everything in life. There is nothing you can rightfully desire that cannot be brought into being through visualization, action and belief.

The keynote of successful visualization is this; See things as you would have them be instead of as they are. Close your eyes and make clear mental pictures. Make them look and act just as they would if they were real. In short, daydream purposefully. Then put foundations under your dreams with your belief.

As James Allen put it: "Dream lofty dreams, and as you dream, so shall you become. Your vision is the promise of what you shall one day be. Your ideal is the prophecy of what you shall at last unveil."

The mental image is what counts, be it for good or ill. It is a devastating or beneficent force, just as you choose to make it. To paraphrase Thackeray . . "The world is a looking glass, and gives back to every man the reflection of his own thought."

Every condition, every experience of life is the result of our mental attitude. We can do only what we think we can do. We can be only what we think we can be. We can have only what we think we can have. What we do, what we are, what we have, all depend upon what we think. We can never express anything that we do not first have in mind.

The secret of all power, all success, all riches, is in first thinking powerful thoughts, successful thoughts, thoughts of wealth and supply. We must build them in our mind first. "Could we rightly comprehend the mind of man," wrote Paracelsus, "nothing would be impossible to us upon the earth." And Buddha told his followers . . "All that we are is the result of what we have thought."

And thought is subject wholly to the control of mind. Its direction rests with us. So learn to control your thought. Learn to image upon your mind only things you want to see reflected in your outer circumstances. Our achievements of today are but the sum of our thoughts of yesterday.

Remember, you can have anything you want if you want it badly enough. You can be anything you want to be, have anything you desire, accomplish anything you set out to accomplish . . if you will hold to that desire with singleness of purpose; if you will understand and believe in your own powers to accomplish.

Just as the first law of gain is desire, so the formula of success is belief. Believe that you have it . . see it as an existent fact . . and anything you can rightly wish for is yours. Belief is the substance of things hoped for, the evidence of things not seen.

It is your BELIEF in yourself that counts. It is the consciousness of dominant power within you that makes all things attainable. You can do anything you think you can. This knowledge is literally the gift of the gods, for through it you can solve every human problem. It is the open door to all good that you desire.

But do not let doubts or fears creep in. Remember the admonition of St. James: "He that wavereth is like a wave of the sea driven with the wind and tossed. Let not that man think that he shall receive anything of the Lord."

Baudouin said the same in different words:

"To be ambitious for wealth and yet always expecting to be poor; to be always doubting your ability to get what you long for, is like trying to reach east by traveling west. There is no philosophy which will help a man to succeed when he is always doubting his ability to do so, and thus attracting failure.

"You will go in the direction in which you face. There is a saying that every time the sheep bleats, it loses a mouthful of hay. Every time you allow yourself to complain of your lot, to say 'I am poor; I can never do what others do; I shall never be rich; I have not the ability that others have;' you are laying up so much trouble for yourself.

"No matter how hard you may work for success, if your thought is saturated with the fear of failure, it will kill your efforts, neutralize your endeavors, and make success impossible." Learn to control your thought. Learn to image upon your mind only the things you want to see reflected in your outer circumstances. Your achievements of today are but the sum of your thoughts and beliefs of yesterday. Your chances of success in any undertaking can always be measured by your belief in yourself.

Suppose your surroundings are discouraging. Just bear in mind that your real environment is within you. All the factors that make for success or failure are in your inner world. YOU make that inner world . . and through it your outer world. You can choose the material from which to build it. The richness of life is within you. No one has failed as long as he can begin again.

So start now to do the things you feel you have it in you to do. Ask permission of no man. Your belief that you can do the thing gives you thought-force their power. Fortune waits upon you. Seize her boldly, hold her and she is yours. She belongs rightfully to you. The men who have made their mark in this world all had one trait in common . . they believed in themselves. So what do you want most from life? Whatever it is, you can have it . . if you can believe in it . . if you can see in it in your mind's eye as yours. You must be able to hold it in your thought, visualize it, see yourself having it. You must make your model clearcut and distinct.

1. Remember, the first thing necessary is a sincere desire, concentrating your thought on one thing with singleness of purpose.

2. The second is visualization, seeing yourself doing it, imaging the object in the same way that God first imaged everything He created.

3. The third essential is to take whatever action is necessary to start your nucleus revolving and growing.

4. Next is faith, believing that you HAVE the thing you want, affirming constantly to your image in the mirror that you ARE rich or successful or healthy or happy. Not that you are going to be, mind you but that you ARE!

5. And the last is gratitude, gratitude for this thing that you have received, for the power that enabled you to create it, for all the gifts that Mind has given you in such profusion. Thank God that you HAVE received.

The Law of Attraction

What is the greatest evil in the world today? What causes more misery, more sin, than all other vices combined? What is the worst enemy of morality and peace and happiness that mankind knows?

POVERTY!

Poverty is responsible for most commercialized vice. Poverty fills our prisons with thieves and murderers. Poverty causes most disease. Poverty is back of nine-tenths of the unhappiness and misery in the world. It drives men to drink and to suicide, women to that and more. It makes people do things that otherwise they would look upon with loathing. Poverty is a vice. It is true that some of the churches still catalog it among the virtues, but that is a relic of the old feudal days when the few had all the riches and the many were left to wallow in misery. To keep the masses from revolution, it was necessary to teach them that God ordered it thus that there was not enough of the good things of life to go around, so that the many must suffer here that the few might enjoy, but it would all be made right in the next world.

We know now that this was mere "pap" to keep the masses quiet. We know that if, as the Master said, a tree is known by its fruit, poverty is as bad as the deadly upas tree of Java, which kills even the birds with its poisonous exhalations. We know that, for every individual to whom poverty has acted as a goad to high achievement, a thousand others have spent lives of squalor and misery. We know that the old idea that there was not enough to go around was just as foolish as that God would pick a particular class of "nobility" and give them everything good while letting the common people starve.

There are more riches in this old earth than mankind can ever exhaust. There is more power in the atom alone than man can ever use. There are unlimited resources of food and riches and comfort as yet undreamed of by man.

Why then do so many live in squalor, even in this richest country in the world? Why do millions die of famine in India and China? For the same reason that a party of explorers, driven by a west wind from the Amazon River far out to sea, and drifting in a river of fresh water, they almost perished of thirst! In much the same way, millions of human beings, living in a world of plenty, perish of want.

God is not partial to a fortunate few. He does not give to them and let the rest starve. He gives freely to all!

But there are certain laws governing these riches of His. There are rules that must be complied with. And until you learn the rules, you are like Ali Baba without the magic "Open, Sesame!" to open the doors of the treasure trove.

You have heard of Einstein's "Law of Relativity." And you probably wondered at times why such a to-do should be made over an obscure scientific law that could have no bearing, as far as you could see, upon everyday life.

But do you know that Einstein's theory is as important to you as any law in the land? For on what is his theory based?

1st, that there is only one material in the Universe.

2nd, and this is the part with a direct bearing upon you . . that there is only one fundamental Law of the Universe. That law is the Law of Attraction.

Perhaps you will get the connection more readily if I give you this law as it is expressed in the Bible. There it reads "To him that hath shall be given, and from him that hath not, shall be taken away even that which he hath."

To put it in ordinary, everyday language Einstein's Law of the Universe and the Biblical precept both mean that you must either be an Attracter, drawing things to you, or else be willing to sit back and see everything that is yours attracted to some stronger personality. Does that seem unjust? If so, it is still the way that all of Nature works.

Take any seed of plant life. Take an acorn, for instance. You put it in the ground . . plant it. What happens? It first gives of all the elements it has within itself to put forth a shoot, which in turn shall draw from the sun and the air the elements that they have to give; and at the same time, it puts out roots to draw from the earth the moisture and other elements it needs for growth. Its top reaches upward to the sun and air, its roots burrow deeply into the ground for moisture and nourishment. Always it is reaching out. Always it is creating a vacuum, using up all the materials it has on hand, drawing to itself from all about every element it needs for growth.

Time passes. The oak tree stops growing. What happens? In that moment, its attractive power ceases. Can it then live on the elements it has drawn to itself and made a part of itself through all those years? No, indeed! The moment growth stops, disintegration starts. Its component elements begin to feel the pull of the growing plants around them. First the moisture drains out of the tree. Then the leaves fall, the bark peels off . . finally the great trunk crashes down, to decay and form soil to nourish the growing plants around. Soon of the noble oak, nothing is left but the enriched soil and the well-nourished plants that have sprung from it.

The Fundamental Law of the Universe is that you must integrate or disintegrate. You must grow . . or feed others who are growing. There is no standing still. You must speed up your rate of motion until you are attracting to yourself all the unused forces about you, or you must give your own to help build some other man's success.

"To him that hath, shall be given." To him that is using his attractive powers, shall be given everything he needs for growth and fruition. "From him that hath not, shall be taken away even that which he hath." The penalty for not using your attractive powers is the loss of them. You are demagnetized. And like a dead magnet surrounded by live ones, you must be content to see everything you have drawn to yourself taken by them, until eventually even you are absorbed by their resistless force.

That is the first and fundamental Law of the Universe. But how are you to become an Attracter? How are you to make your start? In the same way that it has been done from the beginning of time.

Go back to the first law of life. Go back to the beginning of things. You find Nature logical in all that she does. If you want to understand how she works, study her in her simplest, most elementary forms. The principle established there hold good throughout the universe. The methods there used are used by all created things, from the simplest to the most complicated.

How, for instance, did the earliest forms of cell life, either plant or animal, get their food? By absorbing it from the waters around them. How does every cell in your body, every cell in plant or tree or animal, get its food today? In exactly the same way by absorbing it from the lymph or water surrounding it! Nature's methods do not change. She is logical in everything. She may build more complicated organisms, she may go in for immense size or strange combinations, but she uses the same principles throughout all of life.

Now, what is Nature's principle of Increase? From the beginning of time, it has been . .

Divide and Grow

That principle, like every other fundamental Law of Nature, is the same in all of life. It has remained unchanged since the first single-celled organism floated on the surface of the primordial sea. It is the fundamental Law of Increase.

Take the lowest form of cell life. How does it grow? It DIVIDES . . each part grows back to its original size . . then they in turn divide and grow again.

Take the highest form of cell life, MAN. The same principle works in him in exactly the same way in fact, it is the only principle of growth that Nature knows!

How does this apply to your circumstances, to the acquisition of riches, to the winning of success?

Look up any miracle of increase in the Bible, and what do you find? First division then increase.

When the widow of Zaraphath told Elijah she had only a handful of meal and a little oil, he bade her make from these a cake and give it to him . . and after that, to make herself and her son. She did so, and it is written that the barrel of meal wasted not, neither did the oil fail.

When another widow came to Elisha to beg that he save her sons from bondage for debt, he asked her . . "What hast thou in the house?" And when she answered . . "Naught save a pot of oil," he bade her borrow vessels from the neighbors and pour out the oil into them. In other words, start the flow. And so long as she had vessels to receive it, the oil kept flowing.

When the multitude lacked for bread, and the Apostles came to Jesus to ask what they should do, He said . . "How many loaves have you?" And when they told Him five, and two fishes, "He blessed and broke the loaves and gave them to set before the multitude. And the fishes divided He among them all. And they did eat and were filled. And they took up twelve baskets full of the fragments." In each case, God required that they start the flow . . that they give what they had in perfect faith.

When Russell Conwell was building the famous Baptist Temple in Philadelphia, his congregation was poor and greatly in need of money. Through prayer and every other means known to man, Conwell was constantly trying to help his flock.

One Sunday it occurred to him that the old Jewish custom had been, when praying to God, to first make an offering of the finest lamb of the flock, or of some other much prized possession. Then, after freely giving to God, prayer was make for His good gifts.

So instead of first praying, and then taking up the collection, as was the custom, Conwell suggested that the collection be taken first and that all who had special favors to ask of the Creator should give freely as a "Thank Offering."

A few weeks afterwards, Conwell asked that those who had made offering on this occasion should tell their experiences. The results sounded unbelievable. One woman who had an overdue mortgage on her home found it necessary to call in a plumber the following week to repair a leak. In tearing up the boards, he uncovered a hiding place where her late father had hidden all his money . . enough to pay off the mortgage and leave plenty over! One man got a much-needed job . . A servant some dresses she badly wanted . . A student the chance to study for his chosen vocation. While literally dozens had their financial needs met.

They had complied with the law. They had sown their seed . . freely . . and they reaped the harvest.

Many people will tell you "I don't see why God does not send me riches. I have prayed for them, and promised that if I get them, I will use them to do good." God enters into no bargains with man. He gives you certain gifts to start, and upon the way you use these depends whether you get more. You've got to start with what you have.

It's no use saying you have not enough to be worth starting with. Just remember the parable of the talents. The servant who was given five talents put them out at interest and made more, as did the one who was given two talents. The servant who received only one talent felt that it was too little to do much with, so he buried it. And you know what happened to him when the Master came back.

You have a mind. You get ideas in abundance . . ideas that might better the lot of those around you, ideas for service, ideas for making people happy, for improving conditions, for anything of good.

Put them to work! Use them! ACT upon them! In your mind, they are no more than daydreams . . Castles in the Air. Put foundations under them by DOING something to start them into action.

Remember, everything in this universe starts with a nucleus. It can be an idea, an ambition, or your Heart's Desire. But a nucleus of itself has no power. It cannot attract to itself even a single element. YOU have to set it in motion. YOU have to give it life. "Divide and grow!" Give it something of yours to get it started, whether it be money or time or action or all of them. Start it whirling. Give it attractive power.

How can you do it? First, by starting something. If you want a particular job, for instance, a particular work or opportunity, start the wheels in motion that should bring it to you. If it requires special knowledge, study until you have that knowledge. If it requires influence, cultivate those who have that influence. Whatever it requires, do those things and while doing them, stand before your mirror each morning and night, and convince your image there that you HAVE what it takes to get it.

Speed up the rate of motion of your nucleus by your faith in yourself. See yourself in your mind's eye doing the things that will be required of you when you land the job. If it is possible to do so, act out the things that will be expected of you before your mirror. Never pass a mirror without looking your image in the eye and telling him you ARE a success, you ARE accomplishing whatever it is that you have in mind.

Remember always . . first comes the mental image, then the fulfillment. Get that mental image clearly in mind, do something to start it into being, believe in it and the materialization will soon follow. But until you get it clearly in your own mind, you have a poor chance of putting it into the mind of anyone else.

"For anything that you want in life," writes Emmet Fox, "a healthy body, a satisfactory vacation, friends, opportunity, and above all the understanding of God, you must furnish a mental equivalent. Granted the mental equivalent, the thing must come to you." And what is the mental equivalent? What but the image you hold in your mind's eye of the things you want.

Thousands of books have been written on how to be successful, how to win your Heart's Desire, but here is the meat of all:

Every nucleus has power to draw to itself anything it needs for growth and fruition, if started into action and speeded up by constant faith.

That knowledge should enable anyone to succeed. That knowledge is worth any price you may pay for it. It can enable you to overcome any handicap, to surmount any obstacle. It is literally the Gift of the Gods.

So start something . . no matter on how small a scale. To begin, you know, is to be half done. Making a beginning starts your nucleus whirling, and that in turn affects everything about you of a like nature, drawing it to you, setting it in motion likewise.

A strong desire, backed by a firmly held purpose, is like a powerful magnet, drawing to it everything it needs for growth and fruition.

But remember that the power of this magnet is dependent entirely upon your belief in it. Perhaps you will recall the experiment made many years ago by Professor Henry of Princeton. He took an ordinary magnet of large size and with it lifted a few pounds of iron. Then he wrapped the magnet with wire charged from the current of a small battery. Instead of only a few pounds, the magnet lifted 3,000 pounds of iron!

Your belief in yourself is like the current from that battery. It magnetizes you tenfold . . even a hundredfold. It enables you to draw to you anything you need for success.

Working up this necessary belief may be difficult, but it is absolutely essential for without it you cannot succeed. Affirmation can be a great help, as suggested in the forgoing pages, and further study along these lines will help, too.

25 years ago, we wrote a set of little books called THE SECRET OF THE AGES, which explained in far greater detail the power that is in you and how to use it. Through the reading of these books, one man developed such a belief in himself and his mission in life that he started a new religion that now numbers more than a hundred thousand members. Through them, Lewis E. Sherbert of Reno learned to use the power that was in him to such good purpose that he wrote us a short time ago . . "When I began reading THE SECRET OF THE AGES, I was a peddler earning perhaps $15 a week. Since then, thanks to Robert Collier, I have enjoyed many $25,000 years of prosperity."

Through these books, M. D. Couch found the inspiration that enabled him to start a new company which made him more than $100,000, where his previous income over a period of years had been only $7,500 a year.

There were hundreds more who wrote in similar vein, so that the Commercial Reporter said of them . . "These little books have changed hundreds of lives from humdrum drudgery, business worry, and unsettlement, into sunshine and achievement." "This book has been the greatest help and influence that ever came into my life," wrote K. W. U. of Montgomery, Ala. "I have accomplished wonders by the application of its teachings."

We believe that you, too could accomplish wonders with its help. But whether you send for it or not, use what we have given you here in this book. You may find it easier if you have one or two friends, working with you. You remember Jesus told us "If two of you shall agree as touching anything they shall ask, it shall be done unto them. For when two or three are gathered together in my name, there am I in the midst of them, and I shall grant their request."

Remember, though, on the great clock of time, there is only one word "NOW!" If your expectations of health or abundance are all for the future, you may get them in the distant future but never NOW! You will never quite catch up with them. "Behold now is the day of salvation."

What will carry you to your goal tomorrow will carry you there much more surely today. Delays pay no dividends. Remember those lines of Goethe's:

"Are you in earnest? Seize this very minute;
What can you do, or dream you can, begin it!
Boldness has genius, power and magic in it;
Only engage and then the mind grows heated;
Begin, and then the work will be completed."

Prosperity: How To Attract It

By

Orison Swett Marden

Originally Published 1922

Contents

Chapter I -   How We Limit Our Supply
Chapter II -   The Law of Attraction
Chapter III -   Driving Away Prosperity
Chapter IV -   Establishing the Creative Consciousness
Chapter V -   Where Prosperity Begins
Chapter VI -   If You Can Finance Yourself
Chapter VII -   How to Increase Your Ability
Chapter VIII -   Look Like a Success
Chapter IX -   How to Make Your Dreams Come True
Chapter X -   What Discouragement Does to You .. How to Cure It
Chapter XI -   How to Make Your Subconscious Work for You
Chapter XII -   Thinking Health and Prosperity into the Cells of Your Body
Chapter XIII -   How to Make Yourself Lucky
Chapter XIV -   Self-Faith and Prosperity
Chapter XV -   Fear and Worry Demagnetize the Mind How to Get Rid of Them
Chapter XVI -   Good Cheer and Prosperity
Chapter XVII -   The Master Key - To Be Great, Concentrate
Chapter XVIII -   Time Is Money" .. and Much
Chapter XIX -   The Positive vs. the Negative Man
Chapter XX -   Thrift and Prosperity
Chapter XXI -   As a Man Expecteth So Is He
Chapter XXII -   "I Can't Afford It" .. The Habit of Going Without
Chapter XXIII -   How to Bring Out the Man You Can Be

Chapter I

How We Limit Our Supply

- "A man will remain a rag picker as long as he has only a rag picker's vision."

- Why go thru life exhibiting the traits of an underling? If you are a real man, don't go around looking like a beggar,, talking like a beggar, acting like a beggar.

- Only by thinking prosperity and abundance can you realize the abundant, prosperous life.

- Fixing limitation upon ourselves is one of the cardinal sins of mankind.

- Prosperity flows only through channels that are wide open to receive it. Doubt, fear and lack of confidence close these channels.

- A pinched mind means a pinched, limited supply.

- Everything we get in life comes through the gateway of our thought.

If that is pinched, stingy, mean, what flows to us will correspond.

WHAT would you think of a prince, the heir to a kingdom of limitless wealth and power, who should live in the condition of a pauper, who should go about the world bemoaning his hard fate and telling people how poor he was, saying that he didn't believe his father was going to leave him anything, and that he might as well make up his mind to a life of poverty and limitations?

You would say, of course, that he must be insane, and that his hard conditions, his poverty and limitations, were not actual, but imaginary; that they existed only in his mind; that his father was ready to load him with good things, with all that his heart desired, if he would only open his mind to the truth and live in the condition befitting a prince, the son and heir of a great king.

Now, if you are living in pinching poverty, in a narrow, cramped, limited environment in which there seems to be no hope, no outlook for better things; if you are not getting what you want, though working hard for it, you are just as foolish as the prince who, believing that he was poor, lived like a pauper in the midst of his father's limitless wealth. Your limitations are in your mind, just as the prince's were in his. You are the child of a Father who has created abundance, limitless wealth, for all of His children, but your pinched, limited, poverty stricken thought shuts you out from all this abundance and keeps you in poverty.

A Russian laborer named Mihok, living in Omaha, Nebraska, had carried a "luck" stone in his pocket for twenty years, never guessing that it had any monetary value. Time and again friends, who thought that it might be more than an ordinary stone, suggested that he have it examined by a jeweler. He obstinately refused until; finally, they became so insistent that he sent the stone to a Chicago jeweler, who pronounced it a pigeon-blood ruby, the largest of its kind in the world. It weighed 24 karats and was worth $100,000!

There are millions like this poor day laborer, living in poverty, thinking that there is nothing for them but hard work and more poverty who, without knowing it, are carrying in the great within of themselves possibilities of wealth beyond their dreams. Their wrong thinking is robbing them of their divine inheritance; shutting off the abundant supply provided for them by the Omnipotent Source of all supply.

The majority of people are in the position of a man who went out to water his garden, but inadvertently stepped on the hose, shutting off the water supply. He had a big hose and was very much annoyed, very much disappointed, because he was getting only a mere dribble of water when he had every right to expect . . and should get: . . a liberal flow. Water was at the source in abundance, ready to supply his needs; only one thing was at fault, the man himself was pinching his supply, limiting it to a miserable drizzle. He was standing on the hose and didn't know it.

That is literally what all who are living in grinding poverty are doing. They are pinching their supply by stepping upon the hose through which plenty would come to them. They are stopping the flow of abundance that is their birthright, by their doubts, their fears, and their unbelief; by visualizing poverty, thinking poverty, acting as if they never expected to have anything, to accomplish anything, or to be anything.

Everything in man's life, everything in God's universe, is based upon principle . . follows a divine law; and the law of prosperity and abundance is just as definite as the law of gravitation, just as unerring as the principles of mathematics. It is a mental law. Only by thinking abundance can you realize the abundant, prosperous life that is your birthright; in other words, according to your thought will be your life, your supply, or your lack. Your mental attitude will be flung back to you, every time, in kind. A poverty stricken mental attitude will bring only poverty stricken conditions to you.

We are the creatures of our convictions. We cannot get beyond what we believe we are; what we believe we have.

Hence, if we think that we are never going to be strong or well like other people, or to be successful in our calling, we never will be. If we are convinced that we will always be poor, we will be. You can't get away from poverty when you don't expect to; when you don't believe that you are going to.

Many of the people who are living in poverty today never really expect anything else. Their fixed belief that they can never become prosperous keeps them in poverty; that is, it keeps their minds negative, and the mind cannot create, cannot produce, in this condition. It is only the positive mind that can create prosperity; the negative mind is noncreative, non-productive; it can only tear down, inhibit, prevent the inflow of the good things that we long for.

It is not so much what you do with your hands as what you do with your mind that counts. Everything that has been accomplished by the hand or brain of man had its birth in the mind. The universe itself is the creation of Divine Mind. A hard working man who longs for prosperity, but is headed in the other direction mentally, who doesn't believe he is going to be prosperous, is neutralizing his hard work by his negative, destructive thought; he is standing on the hose that connects with his supply.

When you limit yourself in your thought, you are limiting yourself outwardly in a way which corresponds with your mental attitude, because you are obeying a law which is unchangeable. You will notice that the man who puts a nickel in the contribution box, is not only stingy, close, and mean in all his money matters, but his face, his whole person, has a cramped, worried, pinched look. He is forever saving pennies, watching out for little things and never doing big things. No matter how much natural ability he has, his narrow, limited, poverty thought dwarfs him and cuts off his stream of supply. He cannot do big things because he never thinks big things. His warped mind will admit only a pinched supply instead of the big flow that is literally at his command. It is because we have not learned how to use our thought forces that most of us go about like paupers, never glimpsing the marvelous inheritance left us by the All supply, the All-good. Our parsimonious thought pinches our supply.

We often wonder why it is that certain people, in apparently no better circumstances than we are, get so much better things than we do; why they always insist upon and receive the best of everything. We never see them wearing cheap things . . never see cheap things in their homes, or any pinching anywhere. They buy the best food, the best fruits and vegetables in the market, and everything else in accordance. We think they are extravagant when we compare what they pay for things with what we pay for things of the same kind, and we pride ourselves that we are economizing and saving what they are wasting. But, are we? How does our manner of living compare with theirs? Does the enjoyment we get out of life measure up to what they get? Do the few dollars we save compensate for the great lack in our lives . . the lack of good food, of proper clothing, of the little pleasure trips, the social enjoyments, the picnics and various diversions which make life pleasant, healthful, and above all, much more productive for the neighbors whose extravagance we condemn? As a matter of fact, our skimped, pinching policy leaves us poorer in the end.

Prosperity flows only through channels that are wide open to receive it. It does not flow through channels pinched by the poverty thought, by discouragement, doubt, or fear, or by a strangling narrow-visioned policy. A generous expenditure is often the wisest economy, the only thing that brings a generous success. If a great manufacturer like Henry Ford, a great merchant like John Wanamaker, a big railroad manager, or other business man, should lose his broad vision and wide outlook; should begin to skimp on necessary output; should substitute inferior goods and men and service for the best; should reverse his policy, changing from a broad, generous one to a narrow, stingy one, he would soon find his business dwindling away to nothing.

There is no changing the principle of the law of supply. Whatever your business, your profession or occupation, or your circumstances, your mental attitude will determine your success or failure. A pinched mind means a pinched supply. It means that you try to tap the great fountainhead of supply with a gimlet and then expect to get an abundant supply. That is impossible. Your mental attitude gauges the How of your supply.

Chapter II

The Law of Attraction

- By the law of affinity you may know that your own is always seeking you if you are" seeking it With all your might and are not driving it away with your doubts.

- John Burroughs thus beautifully expressed this: "I rave no more 'gainst Time or Fate, For lo, my own shall come to me.

- "Asleep, awake, by night or day, The friends I seek are seeking me.

- "What matter if I stand alone? I wait with joy the coming years; My heart shall reap where it hath sown, What is mine shall know my face.

- "Nor time, nor space, nor deep, nor high Can keep my own away from me."

IT was never intended that God's children should ever want for anything. We live in the very lap of abundance; there is plenty of everything all about us, the great cosmic universe is packed with all sorts of beautiful, marvelous things, glorious riches, ready for our use and enjoyment. Everything the human heart can crave, the great creative Intelligence offers us. We can draw from this vast ocean of intelligence everything we wish: all that it is necessary for us to do is to obey the law of attraction, . . like attracts like.

To realize prosperity and abundance does not depend upon man's own little brain, his own little one sided efforts. It is a question of his making his minds a magnet to attract the things he wants, to attract his desires.

Everything that the race enjoys has been attracted out of the great ocean of intelligence according to a law. All inventions, all discoveries, all the marvelous facilities of civilization, . . our hospitals, our schools, our churches, our libraries, and other institutions, our homes, with their comforts and luxuries, . . have all been attracted from this great cosmic storehouse of intelligence by the same law.

It was intended that our longings, our yearnings, our legitimate desires should be satisfied, that our dreams should come true. It is our ignorance of the law that would bring our own to us which keeps it from us.

When you were a boy experimenting with your little steel magnet, didn't you often try to make it pick up wood, copper, rubber, or some other substance different from itself? And, of course, you found it would not, because it had no affinity for things that were unlike itself. You found that it would pick up a needle but not a toothpick. In other words you demonstrated the law that . . Like attracts like.

Not a day passes that we do not see this law demonstrated in different ways in human life. Sometimes the demonstrations are very tragic. Only a short time ago a little eight year old girl, the daughter of a Pennsylvania farmer, died from fright in a dentist's chair, where she had been placed to have a tooth extracted. Although the child knew nothing about the law, it worked just the same; and, Like Job, the thing she feared had come to her.

By the operation of the same law that draws to us disease and death, we draw to ourselves poverty or opulence, success or failure. The mind at any given time is a magnet for something. It is a magnet for whatever thought, whatever convictions dominate the mind at the time, and the blessed, glorious thing about it all is that we can determine what the mind shall attract, what sort of a magnet it shall become. Now, you may attract to you that which is not good for you, that which will damn you, that which will pain and humiliate. By concentrating upon and working for it you become a specialist in that line and the law of attraction brings it to you. If you have a prosperity mental attitude, if you have a vigorous faith that you are going to get away from poverty, that you are going to demonstrate prosperity, abundance, and strive intelligently and persistently to realize your vision, you will do so. That's the law. If you obey the law you will get good results.

If we could only see a picture of the mental processes of whatever is held in the mind, pulling the things which correspond to our thought; if we could see more failure, more bad business, more debts, more losses starting towards us because we have contacted with these things in our thought, we would quit worrying about the things we don't want and think the things we do want, attracting more instead of less, attracting abundance instead of poverty, prosperity instead of failure.

Oh, how often we make our mind a magnet to attract all sorts of enemy thoughts, poverty thoughts, sick thoughts, fear thoughts, and worry thoughts, and then somehow we expect that a miracle will be performed, and that out of these negative causes we will be sure in some way to enjoy positive results. No miracle could perform such a change as this. Results correspond with causes.

Before we can be conquered by poverty, we must, first of all, be poor mentally. The poverty thought, the acceptance of a poverty stricken environment as an inevitable condition from which you cannot get away, keeps you in the poverty current and draws more poverty to you. It is the operation of the same law which attracts good things, a better environment, to those who think abundance, prosperity, who are convinced that they are going to be well off, and work confidently, hopefully, toward that end.

Not the things we long for most, not the things we wish for, but our own, that which has lived in our thoughts and mind, dominated in our mentality, in our mental attitude, that is what the law of attraction brings to us. It may be that this law has brought us the very things we hated and wanted to get rid of, but we have dwelt upon them, and, because they formed the mental model, the life processes built them into our lives. The law of attraction often brings us hated bedfellows, but they have lived so long in our minds, that they must become a part of our lives, by the very law that like attracts like.

Until recently many of us did not understand what Job meant when he said, "The thing which I greatly feared has come upon me." Now we know that he expressed a psychological law that is as inexorable as the laws of mathematics. We know that the things we fear most, the things we have a horror of and want to flee from, we are really pursuing by our very fear of them. By predicting them and visualizing them in our minds, we are attracting them to ourselves, and when we do this we are turning our backs upon the very things which we long for most.

The time will come when the law of attraction will be known as the greatest power in creation. This is the law upon which all successes, all characters, all lives are built. Mental attraction is the only power upon which we can build anything successfully. It is an inevitable law, an inexorable principle, that everything attracts to itself everything else like itself, that air affinities tend to get together, and when you make your mind a magnet it will attract according to its quality, according to your mental vision, your thoughts, your motives, your dominant attitude.

The saying "Money attracts money" is only another way of stating the law, . . "like attracts like." The prosperous classes think prosperity, believe in it, work for it, never for a moment doubt their right to have all the money and all the good things they need, and of course they get them. They are living up to the very letter and spirit of the law of attraction. A Rockefeller, A Schwab, uses this law in a masterly way to amass a large fortune. The newsboy uses the same law in selling his newspapers, running a news stand and climbing gradually to the mayoralty of his city or town. We all use this law of attraction no matter whether we know it or not. We use it every instant of our lives.

Many people wonder that bad men, wicked men, vicious men are successful in business, at money making, in amassing a fortune, while the good man, the upright man, doesn't seem to be able to make any headway. They haven't the knack of accumulation in the way of making money. Good things do not seem to come to them. If they make an investment they almost always lose; they buy in the wrong market, or sell in the wrong market.

Now, a man's morals do not have anything specially to do with his money making faculties, except that honesty is always and everywhere the best business policy. It is just a question of obeying the law of accumulation, the law that like attracts like. A very bad man may obey the law of accumulation, the law of attraction, and accumulate a vast fortune. If he is honest, his other defects and immoralities, his viciousness, will not hinder the working of the law. The law is unmoral . . it is neither moral nor immoral.

Multitudes of people are attracting the wrong things because they do not know the law. They have never learned that the great secret of health, happiness, and success lies in holding the mental attitude which builds, which constructs, the mental attitude which draws to us the good things we desire. They have never learned the difference between building and tearing down thoughts; the difference between success and failure thoughts; in fact, they do not know that whatever comes to us in life, in our undertakings, great or small, is largely a question of the kind of thoughts we hold in the mind. We can attract the thing we desire as easily as we can attract the thing we hate and despise and long to get rid of. It is simply a matter of holding the image of the thing in the mind. That is the model which the life processes will build into our environment and which we will objectify.

Like attracts like, failure more failure, poverty more poverty. Hatred attracts more hatred, envy more envy, jealousy more jealousy, and malice more malice. Everything has power to attract its kind. The feeling of jealousy or hatred is a seed sown in the great cosmic soil all about us, and the eternal laws return to us a harvest the same in kind. What we sow we reap, just as the soil will return to us exactly what we put into it. Nothing has the power to reproduce anything but itself. There is no exception to this law.

The law cannot pity or help you if you break a bone, or are injured, any more than the law of electricity can help you when you abuse it. It will kill you if you break the law.

To think about and worry about the things we do not want, or to fear that they will come to us, is but to invite them; because every impression becomes an expression, or tends to become so unless the impression is neutralized by its opposite. If we think too much about our losses, too much about our possible failure, all these things will tend to bring to us the very thing we are trying to get away from.

On every hand we see this law of like attracting like exemplified in the lives of the poverty stricken multitudes, who, through ignorance of the law, keep themselves in their unfortunate condition by saturating their minds with the poverty idea; thinking and acting and talking poverty; living in the belief in its permanency; fearing, dreading, and worrying about it. They do not realize, no one has ever told them, that as long as people mentally see the hunger wolf at the door and the poorhouse ahead of them; as long as they expect nothing but lack and poverty and hard conditions, they are headed toward these things; they are making it impossible for prosperity to come in their direction.

The way to attract prosperity and drive poverty out of the life is to work in harmony with the law instead of against it. To expect prosperity, to believe with all your heart, no matter how present conditions may seem to contradict, that you are going to become prosperous, that you are already so, is the very first condition of the law of attaining what you desire. You cannot get it bydoubting or fearing.

Whatever we visualize and work for we will get. What we most frequently visualize, what we think most about, is constantly weaving itself into the fabric of our lives, becoming a part of ourselves, increasing the power of our mental magnet to attract those things to us. It doesn't matter whether they are things we fear and try to avoid or things that are good for us, that we long to get. Keeping them in mind increases our affinity for them and inevitably tends to bring them into our lives.

It is a curious fact that many people seem to think that one must spend years as an apprentice to become an expert in any line of endeavor, in business or in a profession, but that in regard to prosperity it is largely a matter of chance, of fate, something which cannot be affected very much by anything they may be able to do. They say, "Well, I was not built that way. I am not a natural money-maker, and never can be." Or they excuse themselves on the ground that their parents and those before them were never money-makers, and never did anything more than make a bare living.

There is nothing at all peculiar about prosperity any more than there is about legal efficiency or expertness in law or medicine. Its realization is purely a matter of concentration and of preparation; a matter of focusing all our powers upon the prosperity law in order to attract prosperity and to make ourselves expert in attaining it.

The law of prosperity, of opulence, is just as definite as the law of gravitation, and it works just as unerringly. Its first principle is mental. Wealth is created mentally first; it is thought out before it becomes a reality.

If you would attract success, keep your mind saturated with the success, idea. Develop an attitude of mind that will attract success. When you think success, when you act it, when you live it, when you talk it, when it is in your bearing, then you are attracting it.

When we once get this law of attraction thoroughly fixed in our minds we will be careful about attracting our enemies, contacting with them through our mind, thinking about them, worrying about them, fearing, and dreading them. We will hold the sort of thoughts that will attract the things we long for and are seeking, not the things we dread, and despise, and are trying to avoid.

It is just as easy to attract what you want as to attract what you don't want. It is just a question of holding the right thought, and making the right effort. There is no exception to the law of attraction, any more than there is to the law of gravitation, or the laws of mathematics.

Chapter III

Driving Away Prosperity

- As long as you hold the poorhouse thought you are heading toward the poorhouse. A pinched, stingy thought means a pinched, stingy supply.

- The man who sows failure thoughts, poverty thoughts, can no more reap success, prosperity harvests, than a farmer can get a wheat crop from sowing thistles.

- No matter how hard you may work, if you keep your mind saturated with poverty thoughts, poverty pictures, you are driving away the very thing you are pursuing.

- Stop thinking trouble if you want to attract its opposite; stop thinking poverty if you wish to attract plenty. Refuse to have anything to do with the things you fear, the things you do not want.

- It is doubting and facing the wrong way, facing towards the black, depressing, hopeless outlook that kills effort and paralyzes ambition.

A MAN once told me that if he could be assured that he would never have to go to the poorhouse, and that he would have the necessities of life for his family, he would be perfectly satisfied. He said it was evidently not intended that he should have luxuries or anything more than a bare living; he had always been a poor man and he always expected to be poor, that his people before him had also been poor. Now, it was just this mental attitude, . . for he was a hard worker, . . of always expecting to be poor, believing he would always be poor, that kept him from attracting prosperity. He had not expected prosperity and, of course, could not attract what he did not expect. He only just managed to get along, for that was all he expected to do.

One of the chief reasons why the great mass of human beings live such mean, stingy, poverty stricken lives is because their negative mental attitudes, their doubts and fears and worries, their lack of faith, attract these conditions.

The Good Book tells us that "the destruction of the poor is their poverty." That is, their poverty thought, their poverty conviction, their poverty expectation and poverty belief, their general hopeless mental outlook keeps away prosperity. The worst thing about poverty is the poverty thought, the poverty belief.

Multitudes of people never expect to be comfortable, to say nothing of having the luxuries and refinements of life. They expect poverty, and they do not understand that this very expectancy increases the power of their mental magnet to attract want and limitation, even though they are trying to get away from it; that we always head towards our expectations and convictions.

Poverty begins in the mind. The majority of poor people remain poor because they are mental paupers to begin with. They don't believe they are ever going to be prosperous. Fate, conditions are against them; they were born poor and they expect always to be poor, . . that is their unvarying trend of thought, their fixed conviction. Go among the very poor in the slums and you will find them always talking poverty, bewailing their fate, their hard luck, the cruelty and injustice of society. They will tell you how they are ground down by the upper classes, kept down by their greedy employers, or by an unjust order of things which they can't change. They think of themselves as victims instead of victors, as conquered instead of conquerors.

The great trouble with most people who fail to realize their ambition is that they face life the wrong way. They do not understand the tremendous potency of the influence of the habitual mental attitude in shaping the career and actually creating conditions. It is really pitiful to see people making slaves of themselves trying to get ahead, but all the time side-tracking the good things which would come their way if they did not head them off by their conviction that there is nothing much in the world for them anyway, nothing more than a bare living at the best. They are actually driving away the very things which might flow to them in abundance if they held the right mental attitude.

In every walk of life we see men and women driving away the things they want. Most people think the things they do not want. They go through life trying to build happy, prosperous, healthful lives out of negative, destructive thinking, always neutralizing the results of their hard work. They indulge in worries, in fears and envies, in thoughts of hatred and revenge, and carry habitually a mental attitude, which means destruction to health, growth, and creative possibility. Their lives are pitched to a minor key. There is always a downward tendency in their thought and conversation.

Nine-tenths of the people in the world who complain of being poor and failures are headed in the wrong direction, headed right away from the condition or thing they long for. What they need is to be turned about so that they will face their goal instead of turning their backs on it by their destructive thinking and going in the other direction.

The Morgans, the Wanamakers, the Marshall Fields, the Schwabs, think prosperity, and they get it. They don't anticipate poverty; they don't anticipate failure; they know they are going to be prosperous and successful, because they have eliminated all doubt from, their minds.

Doubt is the factor which kills success, just as the fear of failure kills prosperity. Everything is mental first, whether failure or success. Everything passes through our consciousness before it is a reality. Multitudes of people who work hard and try hard in every way to get on would be shocked if they could see a mental picture of themselves headed toward the poorhouse, in fact, as they actually are in thought. They do not know that, by an inexorable law, they must head toward their mental attitude, that when they continually think and talk poverty and suggest it by their slovenly dress, their personal appearance, and by their environment, when they predict that there is nothing for them but poverty, that they will always be poor, no matter how hard they may work.

They do not know that their doubts and fears and poverty stricken convictions are making prosperity impossible for them. They do not know that as long as they hold such thoughts they cannot possibly head toward the goal of prosperity. The sum total of our life is that upon which we have concentrated. If poverty or opulence, if success or failure, if prosperity or want has occupied our minds, if we have focused our attention upon one of these, that is just what we shall see incorporated in our life.

What you have, my friend, what you have surrounded yourself with, is a reproduction of your thought, your faith, your belief in your efforts; is what you have been conscious of.

Our thoughts, our faith, our beliefs, our efforts, all materialize, and are objectified about us. Our words become flesh and live with us; our thoughts, our emotions, become flesh and live with us; they become our environment and surround us. There is only one way to get away from poverty, and that is to turn your back upon it. Begin right away by putting the poverty thought, the poverty fear, out of your mind. Assume as far as possible a prosperous appearance; think the way you want to go; expect to get what you are after, the thing you long for, and you will get it. Mentally and physically, in your clothing, in your surroundings, in your home, in your bearing, erase, as far as you can, all marks of poverty. Affirm with Wait Whitman, "I myself am good fortune." Don't let slovenliness in your home, shabbiness in your children or wife, be an unfavorable advertisement of you.

The fear of poverty is its greatest power. That is what gives it its stranglehold on the masses. Get rid of your fear of it, my friend. Let the prosperity thought take the place of the poverty thought, the poverty fear, in your mind. If you have been unfortunate, don't advertise your discouragement. Brush up, brace up, dress up, clean up; and above all . . look up and think up. Give an up-look to your home, however humble.

Remember that a stream of plenty will not flow towards a poverty saturated thought. A pinched, stingy thought means scanty supply. Thinking abundance, opulence, and defying limitations will open up the mind and set the thought currents towards greatly increased supply.

If all the poverty stricken people in the world today would quit thinking poverty, quit dwelling on it, worrying about it and fearing it; if they would wipe the poverty thought out of their minds; if they would cut off mentally all relations with poverty and substitute the opulent thought, the prosperity thought, the mental attitude that faces toward prosperity, the change in their condition would be amazing. The Creator never made a man to be poor. There is nothing in his constitution which fits drudgery and poverty. Man was made for prosperity, happiness, and success. He was not made to suffer any more than he was made to be insane or to be a criminal.

Thousands of people have literally thought themselves away from a life of poverty by getting a glimpse of that great fundamental principle . . that we tend to realize in the life what we persistently hold in the thought and vigorously struggle toward. Don't think that by holding the constructive, creative thought only now and then, or just when you may happen to feel like it, that it is going to counteract the influence of holding the destructive thought most of the time.

Lots of people who treat for prosperity and opulence, hold the want thought, the lack thought too, and that is the reason their prayer is not answered. They get just the opposite, because that is the thought, the expectation which predominates in the mind.

Our conviction is much stronger than our will power. No will power can help you to do a thing when convinced that you can't. For instance, if you are convinced that a fatal disease which you believe you have inherited is overcoming you, this thought is infinitely stronger than your will to prevent it.

We cannot get away from our convictions. These are being built into the mind, being built into the life and character. If you are convinced that you are going to be poor, that you are never going to be prosperous, no matter how hard you may work, your convictions will triumph and you will live and die in penury. A man will never be anything but a beggar while he thinks beggarly thoughts.

If you are living in the thought of limitation, the conviction of lack and want, the fear of poverty, the belief that you can never become prosperous, you are holding yourself down, keeping yourself back. You are sowing seed which must produce a harvest like itself.

The boy who sows his wild oats seed might as well expect to get just the opposite harvest as for you to saturate your mind with poverty thoughts, lack, want, limitation thoughts, and expect a prosperity harvest. If you are thinking poverty stricken thoughts, saturating your mind with limitation thoughts, you must expect a corresponding harvest and you will get it whether you expect it or not.

In my youth one of the hardest things in the Bible for me to understand was the statement, "To him that, hath shall be given." I couldn't reconcile this with the Bible. It seemed positively unjust. But now I know that it illustrates a law. "To him that hath shall be given," because in getting what he has a man has made his mind a magnet to attract more. On the other hand, "To him that hath little, that which he hath shall be taken away," because he is headed in the wrong direction mentally.

He is closing the avenues of supply by his little thoughts, his doubts and fears. He is in no mental condition to get more, to attract more. If you want to demonstrate prosperity, you must think prosperity; you must hold your mind everlastingly toward prosperity; you must saturate your mind with it, just as a law student must saturate his mind with law, must think it, must read it, must talk it, must keep with lawyers and in a law atmosphere as much as possible, to be successful as a lawyer.

It was intended that we should have an abundance of the good things of the universe.

None of them are withheld from us except by our poverty stricken mental attitude. There is no more possible lack for a human being of all that the heart can wish for than there is lack of water or food supply for the fish in the great ocean. The fish swims in the ocean of supply, as we swim in the great cosmic ocean of supply that is all around us. All we have to do is to open our minds, our faith, our confidence, to its reality, and use our intelligent effort to get all the good there is in it, . . that is everything we need and desire.

Chapter IV

Establishing The Creative Consciousness

- The beginning of every achievement must be in your consciousness.

- We have unlimited power, boundless resources, in the great within of us, but until we awaken to a consciousness of this hidden power, those invisible resources, we cannot use them.

- The consciousness of power creates power. What we are conscious of, we already possess.

- In proportion to the intensity, the persistence, the vividness, the definiteness of your consciousness of the thing you want, do you begin to create it, to attract it.

- The Creator puts no limit to our supply. There is no limitation of anything we need except in our own consciousness.

THE great trouble with those of us who are living in a world of unfulfilled desires and ambitions is that we do not hold the right consciousness. Dr. Perry Green rightly says that Job's lament . . "The thing which I feared is come upon me" . . should be changed to "The thing 'which I was greatly conscious of is come upon me." In other words, it is the thing we hold in our consciousness that comes out of the invisible world of realities and takes visible form in our lives according to its nature, . . poverty or prosperity; health or disease; happiness or misery.

The whole secret of individual growth and development is locked up in our consciousness, for this is the door of life itself. Every experience whether of joy or sorrow, of health or disease, of success or failure, must come through our consciousness. There is no other way by which it can enter and become a part of the life. You cannot have what you are not conscious of; you cannot do what you are not conscious of being able to do. In short, it is an immutable law that, whatever you hold in mind, believe that you can do or get, is the thing that will manifest itself in your life.

The thing that Job held in his consciousness was the thing that came upon him. Joan of Arc saved her country, because from childhood she held the consciousness that she had been born to do that very thing. This poor unlettered peasant girl knew nothing about the great law of mental attraction, but unconsciously she worked with it. But for her consciousness of victory she never could have accomplished her stupendous work.

It is the victorious consciousness that achieves victory in every age and in every field. After many years' study of the lives and methods of successful men in every department of life, I have found that those who win out in a large way are great believers in themselves, in their power to succeed in the things they undertake. Great artists, scientists, inventors, explorers, generals, business men, and others, who have done the biggest things in their specialty, have always held the victorious consciousness. Success was the goal they constantly visualized, and they never wavered in their conviction that they would reach it.

Men fail, not because of lack of ability, but because they do not hold the victorious consciousness, the success consciousness. They do not live in the expectancy of winning, in the belief that they will succeed in reaching the goal of their ambitions. They live rather in the expectation of possible failure, in fear of poverty, and coming to want, and they get what they hold in mind, what they habitually dwell upon. The pinched, narrow, limited, poverty stricken, fear filled consciousness; the consciousness that expects stingy returns, that expects poverty and does not believe it will get anything better, is responsible for more poverty than any other one thing.

Our consciousness is a part of our creative force; that is, it puts the mentality in a position to attract its affinity, that which is like itself. A penury consciousness cannot demonstrate a fortune; a failure consciousness cannot demonstrate success. It would be against the law. If you are steeped in poverty and failure, you have no one to blame but yourself, for you are working against the law. You are holding the poverty consciousness, living in the thought of failure. Perhaps you are wondering why you can't create something that will match your ambition, your longings when all the time you are filling your mind so full of discouragement, so full of black, gloomy, despairing pictures, that your whole life is saturated with the failure consciousness.

You feel, perhaps, that something, some invisible force, some cruel fate or destiny is holding you back. Something is holding you back, but it is not fate or destiny; it is your discouraged mental attitude, the unfortunate consciousness that you have been holding for years. While you were trying to build on the material plane, you were neutralizing all your efforts by constantly tearing down on the mental plane. You have been obeying the negative law which destroys and kills blights and blasts, instead of the positive law that produces; that creates, builds, beautifies, develops man's godlike qualities and glorifies his life.

All of life and its achievements, its possibilities, depend upon our consciousness, and we can develop any sort of consciousness we wish. The great musician has developed a musical consciousness of which most of us are ignorant, because we are not conscious of this mode of activity. Our musical consciousness has not been developed. The mathematician, the astronomer, the writer, the physician, the artist, the specialist in whatsoever line, has developed a particular consciousness, and he realizes the fruits of that consciousness. He manifests and enjoys a special power just in proportion as he has developed his specialty consciousness.

What sort of consciousness do you want to develop? What do you want to get, to do, to become? Make yourself very positive on this point for the first step toward the development of a new consciousness is to get a thorough grip upon your purpose, your desire, your aim; to get a picture of it firmly fixed in your mind; to make it dominant in your thoughts, in your acts, in your life. This is how the successful lawyer at the start develops a law consciousness; the successful physician, a medical consciousness; the successful business man, a business consciousness. It is of the utmost importance to get started right, because whatever the consciousness you develop, your mind will attract that which has an affinity for it, will draw to you the material for your building.

The next thing is to establish the conviction that you can achieve whatever you desire. This is a tremendous step in the way of accomplishment, for conviction is stronger than will power. That is, you may will ever so hard to do a thing, but if you are convinced that you can't do it, the conviction of your inability will prevail over your will power. Your conviction is your strongest lever of accomplishment. This is what has enabled so many poor boys and girls to climb to high place and power in spite of all sorts of obstacles, and often contrary to the opinion and advice of those who knew them best. They were so thoroughly conscious of their ability to do the thing they wanted to do, and so convinced that they could do it, that nothing could hold them back from their own.

The beginning of every achievement must be in your consciousness. That is the starting point of your creative plan. In proportion to the intensity, the persistence, the vividness, the definiteness of your consciousness of the thing you want, do you begin to create in any line. For instance, consciousness of power reveals power; the consciousness of supremacy is equivalent to supremacy itself; the consciousness of self-confidence is what gives us the assurance that we are equal to the thing we undertake. What we are conscious of, we already possess. But we cannot come into possession of anything we are not conscious of. That is, it cannot be ours until we become conscious of it.

If you are not conscious of the ability to succeed, you can't succeed. If you are not conscious of your own superiority, you cannot become superior. But if you hold in your consciousness the picture of masterfulness; if you hold in mind the thought of superiority, you are putting in operation a little law of mastership, a little law of superiority, and you begin to manifest these things in your life. We have unlimited power, boundless resources, in the great within of us, but until we awaken to a consciousness of this hidden power, those invisible resources, we cannot use them.

Some time ago a friend of mine saw a small, delicate woman leap over a six-bar gate when frightened by the sudden approach of a cow which she mistook for a bull. He said that this woman told him she could no more have done this under ordinary conditions than she could have lifted a corner of her house from its foundations. But she thought her life was in peril, and, in her great extremity, she became for a moment conscious of the power within. Seeing the cow running toward her, and imagining that it was an angry bull, she had no time to allow her doubts and fears as to whether she could leap over the gate to control her. It was the only means of escape in sight, and with the aroused consciousness of the latent power within her, she cleared the gate without difficulty. But when the imagined danger was past she lost the consciousness of her hidden strength and relapsed into her ordinary condition of weakness.

There are numerous instances on record where invalids and cripples, people who had been paralyzed for years, who did not feel that they could do anything whatever, have risen up from their beds when a fire or some terrible accident endangered their own lives or the lives of those dear to them, and then and there performed marvelous feats, in carrying heavy furniture out of a burning house, rescuing children, and doing other things that would have seemed miraculous even for strong men.

Again and again unusual emergencies give us a fleeting consciousness of our vast reserve powers and we perform prodigies that amaze ourselves, but we don't continue to make the demand on them and the consciousness that it is possible for us to do anything out of the ordinary slips from us and our measureless resources remain untouched.

Emerson says: "Every soul is not only the inlet but may become the outlet of all that is in God." The consciousness of this great truth is the secret of all power. It is the full realization of our connection with Omnipotence, with Omniscience, with the Source of all there is that enables us to use the vast powers that are within us, always at our command, waiting to accomplish our ends.

The Creator puts no limit to our supply. There is no limitation of anything we need except in our own consciousness. That is the door, which, according to its quality, shuts us off from, or admits us to, the great storehouse of infinite supply. The pinched, stingy consciousness never gets in touch with this supply. It is the man who has faith in his own power to meet whatever demands life may make upon him, who spends his last dollar fearlessly, because he knows the law of supply and is in touch with a flow of abundance, that gets on and up in the world.

But the one who hoards his last dollar in fear and trembling, afraid to let go of it, even though he must go hungry, who always carries in his mind a vivid picture of the wolf at the door, never conquers poverty, because he never gets the prosperity consciousness.

A wonderful uplift and courage comes to the man who follows the aspiring tendency in his nature that bids him trust and look up, no matter how dark the outlook. Faith in the Power that orders all things well tells him that there is a silver lining to the black cloud which temporarily shuts out the light, and he goes serenely on, feeling confident that his plans will succeed, that his demands will be met. His is the consciousness that assures him, no matter what happens, that "God's in his Heaven; all's right with the world."

If you keep this one thing in mind, that we are always creating, always manifesting in our lives the conditions we hold in our consciousness, you will not make the mistake millions are making today, manifesting the things they don't want instead of the things they want.

When we realize that our enjoyment, our happiness, our satisfaction, our achievement, our power, our personality, all depend on the nature of our consciousness, the aim and direction in which it is unfolding, we will not deliberately build up a consciousness of the very opposite of all that we are struggling to attain. On the contrary, we will hold constantly in mind the consciousness of our ambition, whatever it is, the consciousness of our heart's longings, our soul's desires; we will hold the truth consciousness, the God consciousness, the harmony consciousness, the opulent consciousness, and then we shall really begin to live. Then life will mean something more to all of us than it now does to most of us . . a mere struggle for existence.

Chapter V

Where Prosperity Begins

- Whatever we visualize intensely and persistently and back by intelligent effort we tend to create, vitalize into form, to build into the life.

- It is in the unseen world that man, animated and inspired by the consciousness of his partnership with Divinity, is beginning to find some of the secrets of the universe, . . lifting the race from animalism and drudgery, changing the face of the world, pushing civilization up to new and more glorious heights.

- Limitless wealth, inexhaustible supply to meet our needs, undreamed of possibilities, are in the great cosmic intelligence waiting the contact of man's thought to bring them into visible form.

- The invisible world about us is packed with infinite possibilities, awaiting our thought seed, our desire seed, our ambition seed, our aspiration seed, our prosperity and success seed, backed by our effort on the material plane, to make them manifest in the forms upon which we concentrate.

- There is no lack of anything we need on God's earth any more than there is a lack of sunshine. Who would think of complaining that the sun refuses to shine on him, that its rays will not rest upon him, will not bring his crops to maturity, will not warm and cheer his life? There is no lack of sunshine, but we can cut ourselves off from it. If we choose to live in the shadows, if we go down into the dark cellar where the sun cannot enter, it is our own fault.

DURING his lecture tour in the United States, the great scientist, Sir Oliver Lodge, speaking on "The Reality of the Unseen," said: "Our senses are no criterion of existence. They were evolved for earthly reasons, not for purposes of philosophy, and if we refuse to go beyond the direct evidence of our senses we shall narrow our outlook on the universe to a hopeless and almost imbecile extent."

It is the most difficult thing in the world to convince people of the reality of anything they cannot perceive through the senses. Yet the realest things we know anything about are invisible; have never been seen by mortal eyes.

And right here lies the great difficulty for most people in changing undesirable conditions; in getting away from poverty and the things that are holding them back.

They can't see beyond the present; they haven't learned to visualize the future, to see beyond the material things about them into the unseen world, packed with all creative energies, where the mind starts the creative processes. They do not realize that everything in the visible world that man has produced began in a mental vision; that the power of mind picturing, of visualizing the things we want to come into our lives, is God's priceless gift to man, to enable him to bring into visibility out of the invisible world whatever he wills.

Anyone who knows how to use this marvelous power can begin now to visualize his future; to see himself as he would like to be; to see himself mentally doing the things he would like to do; occupying the position he aspires to; and thus he will draw to himself the means necessary to build, step by step, in the material world the future as he sees it in his vision. By its aid we can bring ourselves out of a poverty stricken, discordant environment into harmonious conditions, a harmonious environment, with the refinements and, if we will, the luxuries of life; or we may pervert it, and hold ourselves in degrading lack and poverty, limited, held back from self-development, the unfoldment of our possibilities, and all the joys of living.

Whatever we visualize intensely and persistently we create, vitalize into form, build into the life, bring into the actual. In other words, the vital substance from which man fashions circumstances, destiny, is in the unseen world where all potencies and power dwell. The very foundations of the universe and the things which are doing most for the world today are the unseen forces, eternal principles. The forces which transport us over the globe and bring its uttermost parts into instant communion; the power of the principles of chemistry, of gravitation, of cohesion, of adhesion, . . all the mighty agencies operating in the universe and producing its phenomena, . . we cannot see, hear, or touch, we cannot appreciate them with our senses only as we feel their effects; they are things we know little about, yet we know they are great realities.

Who knows or who has seen what is back of these great principles, these potencies which we know exist? Gravitation, which is holding the heavenly bodies in their orbits, which keeps the world so marvelously balanced in space, revolving at terrific speed around the sun, none of them varying in their revolutions in their orbits the fraction of a second in a thousand years, is an invisible force. Because we can't see or taste, or smell, or handle it, shall we say it is not a reality? That it does not exist?

We can see and feel the effects of electricity, but who knows what this invisible force is? The Edisons, the Bells, the Marconis have, through experiments, found out certain things, certain laws governing it, through the operation of which we get heat, energy, and light. They have put it to work for us in a multitude of ways. It carries our messages under oceans and across continents. It has already done away with a large part of the drudgery of the world, and is destined to serve mankind in ways perhaps not yet dreamed of by even the wisest scientists and inventors. This mighty force which he has used in his thousands of inventions, Edison confesses he knows nothing about. He stands in awe of this mysterious power which has come out of the cosmic intelligence in response to his efforts. He regards himself merely as a channel through which some of its secrets have been passed along to man, to make life less toilsome, more comfortable, and more beautiful.

It is nonsense for skeptics and materialists to say that they take no stock in anything that they cannot test with their senses, when we know that the real force in the very things we live on, the elements that nourish and keep alive even the material part of us, are all invisible.

We cannot see the life-building, life-sustaining gases in the air we breathe; we cannot see the air, yet we take it into our body eighteen or twenty times a minute and get the silent, unseen power resident in it. The blood absorbs and sends it to the billions of cells in our bodies. None of its mysterious potency can we see or handle, yet we know we could not live a minute without it.

No one has ever seen the force in the food we eat, but we know it is there, that we get strength from it, and that after a time the apparently dead, inert matter comes to life in the body; that it acts, dreams, has experiences, works, and creates.

Notwithstanding all its marvelous discoveries, science has not been able to uncover the secrets of the unseen forces everywhere at work in the universe. Who can see or explain the mystery of the unfolding bud, the expanding flower, the generating of the wonderful fragrance and marvelous beauty of the rose? Yet we know that there is reality back of them, an intelligence which plans and shapes them, brings them to their glorious maturity.

We know that all these things come from the same. Omnipotent Source, that they are the creations of Divine Mind. Scientists are demonstrating that there is but one substance, one eternal force or essence, in the universe, and that all we see is a varying expression of it. To the senses this universal substance, which is the great reality back of all we see, is nonexistent. We can neither see, nor touch, nor taste, nor smell it. Yet all the time science is piling up proof after proof that everything about us is merely a modification, a change of form, change of vibration of this universal substance, just as electricity is a manifestation of force in various forms.

We think we live in a material world, but in reality we live in a mental world, a world of externalized thought, a world controlled and guided by invisible forces. We contact with material things only at a few points in our lives. The corporal part of us is fed, warmed and clothed by material things, but we live, move, and have our being in the unseen.

When we come to the reality of ourselves, the soul, the spirit of man, which is one with God, we live altogether in an invisible world. The real self is the unseen self. The man whose reflection we see in the mirror is but the shadow of the reality. The material body of flesh and blood that we see, and can touch with our hands, is not the real man. That is behind what we see and touch. It is back of the cell, back of the atoms, back of the electrons which make up the body.

The new philosophy is going back of appearance and showing us the real man, the invisible man. It is revealing his hidden potencies and possibilities, and pointing the way to their development and use. It shows us that, the impotent, sickly, ailing man, the weakling, the discouraged, disconsolate, complaining being, the failure, the man full of discord, disease, inharmony, is not the man God made; that this is the unreal creature man himself has made. This is the being that wrong thinking, wrong living, and unfortunate motives have made, the being who is the victim of his passions, of his moods, of his ignorance of realities, the great eternal verities of life.

We all learned as children that man is made in God's image and likeness, but the new philosophy urges us to act on this truth; to look beyond the appearance to the reality, to see with the inner eye the real man, the invisible man, who is one with his Creator. He is strong, vigorous, robust, with Godlike powers and qualities. He matches God's ideal of manhood. There is no suggestion of failure, of weakness, of instability, of sickness about him. He is perfect, immortal, unchangeable as truth itself, because the real man is the truth of being, changeless reality. No matter what his conditions or circumstances, the God stuff, the God principle, the divinity in him is still intact, still perfect, still contains all of his possibilities, is still stamped with nobility, with success, with health, with prosperity, with harmony, with the image of his Creator . . for God's image and likeness is perfect, immortal.

If we could only realize this, and measure life with its infinite possibilities from the standpoint of the changeless reality of man, instead of from that of the changing unreality of the body; if we could only hold the thought that we are a part of the creative intelligence of the universe, copartners with God in our work here on the earth, how much more we could accomplish, how much higher we could climb, how much happier we should be I.

When man realizes the tremendous significance of the reality of the unseen; when he grasps the truth of his unity with his Maker, the unity of life, the oneness of the source of all things in the universe, and that all is a manifestation of Divine Mind, he will come into possession of the illimitable power the Creator has implanted in every one of us.

When Christ emphasized the fact that the kingdom of heaven is within us, he meant that this kingdom within is identical with the Divine Mind, and that it is there man taps the source of all power, of all supply. The kingdom within is the kingdom of power, where all man's creative work is started. It is there he connects with the universal substance, the great creative energy; and thought is the invisible tool with which he fashions his creations. Acting upon the hidden, mysterious substance from which everything in the universe is evolved, the thought tool directs, controls, creates according to his desires. It finds its material in the unseen world, and in proportion as the mind grasps the reality of the unseen, the power and the possibilities are there. It is in the unseen world that man, animated and inspired by the consciousness of his partnership with Divinity, is beginning to find some of the secrets of the universe . . lifting the race from animalism and drudgery, changing the face of the world, pushing civilization up to new and more glorious heights.

Your prosperity, your health, your happiness, your success, the fruition of your ambitions, all are in the great formless creative energy, ready to come into form when your thought does its part in starting the creative processes. Limitless wealth, inexhaustible supply to meet our needs, inventions, great productions of art and literature, music and drama, marvels in every field of human endeavor, are in the great cosmic intelligence waiting the contact, of man's thought to come into visible form on our earth.

All the powers in the great cosmic intelligence are constantly working on the thoughts and desires of men. There is no favoritism in the unseen realities. The thoughts of the meanest man on earth are treated in precisely the same way as those of the noblest. Just as the sun and the rain, the wind and the dew give their potencies to the poor farmer and the good one alike, so the thief, the criminal, the murderer, the failure and the marplot have the same material to work in as the just man, the nobly successful, the great architects and artists, the great engineers, inventors, merchants, the great men and women in every field who are uplifting the race and making the world a better place to live in.

In other words, the creative force of thought puts an invincible power into man's hands, makes him a creator, the molder of his life, his destiny, his fortunes. We cannot think without creating, for every thought is a seed planted in the universal substance; it will produce something like itself. You and I can sow in the invisible, constructive thoughts, beautiful thoughts, thoughts of love, of good will, of health, of prosperity, of happiness, of success in our chosen work; or we can sow destructive thoughts, ugly thoughts, thoughts of hatred and ill-will, of disease, of discord, of failure, of poverty, of all sorts of misery, and, one thing is certain, whatever we sow we shall reap. That is the law, and there is no escape from it.

Most of the poverty, disease, failure and unhappiness in the world come from ignorance of the law. These things do not fit God's plan for his children. The Father never intended that we should be subject to disease, that we should wear ourselves out in drudgery, in unhappiness, in failure, in poverty, in constant anxiety, fearing all sorts of trouble and misery. The specter of disease and the wolf at the door are our own creations. They exist only in our minds; but as long as we visualize them, think on them, fear them, they will become real for us and manifest themselves in our lives. Health, abundance, success, happiness, a glorious, joyful living . . these are the things the Creator intended for all his children.

But most of us drive them from us by our false, pessimistic thinking, and then whine and complain about "fate" and "hard luck," when just the reverse is true; when the invisible world about us is packed with infinite possibilities, awaiting our thought seed, our desire seed, our ambition seed, our aspiration seed, our prosperity and success seed, backed by our effort on the material plane, to make them manifest in the forms upon which we concentrate. If you are poor, ailing and unsuccessful, you are working against the law, and until you come to a realization of the truth about the unseen forces at your command and work with the law you will continue to be poor, ailing, and unsuccessful.

Why not begin now to make the unseen forces your friends? Instead of making them your enemies, why not turn about face mentally and work with the law by simply holding the right thought? Why not turn your back on disease and poverty and failure by continually holding the health and abundance thought, saying to yourself: "I AM the child of the Author of health, joy, and abundance; I AM the child of the All-Supply. Health and success continually flow to me from the All-Supply, which is the Source of my being. Nothing but myself can cut me off from this Source; nothing but my own wrong thinking can cut off my supply, . . the health, success, and happiness that are my birthright.

I claim my inheritance from my Father now. I AM health; I AM success; I AM happiness; I AM free now and forever from all that would hinder my development, from everything that would hinder the realization of the ambitions the Father himself has implanted in me. This is my appointed work, the task he has given me to do here on this earth . . to carry out the details of his plan for me is to realize my ambitions. I am working in partnership with Him and I cannot fail. I AM one with Him; I again make my affirmation: I AM health; I AM success; I AM happiness; I AM abundance. My future is secure. I will go straight on, fearing nothing, for there is nothing to fear when I know that God is all, and that I AM one with Him.'"

No matter what your present circumstances and environment, if you hold fast to this mental attitude, to a firm belief in the reality of the unseen, where your supply is, and work in harmony with the law, you can, through the creative power of thought, acting on the invisible universal substance, fashion and draw out of the unseen realms of supply whatever you will . . knowledge, wisdom, power, health, wealth, happiness, success, . . the realization of all your hopes and visions.

Chapter VI

If You Can Finance Yourself

• Beware of little extravagances. A small leak will sink a big ship. . . FRANKLIN.

• Debt is like any other trap, easy enough to get into it, but hard enough to get out. . . SHAW.

• "The improvident man is a liability to the concern in which he is employed, the community in which he lives, his family and himself."

• A little money in the bank is a great friend both in time of need and in time of opportunity.

• Many people completely fail in life or are forced to live in mortifying poverty, to struggle along perhaps under the curse of debt, miserable, and handicapped all their lives because they never learned how to finance themselves.

THERE is nothing more important to a human being than to be able not only to earn his living, but also to know how to use his money to the best advantage, for on this depends his power to make himself independent and consequently to do his best work in the world. The money sense, if not inherited, should be cultivated. Every child should be taught how to finance himself; he should know how to handle money, how to save money, how to spend it wisely for personal enlargement and for life enrichment.

Every child should be trained in thrifty habits, should learn the true value of money and should be able to feel the backaches in every dollar. If we do not teach our children to know what money means, how can we expect them to show wisdom in handling money in their maturity?

The average man does not use anything like the good judgment, the good sense in spending, in investing his money, which he does in earning it. A self-made millionaire tells me that not more than three men out of a hundred who have made money are able to hold on to it. Multitudes of men die without an independence, without a home, without even having been able to support themselves.

I am constantly running across men in middle life or later who have worked hard for many years and tried to get on; but they have nothing to show for it, have nothing laid by; they have no ready cash to enable them to avail themselves of opportunities and no good, solid investments. They have never made any headway since they were young men, because they never learned how to finance themselves. They are like the frog in the well, which keeps jumping up only to fall back again to the bottom from where it started.

There is no other one thing which will mean quite so much to you in after life, my young friend, as learning the art of handling money and knowing how to finance yourself wisely. If you cannot do this, you will always be an easy mark for any smooth and oily promoter that happens along. Everybody will be aware of your gullibility and know that if you have any money it is not much of a trick to get it away from you.

Money is the slipperiest stuff in the world. The majority of people can't hold on to it any more than they could hold on to an eel or a greased pig. It slips through their fingers and disappears through all sorts of leaks of the pocketbook. Scores of men can make money where only one can hold on to it. There is always somebody who needs money, always some temptation to spend it.

Most people take too much risk with the money they have; they are too greedy, too anxious to keep it at work. They dislike having a dollar on hand that is not earning something, and so they often make the most foolish investments.

There is one man of my acquaintance, an able business man in many respects, who has been in hot water most of his life because of this. He never has ready cash for any unusual opportunity or emergency. He is a fine chap, a popular man, and has much ability, but he cannot bear to keep money lying idle; it must be doing something; so he puts it into anything that offers, and then when good chances come he can't avail himself of them, because his money is tied up in some wildcat scheme.

"Don't take chances with your little savings," is the advice of level-headed experts in financial matters.

Making foolish investments, trying to make large profits has kept vast multitudes of people in poverty all their lives. There is nothing like taking a stand in your early career only to invest in sound, solid, substantial things. The rich man can afford to take chances because if he loses he does not feel it, but you can't afford it. Go slow. The gambling instinct, the effort to make a fortune quickly, a lot of money with a little investment, is the cause of more unhappiness, of the poverty condition in more homes, than anything else I know of. It makes more disappointed lives, thwarts more ambitions, causes more people to die disappointed with their careers than any other thing.

One of the first steps in financing yourself properly is to keep a personal cash account. This is one of the best educators and teachers of economy and system. If the habit is formed when you are young in years it will never be broken. It will mean a competence in later life when otherwise there would have been none.

The world demands that every individual know how to take care of himself, how to be independent, self-reliant, how to finance himself wisely, how to make the most of his income.

However you make your living, whether by the work of your hand or of your brain, in a trade or in a profession, at home or in the shop, whether your income be small or large, you will always be placed at a disadvantage, unless you know how to finance yourself successfully. This is not to be "close," mean, or stingy, but to know how to make the most out of your income; not to expend the margin you should save in silly extravagances or to make foolish investments.

There is one thing that should be indelibly impressed upon every youth's mind, and that is the tragic consequences of debt, especially when incurred in early life. It has ruined many of the most promising careers. The youth should be so trained that under no consideration could he be induced to complicate his life by financial obligations. He should be shown that his success in life, the realizing of his ambition will depend very largely upon keeping his ability free from any sort of entanglement, and that he must keep this freedom at all costs. He should be taught that his unclouded enthusiasm and his zeal are very precious assets, and that nothing will kill these more effectively than the consciousness of being in a trap, the consciousness of being tied hand and foot by the curse of debt. The youth should be taught that to mortgage his future prospects would be fatal.

I have known quite a number of very promising young men to run in debt for automobiles. Many men have even mortgaged their little homes in order to get an automobile, trying to justify themselves by what it would mean to the health and pleasure of their wife and children.

Of course it would mean a lot to them, but, on the other hand, to a young man who is just starting out for himself, the purchasing of that which he cannot afford may handicap him for many years. No one can be happy, no matter how optimistic, who is forever in the clutches of poverty, of harassing debt. I know a man who has literally lived in shame for many years because of early debts which he contracted when he had good credit. When he lost his business he had to struggle with this debt, until the interest doubled and trebled, and sometimes quadrupled. Nothing could have persuaded him to put his head in such a noose if he had realized what the result would be.

"To be broke is bad," says Dr. Frank Crane. "It's worse; it's a crime. It's still worse, for it's silly. Crimes can be pardoned and sins forgiven, but for the plumb fool there is no hope."

Now, the young man who puts nothing by for a rainy day or an emergency is a "plumb fool." And there are so many of them! As the late Marshall Field said, "the present day tendency to live beyond their incomes brings disaster to thousands."

Many people live beyond their means because they cannot bear to have other people think that they cannot afford this and cannot afford that, that they cannot keep up appearances, their social standing. But it is better to be unpopular than to be embarrassed, better to be unpopular than to be in a hole, as someone suggests.

I AM —?

I AM your best friend in time of need.

I can do for you what those who love you most are powerless to do without my aid.

I AM the oil that smoothes the troubled waters of life. I straighten out difficulties and remove obstacles that will yield to nothing else.

I AM a supporter of faith, a spur to ambition, a tonic to aspiration, an invaluable aid to people who are struggling to make their dreams come true.

I give a man a fine sense of independence, a feeling of security in regard to the future, which increases his strength and ability and enables him to work with more vigor and spontaneity.

I AM a stepping stone to better things; a hope builder; an enemy of discouragement, because I take away one of the greatest causes of worry, anxiety, and fear.

I increase self-respect and self-confidence, and give a feeling of comfort and assurance that nothing else can give. I impart a consciousness of power that makes multitudes, who otherwise would cringe and crawl, hold up their heads and carry themselves with dignity.

I open the door to many opportunities for self-culture and to social and business advancement. I have enabled tens of thousands of young men, who made sacrifices to get me, to take advantage of splendid opportunities which those who did not have me were obliged to let go by.

I increase your importance in the world and your power to do good.

I make people think well of your ability, increase their confidence in you; give you standing, capital, an assured position, influence, credit, and many of the good things of life that without me would be unattainable.

I AM a shock absorber for the jolts of life, a buffer between you and the rough knocks of the world. The man or woman who doesn't make an honest, determined effort to get me is lacking in one of the fundamental qualities that make for the happiness, the prosperity and well-being of the whole race.

Millions of mothers and children have suffered all sorts of hardships and humiliations because husbands and fathers lacked this practical quality, which would have saved themselves and those dependent on them so much suffering and misery.

Multitudes have spent their declining years in homeless wretchedness, or eked out a miserable existence in humiliating dependence on the grudging charity of relatives, while other multitudes have died in the poorhouse, because they failed to make friends with me in their youth.

I AM one of the most reliable aids in the battle of life, the struggle for independence; ever ready to help you in an emergency . . sickness in your family, accident or loss, a crisis in your business . . whatever it may be. You can always rely on me to step into the breach and do my work quietly, effectively, without bluster.

I AM . . . A LITTLE READY CASH

Chapter VII

How To Increase Your Ability

- Our ability is as sensitive to our moods, our feelings, our mental attitudes, as the mercury is to the changes of the weather or a weather-vane is to the currents of air.

- The perpetual taunting and haunting of unsatisfied ambition, the consciousness that one has the ability to do the bigger thing, but is obliged to do the lesser because one did not early in life persist in following the path that led to the bigger; to feel cramped and limited in a little seven-by-nine situation in middle life or later, when one knows that he has the natural ability to fill an infinitely bigger place, is a hell on earth.

- Hope, self-confidence, assurance, faith in one's mission, enthusiasm in one's work, optimism, courage, joy, open up the ability accordion wonderfully. Fear, anger, envy, prejudice, jealousy, worry, smallness, meanness, selfishness, close it.

- Happiness in our work, the consciousness that we are doing our best, looking our best, and making a good impression on others . . these are tremendous enlargers of ability, because they increase one's self-respect and self-appreciation. They give one assurance, confidence, and confidence gives a marvelous impetus to initiative and executive ability.

A PROMINENT business man says that the best contract he ever got was one he lost. Why? Because it set him to investigating the cause of the loss, to investigating himself, to finding the weak places in himself and in his business methods. It was the lost contract that led him to the discovery that he was not using more than half the ability he actually possessed.

Most people rob themselves of success and fortune by mistaken ideas about their ability. They are like a young stenographer who told me that if she had the ability to become an expert in her line, she would go to evening school, study nights, and do everything she could to improve her education and to develop herself in all possible ways. But as she was sure that she had only a very moderate share of ability, she was convinced that there was no use in trying, and that she must be satisfied with an ordinary position. In other words, she believed that her ability was a fixed quantity; something which could not be enlarged or diminished, which she could not change in any respect any more than she could change the color of her hair or of her eyes.

Now, the idea that our ability is an invariable quantity, fixed by heredity, or by some immutable law which we can neither understand nor control, is one of the most unfortunate that could take possession of anyone's mind. And nothing could be farther from the truth, for, as a matter of fact, human ability is a very variable and a very elastic quantity. It can be expanded almost indefinitely, or contracted, in a great many ways. It is like an accordion, which the player sometimes draws out to its full extent, and again closes completely. For instance, you can close up your accordion by wrong thinking until but a mere fraction of your possible ability is available, or you can open it up by right thinking and make every bit of it count in making your work, your life, a grand success.

Multitudes of people go through life with their actual ability so cramped, so muzzled and suffocated by their negative, destructive mental attitude, their doubts, fears, worries, superstitions and preconceived ideas, their lack of courage, their lack of faith in themselves and in their mission, that they make but a very small percentage of it count in their life work, even when they make a supreme effort to do so. Everywhere we see men and women, hard workers, who do not accomplish a tithe of what they could accomplish, with half the effort and half the time they now expend, if they would only keep their minds in a positive, creative condition, and face life in the right way.

While the development and sharpening of the different mental faculties is the first essential to the increase of our natural ability, it is a mistake to think that all of our ability expansion is dependent on this. It doesn't matter what amount of natural ability you have, if it is unavailable, bottled up by your pessimism, your doubts, your fears, your cowardice and lack of faith, it is useless to you. If you had a valuable gold mine on your property, and, instead of clearing away all obstructions to get at the ore you should add a lot more, your gold mine wouldn't add one particle to your available wealth. Potentially you had an immense fortune, but so far as you were concerned it might just as well not be there, for you derived no benefit from gold you could not get at and exchange for the good things of fife that you desired. It is just the same with your ability. If instead of doing everything in your power to make it available, to give it outlet, you shut it up within you, covering it over with all sorts of mental obstructions, it will never expand," will never yield you anything.

Many of us think if we only had some other person's talent or opportunities; if we only had the advantages of some other fellows near us; if only we were superbly equipped with facilities for our particular work, that we would do wonderful things.

Now, the Creator never sent anyone into this world without equipping him with just the tools required for the job He meant him to do, the job which He qualified him in every respect to do. He didn't sharpen the tools for us, because if He had done that He would have deprived us of the very thing that is designed for our expansion and growth. It is by drawing out all that is in us, by bettering our work each day, by overcoming obstacles, clearing away the rubbish and mental debris that evoke our growth, and always reaching up to the attainment of our highest ideal, that, day by day, we unfold layer after layer of the wealth of ability that is enfolded in every human being, no matter what his apparent disabilities or handicaps.

Helen Keller is, perhaps, one of the most remarkable examples the world has ever seen of the power of the determined soul to overcome everything that stands in the way of its complete development. Deaf, dumb, and blind at the age of eighteen months, what opportunity was there for a human being so handicapped to do anything of value in the world; to become anything other than despair to herself, a hopeless, helpless burden on her relatives? Yet out of her world of darkness the indomitable spirit within evolved a being of such remarkable ability and power that there are few today who are rendering greater service to humanity than this woman who, apparently, at the outset of life was hopelessly handicapped. She is a wonderful illustration of the truth that there is no limit to man's development, and no insuperable obstacles to his development except those he himself puts in his way.

The eagle is the mightiest and most powerful of all the feathered tribe. It can fly higher and remain longer on the wing than any other bird. Yet if this monarch of the air were held captive, tied by one of its feet to a huge ball or heavy weight, it could not fly as high as a barn-yard fowl. No matter how strong its natural instincts to soar into the heavens, it could not move from the earth.

Now, like the eagle, man was made to fly high, to do great things, but multitudes of people spend their lives doing little things instead of the big things they are capable of doing because of something which chains their ability and holds them down in an inferior position. There is a vast amount of unproductive ability in the great failure army today, which was never given an opportunity to fulfill the purposes for which the Creator meant it. Some of the most pitiable instances of spoiled lives I know of are those of men and women of middle age who really have the ability to do something large and grand, but who have failed to do so because of their unwillingness to make sacrifices in youth for the sake of their ambition. Love of ease enchained their faculties and held them prisoners until their ambition died and they lost even their desire to fly.

Some people are tied down by bad physical or mental habits, which make it impossible for them to put their best selves into their work.

There is a constant leakage of energy and vital force, resulting from preventable causes, which hinders their progress at every step and makes their ability unavailable. Others are held down by character traits or peculiarities of disposition which handicap all their success qualities and neutralize their efforts to advance. A quick temper, a jealous, envious disposition, lack of faith and self-confidence, vacillation, bashfulness, timidity, carelessness, inaccuracy and a host of other faults and weaknesses seriously hamper the development of their ability and act like weights in holding them down when they are eager to go up higher.

Whatever causes in harmony in the mind robs us of power and hinders our advancement. If you would gain control of all your resources and increase your ability, avoid as you would poison everything that tends to make you negative, . . worry, anxiety, jealousy, envy, fear, cowardice, the whole family of depressing, despondent thoughts. They are all confessions of weakness, and may be summed up as power destroyers. Every fit of the blues, every unhappy thought, every feeling of discouragement, of despondency, every doubt, every fear, is a crippler of ability. In other words, our ability is extremely sensitive to our moods, to our mental condition generally.

When we don't feel like it, when we are out of sorts, when for one reason or another we feel blue, discouraged, despondent, full of doubt and anxiety, our ability is very much contracted. On the other hand, when we are in good trim, when our minds are harmonious, not anxious or worried about anything, it is enormously, expanded. That is, all the positive, uplifting, encouraging, cheerful emotions and feelings expand or increase our ability, while all of the negative, depressing, discouraging, gloomy ones contract or lessen it.

This shows that after we have done everything in our power to increase our ability by education, by training for our special work, by sharpening and improving our natural gifts and faculties in every possible way, we can yet so contract or expand it by our mental attitude, that it is safe to say nine-tenths of its availability depends upon our state of mind at any given time. We all know how it is enlarged by a sublime self confidence, an unwavering faith, and how it is contracted by the lack of faith in ourselves, by self-depreciation, by timidity, and lack of courage. You know how much bigger a man you are, how much more capable of planning and doing things, when your courage is up and you believe in yourself, than when you are blue and discouraged. You know from experience that your consciousness of ability expands so you feel as though you could tackle almost anything. Make this your habitual state of mind and your ability will always be available, always at its maximum.

On the other hand, hold a poor opinion of yourself, refuse to assume responsibility, always berate yourself and belittle your powers, and if you had the natural ability of a Plato you would never amount to anything. This sort of mental attitude holds down more real ability, keeps more deserving merit in mediocre positions, than perhaps any other handicap in the gamut of human disabilities. Multitudes who have excellent mental endowments and splendid traits of character remain practically nobodies all their lives because of timidity, a sense of inferiority, a doubting, self-depredating attitude toward themselves. Others with half their natural ability forge ahead, make fortunes, attain places of power and influence, while they remain in poverty and obscurity.

Everywhere in life the timid, retiring, self-effacing man is placed at a tremendous disadvantage, mentally, socially and in a business and professional way. People may be sorry for him, they may pity him, and his friends may say he has great ability and splendid traits of character; but this is not enough. Lacking self-confidence, push, assurance, the courage to demonstrate his ability to the world, he will not win out in anything in a large way. His mean opinion of himself will neutralize a large percentage of his real ability.

Every man has more ability than he thinks he has, more than he ever uses ordinarily. Under the impulse of a strong motive, a new stimulus to exertion, or having a great responsibility thrust upon us, being put in a situation where we must either sink or swim, there isn't one among us that wouldn't respond to the demand and unfold an amount of ability which we never before dreamed we possessed. Some men's ability lies so deep that they are never at their best except in a great crisis. Then the giant in them is unshackled, and great powers, of which they themselves were ignorant, are unlocked within them.

Responsibility is a great ability developer. We often see a good example of this when a young man is taken into partnership in a large concern. His initiative, his executive force, his courage, all the ability expanding qualities, are so strengthened by the stimulus of promotion that he goes ahead and does things that he did not dream he could ever accomplish when he was an employee. Now, taking him into partnership did not add to his latent ability at all, but it gave him more confidence in himself, and the fact that he is put on his mettle to make good in the new position compels him to draw on his ability to the limit, and he does make good. Never sidestep a responsibility. It is throwing away an opportunity to enlarge your ability.

If an Edison should invent an instrument by means of which it would be possible for men and women to increase their natural ability fifty per cent, there is no price we would not be willing to pay for such an instrument. Yet there isn't a man or woman, a boy or girl, living today who can't do this by right thinking, facing life the right way, and using the opportunities that are at hand. Right where you are, no matter what your environment, whatever your disadvantages or handicaps, you have enough ability to make you a success in whatever you desire to do; to lift you out of lack and poverty and make you a millionaire. Expand your ability; do everything that will enable you to stretch your accordion to its limit, and you will be amazed at what you can accomplish.

Chapter VIII

Look Like A Success

- You have no more right to go about among your fellows with a vinegar expression an your face, radiating mental poison, spreading the germs of doubt, fear, discouragement and despondency among them, than you have to inflict bodily injuries on them.

- To be a conqueror in appearance, in one's bearing, is the first step toward success.

- Walk, talk, and act as though you were a somebody, and you are much more likely to become such.

- Let victory speak from your face and express itself in your manner, your conversation, your bearing.

- Never show the world a gloomy, pessimistic face, which is an admission that life has been a disappointment to you instead of a glorious triumph.

- When a man feels like a king he will look kingly. Majesty more regal than ever sat on a throne will look out of his face when he has learned how to claim and express the divinity of his birthright.

WHEN Frank A. Vanderlip, former president of the National City Bank, New York, was a reporter on the Chicago "Tribune," he asked his chief to tell him what he thought would be the greatest help to a man struggling to succeed. "Look as if you had already succeeded" was the prompt reply.

This made a great impression upon young Vanderlip and completely changed some of his ideas on the subject, especially in regard to dress. From that time he began to spruce up, to be more particular about his general appearance. His chief had opened his eyes to the great value of appearances, especially in making a first impression. He became convinced that if a man did not look prosperous, people would think he did not have the right ambition or the ability to succeed; that there must be something the matter with him or he would dress better and make a better appearance.

Charles W. Eliot, President-emeritus of Harvard, said that much of one's success would depend on others' opinion of him, of those to whom he, perhaps, had never spoken a word, had never even seen. One's reputation travels by various routes in every direction and, according to its nature, will have a big influence on one's career. It is a great thing to form a habit of going through the world giving the impression to everybody that you are a winner, that you are bound to be somebody . . to stand for something worthwhile in the world. Let this idea stand out in everything you do, in your conversation, your appearance. Let everything about you make the world say, "He is a winner; keep your eye on him."

If you are anxious to win out in a large way, cultivate the bearing of success, the appearance of a successful man. If you carry about with you a defeated, poorhouse atmosphere; if your appearance suggests slovenliness, slipshodness, the lack of system and order, the lack of energy, of push, of the progressive spirit, you can't expect others to think you are an efficient, up-to-date person, pushing to the front. Of course every employer knows that it sometimes happens that a shabbily dressed man, with baggy trousers and soiled linen, may have a lot of good stuff in him, but they don't expect it. The chances of finding a very valuable employee with such an advertisement of himself is so small that most men won't take the risk. Your dress, your bearing, your conversation, your conduct, should all square with your ambition. All of these things are aids to your achievement, and you cannot afford to ignore any one of them. The world takes you at your own valuation. If you assume the victorious attitude toward it, it will give you the right of way.

One reason why it is so difficult for many young people to get a start, to get on, comes from the fact that they do not create in others the impression of power, of the force that achieves, that does things. They do not realize how much their reputation has to do with their getting on in the world. They do not realize that other people's confidence is a tremendous force.

A great physician or lawyer gets his reputation largely from the impression which he makes upon people, not only in the way he performs the duties of his profession, but also in his general attitude. We weigh, measure, and estimate people by the impression they make upon us, everything considered. The victorious attitude inspires confidence in others as well as in oneself. Its psychological effect is compelling. Walk, talk, and act as though you were already the man you long to be, and you are unconsciously putting into operation unseen forces that bend circumstances to the accomplishment of your will. Let your air be that of a winner, of a man who is resolved to make his way in the world . . to make himself stand for something. Put energy and life into your step; vim, force, vitality, pep into every movement of your body. Look straight forward; never wince. Don't apologize for taking up room on the earth which might be filled to better advantage by another; you have just as much right here as any other human being, if you are making good, and if you are not making good you should be.

No matter what comes to you, defeat, threatened failure, never lose your victorious consciousness. Let people read this declaration in your bearing, in your life generally: "I AM a winner; I have not shown the white feather. I have not shirked; I have done my part; I have not been a sneak; I have not been a thief or a cheat, wearing and using what others have earned and giving nothing back in return. I have done my part and can hold up my head and look the world in the face!"

The more trying your situation, the harder the way looks to you, the darker the outlook, the more necessary it is to carry that victorious consciousness. If you carry the down-and-out expression, if you confess by your very face that you are beaten, or that you expect to be, you are a goner. The victorious idea of life, not the failure idea; the triumphant, not the thwarted, ambition is the thing to keep ever uppermost in the mind, for it is this that will lead you to the goal you aspire to reach. Have faith in your God-given power to succeed in a worthy ambition. Concentrate your efforts on its realization, and nothing on earth can keep you back from success. Such a mental attitude will make you a winner from the start, because you always head toward your thought, toward your conviction of yourself. The conviction that you are born to win is a tremendous creative force in your life, just as the conviction that you are a failure will keep you down till you change the model of yourself. Life is not a losing game. It is always victorious when properly played. It is the players who are at fault.

God did not make a man to be a failure. He made him to be a glorious success. The great trouble with all failures is that they were not started right. It was not drilled into the very texture of their being in youth that what they would get out of life must be created mentally first, and that inside the man, inside the woman, is where the great creative processes of all that we realize in our careers are carried on. Most of us depend too much upon the things outside of us, upon other people, when the mainspring of life, the power that moves the world of men and things, is within us. Think what it would mean to the world today if all the people who look upon themselves as nobodies and failures, dwarfs of what they might have been and ought to be, would get this triumphant idea of life into them! If they could once get a glimpse of their own possibilities, and would assume the victorious, the triumphant, attitude, they would revolutionize the world.

How many people form the chronic habit of indulging in frequent fits of depression! They allow the "blues" an easy entrance to their minds, in fact, are always at home to them, and are susceptible to every form of discouragement that comes along. Every little setback, every little difficulty, sends them into the "blues" and they will say "What's the use!" As a result their work is poor and ineffective, and they do not attract the things they desire.

Every time you give way to discouragement, every time you are blue, you are going backward, your destructive thoughts are tearing down what you have been trying to build. One fit of discouragement, visualizing failure or poverty stricken conditions, will rapidly destroy the result of much triumphant thought building. Your creative forces will harmonize with your thoughts, your emotions and moods; they will create in sympathy with them.

Saturate your mind with hope, the expectation of better things, with the belief that your dreams are coming true. Be convinced that you are going to win out; let your mind rest with success thoughts. Don't let the enemies of your success and happiness dominate in your mind or they will bring to you the condition that they represent. Destroy the thoughts, and emotions and convictions which tend to destroy your hope, your ambitions, to tear down the results of your past building. If you don't they will create more failure, more poverty. If you want to realize success, think creative, successful conditions.

Set your character and your whole life towards triumph, towards victory. Hold the victorious thought towards yourself, towards your future, towards your career; it will tend to create the conditions favorable to the carrying out of your ambition, the fulfilling of your desires.

"Go boldly, go serenely, go augustly; Who can withstand thee then!"

I know of nothing that gives more satisfaction than the consciousness that we have formed the habit of winning, the habit of victory, the habit of carrying a victorious mental attitude, of walking, acting, talking, looking like a winner, a conqueror. That sort of attitude always keeps the dominant, helpful qualities in the fore, always in the ascendancy.

One of the most obstinate habits to overcome in mature life, and one fatal to efficiency, is the habit of being defeated. Never allow yourself to fall into it. You may learn a lesson from every defeat that will make a new stepping-stone to your ambition.

Success is every human being's normal condition; he was made for success; he is a success machine, and to be a failure is to pervert the intention of his Creator. Every youth should be taught to assume a triumphant attitude towards life, to carry himself like a winner, because he was made to win. No child is really educated until he has learned to live a victorious life. That is what real education spells, victory. The habit of winning out in whatever we undertake can be formed almost as easily as the habit of being defeated, and every victory helps us to win other victories.

From the cradle a child should be taught that he is divine, a god in the making, and that he should hold up his head and go forth with confidence, because he is destined for something superb. Teach the child that he came to the earth with a message for mankind, and that he should deliver it like an ambassador. Show him that wrestling with difficulties is like practicing in a gymnasium where every victory over his muscles makes him so much stronger, and makes the next attempt so much surer and easier. Let him fully understand that every problem solved in school, every errand promptly and courteously performed, every piece of work superbly done is just so much more added to, his winning power, to the strength of his success possibilities.

The great prizes of life are for the courageous, the dauntless, the self-confident. The man who is timid and hesitating, who stops to listen to his fears, lets many a good opportunity pass beyond his reach.

If you find you are inclined to be timid; if you lack courage and initiative; if you are too bashful to speak or express your opinions when it is desired; if you blush, and stammer, and are awkward when you would appear calm and self-possessed, you can overcome your defects and build up the qualities you lack by training your subjective self to be courageous, unembarrassed, at your ease in any surroundings. Constantly suggest courage and heroism to this inner self. Stoutly deny that you are timid, cowardly, afraid to speak or to be natural in public or before anyone. Assert that you are brave, that you are not afraid to do anything that it is right and proper you should do.

Practice walking about among your fellows as though you were brave, courageous, self-confident, perfectly sure of yourself, as capable of carrying on a conversation creditably, or of entering a room gracefully as you are of discharging your daily duties.

Hold the triumphant thought towards your future, towards your ideal, your dream. Carry the atmosphere of the victor. Learn to radiate power. Let everything about you bespeak confidence, strength, masterfulness, victory. Let everybody who has anything to do with you see that you are a born winner.

You must not go about as though life had been a disappointment, as though you had no special ambition in life. If you want to stand for anything unusual; if you want to carry weight in the world; if you want to make your neighbors proud that you live near them, you must brace up in every respect. Keep yourself up to standard. Don't go about like a failure, like a nobody. Don't go about in a sloppy, slovenly way. Dress up, brace up, look up, struggle up. Let the world see, as you walk about, that you think well of yourself, and that there is a reason for it. Let people see that you are conscious you are on a superb mission, playing a superb part in the great life game.

You will soon begin to see the thing you are looking for instead of the thing you are afraid of, and will find your dreams coming true.

Chapter IX

How To Make Your Dreams Come True

- Our heart longings, our soul aspirations are prophecies, predictions, forerunners of realities. They are indicators of our possibilities, of the things we can accomplish.

- The moment you resolve to make your life dream come true, you have taken the first step towards its realization, but you will stop there if your efforts cease.

- Keeping right after your ideals, nursing your visions, cultivating your dreams, visualizing the thing you long for vividly, intensely, and striving with all your might to match it with reality . . this is what makes life count.

- Our dreaming capacity gives us a peep into the glorious realities that await us further on.

- Dreams are true

WHEN Gordon H. Selfridge, former manager of the Marshall Field Company, went to London and there established a great department store of the Marshall Field type, he only took the final step in the realization of a dream which he had nursed for years. Long before he stepped foot on the shores of England, he had had the department store all worked out in his mind. He had built it mentally before he crossed the Atlantic, and already in his mind's eye, saw it a marvelous success. "I pictured the great crowds of customers headed toward my new store," he said, "and could see it full of eager buyers long before I went to England."

From the time that the idea of a department store in London took form in his mind, Mr. Selfridge kept visualizing the completed structure. He kept his dream alive and vivid by the determination to make it come true. He would not allow it to be shattered, or let his idea be driven out by doubts, fears, and uncertainties, or by the well meant advice of his friends: to keep out of England because the English people were so slow to new ideas that he would fail if he went there. He didn't heed what they said, for he didn't believe that the English people were so unprogressive as they thought. He believed that they would respond to the American idea, the Marshall Field idea, and that the methods which had proved so successful in the United States would also be successful in England.

The amazing popularity of the Selfridge Department Store, which has long been one of the sights of London, is but another proof that the dreamer who dreams and sees visions is always wiser than, and always ahead of, the so-called practical, wise ones who discourage him and try to turn him aside from his vision. The men and women who, in all ages, have done great things in the world have always been dreamers, have always seen visions, and always pictured their dreams as realities; visualized themselves accomplishing the things they were ambitious to do long before they were able to work them out in the actual and make them realities.

Columbus, Stephenson, Charles Goodyear, Elias Howe, Robert Fulton, Cyrus W. Field, Edison, Bell . . all the great discoverers, scientists, explorers, philanthropists, inventors, philosophers, who have pushed the world forward and done immeasurable service to mankind, have visualized their dreams, nursed their visions through long years, many of them in the midst of poverty, persecution, ridicule, opposition, and contumely of all sorts, until they brought their dreams to earth and made them realities.

In making a study of the methods of successful men and women I have found that they are almost invariably strong and vivid visualizers of the things they are trying to accomplish. They are intense workers as well as dreamers, and nurse their vision tenaciously until they match it with reality. They build castles in the air, but they put the solid foundation of reality under them.

When Lillian Nordica was a poor girl, singing in the little church choir in her native village in Maine, when even her own people thought it a disgrace for a girl to appear on the stage, to sing in public concerts or in opera, she was picturing herself a great prima donna singing before vast audiences in her own country, in foreign capitals, and before the crowned heads of Europe.

When young Henry Clay was practicing oratory before the domestic animals in a Virginia barn and barnyard, he visualized himself swaying vast audiences by his eloquence. When Washington was a lad of twelve he pictured himself as a leader, rich and powerful, a man of vast importance in the colonies, and the ruler of a nation he would help to create.

When the young John Wanamaker was delivering clothing in a pushcart, in Philadelphia, he saw himself as the proprietor of a much larger establishment than any then in that city. He saw beyond that and glimpsed the Wanamaker of later days, the great powerful merchant, with immense stores in the world's leading capitals. Young Carnegie pictured himself a powerful figure in the steel world, as did the youth Charles M. Schwab, even when an ordinary employee. When working at the Homestead plant Schwab told Mr. Carnegie what he wanted was not more salary, not a larger position as a mere employee; that his ambition was to be a partner in the concern. That was the only thing that would satisfy him.

Now this sort of visualizing is not mere vanity, or petty egotism, it is the God urge in men pushing them out beyond themselves, beyond what is visible to the physical eye, to better things. The Scriptures tell us that without a vision the people perish. I have never known a man to do anything out of the common, who was never able to see beyond the visible into the vast invisible universe of the things that might be; who did not keep clearly in his mind the vision of the particular thing he was trying to accomplish. It is the man who can visualize what does not yet exist in the visible world about us and see it as a reality; the man who can see thriving industries where others see no chance, no opportunities; the man who sees teeming cities, great populations on the prairies where others see only sagebrush, alkali plains, desolation; the man who sees power, opulence, plenty, success, where others see only failure, limitation, poverty, and wretchedness, who eventually pushes to the top and wins out.

It was this sort of vision that made James J. Hill the great "empire builder" of the Northwest. His dream of a great system of railroads that would cause millions of fertile farms to spring up along their route and make the desert blossom like a rose, was laughed at as a visionary, scheme by many of those who were working for him when he died. They were men who had never been able to make a place and a name for themselves, because they had never learned that the great secret of success lias in visualizing dreams and making them come true. Perhaps they did not believe in their dreams, and put them out of their minds as mere idle fancies.'

Many people seem to think that the imagination, or visualizing faculty, is a sort of appendix to the brain, which it is not a fundamental or necessary part of man, and they have never taken it very seriously. But those of us who have studied mental laws know that it is one of the most important functions of the mind. We are beginning to discover that the power to visualize is a sort of advance courier, making announcement of the things that the Creator has qualified us to bring about. In other words, we are beginning to see that our visions are prophecies of our future; mental picture programs, which we are supposed to carry out, to make concrete realities. For instance, a youth whose bent is entirely in another direction is not haunted by an architectural vision, an art vision, a. mercantile vision, or a vision of some other calling for which he has no natural affinity.

A girl does not dream of a musical career for years before she has the slightest opportunity for taking up music as a career if she has no musical talent, or if her ability in some other line is much more pronounced. Boys and girls, men and women, are not haunted by dreams to do what nature has not fitted them for. We dream a particular dream, see a particular vision, because we have the talent and the special ability to bring the dream, the vision, into reality. Of course, I do not mean by dreams and visions the mere fantasies, the vague, undefined thoughts that flit through the mind, but our real heart longings, our soul yearnings, the mental pictures of a future which haunts our dreams, and the insistent urge which prods us until we try to match them with their reality, to bring them out into the actual. There is a divinity back of these visions. They are prophecies of our possible future; and nature is throwing up these pictures on our mental screen to give us a glimpse of the possibilities that are awaiting us.

One reason why most of us do such little, unoriginal things is because we do not sufficiently nurse our visions and longings. The plan of the building must come before the building. We climb by the ladder of our visions, our dreams. The sculptor's model must live in his own mind before he can call it out of the marble. We do not half realize the mental force we generate by persistently visualizing our ideal, by the perpetual clinging to our dreams, the vision of the thing we long to do or to be. We do not know that nursing our desires makes the mental pictures sharper, more clean cut, and that these mental processes are completing the plans of our future life building, filling in the outlines and details, and drawing to us out of the invisible energy of the universe the materials for our actual building.

There is no other one thing you will find so helpful in the attainment of your ambition as the habit of visualizing what you are trying to accomplish, visualizing it vividly, just as distinctly, just as vigorously as possible, because this makes a magnet of the mind to attract what one is after. All about us we see young men focusing their minds with intensity and persistence on their special aims and attracting to themselves marvelous results. A medical student holds in his mind a vision of himself as a great physician or surgeon, and in a few years we are amazed at the size of his practice. He called it out of the great universal supply by his perpetual visualizing, the constant intensifying of his desire, and the unceasing struggle on the material plan to make his dream come true.

Even if you are only a humble employee, visualize yourself as the man you long to be; see yourself in the exalted position you long to attain, a man of importance and power carrying weight in your community. No matter if you are only an errand boy or a clerk, see yourself as a partner in your concern, or a proprietor of a business of your own.

There is nothing more potent in drawing your heart's desire to you than visualizing that desire, dreaming your dream, seeing yourself as the ideal man of your vision, filling the position in which your ambition would place you. Do this, and work with all your might for the attainment of your object on the physical plane, and nothing can hinder your success.

These are the means, consciously or unconsciously adopted, by which every successful man has ultimately attained his heart's desire.

Reading and thinking, visualizing and working along the lines of his ambition, the boy, Thomas Alva Edison, at the very first opportunity, when a newsboy on the Grand Trunk Railway, begins to actualize his desires by experimenting with chemicals in a baggage car which he had fitted up as a laboratory. He clings to his vision constantly, visualizes his dream of-the-magic possibilities of electricity; goes on discovering, experimenting, inventing, until we find him the world's greatest electrical inventor, the "Wizard of Menlo Park," His mind, working in harmony with Divine Mind, has wrought marvelous inventions out of the great cosmic intelligence, which is packed with potencies for those who can visualize with intensity and work with constancy. What Edison has done, what all aspiring souls have done to make their dreams come true, you can do. Cling to your vision and work.

There is a power in man, back of the flesh, but not of it, working in harmony with the Divine Intelligence in the great cosmic ocean of energy, of limitless supply, that is, today, performing miracles in invention, in agriculture, in commerce, in industry. This power, which is creative and everywhere operative, is destined to lift every created thing up to the peak of its possibilities. It is latent in you, awaiting expression, awaiting your cooperation to realize your ambition. The first step toward utilizing it is to visualize the ideal of what you want to make real, the ideal of the man or the woman you aim to be, and the things you want to do. Without this initial step the further process of creating is impossible.

No matter what happens, always hold fast to the thought that you can be what you long to be; that you can do the thing you want to do, and picture yourself always as succeeding in what you desire to come true in your life. No matter how urgent duties or obligations may for a time hold you back, how circumstances and conditions may contradict the possibility of your success; how people, even your own people, may blame or misunderstand you, may even call you a crank, crazy, a conceited egotist, hold fast to your faith in your dream, in yourself. Cling to your vision, nurse it, for it is the God-inspired model by which He is urging you to shape your life.

Chapter X

What Discouragement Does To You And How To Cure It

- Discouragement has done more to dwarf the efforts of the race, has thwarted more careers, stunted and starved more lives, than any other one agent.

- Never make a decision when downhearted. Never let the weak side of your nature take control.

- You are not capable of correct judgment when fear or doubt or despondency is in your mind. Sound judgment comes from a perfectly normal brain.

- Have you the grit and pluck to stand all sorts of discouragement and to struggle on after failure without losing heart; to get up again every time you fall? Can you stand criticism, misunderstanding, abuse, without flinching or weakening? Have you the perseverance to go on when others turn back, to continue the fight when everybody around you is giving up? If you can do this you are a winner. Nothing can hold you back from your goal.

- "You can't do it!" keeps more people with splendid ability in mediocrity than almost any other thing. "You can't do it!" meets you everywhere in life. At every turn you propose to take, you will find someone to warn you away, to tell you not to take that road, that it will lead to disaster. Unless you have unusual pluck, an iron will and a determination which never wavers, you are likely to become discouraged, and when you are once discouraged your initiative is deadened and your power paralyzed.

Someone says: "Discouragement hides God's means and methods." It does more. It hides God himself; it blots out of sight about everything that is helpful and friendly to us. It paralyzes our ability, our courage, our self-confidence; it destroys our efficiency and cuts down the effectiveness of every one of our faculties.

Every physician knows how discouragement affects the cure of a patient, . . delays it, and often makes it impossible. The sick man who is cheerful, hopeful of his restoration to health, has ten chances to one for recovery compared with the one who is blue and despondent. Discouragement breaks the spirit, and when a man's spirit is broken he has no heart for anything. He is beaten in life's battle. A broken spirit, the loss of hope and courage, causes more failures, more suicides, more insanity, than almost anything else. I wish it were possible to show victims of discouragement what it does to them . . how it destroys their morale, and tears down what they have built up in their creative, hopeful moments.

Only a short time ago I read the story of a fine young man who became the victim of discouragement. After losing his position, during a period of business depression, this man would start out every morning to hunt for another; and every night he would come home disappointed, but, for a long time, not discouraged, always believing that he would ultimately get a job.

This had been going on for weeks, when one night he was late in returning, and his wife, watching at the window until it was too dark to see any more, drew down the shades and tried in busying herself with house-wifely tasks to dispel the sudden feeling of anxiety that gripped her. When her husband came an hour later, she noticed that some depressing influence seemed to have been working upon him; that he was not quite as hopeful as he had been. She cheered him up as usual, gave him his supper, encouraged him in every possible way, and sent him to bed comforted. Next morning he tried to talk hopefully, and when he was ready to start for the city, assured her that he was going to do his best. But it was evident he didn't feel quite as sure of himself, quite as self-confident, as he had been.

Watching at the window for his return that evening, the faithful wife was surprised to see that he was not alone. A shadowy, sinister figure was at his side, talking very earnestly to him. It accompanied him to the gate and then suddenly vanished. The next evening the same sinister figure walked at his side, and the look of despair on the man's face frightened her. The third evening the wife waited and watched until long after dark, but no husband came. Numb with fear, she sat through the long night at the window, where she kept a light burning until daylight, but no husband, and no word from him, came to her.

As soon as life began to stir in the neighborhood she went out for a morning paper, and the first item that caught her eye was the suicide of a man who had thrown himself into the river and was drowned. Filled with foreboding, she rushed to the morgue where the newspaper stated the body had been taken, and there her fears were verified. The body of the drowned man was that of her husband.

The young man had toward the end become so discouraged by the hideous pictures his doubts and fears threw upon the screen of his mind that he became mentally unbalanced, and in despair ended his life. In those last days discouragement was so persistently at his side, telling him it was no use looking for a job, that he would never get one, that it was visualized by him as a reality, and actually became visible to the sensitive, sympathetic eyes of his wife.

Right now I know a number of people who are so depressed and demoralized by pessimistic, discouraged thinking, that they are seriously endangering their future success and the happiness of their whole lives. Because they are temporarily out of employment, discouragement has taken hold of them and filled their minds with such black, depressing pictures that they go about as do the insane in the beautiful grounds allotted to them. They see only the gloomy mental world their thoughts have constructed, and are unaware of the bright, cheerful, sunlit world all around them.

They are, in fact, temporarily insane, because all mental depression, whatever the immediate cause, is in some degree mental derangement, the confusion and unhappiness which are always the results of wrong thinking. It is well known that worry and discouragement cause chemical changes in the body, which actually produce chemical poisons.

These poisons lower the resisting power of both body and mind and leave the sufferer a prey to all sorts of unfortunate results. There are multitudes of people today in poor health and in poor circumstances, plodding along in discontent and unhappiness, when they might be happy and doing superb things were they not the victims of discouraging conditions, conditions which are largely the result of their fear and worry. Their minds are out of joint, unhinged, and unfit for the work of today, because they are divided between looking forward to the future, anticipating all sorts of evils and misfortunes, and looking backward to the past, regretting whatever they had or had not done.

One of the saddest things in my work is the cry of unhappiness that comes to me from people who have lost their courage and ambition. They write me that they have ruined their careers, and that all they can do now is to live on in a very hopeless and unhappy way. "Oh, if I hadn't quit in a moment of discouragement!" they wail: "If I hadn't yielded to homesickness and left college!" "If I had only stuck to my trade, to my law practice, to my engineering work a little longer, until success came to me; if I had only kept on, how different things would be today! But I lost heart, got blue and discouraged and decided to try something easier. I have never been happy or satisfied with myself since I played the coward and turned back, but it is too late to make a change."

There are millions of people in inferior or mediocre positions today who might be doing big things had they not yielded to discouragement at the start and ruined the promise of their lives. Nine-tenths of the men and women in the great failure army are there because they were not prepared to meet obstacles, setbacks, and were frightened when they confronted them. They didn't have the vision that sees beyond obstacles and holds on in spite of unexpected difficulties, disappointments, and reverses.

Some people are always at home to the "blues." They are, as Carlyle says, "rich in the power to be miserable." I know a woman whose mind is so adjusted to despondency and discouragement that a very little thing brings on a fit of the "blues." She seems to be always ready to receive the whole blue family, and the first one that gets admission to her mind drags in his relatives, . . . discouragement, despondency, despair, fear, worry, and all the rest. They hold her in thrall for days together, driving out everything else, all happiness, courage, confidence, her very sanity.

Indulgence in the "blues," in morbid, despondent moods, is dangerous to character development and success. After a while it becomes a settled habit, a disease, and every little setback, every little disappointment, throws the sufferer off his balance, kills his enthusiasm and his zest for work, lowers his efficiency and, for the time being, his ability. In the end it acts like creeping paralysis and robs him of all initiative, all power and energy, all desire even to do. I am acquainted with a man whose habitual despondency has starved and stunted his whole life. He is a striking illustration of the destructive power of unhappy thoughts. He gives one the impression of great possibilities never expressed.

His forces are shut up within him. He is always full of fear, worry, and anxiety. Discouragement envelops him like a mantle. His attitude, his manner, his expression, his speech, all indicates a shrinking and shriveling, an impotence which is due to his unfortunate moods. He is discontented, restless, unhappy, suffering from the sense of a thwarted ambition, and although he has worked very hard all his life his morbid mentality and discouraged outlook have cut down his efficiency more than fifty per cent, and left him away behind where a man of his natural ability should be.

One of the marks of a strong soul, one who is anchored in faith, is the ability to conquer discouragement, melancholia, the "blues," all tendencies to cowardice and self-pity. No matter what happens, what obstacles or trials push such souls back, or for a time press them down, they never lose hope or give way under disappointments and failures. It is not that they do not feel those things, but that they will not suffer them to turn them aside from their purpose, to defeat their ambition.

Now the greatest obstacles to our success are in our minds, and there is no one so weak that he cannot overcome the most destructive enemy thoughts by the application of mental chemistry; that is, by calling to his aid the antidotes for the enemy thoughts, and training his mind to face the light instead of the darkness. A discouraging, despondent thought can instantly be neutralized by a courageous, hopeful thought, just as an acid can instantly be neutralized by an alkali. The mental law is as scientific as the physical. We cannot hold two opposite thoughts in the mind at the same time, one neutralizes or drives out the other. We can always crowd out a negative, destructive fear thought, by persistently holding in mind its opposite, . . a positive, courageous, constructive thought.

"Whistling to keep up courage is no mere figure of speech," said William James, the great psychologist. "On the other hand, sit all day in a moping posture, sigh and reply to everything in a dismal voice and your melancholy lingers." That is, by our thoughts and acts we can draw to ourselves courage or discouragement. In other words, we can change our mental attitude as we will; and to change our thought is to change our condition.

For instance, if you are looking for a job and don't find one; if you have had reverses, and don't know where your next dollar is coming from; if you are a round peg in a square hole; if you have made mistakes; if for any reason you are discouraged and tempted to retreat before the enemy, instead of going about with a defeated, gloomy, despondent air, turn about face at once and assume the attitude of a victor in life. Say to yourself: "God did not create any man to be a failure. He gave to all his children qualities that command success, each in his own field. All we need is to use them. I AM success-organized, because I partake of the attributes of the Creator of the universe, the Omnipotent One. I will now use the divine power within me to do the thing I want to do; to get the position I desire; to satisfy all my needs. Failure cannot come near me. I AM a success now, because I AM one with All Power."

Resolutely hold this mental attitude, and you will be surprised to find what courage it will give you, and how your difficulties will wilt before it. General Foch says that a lost battle is a battle you think you can't win. Multitudes of battles have been won by the persistent determination of a single general who had not given up hope when all others had.

"You are beaten; this army is not beaten," has ever been the reply of great generals to the discouraged one who wanted to give up the battle as lost. It is the Joifres, the Fochs, the Grants, the men of indomitable faith and courage, who have ever wrung victory from defeat.

All down through history glorious victories have been won, not by masses of men, but by single individuals who had superb courage, a mighty faith in themselves and in their undertaking, an unflinching determination to succeed. In innumerable instances such brave souls had saved the day when their comrades had given up because they saw nothing but defeat, where the will to conquer had seen only victory. There is somebody not far from you at this moment, my doubting, discouraged friend, who could step into your place and command victory with the resources which you think so inadequate for the work you have to do. There is somebody who has no more ability than you have who could see an unusual opportunity in the situation which you find so hopeless, so discouraging.

A great scientist said that when he encountered what seemed an unconquerable obstacle he invariably found himself upon the brink of some important discovery. The time above all others when it is most important for a man to hold fast to his faith and courage is when the way is so dark that he cannot see ahead. If you push on toward your goal when everything seems going against you, when doubt and discouragement are doing their best to make you give up, turn back, turn coward and quitter, then is the time when "you are closer to victory than you dream of. If you never lose your conviction in your divine God-given power to win out in spite of handicaps or any obstacles that may arise in your path, nothing can defeat you, because you are in conscious partnership with Omnipotence.

WHAT AM I?

I am the great paralyzer of ability, the murderer of aspiration and ambition, the destroyer of energy, the killer of opportunity.

I am the cause of more suffering, more human misery and loss, more tragedies and wretchedness than any other one thing.

I have cursed more human beings, arrested the development of more fine ability, strangled more genius and stifled more talent than anything else in the world.

I have shortened vast multitudes of lives and sent more people to the insane asylum, to crime and suicide than men dream of.

I cause chemical changes in the brain which cripple efficiency and ruin careers.

I deprive human beings of more things that are good for them, things that fit their nature, and that they were intended to enjoy, than any other one agent.

I cause men and women to wear poor, shabby clothes, to look dejected and forlorn, when it is the right of every human being to look up, to be well dressed, attractive, and happy.

I shut out the sun of hope and cause men to see everything in a distorted light because I make them look on the shadow side of things.

I devitalize people and make chronic invalids of men and women who should be enjoying perfect health.

I am the devil's most effective instrument. If he can once get the bare suggestion of me into the human consciousness at the psychological moment, he can work destruction to the most ambitious, the greatest genius.

I starve and stunt minds, and keep vast multitudes of people in ignorance.

I usually attack a man when he is down, when things have gone wrong, and he is feeling blue. When he is tired, fatigued, devitalized, I find an easy entrance to his mind, because then his courage is not so keen, his brain is not so alert, and he has less dare in his nature.

I find that the best time to work on my victims is in the afternoon. In the morning men are too vigorous mentally, have too much vitality and energy, too much courage, to give in to me, but along in the afternoon when the body and brain begin to weary of work, and the whole man feels a bit fagged, I can tackle the great mental scheme which was in the forefront of the brain in the forenoon, when the faculties were clean-cut, and unless my victim is alert I soon have him under my control.

I am the greatest human deceiver. Once I get into the mind, I can make a giant believe he is a pygmy, and of no account. I can cut down his self respect until in his own estimation he is a very ordinary man.

I have a twin brother, Doubt, who is called the great traitor. He is always ready to help me to finish my little game. We work together, and when under our control it is impossible for a man to be resourceful, original, or effective.

I creep into a man's mind after he has resolved to branch out on new lines, to step out from the beaten path and blaze his own way, and weaken his ardor, dampen his enthusiasm, and make him feel inefficient and helpless.

I whisper in his ear, "Go slow; better be careful. Many abler men than you have fallen down trying to do that very thing. It is not the time to start this thing; you had better wait, wait, wait."

I haven't a single redeeming thing in my nature, and yet I have more influence with the human race than has any one of the finer, nobler qualities which help to bring man up to the height of his possibilities.

I AM DISCOURAGEMENT

Chapter XI

How To Make Your Subconscious Work For You

• When all men know how to make the subconscious work for them there will be no poor people, none in distress or suffering, in pain or ill health; no one will be unhappy, no one will be a victim of thwarted ambitions.

• Your subconscious mind is like a garden, and you must be very careful what you plant there. Every thought, every emotion, every suggestion is a seed planted in the subconscious soil, and will bring you a harvest like itself. It doesn't matter what kind of thought seeds you plant, whether poverty or prosperity, failure or success, happiness or misery, you will reap a harvest in kind.

• If you impress vividly, intensely, and persistently, upon the creative mind in the great within of you, your determination to be what you long to be; if you register your vow to succeed in doing what you long to do; and do your level best to actualize your longings, nothing in the world can stand in the way of your success.

• Every great inventor, every great discoverer, every great genius has felt the thrill of the divine inward force, that mysterious power back of the flesh but not of it, which has come to his aid in working out the device, the discovery, the book, the painting, the great musical composition, the poem, whatever he was trying to create or discover.

I predict that within the next twenty-five years the average man, through his knowledge of the infinite power and possibilities of the subconscious mind, that mysterious force in the great within, will be able to accomplish more than the greatest minds of all time have ever dreamed of doing. Science has revealed the mechanism of the body and mastered the secrets of its marvelous construction and action; but the mystery of mind is as yet but dimly understood. Very few have even a faint realization of its immense hidden powers.

The body becomes unconscious in sleep and all its voluntary activities cease. But the mind . . what does it do when the body sleeps? We know it does not sleep, for when the body is wrapped in slumber the memory and imagination slip out of their house and go where they will. They wander in scenes of the past or they project themselves into the future. Now they are visiting in California, now in London, now in Paris, now they are among the stars. What embodiment do they assume? Or do they take visible form? They certainly seem to be completely independent of the body during sleep.

The new psychology explains the mystery of mind in a very simple way. It claims that that part of the mind which continues active when we sleep is that marvelous force in the great within of us which, understood and rightly used, will enable man to reach the heights of his limitless possibilities.

We know that we are tapping a new source of power. When we can do this intelligently, scientifically, we shall all be performing what hitherto have been regarded as miracles. We are just beginning to realize that the subconscious mind is the channel by which we connect with infinite supply; with the great creative processes of the universe; that through it man can tap the Infinite Mind and accomplish things that will dwarf to insignificance achievements that now excite our wonder and admiration.

Everything, so far as results are concerned, depends upon the degree of intelligence and conscious purpose with which we use the subconscious mind, for it is forever occupied registering on the invisible creative substance your every thought, emotion, desire, wish, or feeling. It never sleeps, but is incessantly working on the suggestions it receives from the conscious or objective mind. Your habitual thought, your convictions, your visions, your dreams, your beliefs, are all impressed upon it, and will ultimately be expressed in your life. In other words, your subconscious mind is your servant, and proceeds instantly, without quibbling, without questioning, no matter whether it is a big thing or a little thing, whether it is right or wrong, to obey the order, to follow the suggestion, you give it.

For instance, when you want to take an early train, or to get up in the middle of the night for some purpose, when you haven't been accustomed to do so, and you say to yourself, or hold the thought in mind before dropping to sleep, "I must wake up in time to get that train in the morning," or, "I must get up at one o'clock tonight," you are sure to awaken at almost the exact time you register, when, perhaps, you haven't been awake at that hour before in a year. You have no alarm clock; no one calls you; what wakes you up at just the right time? You probably never asked yourself the question, or thought about it. But it was that little faithful subconscious servant who was on the watch for you while you slept.

A similar thing is true of our appointments; making dates or engagements for some time in the future. You agree to meet a man tomorrow or someday next week at a certain place and hour. You don't make any written record of it and the thing passes out of your mind. But when the time comes round you are reminded of your engagement. From long experience I know that that something inside of me will bring every engagement I make to my consciousness in time for me to attend to it. I don't keep thinking of it all the time. Not at all. I file it away in the within of me as I would file a business letter in my office for future reference. Then I dismiss it from my thought, knowing that it will be taken care of at the proper time.

The trained man learns to commit all sorts of things to his subconscious secretary, knowing from experience that it will serve him faithfully, not only in comparatively small things, such as awakening him at any desired hour in the night or early morning, constantly reminding him of his engagements, but also in the serious problems of life. Edison says that when he is right up against a great problem in his work and has no idea in the world how to solve it, he simply sleeps over it, and many a time he wakes up in the morning to find his problem solved; it has been worked out for him while he slept in ways which he never dreamed of. The details of various inventions have been completed for him in this way.

I know a great many business and professional men who do as Mr. Edison does when serious problems confront them; they sleep on them before they make any decision. In fact, it is the commonest thing in the world, when we are considering some serious problem, for all of us to say: "I must sleep over that matter before deciding; it is so important." What does sleeping over such a matter mean? We may not understand or be able to explain, but what it really means is this: Your subconscious mind takes up the problem at the point where your conscious mind left it when you went to sleep, and in the morning you will find that it has been thought out for you. Your subconscious wisdom has entered into the transaction, given you the benefit of its advice and enabled you to make the right decision.

When all men know how to make the subconscious work for them there will be no poor people, none in distress or suffering, in pain or ill health; no one will be unhappy, a victim of thwarted ambitions. We shall know then that all we have to do to make our dreams come true, to be prosperous and happy, is to give our invisible secretary the right instructions and follow this up with the necessary effort. Establishing in your subconscious mind the things that you want to come true, that you are ambitious to attain; impressing upon it the ideal of the man or woman you long to be, is the first step toward achievement.

Hold the conviction in your consciousness that your own is already headed your way, work for it confidently in the realization that you can draw from the creative energy of the universal mind anything you desire, and it will surely come to you, because you will thus start the process of creation in the great within of you.

Consciously or unconsciously put in motion, these are the initial steps that have led to the production of every great work of art and genius in the world. They were adopted in the production of our railroads, our ships, our homes, our great monuments and buildings, our cities, our telegraph, telephone, and wireless systems, our airplanes, and all the marvels of modern inventions. Edison says he is only a medium for transmitting from the great cosmic intelligence and energy which fill the universe a few of the infinite number of devices which are destined to emancipate human beings from every form of drudgery. He believes that the best things he has given to the world have been merely passed along through him to his fellow men from the Infinite Source of all supply.

While the subconscious mind is all-powerful in working out the pattern or idea we give it, of itself it does not originate, so it will make all the difference in the world to you what sort of material you give your subconscious mind to work on. You can make it an enemy or a friend, for it will do the thing which injures you just as quickly as the thing which blesses you. Not through malice, but because it has no discriminating power any more than the soil in which the farmer sows his seed. If the farmer should make a mistake and sow thistle seed instead of wheat, the soil doesn't say to him, "My friend, you have made a mistake. You have been sowing thistle seed instead of wheat, so we will change the law, which you may get what you thought you were going to get." No, the soil will always give us a harvest like our sowing. If we sow thistle seed it will be just as faithful in producing thistles as it will in producing wheat or cabbages or potatoes.

We sow the seed and nature gives us a corresponding harvest; that is the law on the physical plane. It is exactly the same on the mental plane. The subconscious mind is like the soil, passive. The objective mind uses it, gives its commands or suggestions, which it carries out according to their nature. That is, the objective or conscious mind sows the seed in word, motive, thought or act, and the subconscious mind gives us back our own; always the thing that corresponds to what we impressed on it.

In other words, the subconscious mind has no choice but to follow the lead we give it. Hence, how important it is that our instructions to this invisible servant should be for our good and not for our harm; that we should saturate it, not with the things we do not want, the things we hate and fear and worry about, but the things we long for and are striving to attain.

If you are working hard, and yet not progressing toward your ideal; if you are in poverty and wretchedness, though constantly struggling to get away from those conditions; you are not obeying the law "which governs the subconscious.

Your thought is at fault; you are thinking poverty, thinking failure; your mind is filled with doubts and fears; you are working against the law instead of with it; you are neutralizing all your efforts by your wrong mental attitude.

Some people by their indomitable faith and self-confidence get hold of the dormant powers of the great within of themselves and unconsciously work with the law which governs them. Wherever a man or a woman is doing unusual things, struggling heroically to accomplish some great purpose, you find one who consciously or unconsciously is obeying this law, by making tremendous demands upon the subconscious; by registering his life purposes with such tremendous intensity and working so persistently, so confidently, along that line that his purpose is unfailingly carried out.

Luther Burbank, for example, has done and is doing tremendous things in the plant world because he makes tremendous demands upon the mighty agent within, his subconscious mind or self. He does not neutralize the demands by doubts and fears as to whether they will be carried out or not. He makes his demands, gives his orders, persistently, emphatically, with vigor and determination, and they are faithfully executed. By the same means, consciously or unconsciously used, Madam Curie has made some of the most remarkable discoveries in the scientific world.

We can all accomplish our ends, attain our life ambition by doing as they and all other great achievers are doing . . working with law. We are not, as we were taught to believe in the past, so many separate little bits of mind thrown off into space to struggle for ourselves; we are all a part of the infinite mind, the cosmic intelligence and energy of the universe. We are the creation of the one Supreme Mind which called all things out of the unseen, and since the created must partake of the qualities of the Creator, man must partake of the qualities of omniscience, of omnipotence, of the Supreme Mind that gave man dominion over the earth and everything on it. This means that we are really, so far as this earth is concerned, in partnership with God, that we are co-creators with the great creative intelligence which is everywhere active in the universe.

The marvelous accomplishments of man within the past few centuries can only be accounted for through his cooperation with his Creator. It is the spirit of God in man working in harmony with the spirit of God in the great cosmic intelligence of the universe which has made possible within the past half century achievements in science, in invention, in discovery that our ancestors would have ridiculed . . if anyone dared to suggest them as possibilities . . as the imaginings of the insane.

Wireless telegraphy and telephony, the automobile, the airplane; the harnessing of electricity to do the work in our factories, in our homes; the reconstruction of the body by great surgeons, the discoveries in astronomy; cables under oceans, connecting the ends of the earth; the construction of railroads under rivers and under the streets of our teeming cities; the works of scientific men in every field, of the great agriculturists, horticulturists and naturalists, and the great animal breeders who are doing in the animal world what the Burbanks are doing in the plant world . . all these things are the results of man's reaching out into the great creative energy and in cooperation with Omnipotence molding it to his purposes.

The dictum of science is that "Nature unaided fails." In other words, man is God's working partner on this earth, his work being to lift everything upon it, including man himself, to the highest possibility of the divine plan. There is a power in man back of the flesh, which, working with the divine cosmic intelligence, will enable him to do things that at present we can hardly conceive of. Nothing we can imagine or dream" of will be impossible of achievement, because we are a real part of the creative power which performs miracles throughout the universe. That is, apparent miracles, for everything follows a law which is never violated in order to perform what seem to us miracles.

In the consciousness of the mighty possibilities of the subconscious mind to tap the great universal mind lies the secret of infinite creative principle, of limitless power. There are powers in your subconscious mind which, if aroused and utilized, would help you do what others tell you is "impossible." Your ideal, your heart's desire, however unattainable it may seem at present, is a prophecy of what will come true in your life if you do your part.

It is only in our extremities that we touch our real power, that we unconsciously have recourse to the great within. There are multitudes of people in the failure army today, with scarcely energy enough to keep them alive, who have forces slumbering deep within themselves which, if they could only be awakened, would enable them to do wonderful things.

The great trouble with most of us, even those who have studied along this line, is that our demands upon ourselves are so feeble, the call upon the great within of us is so weak and so intermittent, that it makes no vital or permanent impression upon the creative energies; it lacks the force and persistency that transmute desires into realities. When we realize that it is through our subconscious selves, in the great within of us, that we make wireless connection with the All-Supply, with all possible joy and satisfaction; that it is here the great creative processes which make our dreams come true are started, it seems strange that we don't use this great force to better advantage.

When the necessary conditions are fulfilled the law that governs the subconscious operates unerringly. Work with the law instead of against it and nothing can hinder your success. In other words, let your subconscious mind help instead of hinder you. Give it the right thought, the right instruction, the right ideals to work on; give it success thoughts instead of failure thoughts, bright cheerful, hopeful thoughts instead of gloomy discouraging ones; never hold a thought that does not correspond with your ideal or ambition; no matter what conditions are, what obstacles stand in your way, persist in vividly visualizing your success, never letting a doubt or fear thought come between you and the confident belief that you will get the thing you long for and are working for with all your heart, and you will be amazed at what your faithful secretary, working in harmony with creative intelligence, will do for you.

The interior creative forces are more active during the night than in the day time, and are especially susceptible to the suggestions they receive before we fall asleep. During sleep the conscious mind is not active, and consequently the subconscious mind operates uninterruptedly, without any of the objections or hindrances which it is constantly bringing up during the day. Therefore it is of the greatest importance that you give the subconscious the right message, the right model on which to work during the night.

Do this before you drop to sleep and it will work for the attainment of your ambition, your desire, all night. Never allow yourself to fall asleep in a doubting, despondent mood. Do not hinder the operation of the creative intelligence at any time by doubt, or fear. Doubt is the great enemy which has neutralized the efforts, and killed the success of multitudes of people. Live always in the consciousness that you are a success in whatever you are trying to do and the creative processes within you, faithfully working according to the model you give them, will produce whatever you desire.

Chapter XII

Thinking Health And Prosperity Into The Cells Of Your Body

- Every cell in us thinks... Thomas A. Edison

- Each cell in the body is a conscious intelligent being. - Professor Nels Quevli

- Think and say regarding yourself and your future only that which you wish to come true.

- As every cell in your body is constantly being made new, why not put new thoughts, new life, into your cells and not drag along with you all the old skeletons of the past?

- The cell minds all through your body know whether you are master or not. They know whether you go through the world as conqueror or conquered, as a master or a slave, and they act accordingly. They fling back into your life the reflection of your thoughts, your motives, your convictions. Your condition will correspond with the mental attitude they reflect.

- Thinking wholeness, completeness, perfection, into the cells will encourage and stimulate them. The functioning of all the cells of the body, of the various organs, is lowered when we are thinking black, discouraging thoughts, and all of our mental faculties correspond with our physical condition.

When physicians told Jane Addams, a young girl just graduated from college, that she could not live more than six months, she said, "All right, I will take that six months to get as near as I can to the one thing I want to do for humanity."

What happened? The firm expression of her determination to do the thing that lay nearest to her heart registered itself so indelibly on the cells in every remotest part of her body, from her brain center to the tips of her fingers, and downward to the points of her toes, that they began immediately to build for health. Eight years after the medical authority of that time had given her six months to live; she started Hull House, the world-famous Chicago settlement. Today she is an international figure, a leader in different phases of the great modern movement for world betterment. If instead of giving them her positive ringing message for life and work, Jane Addams had impressed upon the cells of her body the negative pronouncement of her physicians, and told them that she was going to die in six months, what would have happened? She would have died; for the cells would have accepted one suggestion as readily as the other. Instead of setting to work to repair and build up the body, they would have quit work; the various organs and tissues would have disintegrated, and the world would never have heard of Jane Addams or her great work.

When we get a thorough understanding of the power that Miss Addams unconsciously used when she cast the thought of death out of her mind and replaced it with the life thought, we can build into the very structure of our bodies whatever we wish them to express. If we are dissatisfied with the bodies we now have, we can literally build new ones, for every one of the billions of tiny cells that compose the human body is a living, thinking, working entity, which, like the sensitive plate of a camera, records in its structure the image of every emotion, thought, impression, or passion that passes through our consciousness.

The author of that marvelously interesting book, "Cell Intelligence" says: "The cell is a conscious intelligent being, and by reason thereof plans and builds all plants and animals in the same manner as man constructs houses, railroads, and other structures." That is, every cell does its part in building the body, setting the life along the lines we suggest, just as the mason, the bricklayer, the carpenter, and other workers construct a house in accordance with the lines of the architect's plan. Not only that, but scientists now believe that the cells which constitute the various organs of the body, the brain, the heart, the liver, the kidneys, the lungs, etc., . . have what is called "organ intelligence," and that these cells are susceptible to mental suggestion for the health or disease of their particular organ. In other words, the little community of cells that form the heart think and work for the heart; the brain community work for the brain; the stomach community, for the stomach, and so on; and all together make a huge army of little body workers, responding instantly to whatever thought we impress on them.

If, for instance, there should be a disease tendency lurking in any part of your body; if your digestive organs, your heart, your kidneys, your liver, or some other organ, should not be functioning normally, by sending encouraging, energizing, uplifting thoughts, the suggestion of health and wholeness, to the community cells, and by living rightly, you can neutralize the disease tendency and bring the organ back to normalcy. The intelligent cells will do exactly as your thought suggests . . work for health and the elimination of the disease tendency. On precisely the same principle, the opposite thought, . . the thought of disease, of abnormalcy, . . suggested to these little cell minds, which are already tending to disease, to abnormalcy, will aggravate the trouble and hasten the development of the lurking disease in the system.

I have heard a man curse his stomach and his digestive organs for not digesting his food properly. Every time he sits down to the table he begins to complain about the food hurting him: "I can't eat this," he will say. "My stomach can't take care of it. I can't digest this; I can't digest that. It is bound to come back on me if I attempt to eat it. I wish I had a decent stomach instead of the good-for-nothing thing I have." Now, how can any intelligent man expect the cooperation of his stomach and his digestive organs when he is sending such discordant thoughts into their cell minds? When he is constantly blaming and cursing those organs for not functioning normally, upbraiding them for giving him pain and distress, how can he expect them to do their best work and serve him cheerfully and efficiently? Those organs are like children or employees, and a man might just as reasonably expect to get cheerful, willing, efficient service from his children or his employees by cursing, scolding, and abusing them as to get it from his bodily organs when he does this.

The state of your body is a reflection of your habitual thought about it, your general mental attitude and beliefs regarding your various organs. When you think of your heart as weak, of your liver as sluggish, of your kidneys as diseased; when you say, "I'm sick; I'm discouraged; I'm tired; I'm down and out; I'm all in; all used up; I don't feel like anything," do you know what you are doing to the little cell minds all through your body? You are weakening and demoralizing them; you are stamping your discouraged, despondent thought, the picture of weakness, of inefficiency, on their very structure, and their functioning will be accordingly deteriorated. The weak, discouraged, pessimistic, sick or diseased thought produces a condition like itself in every cell in the body, and the body suffers in proportion to the persistence of such thoughts. They tend to tear down, to destroy the body tissues, to paralyze the life functions.

The real basis of all forms of mental healing is the fact that the cells of the body are all alive and intelligent; that they respond to our thought, to our intelligence, to our suggestions to them. It makes a great difference to the mental healer to know that instead of sending his thought into a mass of dead cells, everyone is not only alive, but is just as responsive to his mental attitude as an intelligent child would be. He knows that his health thought, his uplift thought, the thought of their wholeness and completeness, the suggestion of their divine origin, of their power to build up the body, to renew its strength and vigor, sends a thrill of encouragement, of hope and assurance through every one of them, and starts them on their task of neutralizing the disease thought and renewing the health and vitality of his patient.

Be careful what you think into these little cell minds of your body, my friend, for it will come back to you not only in your physical condition but in every aspect of your life. For example, when you think bad luck into them, when you are thinking how unlucky you are, telling everybody about it, saying that fate is against you, and that no matter what you do you can't get ahead, you are discouraging these little cell minds, just as you do when you think disease and ill health into them. You paralyze them, in other words, and instead of functioning normally, they function abnormally, and your health, your chances of success, your mentality, your power to overcome the obstacles in your way, are all seriously affected. There is a letting down all along the line. Your discouraged, pessimistic thoughts have robbed you of energy and pep; demagnetized you for the very things you are trying to attract, .. health and prosperity.

The problem of maintaining physical vigor, abounding health, the magnetic energy that draws things to us out of the cosmic intelligence, is solved when you learn how to keep all of the little cell minds which form the different tissues of the body organs in perfect condition, so that they will be alert, happy, cheerful, hopeful. They will then reflect the maximum of your creative thought, the maximum of vigor and robustness, of physical and mental power, for it is in these little building, creative centers that our grit and our determination are nourished. Here is where we get our energy, our motive power, and hence we must be very careful what we whisper into these little cell minds, whether encouragement or discouragement, hope or despair, health or disease, poverty or prosperity. They are, so to speak, the tiny children of the larger mind and are very susceptible to what the larger mind thinks, the instructions it sends them, the various impulses which go out from the central station of the body . . the brain.

If a sick, weak man wants to be strong and well, he must impress a strong, healthy picture of himself on the cells that are trying to repair, to rebuild him. He must hold the image of himself as he would like to be, not as he is. Instead of this many sick people think or say to themselves something like this: "Oh, how sick I am. I feel so weak that I'm afraid I never shall be well again. I shall never be able to do anything in the world. My ambition only mocks and tortures me, because I shall never be able to realize it. Looks as if my work here was done. This disease has gotten such a hold upon me that it will never let go. Why is it that the Creator allows human beings to suffer this way, tortures them with the ambition to do something which they can never do, never have the strength to do?"

How little people realize that when they hold such thoughts, visualize themselves in a weak, despairing, dying condition, they are just as surely committing suicide as if they were to take a slow poison. Every cell in the body is poisoned and made helpless by the wrong thought.

If you picture the billions of cells in your body as tiny individualities, little dancers, who are dancing to whatever tune you give them, you will get some idea of the action of your mind upon them in uplifting or depressing you; for they dance the life dance or the death dance, the sick dance or the health dance, the poverty dance or the prosperity dance, the love dance or the hate dance, the happiness dance or the misery dance, the success dance or the failure dance, in response to whatever thought tune you give them.

Many people make themselves invalids or semi-invalids all their lives by their down-dragging thought tunes, holding the discouraged conviction that they never will be well, that they are always going to be more or less helpless. If they changed their conviction their physical condition would immediately change. This has been proved true time and time again by the apparent miracles wrought by mental healers, who simply changed the trend of the patient's mind, turned his thought from abnormal, diseased conditions to healthful, wholesome conditions. Then the little cells began to dance to the new tune, the tune of life, of wholeness; and the body at once responded in renewed vitality and vigor.

Nothing will do more toward making your life, your personality, your environment what you want them to be than the daily habit of thinking into the cell minds of your body what you wish them to express, . . health, prosperity, success, happiness, joy, goodwill, harmony peace, divine power and energy. You can do this every morning before you start out to your daily task and every little while during the day when you have a bit of leisure.

The important thing is to keep out of the mind all enemy thoughts. The moment any of these gain entrance, and are permitted to remain, they begin to tear down and destroy. They play havoc with your efficiency, with your health and happiness. If anything occurs during the day to disturb your poise or your self-control, if you feel angry impulses rising within you, recollect yourself as quickly as possible and get control again, for nothing is more hurtful to the whole man or woman than mental in harmony of any nature. You can speak peace into the billions of turbulent cells, just as Christ spoke peace to the turbulent waters of the sea. When you give them the harmony keynote they will respond. They will always reflect what you suggest to them.

When the master mind speaks they obey. Change your inharmonious thought and you change the condition of the billions of little cell entities in your body. In short, whatever you want your life to express, think it into those entities and it will come to pass; for they are your partners, doing team work with you. Think of every cell in your body as a little worker for you, a little producer, a little intelligent separate entity, cooperating with the one great universal intelligence, the great cosmic purpose. Picture the cells collectively as a myriad army welded together by Supreme Power and working together to make you a dominant, forceful personality, a man or a woman capable of conquering any environment, mastering any unfortunate conditions that wrong thinking may have brought into manifestation.

Never allow yourself to think weakness, poverty or poverty stricken conditions into them or want or limitation of any kind. You are God's child; think accordingly. Think in keeping with your immortal inheritance. Think big, because you are big. Think generously, because you are made to express generosity. You are not made for cheeseparing economy, but for largeness of living; you were made for the life abundant, not for the pinched, stunted, starved life. The possibilities of the life which keys the cell minds to the right thought is beyond all calculation. Every thought of power, every thought of health, every thought of love, every truth thought, every beauty thought, every thought of perfection, of wholeness, of vigor of mind and body, every thought of God will attune your mind and body to the power and perfection of the creative plan of Divine Mind.

Thinking health, thinking happiness, thinking truth, thinking power and perfection, prosperity, success, into the little cell minds of the body will, in the future, be a very important part of every child's training. Their lives from the start will be keyed right; the little cell workers will get the right command, the right mental picture, and they will build for health, prosperity, and success, not for weakness, poverty, and failure. Right thinking, making the cells work in the right way, of construction instead of destruction, will banish from the earth two of the greatest handicaps of the race . . disease and poverty.

WHAT AM I?

I AM the vital principle of life . . the greatest of all success and happiness assets.

I AM that which gives the plus quality to human beings. I put pep, ginger, vim, into human effort.

I AM the source of physical and mental power. I give the body vigor and buoyancy, the brain vital energy and originality.

I AM your best friend . . the friend of the high and lowly, the rich and the poor alike . . but, be he king or beggar, who violates my laws must pay the penalty.

I AM often sought in vain by the man who rides in his limousine, but am generally found in the company of the man who walks to his work and takes plenty of exercise.

I AM the great multiplier of ability, the buttress of initiative, of courage, of self-confidence, the backbone of enthusiasm, without which nothing worthwhile was ever accomplished.

I AM the greatest constructive power in the life of man. Without me his faith weakens, his ambition sags, his ardor oozes out, his courage faints, his self-confidence departs, his accomplishment is nil.

Without me wealth is a mockery, a palatial home a bitter disappointment.

Next to life itself, I AM the greatest gift God has given to man; the millionaire who has lost me in piling up his fortune would give all his millions to get me back again. I AM that which gives buoyancy to life, which makes you magnetic, joyous; forceful, which brings out your resourcefulness and inventiveness, that which raises efficiency to its maximum and enables you to make the most of your ability.

I increase every one of your forty or fifty mental faculties a hundredfold.

I AM the leader of them all. When I AM present they are up, at their best; when I AM absent, they are down, at their worst.

I AM the friend of progress, the stimulator of ambition, the encourager of effort, the great essential to efficiency, to success, the promoter of long life and happiness.

I AM a joy bringer. Where I go, good cheer goes. Where I AM not, depression, discouragement, the "blues," are present. My absence means declining powers, often thwarted ambition, blighted hopes, mediocrity, failure, a shortened life.

The wise man guards me as the apple of his eye; the fool often abuses and loses me through ignorance, indifference or neglect.

I AM GOOD HEALTH

Chapter XIII

How To Make Yourself Lucky

- Believe with all your heart that you can and will do what you were made to do.

- The "lucky" man never waits for something to turn up.

- "Luck is the ability to recognize an opportunity and take advantage of it."

- To make yourself lucky, choose the vocation nature fitted you for and then fling your life into it. Be all there.

- Self-confidence and industry are the friends of good luck.

- Good luck follows good sense, good judgment, good health, a gritty determination, a lofty ambition, and downright hard work. It follows the man who cultivates tact, courtesy, courage, self-confidence, will power, optimism, health, and goodwill to all men.

A New York broker not long ago committed suicide because he thought luck, which had been a dominant factor in his life creed, had forsaken him. He had such faith in the fetish, luck, that, when he met with a series of Wall Street losses, he believed there was no further use in struggling against his destiny. Luck had turned its back on him, he declared, and he had nothing more to live for. His dying words to his wife were, "Good luck to you."

Many a man, though he may not go so far as this Wall Street broker did, limits himself by a superstitious belief in good or ill luck. He is convinced that there is some fate or destiny, something beyond his control which determines the extent of his achievement, and that if this mysterious power fights against him, he will fail; if it helps him, he will succeed.

Nothing is so fatal to achievement as the belief in a blind destiny, in the fallacy that an effect can be brought about without a sufficient cause. Yet how many able-bodied people are waiting around for luck to solve their problems, waiting to get a lift from that mysterious, indefinable something which helps one man on and keeps another back, regardless of his own efforts. One might as well wait for luck to solve mathematical problems as to wait for it to solve any of his own life problems. Man is master of his own destiny. The power to solve his problems is right inside of him. He makes the fate which downs him or lifts him up. Life is. not a game of chance.

The Creator did not put us here to be the sport of circumstances, puppets to be tossed about by a cruel fate, which we could not control. He has given man a free will, an unfettered mind, and . .

"Man makes his fate according to his mind; The weak, low spirit Fortune makes her slave, But she's a drudge when beckoned by the brave. If Fate weave common thread I'll change the doom And with new purple weave a nobler loom."

"Why art thou cast down, oh, my soul!" There is that within you, my good friend, which is a great deal more than a match for anything that can try to down you. You have inherited a power from your Divine Parent which infinitely more than matches any defect or deficiency you may think you have inherited from your earthly parents, or any handicap in your environment. There is something of omnipotence in you, for you are the child of Omnipotence, and you must have inherited the qualities of your Creator.

No matter what happens to you, remember there is something in you bigger than any fate, something that can laugh at any cruel destiny, for you are your own fate, your own destiny.

There is a God in you, my friend. Assert your divinity. All you have to do is to tap the Eternal Mind, the great cosmic energy, and all power is yours. You are at the very source of the All Supply.

"Luck is the ability to recognize an opportunity and take advantage of it," says Beatrice Fairfax, and if we accept her definition we must admit that there is such a thing as luck. Perhaps you have heard of the young man who happened to be the only physician present in a crowd which gathered around a king's carriage when he was stricken with a fit in a street in London. The young doctor pressed through the crowd and said he could relieve the king by bloodletting. The king revived and this incident was a great stepping-stone to the marvelous career of Ambrose Pare.

It sometimes happens that in a railroad wreck or some other great catastrophe an unknown man leaps into notoriety by some simple act which thousands of others could have performed as well. But the ability to seize the opportunity, and do the needed thing promptly and accurately, is due to the cultivation of one's initiative, the daily development of promptness and precision in caring for business affairs. What you, my friend, may right now be calling your hard luck, may be the result of some weakness, some bad habit, which is thwarting your efforts, keeping from you the prosperity you desire. You may have peculiarities, objectionable traits, which are bars to your progress, stumbling-blocks in your path. Your bad luck may be lack of preparation, a poor education, insufficient training for your special work. Your foundation may be too small for any sort of a respectable life structure. Or, your bad luck may be indolence, a love of ease and pleasure, a desire to have a good time first of all, no matter what happens.

Good luck is the very opposite of all this. Every successful man knows that good luck follows the strong will, the earnest, persistent endeavor, good hard work, thorough preparation, the ambition to excel and a dead-in-earnest purpose. The "lucky" man is the man who has been a closer thinker, a harder worker, than his "unlucky" neighbor. He is more practical, his life has been ruled by system and order.

Luck is like opportunity, it comes to those who work for it and are ready for it. Make the best possible use of your time, this will make you lucky. If you are handicapped by the lack of an education you can get a fair equivalent of a college education, no matter how busy your life may be. Read and study during your spare moments. A multitude of men and women are educating themselves in this way every day, and are climbing up in the world in spite of a thousand obstacles and handicaps which you have never known. If we should examine the careers of most men who are called "lucky," we should find that their success has its roots way back in their early youth, and that it has drawn its nourishment from many a battle in the struggle for supremacy over poverty and opposition. We should find that the "lucky" man is not a believer in luck, but in himself; that he has never waited for things "to turn up," or for luck to come his way.

He has gone to work and turned things up, made luck come his way. My experience has been that the men who are made of winning material do not talk of hard luck or cruel fate; they do not talk of being" kept back by others. If a man has yeast in him he will rise; nothing can keep him back. Clear grit will attract more good luck than almost any other one thing I know of.

It is usually the lazy, the indolent, the pleasure-loving good-for-nothings, the weaklings, who are the firmest believers in luck. The mere fact that a man is always talking about his "hard luck," blaming his non-success, his defeats on someone else, or on unfortunate circumstances, is an admission that he is a weak man. It shows that he has not-developed independence or strength of will, the mental fiber which overcomes obstacles.

There is everything in forming this habit of thinking of yourself as lucky, fortunate, of always seeing yourself as you would like to be, not as one who is inefficient and always blundering. Talk about yourself and of things as you wish they were, otherwise you will drive away what you long for and attract things which you wish to get rid of.

A business man whom I have known for some years has formed what might be called "the hard luck habit." If he invests in anything, be will say: "Of course, I'm sure to lose. It is just my luck. When I buy the market always begins to fall. The good things fly away when I purchase." He always thinks he is going to get the worst of it in whatever he undertakes. If he starts something new in his business, he immediately begins to talk gloomily about it. "It won't go, I have a feeling that it won't win out," he declares. :

He is always talking "hard luck," predicting that things are going to the bad, and that "it will have to be worse before it is better." This man hasn't nearly as much money as he had several years ago, and his losses have come largely from his sour mental outlook, his lack of confidence in his judgment, his perpetual anticipation of loss and evil, and his belief in an unkind fate.

There are multitudes of hard working people who are continually driving away from them the very thing they are trying to get, because they do not hold the right attitude of mind. They lack the enthusiastic man's optimism, his faith and self-confidence, . . all friends of good luck. If you persist in looking and acting like a failure, or a very mediocre or doubtful success; if you keep telling everybody how unlucky you are, and that you do not believe you will win out, because success is only for a favored few, those who have a pull, someone to boost them, you will be as much of a success as the actor who attempts to impersonate a certain character while looking, thinking, and acting exactly like the opposite.

Our thoughts and words are real forces which build or tear down. Who sees only failure is never a winner. It is the man who never sees anything but victory, who never acknowledges the possibility of defeat, that wins out. The man who tries to excuse his failure on the ground that he was doomed from the start by the bad cards fate dealt him, that he had to play the game with them, and that no amount of effort on his part could have materially altered the results, deceives himself.

I know a man who, whenever he misses a train, says, "I knew I wouldn't catch it! It was just my luck to miss it! I must have been born late." If he makes a blunder or an unfortunate mistake he will say, "I am unlucky about everything. I might have known it would turn out bad. If I bought gold dollars today they wouldn't be worth more than fifty cents tomorrow."

Now, my friend, talking disparagingly about yourself, depreciating yourself, is self deterioration.

The constant suggestion of your inferiority, of your defects or weaknesses, will interfere with your success in anything. You can't be lucky, you can't be successful, if you are all the time talking against yourself, for this will undermine your confidence in yourself and in your efficiency.

Hold a good opinion of yourself. Think highly of yourself. Learn to appreciate your ability and to respect yourself, not egotistically or from a selfish standpoint, but because you appreciate your marvelous inheritance of divine qualities.

Remember that every time you talk depreciatingly of yourself, no matter if you do not really believe it, if you do it for effect, that is, telling others of your hard luck, admitting that you cannot get along as do other people, that you cannot make money and save it, that you don't seem to have any money sense, you are lowering your estimate of yourself, your ideal of yourself, and this is the pattern for your life building.

There is a, sculptor in you who is working to the pattern which; you hold up to him, and if you hold up a defective, weak, deficient, dwarfed pattern,; it will be built into the very structure of your being.

What you think of yourself will come to you; what you believe regarding yourself, your ability, your future, will tend to come to you. What you expect of yourself is this very instant being wrought into the texture of your being.

Always think of yourself as lucky. Never allow yourself to think of yourself in any other way. Say to yourself: "I AM good luck. I must be lucky, because I AM a part of the divinity which can never fail. I partake of omnipotence because I AM a child of Omnipotence, a partner of the Almighty. It is my nature to be lucky. I was made to be lucky. I was born to win. I AM the child of the King of kings. A princely inheritance is coming to me, and I must conduct myself with that respect for myself and for my ability which becomes a prince of the Most High."

Constantly meditate on what a marvelous thing it is to have such an inheritance, to be conscious that you are really are a god in the making, that there is a divinity within you which can never be lost, an omnipotence which can triumph over any handicap, of earthly, inheritance or accident.

Learn to reinforce yourself, to refresh and reinvigorate yourself by tapping the great cosmic intelligence through the subconscious mind, by going much into the silence, and communing with the All-Good. You should no more harbor a fear thought, a worry thought, a jealousy, envy or hatred thought, a selfish thought; than you would listen to the temptation to steal. These things rob you of your peace of mind, your power, force and vitality, your poise as well as your comfort.

You would not allow a thief to ramble through your home to steal. Why should you allow your enemy thoughts to roam through your mind without a protest? A dwarfed ideal means a dwarfed mind, a dwarfed future, a dwarfed career. Your conviction of yourself, your belief regarding yourself, your future, your ability, will all reappear in your career.

Someone says: "Dare to fling out into the great cosmic mind greater assurance about yourself; dare to have greater confidence; dare to believe in yourself and your mission. Have a grander ideal, a nobler aspiration."

A man must have faith in the thing he is trying to do or trying to get. His hope, his confidence, his expectation are powerful factors in the gaining of his ambition. They are searchlights on the horizon, descrying opportunity from afar.

Nothing can defeat you or rob you of success but yourself. No conditions, however inhospitable, can swamp you, or thwart your life aim . . if you have a life aim. Your own weakness only can do that . . your lack of determination, your lack of energy, your lack of backbone, your lack of confidence in yourself. Nothing in the world can make you a nonentity; no mischance's, no conditions, no environment, nothing but yourself can do that. You can be a nobody if you will, or a somebody if you will; it is right up to you.

You can make a success of your life; you can send your influence down the ages, or you can go to your grave a useless nobody, without ever having made a ripple in the current of the life of your day. Your luck, good or bad, is in yourself.

Thinking of your misfortune or hard luck in not being as well placed or as well conditioned as others is fatal to success and happiness, because we must go in the direction in which we face, and we face the way we think, the way we talk, the way we act. We are like weather vanes and we turn this way and that way according as we think. Our thoughts, our emotions, our feelings are like the wind which turns the weather vane.

I know of no one thing that will have a greater influence upon your life than the forming of the habit of thinking of yourself as lucky, regarding yourself as extremely fortunate in your birth, in your location, in your adaptation to your particular line of work, as fortunate in your ambition and in your chance in life to make good. We are just beginning to learn that we are made, fashioned and molded by our thoughts, which are forces as real as is the force of electricity. Our thought is constantly shaping us to correspond with it. We are our own architects, our own sculptors. We are always reshaping, remolding ourselves to fit our thoughts and our emotions, our motives, our general attitude towards life. If we think of ourselves as being always lucky, we may not be extraordinary examples of good luck, but we shall always be happy, smiling and contented, believing that everything that comes to us is the best that we could possibly attain.

WHERE LUCK HAS BEEN FOUND

In thrift and foresight.

In thorough preparation for one's life work. In mental alertness.

In always being ready to lend a helping hand wherever and whenever needed. In being tactful and a good mixer.

In holding the efficiency ideal of oneself and one's capabilities. In downright, constant hard work.

In being ready for the opportunity when it came.

In courtesy, kindness, and consideration toward everybody.

In helping oneself instead of looking to others for boosts, capital, or favors of any sort.

In doing one's work a little better than others did theirs.

In not being satisfied with anything but one's best, never accepting one's second best or a botched job.

In always carrying some reading matter in one's pocket, so that spare time could be utilized while waiting for trains, or for those who were tardy in appointments, by reading for self improvement.

In being cheerful, no matter how dark the outlook. In trying to make good in every possible way, while never taking advantage of others.

In beginning the thing which something within one said one could and ought to do, no matter what obstacles stood in the way; by obeying one's good impulses promptly, before they quit prodding one.

In never allowing oneself to believe that he was born to be poor, a failure, a mediocre sort of a man or woman.

In carrying the victorious attitude in everything,' looking like a winner, talking like a winner, and radiating the confidence of a winner.

In holding that the good things of the world were not made for a favored few, but for all God's children.

In substituting clear grit and persistency for the advantages which many others enjoyed from birth.

In believing that the best part of one's salary was not in one's pay envelope but in the chance to make good in every bit of work that passed through one's hands.

In the opportunity to absorb the secrets of one's employer's business; to learn for pay what he bought dearly, perhaps, after failure and an enormous expenditure of money and time, and, possibly, the shortening of his life in the process.

In keeping eyes and ears open, and mouth closed most of the time.

In indomitable perseverance, a determination which knew no give up or retreat; in everlastingly pushing ahead whether one could see the goal or not.

In the right attitude towards life, towards one's work, towards everything and everybody.

In choosing one's company, associating only with people who were doing their best to get on and get up in the world.

In the consciousness of one's partnership with the All-Good, the All-Supply, with the Infinite Mind.

In learning, through mental chemistry, to neutralize the things which kill one's best efforts . . fear, worry, anxiety, jealousy, envy, malice, touchiness, anger, and thus to keep one's mind free for the larger things.

Chapter XIV

Self-Faith and Prosperity

- Faith unlocks the door to power.

- It is the men and women with a stupendous faith, a colossal self confidence, who do the great deeds, accomplish the "impossible."

- No matter what your need is, put it into the hands of faith. Do not ask how, or why, or when. Just do your level best, and have faith, which is the great miracle worker of the ages.

- Faith opens the door, sees the way. It is a soul sense, a spiritual foresight which peers far beyond the vision of the physical eyes and sees the reality long before it takes material form.

- A one-talent man with an overmastering self-faith often accomplishes infinitely more than a ten-talent man who does not believe in 'himself.

- Faith increases confidence, carries conviction, multiplies ability. It doesn't think or guess. It is not discouraged or blinded by mountains of difficulties, because it sees through them . . sees the goal beyond.

- There is a tremendous creative power in the conviction that we can do a thing.

- You may succeed when others do not believe in you, when everybody else denounces you even, but ever when you do not believe in yourself.

A colossal faith in himself, a sublime self-confidence that never wavered in any situation, was the great secret of Theodore Roosevelt's many-sided success, for he believed in Roosevelt, as Napoleon believed in Napoleon. There was nothing timid or half-hearted about him. He went at everything he undertook with that gigantic assurance, that tremendous confidence, that whole-hearted belief in his power to do the thing, that half wins the battle before it begins. Without any pretension to genius, as he himself said, with only the qualities of the average man, by intensive application he so developed every power of mind and body that he raised himself head and shoulders above the average man.

"According to thy faith be it unto thee," is just as scientific in the world of affairs as any demonstrated truth of science. Whether your ambition be to build up a great business, to accumulate a fortune, to win political power and influence, to make a great name in science, in politics, in journalism, in whatsoever field your bent inclines, a superb faith in yourself is the imperative price.

Most of the people in the great down-and-out army failed because they lacked faith in themselves. They doubted their power to make good. They did not believe enough in themselves, while they believed too much in circumstances and in help from other people. They waited for luck, waited for outside capital, for a boost, for influence, for a pull, for someone or something outside of them to help them. They depended too much upon everything else but themselves. And now they remain in the great failure army because they are not willing to pay the price for what they want, or they haven't the courage to try again. They lack that which faith gives . . bulldog grit, tenacity, determination.

Self-confidence has ever been the best substitute for friends, pedigree, influence, and money. It is the best capital in the world; it has mastered more obstacles, overcome more difficulties, and carried through more enterprises than any other human quality. It has made more American millionaires than any other human force or quality.

It was the ambition to succeed, backed by the "I can and I will" spirit of self confidence that enabled a poor boy, after repeated and disheartening failures, to give New York City its most beautiful business structure . . the Woolworth Building. Foreign architects have pronounced this one of the most beautiful in the world, "a dream in stone."

The man who brought it into being was Frank W. Woolworth. Born on a small farm in New York State, this man had no other heritage than a sound body and the native grit and self-reliance which have carried so many Americans to their goal. He began his career in a little grocery store, in the corner of a freight shed, owned by the station-master at Great Bend, N. Y. There he acted as grocery clerk and assistant station-master without pay. His first salary in a larger store was $3.50 a week. In spite of persistent hard work for years, disappointment and failures were the only visible results of his efforts.

But in spite of hard luck and desperate poverty he hung on until fortune smiled, and then he began to establish the Woolworth five and ten cent stores, with the result that before his death, a few years ago, he had over a thousand stores with a capital of $65,000,000, giving employment to many thousands of people. He had also erected the great Woolworth Building, and, overtopping all, he had built a manly, lovable character. He left an example of honest success, wrung from the hardest conditions, that will be an inspiration to every youth who has an ambition to lift himself from poverty to power, while at the same time rendering great service to the world.

Henry Ford is another American who started in life with nothing but brain power and a belief in Henry's ability to do the thing he wanted to do. After many ups and downs, working first as a youth on the home farm near Detroit, later as a machinist, and as chief engineer of the Edison Illuminating Company, always plugging away in his spare time, developing the invention on which he began to work as a small boy, his farm tractor, he had passed the age of forty before he made acquaintance with success. Indeed, at forty he was supposed by those who could not gauge his character, his indomitable will, his faith in himself and his power to wring victory from defeat, to be a failure. But he was even then engaged in organizing the Ford Motor Company and well started on the way to the phenomenal success that has made his name known all over the world.

Now, at fifty-eight, Mr. Ford, many times a millionaire, is the head of an army of over 80,000 industrial workers, besides many others indirectly identified with his interests. He is owner of thirty-five manufacturing plants in the United States. The largest of these, which is at Highland Park, Detroit, employs 40,000 people in making Ford cars, while at the River Rouge, plant, nine miles from Detroit, auto parts and tractors are turned out. He has a $5,000,000 tractor plant at Cork, Ireland, also assembling plants at Cadiz, Copenhagen, Bordeaux, and Manchester, England, and two in South America.

In addition to all this, Mr. Ford owns The Dearborn Independent, a weekly publication, the Detroit, Toledo & Ironton Railroad, and a farm of 5,000 acres, west of Detroit, the food producer of which is sold to the employees of the Ford factories at cost prices. Nor is this industrial giant satisfied to stop here. His benevolent activities go hand in hand with his industrial achievements. His $5,000,000 hospital in Detroit, and his school for boys where they can "learn while they earn," are samples of what he is doing in this direction.

It is men of this type, men with one hundred per cent, of faith, who kill their doubts, strangle their fears, get up every time they fall and push to the front regardless of obstacles, who win out in life. As long as you live in an atmosphere saturated with failure thought you cannot do the biggest thing possible to you, because you cannot have a hundred per cent, of faith; and, remember, that your achievements, your success, will depend upon the percentage of your faith in yourself and in what you are trying to do.

A great many of those who fail in life, or who attain only mediocre positions, keep themselves back by self-depreciation, by a lack of faith in their own powers, the suggestion of their own inferiority. Nothing is more detrimental to success than this sort of mental attitude. It would take the stamina out of a Napoleon. The instant you acknowledge that you are incapable of doing the thing you attempt to do, or that anything can permanently block the way to the goal of your ambition, you set up a barrier to your success that no amount of hard work can remove. He can who thinks he can, holds true in every situation of life.

When someone asked Admiral Farragut if he were prepared for defeat, he said: "I certainly am not. Any man who is prepared for defeat would be half defeated before he commenced."

It makes a great difference whether you go into a thing to win, with clenched teeth and resolute will; whether you are prepared at the very outset to make your fortune, to succeed in your business or profession, to put through the thing you have set your heart on, or whether you start in with the idea that you will begin and work your way along gradually, and continue if you do not find too many obstacles, but that if all doesn't go well there is always a way to back out. To go into a thing determined to win, to feel that self-assurance, that inward sense of power that makes one master of the situation, is half the battle; while, on the other hand, to be prepared for defeat; to anticipate it is, just as Admiral Farragut said, to be half defeated before one commences. You must bum all your bridges behind you, leaving no temptation to retreat when things look black ahead.

The men who built up America's great industries and made enormous fortunes . . the Peabodys, the Astors, the Goulds, the Vanderbilts, the Morgans, the Rockefellers, the Carnegies, the Schwabs, the Hills, the Fords, the Marshall Fields, the Wanamakers, . . all the people who have done and are doing big things in the world, . . not only had the faith which does the "impossible" but they have been exacting trainers of themselves. They do not handle themselves with gloves. They hold themselves right up to stern discipline. They do not allow dawdling, idling; they put a ban on laziness, indifference, vacillation; they fix their eye on the goal and sacrifice everything which interferes with their ambition, everything which stands in the way of the larger success. They know that he who is enamored of his easy chair, who thinks too much of his comfort and ease, his good times with his companions evenings, who thinks too much of the pleasures of the senses, will never get anywhere.

There is no possible way of defeating a human being who is victory organized. If he has the faith that moves mountains, if he has winning stuff in him, he is going to win, no matter what stands in the way. There is no holding him down, because, in addition to his unswerving belief in himself, he is ready to pay to the last cent the price that even the most gifted among men must pay for success. Nothing is denied to one who is willing to pay the price for it. Only your own inertia, your own lack of faith in yourself, your own lack of push and' determination, can thwart your ambition.

Your longings are the proofs that you can back them up with realities. Faith makes light of obstacles, because it increases ability and multiplies power. Joan of Arc multiplied herself ten thousand times by her faith; multiplied her ability a million times by her conviction that she was God-ordained to restore the throne of France and drive the enemy from her soil. She was ready to make any sacrifice to save her country, and every sacrifice she made, every obstacle she overcame, made her stronger to accomplish the great task she had undertaken. Without work we know that faith is of no avail. Everything depends on the "hustle" with which we back it.

The only real power one ever gains is won in the struggle to overcome obstacles. It is the effort of brain and muscle put forth in the actual doing of the thing, the downright hard working, the vigorous thinking and planning that make the strong man, the man who reaches the goal of his ambition.

It was everlasting hustling, added to his indomitable self-confidence that made Alfred Harmsworth, now Lord Northcliffe, one of the wealthiest men in England, and one of the most successful publishers in the world. In an interview he said, "I feel that whatever position I have attained is due to focusing my energies and time. When I went into journalism I made up my mind that I would master the business of editing and publishing. This is a vast specialty, but then I was very young and had a good deal of self-confidence."

This self-confidence was one of his most marked characteristics even as a boy. When only fifteen, while attending an English grammar school, he started a little school paper in which he said: "I have it on the best authority that this paper is to be a marked success." And a marked success it proved, as has every enterprise to which this hustling, self-confident journalist has put his hand. At twenty-one young Harmsworth started in the regular publishing business with a little weekly called "Answers," which was also a success. Before he had reached the age of thirty he was a millionaire publisher and at thirty-six he was the head of the largest publishing business in the world. Today Lord Northcliffe, who is regarded as one of the most powerful and influential men in England, is worth a great many million dollars, besides owning two million dollars' worth of paper-making timber-land in Newfoundland.

We get in this life whatever we concentrate upon with all our might and main. Our success or failure is in our own hands. Many who are complaining that the door to success is locked and barred against them, because they are too poor to get an education, or they have no one to help them to get the position they desire, are not succeeding, are not getting the thing they want, because they are not willing to make the necessary effort to succeed. They are not willing to do the hard work, not willing to get right down on their marrow bones and hustle. They may have faith in their ability, but they haven't the energy to put the ability to work and make it do things for them. They want someone else to do the pushing, to make things happen for them.

No man ever climbed to success on another's back. He must hustle, make things happen himself, or fail.

Joseph Pulitzer, a young boy who came to America from Germany, was so poor when he landed he had to sleep on the benches in City Hall Park, New York, in front of the space now occupied by the World Building, which he built later. This poor youth had so much faith and so much energy that he made millions out of a paper which was pretty nearly a failure in the hands of the people from whom he bought it. No matter how humble your position, though you be but a section hand on a railroad, a street cleaner, a day laborer or a messenger boy, if you have faith in yourself, in your vision, and back up your faith with downright hard work, nothing can keep you from realizing your vision. A fortune is accumulated by the same means that make a man a successful musician, or politician, or inventor. Faith and work have magic in them. It is faith that leads the way in all undertakings. It is the divine faculty which connects men with the great Source of all supply, the Source of all intelligence, the Source of all power, of all possibilities. If you only have faith, one hundred per cent, faith in yourself, in your life work, in anything you undertake, you cannot fail.

THE GREAT CONQUEROR

I AM that which is back of all achievement, which has led the way to success, to happiness, through the ages.

I crossed an unknown ocean with Columbus, who without me would never have discovered America.

I was with Washington at Valley Forge; and but for me he would not have succeeded in liberating the American colonies and making them a nation.

I went through the Civil War with Lincoln, and guided his pen when he wrote the Emancipation Proclamation that freed millions of human beings from slavery.

I was with the English patriots who forced King John to sign that great charter of human rights . . the Magna Charta.

I was back of those who forced the French Revolution . . and of those who signed the American Declaration of Independence.

I was with Christ when all his disciples and friends had fled; and I cheered and comforted the martyrs at the stake . . all the men and women who gave their lives to maintain the truths he taught.

I crossed the ocean with Cyrus W. Field fifty times before his great undertaking, the ocean cable, was perfected. I was on the ship with him when the cable parted in mid-ocean, after the first message had passed over it, and gave him courage to persist when the work had to be done all over again.

I AM the locksmith who can unlock all doors, whom no obstacle can hold back, no difficulty or disaster dishearten, no misfortune swerve from my purpose.

I AM a friend to the down-and-outs, the unfortunates, those to whom life has been a great disappointment. If these people would take hold of me I would turn them around so that they would face their goal and go toward it instead of turning their back on it and going in the opposite direction; they would face the sun and let the shadows fall behind instead of in front of them as in the past.

I AM a booster, an optimist, one who always sees something of hope in every human being, for I know that there is a God in every one; that men and women are gods in the making; that they are all capable of doing infinitely more, infinitely better things, than they have yet done.

No matter how bad the conditions which confront me, I wear a smile, for I know that the sun is always behind the clouds and that after a time the storm will pass and the sun will shine again.

I see triumph beyond temporary defeat. I look past obstacles which discourage most people, for I know that they become smaller as one approaches them; and experience has shown me that but a very small fraction of the things which people dread, fear, and worry about ever happen.

If you know me, if you believe in me, work with me, cling to me, no matter how full of failures and disappointments your past has been, I will help you to overcome adverse conditions and crown you with success, for I conquer all difficulties.

I AM FAITH

Chapter XV

Fear And Worry Demagnetize The Mind .. How To Get Rid Of Them

• A day of worry is more exhausting than a week of work.

• Fear impairs health, paralyzes efficiency, kills happiness, shortens life.

• Crossing bridges before they come to them puts more victims in the great failure army, in the ranks of the unhappy and inefficient, than almost anything else. The fear of tomorrow, anticipation of the trials and troubles just ahead, robs multitudes of the strength and enthusiasm that would enable them to make today a glorious success.

• The man who fears tomorrow is afraid of life, and that sort of man is a coward. He has no faith in God or in himself. He will never amount to much.

• If you have had an unfortunate experience; if you have made a failure in your undertaking; if you have been placed in an embarrassing position; if you have fallen and hurt yourself by a false step; if you have been slandered and abused .. forget it. There is not a single redeeming feature in these memories, and their ghosts will rob you of many a happy hour.

• It is not the work we have actually done, the burdens we have actually borne, the troubles that have actually come that have furrowed deep wrinkles in the faces of many of us, and made us prematurely old; it is the useless fears and worries we have lugged along with us that have done all the mischief.

Dr. William F. Warren, a former president of Boston University, in an address to the students said: "No command or entreaty occurs so many times in the Bible as this emphatic one, 'Fear not!' I once thought to prepare a sermon on it, but it proved too fruitful for me. From Genesis to Apocalypse 'Fear not' seemed an unending refrain. I began to count the occurrences; soon I had twenty, then thirty, then forty, then fifty.

Glancing from fifty to seventy I noticed that other words, like those of our Lord, 'Let not your heart be troubled, neither let it be afraid,' meant exactly the same thing; so that my count, however complete, never represents the true total."

Yet there are millions of people in America, in every part of the world, whose minds are constantly filled with the fear of something. From the cradle to the grave, fear throws its black shadow over mankind, marring and stunting vast multitudes of lives, making people wretched, keeping them in poverty and inferiority, driving many to insanity and death.

Not long ago a girl in New York slipped on an icy pavement and fell to the street. At the moment an approaching truck passed so close to her that the wheels almost touched her. Terror-stricken at the thought of her danger, the girl imagined that the horses and the truck had actually passed over her. When picked from the street and taken to a nearby hospital in an ambulance she was raving about the horses and the truck running over her, and finally became insane.

This tragedy was purely the result of imagination, for there was not a scratch of any kind on the girl's body, not even her clothes having been touched. Like the fears and worries that makes the lives of so many people wretched failures, the thing that drove away her reason had no reality. The thing she feared never happened, but the effect of her fear, the conjuring up in her mind a picture of death, or of a mutilated body, brought upon her something worse, something more disastrous; for no other loss can compare with the blotting out of the light of reason.

The wrong kind of thought is daily bringing disaster, frightful tragedies and misfortunes into the lives of men and women everywhere. A short time ago during a severe thunderstorm, a woman became unconscious from fright and died. An examination showed that there was no heart trouble, and that the lightning had not touched her; but it appeared that all her life the woman had felt a great nervous dread of thunder and lightning, and finally the thing she had long feared and expected came to her. It was not the lightning, however, but her fear of it that had killed her.

Multitudes today are seriously affected through fear of disease. They fear and expect influenza or pneumonia, and so invite these diseases. Their fear destroys their disease-resisting power and predisposes them to become victims. We had a striking example of this soon after America entered the World War, when the influenza epidemic made its appearance in the soldiers' camps, and then spread through the country like wildfire. In an incredibly short time, thousands of victims, mostly young people, were carried off by the dread disease. Fear was at the bottom of its widespread destructiveness.

Through the influence of the fear thought, the gloomy, discouraged thought, the disease thought, the failure thought, . . all sorts of morbid thoughts and imaginings . . people are cutting off their divine supply, ruining their health, their possibilities of success and happiness. The fear of death, the fear of disease, the fear of coming to want, the fear of failure, the fear of what our neighbors will think and say, the fear of accidents, anticipating misfortunes, bad luck generally, the fear of the future, of the miscarriage of our plans, fear of this, fear of that and the other, makes this, the most negative and destructive of all human emotions, the closest companion of our daily lives. Fear is the damnable ghost that is always bobbing up to rob us of our legitimate enjoyment, of our peace of mind, of our courage and strength, of our faith in ourselves and our ability to rise above conditions that cramp and hold us in thrall.

Take the fear of poverty alone. Consider the misery it has caused. Who can ever estimate what havoc this single fear has played in the race history, . . the fear of coming to want, the torture of visualizing the wolf approaching the door; the agony of possible suffering for our loved ones if we cannot provide for their needs! Oh, this terrible fear of want! We read it in the faces of multitudes of people who never have learned to demonstrate supply, who know nothing of the law of prosperity and never dream that holding in mind this fear of want, this horror of poverty, having the conviction that they are doomed to be poor all their lives, is driving away from them the supply, the opulence they long for. They do not know that it is only by holding the prosperity thought, the thought of abundance; by picturing themselves in connection with limitless supply, visualizing what they want instead of what they don't want, that they will get away from the poverty they hate and connect with the very fountainhead of supply.

How many men and women deplete their strength and thus lessen their earning power by lying awake at night worrying over their business problems, their home problems, the expanding needs of their growing families, and wondering where their supply is coming from! Has this fear and worry business ever done anything for you?

Has it ever added to your income, to your health, to your comfort or your happiness? Has it ever solved your problems or helped you in any way? Hasn't it always done just the reverse? Most of us know from bitter experience how the vicious fear and worry habit uses up our mental powers, saps our life forces, cuts down our efficiency, robs us of hope, courage, and enthusiasm; in fact, cuts down our success chances fully seventy-five per cent.

The great secret of success, and of happiness, too, is to have faith; to face life with courage and confidence, and not to anticipate trouble. It is greatly to our discredit that, in spite of the fact that America is the richest, the most prosperous, the most productive and resourceful country in the world, we are a nation of worriers. The majority of us don't face life in the right way; we fear and worry more than any other people on earth. The Public Health Service in Washington realizing this, and knowing the evil effects of such a mental attitude in breeding nervous diseases and other life stranglers, some time ago issued a bulletin, the burden of which was, "Don't worry." "So far as is known," it said, "no bird ever tried to build more nests than its neighbor.

No fox ever fretted because he had only one hole in which to hide. No squirrel ever died of anxiety lest he should not lay by enough nuts for two winters instead of for one, and no dog ever lost any sleep over the fact that he did not have enough bones laid aside for his declining years."

In other words, we might take a lesson from what we call the "lower animals" in not worrying about our future supply, which is one of the chief sources of our anxiety. We say they cannot reason, but they show far more intelligence in this matter than we do; they show that faith we lack, that faith which the Christ so constantly tried to implant in his disciples: "Therefore take no thought [that is, no anxious thought] saying what shall we eat? or What shall we drink? or, Wherewithal shall we be clothed? . . . For your heavenly Father knoweth that ye have need of all these things . . Take therefore no thought for the morrow; for the morrow shall take thought for the things of itself. Sufficient unto the day is the evil thereof."

Rich and poor alike are victims of the unreasonable fear of lack of supply, lack of means, as all panics and business depressions show, for it is the wealthy who through withdrawal of cash from business and banks, first disturb public credit. Of course not all of us anticipate financial shortages. There are many who, though not what the world calls wealthy, do not worry over money matters: instead they allow fear and worry to get hold of them through some other obsession, the anticipation of failure in their work, a breakdown in their health, some misfortune to their children, the fear that some member of the family may go wrong, bring disgrace upon themselves and all connected with them.

Now, the man or the woman who is constantly afraid of some impending evil, always dreading, anticipating something that will work to his or her injury, or who is worrying about something that has already happened, is lacking in the most essential character and success elements . . courage, self-confidence, and faith in the divine God-power in the great within of man, which makes him greater than anything that can happen to him. Such a fear-stricken, worrying soul shows by his mental attitude that he does not believe in God; that he is not anchored in the consciousness of the limitless power and resources that are at his command; that he lacks confidence in the infinite Power that creates, preserves, and upholds the universe.

Don't be one of those craven souls; don't allow yourself to be robbed of your birthright . . success and happiness. Even if you have the fear and worry habit, you can free yourself from it. Professor William James says that fear is conquerable; that it has at last become possible for large numbers of people to pass from the cradle to the grave without ever having a pang of genuine fear. There is no doubt that fear and worry, those terrible evils that have so long cursed mankind and held back the development of the race can be absolutely driven out of our lives. And you will not get very far, my friend, nor climb very high, until you rid yourself of your fears and doubts, of the worry and discouragement which are blighting your life, strangling your aspirations and obscuring your ideals. How many really able people are struggling along, barely making a living, getting nowhere near the realization of their youthful dreams, because they listened to the whisperings of those human traitors, the fears and doubts and worries which held them back from doing what they were sent into the world to do!

It is for you to determine now whether you shall continue to be the slave of fear and worry; to lead the narrow, pinched life, limited in all its possibilities and power of expression, that you have so long been living, or whether you shall leave it forever behind you and rise to the height of your divine power and possible achievement through claiming your kinship with God . . with whom all things are possible. You don't need to make any preparations, to delay for anything, or to ask anyone's assistance. You can break away from your discouraging past; you can change your poverty stricken environment and plant your feet firmly in the path of attainment; you can do this instantly by reversing your thought. Through the exercise of your divine power you can change your thought at will; and to change the thought is the first step in the cure of any evil condition.

Worry, anxiety, lack of faith, self-depreciation, timidity, lack of self-confidence, these are all expressions of fear, and cannot exist in your mind for a moment in the presence of the courage, thought, the mental suggestion of fearlessness, self confidence, self-reliance; the image of yourself as strong, resourceful, courageous, in touch with the infinite reservoir of divine power and energy that flows to you from your Source, the Omnipotent One, the Creator of the universe. Instead of picturing trouble and misfortune ahead, brooding over the difficulties that confront you, and fearing you will never be able to get past them, flood your mind with triumphant thoughts, with the thought of the power that is stored in the great within of you, always wanting to be used, always more than a match for the giant fear that tries to frighten you with bogies, with unrealities that have no existence outside of your troubled imagination.

No fear, no anxiety, no discouragement, no doubt or apprehension regarding the future, can possibly enter your mind while it is filled with thoughts of hope, of courage, of assurance, of all power and strength through your connection with Infinite Power.

You will find it a great help in driving out fear and worry to express strong, courageous sentiments aloud. When alone say to any enemy thoughts that would frighten or harass you: "Get out of my mental kingdom. I will not allow you to come between me and my Father. I AM a son of God, and I was never made to cower before anything; to be frightened and turned from my purpose by a mere thought. I AM brave, courageous, afraid of nothing; I AM a conqueror of fear, not its slave."

Remember, that as God's child you have nothing to fear, for through your kinship with Omnipotence, the Source of all courage, of all supply, of all beauty, of all good, no evil thing has power over you. The next time that something which you feel is holding you back whispers to you, "Don't do that; you'll make a fool of yourself. Many a stronger, abler man than you are has failed in trying to do that same thing. Many with more ability, in more favorable circumstances, with more influence, and with outside help, have failed in the ambitious undertaking you are going to attempt, poor and ill-equipped as you are. You had better be careful; make sure that you are going to succeed before you begin," . . don't listen to the evil thing, for it is fear that is whispering to you. And it is lying as it has lied to millions who came before you, as it will lie to millions who come after you. He who listens to it will never enter into his heritage as a child of God, his birthright of peace, power, harmony, success, abundance.

Fear and doubt, discouragement and worry are always found together. They belong to the same family, and work for the same end . . to rob people of energy and ambition, and to keep them from doing what they were made to do. They have ever been the great retarders of human progress, the great killers of ability, the blighters of happiness, the stranglers of aspirations, the murderers of success. They have kept untold millions in mediocrity and have caused utter failure and ruin of other millions who could have done big things had they gone ahead, made the most of their ability and worked steadily for the realization of their early visions. God never meant any of His children to be victims of fear, worry, discouragement or any evil specter of the imagination.

He intended that their lives should be triumphant achievements, glorious successes, and not miserable failures.

Whatever tries to hold you back from the pursuit of a high ambition is your enemy. When fear tries to shake your confidence in yourself, to keep you from beginning the things which you long to do and feel that you have the ability to carry through; when you feel yourself weakening before some unusual difficulty and think of turning back; when you are tempted to worry about something that has happened, or that you think may happen; when you doubt your ability to do this or that, and think you would better not undertake anything that is not perfectly sure to come out all right, drive all such suggestions out of your mind. Asserting your divine power as a son of God, say to yourself: "Now, it is right up to me to make good. I can't give up this way and turn coward. It would be unmanly, contemptible. I AM able to overcome this thing; it has no power to keep me down.

No matter whether I can see the way or not I shall keep going, forging ahead. No matter what obstacles may come up I shall keep headed toward the port of my ambition. Nothing has power over me, but what I give it. I will not allow anything to thwart my purpose and destroy my career. I can and I will rise above all my troubles, above all my mistakes and errors. Nothing can keep me from my own, for from now on I will work with the God in me. I will not be overcome by any enemy; I will overcome."

Nothing but ourselves can make God's promise to man void, . . "Behold I have set before you an open door which no man can shut." The door that leads to your ambition, to the fuller, happier, more abundant life you desire is wide open. No one can close it but yourself. Nothing but your doubts, your fears, your pessimism, your worry, your lack of faith in the Creator and in yourself can prevent you from matching your desires with reality.

Chapter XVI

Good Cheer and Prosperity

- Smiles attract dollars as they attract everything that is good and wholesome.

- The man who keeps his machinery well lubricated with love, goodwill and good cheer can withstand the hard jolts and disappointments of life infinitely better than the man who always looks on the dark side.

- "No smiles, no business."

- Good cheer is one of man's greatest benefactors. It has helped him from giving up to despair even when starvation has stared him in the face and all mankind seemed against him.

- When a man chooses good cheer for his companion he never talks of hard times or carries a picture of poverty or want in his mind.

- The cheerful man is preeminently the useful man.

If I were asked to name the one thing that would help the human race more than any other, I would perhaps say, "More cheerfulness, . . good cheer, keeping sweet under all circumstances."

More cheerfulness means more life, more happiness, more success, more efficiency, more character, a larger future. The cheerful man does not cramp his mind and take half views of things.

Have you never noticed that, as a rule, it is the cheerful, hopeful, optimistic people who succeed, and that it is the sour, morose, gloomy natures who fail or plod along in mediocrity, who never amount to anything? A habit of cheerfulness enables one to transmute apparent misfortunes into real blessings.

More cheerfulness will help you all along the line of hie. It will help you to bear your burdens; it will help you to overcome obstacles; it will increase your courage, strengthen your initiative, make you more effective, more popular, more helpful. It will make you a happier, more successful man or woman; it will transform and beautify the humblest and homeliest surroundings.

Cheerfulness means poise, serenity, a sane, wholesome, well-balanced outlook on life. The cheerful man knows that there is much misery, but that misery need not be the rule of life. There is no philosophy like cheerfulness. No one can estimate the healthful, uplifting power of one cheerful life, one serene, balanced soul. The hopeful, cheerful nature is constructive. He who has formed a habit of looking at the bright side of things has a great advantage over the chronic dyspeptic who sees no good in anything. Shakespeare says:

> "A merry heart goes all the day,
> Your sad tires in a mile — a"

There is no other life habit which can give such prolific returns in happiness and satisfaction as that of being cheerful and sweet under all circumstances. The cheerful man's thought sculptures his face into beauty and touches his manner with grace.

Why not resolve that, whatever comes or does not come to you, whether you fail in your undertaking or succeed, you will keep cheerful, hopeful, optimistic, and be grateful for the good things that are yours? In almost everything we can find some happiness if we look for it. The trouble with us is that we generally want more to make us happy than we deserve, and we are not grateful enough for the many things that are ours to enjoy.

How many of us might learn a lesson from the poor little girl living in the slums of a great city who took a prize at a flower show. When asked how she managed to raise her beautiful plant in the dark alley where her home was, she answered that there was a little space between two tall buildings through which a bit of sunshine came in, and that by moving the plant as the sun moved she had managed to keep it in the sunshine and to produce the prize flower. We all have at least a little sunshine in our lives, something to be thankful for, and by turning our faces to it, we could manage somehow to keep growing, but we don't make the most of the little sun we do have, as the little girl did.

There is much that even the poorest of us might enjoy in the common, everyday life, if we would only now and then stop, look, listen, think and contemplate; if we would only try to see things in their true light, to hear the voices of Nature, to see the miracles going on about us on every hand in God's great laboratory. We could be happy in the most ordinary situations in life if we would only learn to delve down into the common things, to appreciate them, to see their marvelous beauty.

But no, it is always what we want, not what we have, that claims our attention. It's the far-away thing, it's tomorrow, next year, when we are better off, when we are a little better able to have luxuries, to have an automobile, to travel, then we'll enjoy ourselves and have a good time.

I know a man who, although very poor, can manage to get more comfort out of a real tough, discouraging situation than anyone else I have ever known. I have often seen him when he did not have a dollar to his name, with a wife to support, yet he was always buoyant, happy, cheerful, contented. He would even make fun out of an embarrassing situation; see something ludicrous in his poverty. He never was in a difficulty that blotted out the sun for him, for he always saw light ahead; and there is no doubt in my mind but that ultimately he will be a big success in his business.

If we are cheerful and contented all nature smiles with us; the air is balmier, the sky clearer, the earth has a brighter green, the trees have a richer foliage, the flowers are more fragrant, the birds sing more sweetly, and the sun, moon and stars are more beautiful.

Money itself has very little to do with happiness. Some of the most wretched men and women I have ever known anything about have been very rich. They could have everything that money could buy, but their money didn't bring them happiness; it didn't bring contentment or harmony into their homes. In fact, if many of these men and women had been poor, they would have been infinitely happier.

High-minded cheerfulness is found in great souls, self-poised and confident in their own heaven-aided powers.

Epictetus, the pagan philosopher, proved in his life the truth of his own words . . "A man can be happy without wealth, without family, without office or honor, without health, without anything that the world seeks after." There are few of us lacking in all these things, but we are not happy because we are not normal as Epictetus was.

Multitudes of people think that happiness consists largely in getting rid of disagreeable things, disagreeable duties, in getting rid of the dry, dreary, routine of life, the compulsory drudgery: in getting rid of the responsibility of providing ways and means. They think they would be happy if they could only get freedom from the irksome things of life, the pinching, the hitching along from day to day, which comes from trying to do business on limited capital; freedom from duns, frets, and naggings; freedom from the thousand and one pricks and annoyances of the daily workaday life. In short, most of us think we would surely be happy if we were released from the anxiety of the bread-and-butter question; if we did not have to think about the cost of things or the ways and means of getting them.

But, as far as we know, rich people are no happier than poor people. With them it is largely a question of shifting anxiety and worry to other things. The moment people get beyond the necessity of working, beyond anxiety about the cost of living, there are many other enemies of their happiness to creep into their lives and destroy their harmony . . if they allow them.

The things which torment us, which keep us from being cheerful and happy are the boomerangs that come back to us from our wrong doing; all the mental wounds from which we suffer are self-inflicted. No human being can possibly injure another without injuring himself more. He cannot do wrong without paying for it in corresponding suffering. In a similar way our thoughts react upon our prosperity and happiness.

The new philosophy shows us that we do not have to die to come to our own, to reach our heaven, the heaven of our dreams, that the grave is not the portal of paradise, but that paradise is here and we are living in paradise but don't know it, because we can't see it, except as we get a glimpse of heaven shining through in all that is beautiful and sweet and lovely and kindly. It teaches us that paradise is gained by right living and right thinking, right acting, by practicing the God qualities. It teaches us that we can never awake in His likeness until we practice His qualities, the qualities which make up divinity. It teaches us that our consciousness of our oneness with the One is the source of all our strength, the source of all our power, the secret of all our success that is worthwhile," the source of our healing.

The new philosophy teaches us to face toward the light whether we can see the goal or not, always to look in the hopeful direction. It teaches us to look toward success, toward opulence, toward prosperity, no matter how poverty stricken our environment seems. It teaches us to look toward the perfect man that God planned, that God intended, not to see the sick or the diseased or the immoral, sinful, criminal or defective man. It teaches us that when we look at human beings through suspicious eyes, through distrusting eyes, through doubting eyes, through envious, jealous, or hatred eyes, we arouse in them, by an inevitable law, the very qualities which we hold in our mind, the qualities which we see in them. If we wish to appeal to the best, if we wish to draw the best out of others, we must look for the best in them; we must think the best of them; we must trust them; we must believe in them.

The man who smiles and sees the best in everything and everybody is the man who draws the best out of others. He attracts others and wins out in life, while the gloomy, sour face repels everyone. "No smiles, no business," is the motto of a successful business house. At first this struck me as rather a peculiar motto, but on second thought, I realized how apt it is.

Do we not all know that sour, gloomy faces drive away business, and that pleasant, sunny faces attract it? Cheerfulness will attract more customers, sell more goods, do more business with less wear and tear than any other quality.

Nobody but himself may be helped by the money millionaire, but everybody is enriched who knows or comes in contact with the millionaire of good cheer, and the more he gives of his wealth the more it multiplies.

Andrew Carnegie owed his popularity and much of his success and happiness to his cheerful disposition. In his later years he said: "My young partners do the work and I do the laughing, and I commend to you the thought that there is very little success where there is little laughter."

Whoever strikes the keynote of joy and happiness is a dispenser of the balm of Gilead, of a healing force. A man without cheerfulness is a sick man. The sadness of his spirit lays a withering blight on all the beauty of his life. He becomes prematurely old. His strength decays. "A broken spirit drieth up the bones."

But cheerfulness is a medicine. It promotes health. The habit of cheerfulness lubricates the human machine and very greatly increases and sharpens every one of the mental faculties.

It improves every function of the body. Cheerfulness keeps one young; it is one of the secrets of eternal youth.

One who admits to himself and others that he is sick is indeed sick; but one who declines to make such admission, and cheerfully goes on as if he were well, conquers many an ailment, which if he had succumbed to it, might have proved serious.

Beecher used to speak of sunny natures who moved through the world like cheering music, spreading joy and gladness wherever they went. We have all met rare souls who live in the sunlight all the time. No matter how poor they may be in worldly goods they see something in life to be thankful for. They are always helpful, hopeful, encouraging, happy. Wherever they go they scatter sunshine.

If we cannot always so control our moods as to be really happy we can always appear cheerful. This is a duty we owe society and ourselves. It is weak and cheap to go about radiating mental poison, the poison of discouragement, of gloom; the poison of worry and anxiety. It is weak to go about the world wearing mourning in our expression. It is a sin to peddle gloom and despondency. We owe it to the world and to ourselves to scatter sunshine, to appear at our best, not at our worst.

There is significance in the fact that man is the only animal that has a sense of humor . . that can laugh. The Creator meant us to have fun; to rejoice and be glad always. Happiness is man's birthright. Laughter is a token of saneness. Abnormal people, insane people, seldom laugh. It is as natural to a normal human being to want to laugh and have a good time as it is to breathe. There is something wrong about a person who never laughs, who is always serious. Things which amuse and make us enjoy life have a healthful physical and moral influence.

The happiness habit is just as necessary to our best welfare, to any success that is worth the name, as the work habit, or the honesty habit, or the square-dealing habit. We can cultivate the habit of being cheerful and happy just as we can cultivate the habit of being polite to everyone with whom we come in contact. Anything that will make a man feel joyous and happy, that will clear the cobwebs of discouragement from his brain and drive away fear, care, and worry, is of practical value and should be encouraged. Innocent, hearty fun will do this as nothing else can.

It is the shrewdest kind of business policy to do what will recreate, refreshen, and rejuvenate one for the next day's work. Then why not have a lot of fun and laughter in the home?

One of the greatest sins multitudes of parents commit against their children is suppressing their love of play in the home. Many parents insist that their children must not talk or laugh at meals. This is a crime against childhood. It is actually unfitting them to be pleasant and agreeable companions, "good mixers" when they grow up and go out in the world, for the habits of childhood become a part of the grown man and woman.

Fun is as necessary as bread. He makes a mistake who regards laughter and humor as transitory, superficial things that pass away and leave nothing behind. They have a permanent, beneficial influence on the whole character and career. Having a good time should be a part of our daily program. Why should this not enter into our life-plan? Why should we be serious and gloomy over our work, over our meals? Why not do everything with joy and gladness?

Cheerfulness will help you all along the line of life. It will help you bear your burdens; it will help you to overcome obstacles; it will increase your courage, strengthen your initiative and make you more effective. It will not only make you a happier, but also a more successful and progressive man. Cheerfulness, more joy in the life, is our greatest need.

Struggles, disappointments, difficulties are not meant to make us sad, but to make us strong . . for if we do not whine and complain, we shall be given strength to overcome all these.

The cheerful man sees that everywhere the good outbalances the bad, and that every evil has its compensating balm.

Robert Louis Stevenson said, "A happy man or woman is a better thing to find than a five-pound note. He or she is a radiating focus of good will and their entrance into a room is as though another candle had been lighted."

We were all made for happiness, to rejoice and be exceeding glad. Any inharmony or discord in our nature is contrary to divine law and diving will. It was the Creator's intention that everybody should be happier than the happiest beings are today.

If you, my friend, have not found that source of happiness which will keep you in poise and serenity, no matter what may happen to you or yours, if you have not found that poise which gives the peace that provides understanding under all conditions, you have not yet found the great secret of life. You have yet to learn that real enjoyment, real satisfaction does not come from the possession of things, does not come from outside sources, but that our highest satisfaction, our highest enjoyment, our highest happiness, ever comes from within. Here is the fountain of all supply; here is where we touch God, the Source of all good; here is where we tap the divinity in the great within of us.

If your supply is limited and you feel unhappy, dissatisfied, gloomy, you may be sure that there is something wrong inside of you. There is something wrong in your thought, in your motive, in your acts, something wrong in your view of life. You are violating your nature in some way or you are not using your powers rightly.

Chapter XVII

The Master Key To Be Great

Two friends set out on a journey once, oh, many years ago, The one bestrode a mettled steed, the other trudged below; And he that rode raced everywhere, save to the place he should, "Because," said he, "there's time enough, and this, my mount, is good." Time journeyed, too, and when, at last, the limit's hour did toll, The one that pleasure's bubble sought was still far from the goal,. While he that came with tedious pace was at his travel's end, With but one shadow on his heart, . .the failure of his friend. - T. H. Winton.

THE son of a poor Welsh schoolmaster, without advantage of birth or fortune, without pull or influence of any kind, David Lloyd George succeeded in raising himself to the highest position in the British Empire. As Prime Minister of England, he ranks next to King George, while his power and responsibility greatly overtop that of the King or any other man in the empire.

What is the secret of his success? One word tells it: concentration.

Before the boy was two years old, his father died. His mother then took her family to live with her brother, Richard Lloyd, a humble cobbler. The cobbler's shop was a sort of political forum for workingmen of the neighborhood, and there young David got his early training in politics. In his teens he studied law, and at the age of twenty-one began to practice. But long before he was admitted to the bar, when he first visited the House of Commons, he made up his mind that that was to be his future domain, and then and there resolved to enter parliament. With all the vigor and tenacity of his nature he concentrated on his ambition, with what result the world knows. One of the ablest and most brilliant statesmen England has produced; he is today the most dominant figure in world affairs.

What David Lloyd George has done in his field you can do in yours, as millions of others have done, by the same means, . . concentration.

There is no more powerful magnet in the world for attracting the thing we desire, no force more effective in realizing the ambition we long to attain than concentration. It has been the chief factor in all the great achievements of history. It is the cornerstone of success in every line; the principle upon which all progress is based. All the inventions, all the discoveries, all the modem facilities, which the world enjoys are the children of focused minds. Whatever you long to be, or to have, you can be, you can have, by focusing your mind and concentrating your efforts on that one thing.

When Franz Liszt, the great composer, was a mere youth, his elder brother chided him for spending his time on music and told him that he himself was going to be a great landowner. The would-be landowner scorned his young brother's musical bent, holding that a talent for music would only ruin a man. Franz, however, stuck to his bent, and even ran away several times in order to gratify the ambition for a musical career, which was discouraged at home.

Years later when the elder brother had become a wealthy landowner he called on Franz, who was still a struggling musician. Not finding him at home he left his card which bore the inscription, "Herr Liszt, Landowner." When more years had passed and the young composer had finally won out, he returned the call of his landowner brother and presented his card, which read, "Herr Liszt, Brain-owner."

Aside from the humor of this little story, the point is that each of the brothers got what he concentrated on; the one became a wealthy landowner, the other a world famed musician and composer.

If your ambition is like that of the elder brother, to become a wealthy landowner, a prosperous man of affairs, then you must concentrate on prosperity, on the acquisition of wealth in some form. We all know men who seem to attract money from every direction. Everything they touch turns to money, as we say, while others who work just as hard for the same end have no success at all. The different results are due to the difference in intensity and persistence of concentration. The natural, the born money-maker thinks in terms of money; he is making money mentally all the time, so to speak, because his mind is focused on money. He is always nursing his money vision. He is positive in his conviction that he will make money, will be wealthy, and he concentrates on his object with such intensity and singleness of aim that he literally creates money.

The man who wants money, but who doesn't concentrate intensely on getting it; who doesn't believe very much in his ability to get it, who fears he will never be even what we call a well-to-do man, is like one who wants to be successful, but is always thinking about failure, worrying about it, fearing, believing, that he never will become a success. Or like a man of average ability who should scatter his forces in a dozen different directions, hoping that by chance he might manage to succeed in someone of them.

There is no such thing as succeeding in anything by chance. The greatest genius in the world never created a masterpiece in any line . . by chance. Concentration is the master key to all success. It is the fundamental law of achievement. The man who does not concentrate will be either a half success, a mediocrity, or a complete failure.

The French have a proverb, "He who does one thing is terrible." In other words, he who sticks to one thing is irresistible. No matter if a world opposed his progress he would forge his way through to his goal. It was bending all his energies to the accomplishment of his purpose that made Napoleon one of the most notable figures in history. His intense concentration on his one unwavering aim enabled him to write his name on the very stones of the capital of France; to stamp it indelibly upon the heart of every Frenchman. Even today, a century after his death, France, though a republic, is still under the spell of Napoleon's name.

"To make a success of the shoe business is my one great ambition," said the head of one of the largest shoe houses in the world not long ago. "I am not a director or trustee of any bank. I do not scatter my energies. I don't pretend to know many things, but I do know something about the shoe business. I have put my ability, my energy, my life into the work of making good shoes"

This man, who began life on the lowest round of the ladder, without capital or influence, built up a business which keeps a force of two hundred traveling salesmen on the road today and is turning over some $25,000,000 a year.

Emerson says, "The one prudence in life is concentration; the one evil is dissipation." Scattering our energies, dissipating our creative force, failing to bring our mind to a focus and to hold it there, is responsible for nine-tenths of the failures in life and most of the poverty of the world. I know one of those dissipaters who generates more new ideas and outlines more new schemes than anyone else I have ever met.

Yet he has never accomplished anything more than the making of a meager living, because he never sticks long enough to any one thing to make it go. His brain power and all of his energy are scattered in following one new thing after another without ever carrying any of them forward to completion. Every time I talk with him he amazes me with the fertility of his mind, his resourcefulness in developing original ideas, many of which would prove valuable if they were only put into execution, but they never get beyond the mental stage. The concentration necessary to bring them down to earth, to put them to work, is lacking. There are thousands like this man, getting small salaries in very ordinary positions, whose knowledge of a dozen different occupations, concentrated in one line, would have made them efficient specialists. Everywhere we find men who early in life studied law, medicine, theology, who taught school a few years, worked in a store a little, took a hand at railroading did a little business, traveled for some house, and finally settled down at one thing, only to find that their training years, the years of largest opportunity, when they were susceptible to discipline, had gone by.

No matter how brilliant or versatile you may be you cannot afford to divide your ability, to throw away valuable experience in jumping from one vocation to another. If you would succeed in a worthwhile way, you must be a whole man with undivided interests, able to fling the weight of your entire being into one calling. No one is large enough to be split up into many parts; and the sooner a man can stamp this truth upon his mind the better his chances for being a profitable member of society. Elbert Hubbard says: "The master man is a person who has evolved intelligent industry, concentration, self-confidence until these things become the habit of his life."

Coleman Dupont furnished a good example of the master-man at a critical stage in the affairs of the Dupont Powder Company. When he was called to the head of the business it was losing ground rapidly, but through his amazing industry and concentration, backed by confidence in his ability to do what he undertook, he very soon turned the tide and headed the company toward success. When an interviewer asked Mr. Dupont how he did this, he said: "I talked powder, I ate powder, I dreamed powder. I thought of little else but powder." This concentration on one unwavering aim built up an enormous institution of worldwide fame.

No matter what your business, trade, or profession, you cannot make a mistake in following Mr. Dupont's remarkable methods of concentration which make him a master-man in his line. Think the thing you want; talk it; live it; breathe it; dream it; act it; radiate it from every pore of your body; saturate your life, with it; visualize it; believe that it is already yours. That's the only way to get anything of value in this world. If we could only realize the marvelous power of thought, the creative force in concentration, the drawing power of intense visualizing, how much more we could accomplish! It is this, which really makes the mind a powerful magnet to attract what it desires, what it longs for most. Everywhere we see illustrations of the attractive force of positive, definite thought concentrated on one point.

Take the little Hebrew boys who come from other countries to America when very young. From the start they have the concentrated commercial instinct of their race. They think in terms of money making; they keep their minds on ways and means of making money until they become powerful magnets, attracting money from every direction.

That's why they succeed and become wealthy where American youths with far better opportunities attract poverty and remain poor all their lives. From the time the Hebrew boy starts to shine shoes on the street, to sell papers, or to peddle some small articles, he is all the time thinking of the money he is going to make; counting what he has and planning what he will do with it; how he can increase it; how he can enlarge his little business, put his profits to work for him and accumulate more money. In a very short time he has a newsstand or a little shop of his own; he invests in a little real estate; by and by he borrows some money and puts up a house, and so he goes on trading in one thing and another, his mind always bent on making more money, until one day this little newsboy, or bootblack, or peddler becomes a man of Fortune . . a millionaire.

To demonstrate prosperity, you must concentrate on prosperity; you must hold the prosperity attitude; to demonstrate abundance, you must think abundance, just as you must think health, think vigor, if you would be healthy and vigorous. It is not enough to long for health; you must believe that you will be, that you already are, well and strong. You must expect it. According to thy faith be it unto thee. You must hold in mind that thing, whatever it is, you wish to express in your life, and you must believe it will come. The student who is trying to become a lawyer saturates his mind with law. He thinks law, reads law, studies law, keeps his mind focused upon a future as a lawyer; keeps in a law atmosphere; he pictures himself practicing at the bar, a man of mark in his profession; he continually fills his life with the law ideal, and by the force of his powerful concentration fits himself for the practice of law.

The medical student must follow the same method; so must the aspirant to the ministry or any other vocation. And so must the aspirant to wealth.

You can't expect to become prosperous if you don't hold fast to the prosperity vision, if you don't believe with all your heart you are going to be prosperous. If your mind is occupied with something else most of the time; if it is filled with doubts about ever accumulating property or becoming prosperous in any line of business, don't deceive yourself with the idea that prosperity will come to you if you only work hard. It won't. Nothing will come into your life except by the doorway of your thought, of your expectation, your faith. Concentration is indispensable to success in anything. As Dr. Julia Seaton says: "Concentration is the vital essence of all life, and without it there is no real purpose, no real control. Upon the power of concentration more than upon any other one thing, depends" our law of attracting, controlling and mastering life's conditions."

If you feel discouraged because you are not getting on as you hoped you would, something is wrong. Your mind is not pulling in harmony with your effort on the physical plane. Something has arrested your progress, and that something is a mental stumbling-block which you yourself put in your path. You are not thinking yourself on, you are not putting yourself in the getting-on current by concentrating with confidence, with faith, along the line of your ambition. Discouragement, doubt, a wavering, divided mind, the scattering of your efforts, something or other is neutralizing the force which would naturally take you to your goal. Perhaps you are frittering away your energies by giving your spare time to side-lines, trying to make a little success here, a little there, not giving the whole of yourself to your life work.

In Maine, the farmers say that it makes a horse a gawk to drive it without blinders, because its attention is drawn this way and that, which ruins the animal's gait and speed. Many a man has been ruined by not confining himself within sufficiently narrow limits to give concentration and direction to his energies. Said Andrew Carnegie: "One great cause of failure of young men in business is lack of concentration. They are prone to seek outside investments, side-lines. The cause of many a surprising failure lies in so doing. Every dollar of capital and credit, every business thought, should be concentrated upon the one business upon which a man has embarked. He should never scatter his shot. It is a poor business which will not yield better returns for increased capital than any outside investment. No man or set of men or corporation can manage a businessman's capital as well as he can Manage it himself. The rule, 'Do not put all your eggs in one basket,' does not apply to a man's life work."

Don't be afraid of being known as a man of one idea. The men who have moved the world have been men of this kind. It is the man who has his purpose burned into every fiber of his being, who has the faculty of focusing his scattered energies on one point as a burning glass focuses the scattered rays of the sun, which succeeds. "When I have a subject in hand I study it profoundly," said Alexander Hamilton. "Day and night it is before me. My mind becomes pervaded with it. Then the success I make, the people are pleased to call genius. It is the fruit of thought and labor." Concentration without genius will accomplish more than genius without concentration.

Chapter XVIII

Time Is Money .. And Much More

- Few of us realize the connection between the day, the hour, in which we are living, and our success, our happiness, our destiny.

- It is so much easier to dream of a great big success tomorrow than to try to make today a big success.

- When I see a young man who seizes every odd moment for self improvement, who has an ambition to make each day count, then I know that there is something, a very big something, coming to him in the future.

- Our today's are the blocks with which we build our future. If these are defective, the whole structure of our life will correspond. That marvelous future which you have dreamed of so long will be exactly what you put into your todays.

- The world grants all opportunities to him who can use them. Power and fortune are hidden away in the hours and moments as they pass, awaiting the eye that can see, the ear that can hear, the hand that can do.

WHEN Queen Elizabeth of England was dying she said, "My kingdom for a moment!"

One of the richest men in the world said he would give millions of dollars to be assured of a few more years of life.

The late J. Pierpont Morgan used to say that every hour of his time was worth a thousand dollars. It was probably worth many thousands of dollars, even if measured by money alone, for the accumulation of a vast fortune was only an incident in Mr. Morgan's many-sided career.

But time is infinitely more valuable to us than is shown by its money-making power. I have never known of any person to make his life worthwhile in any direction until he came to the realization of the immense value of time. Time is our most precious asset, our greatest riches; because in it live our success, our happiness, our destiny.

Yet multitudes are engaged in killing time. Their chief aim in life is to fritter it away as rapidly as possible. They do not realize that this is infinitely more wasteful than it would be for a rich man to throw hundred dollar bills or valuable diamonds into the sea, or to do as Cleopatra did, dissolve priceless pearls in a glass of wine and drink them.

The future of a young man can be gauged to a nicety by the value he puts upon his time, especially his spare time. From the foundation of the American republic the greatest and most successful Americans have been men who not only in their youth but all through their lives made use of every spare moment in broadening their minds, adding to their knowledge, and developing their ability along their special line. The Washingtons, the Franklins, the Lincolns, the Burritts, the Morses, the Fields, the Edisons, the men in every line of endeavor all over the civilized world who have done great things for mankind and made themselves famous, achieved their great work not because they were geniuses, but because they got from every minute of time its full value.

"I have in my time known many famous in war, in statesmanship, in science, in the professions, and in business," said the late U. S. Senator Hoar of Massachusetts. "If I were asked to declare the secret of their success, I should attribute it, in general, not to any superiority of natural genius, but to the use they made in youth, after the ordinary day's work was over, of the hours which other men throw away or devote to idleness, or rest, or society. The great things in this world have been done by men of ordinary natural capacity, who have done their best. They have done their best by never wasting their time."

There are many so-called common or ordinary employees today, who, perhaps, think they haven't nearly as good a chance to rise as their more brilliant or showy companions, who will within a few years be filling high positions. The history of the past shows that every year brings out multitudes of giants from the ranks, often young fellows who are more surprised at their rapid advance than the employers who are watching them.

The only reason why anyone remains a common, ordinary employee, doing routine work and drawing a small salary, is not because he doesn't have the ability to rise higher, but because. He is not awake to the possibilities in his spare time.

Charles M. Schwab had no more ability perhaps and no better chance to rise than the hundreds of other young men who were working with him at the Homestead plant of Andrew Carnegie when he started in at a dollar a day. The reason why he has become a millionaire and a king in his line is because he saw the necessity of a better education than he had had a chance to get up to that time, and devoted his evenings and spare time to making good his deficiencies, and particularly to acquiring special knowledge in regard to iron and steel. He was always on the alert to improve his opportunities, always preparing himself to be ready to fill positions next above him in case of a vacancy. That is why his rise was so rapid, why he is today one of the richest and most prominent business men in his line in the world, while his early fellow workers who preferred "a good time" to self-improvement in their spare time have never been heard from. Speaking of those early days when he was beginning to attract attention at the Carnegie works, Mr. Schwab said: "At that time science began to play an important part in the manufacture of steel.

My salary at the age of twenty-one warranted me in marrying, so I had a home of my own. I believe in early marriages, as a rule. In my own house I rigged up a laboratory and studied chemistry in the evenings, determined that there should be nothing in the manufacture of steel that I would not know. Although I had received no technical education, I made myself master of chemistry, and of the laboratory, which proved of lasting value.

"The point I wish to make," continued he, "is that my experimental work was. not in the line of my duty, but it gave me greater knowledge. Achievement is possible to a man who does something else besides his mere duty that attracts the attention of his superiors to him, as one who is equipping himself for advancement. An employer picks out his assistants from the best informed, most competent and conscientious."

"One is so tired after a day's work he does not feel like studying," is an excuse often urged by young people when reminded that they are not doing anything to advance themselves. It is only the excuse of those who are too lazy to work for what they want, or who lack the ambition to climb. It is well known that a change of occupation in the evening, . . the bringing into play of a different set of muscles, brain tissues, ideas, and thoughts, generally rests rather than tires one. Of course everyone should take a proper amount of time for needed recreation, exercise and rest, but very often those who claim they are too tired to study evenings waste more energy in foolish dissipation or dawdling aimlessly around doing nothing than they would spend in reading or study.

Only a short time ago I read of a young school teacher who learned six or seven languages in her spare time, and who managed, by earning some extra money evenings in teaching private pupils, to save enough money to go to Europe, to perfect herself in these languages. The enjoyment and breadth of culture she got out of her travels in the different European countries would have been a great reward for the sacrifices she made; but she got much more than that, for she advanced rapidly in her profession, and is now an instructor in French, German, and Italian in a high school for girls.

"The whole period of youth," says Ruskin, "is one essentially of formation, edification, instruction. There is not an hour of it but is trembling with destinies . .not a moment of which, once passed, the appointed work can ever be done again, or the neglected blow struck on the cold iron." Millions of down-and-outs are today bemoaning the loss of the golden opportunities they allowed to slip by in youth, the evenings and holidays they idled away when they might have been laying the foundations for a happy, successful future. But they couldn't eat their cake and have it too, arid now they feel it is too late even to try to make good.' They feel that they have nothing to look forward to but an old age of poverty and bitter regrets.

There is no magic which can give a youth a golden future when he is slipping careless, slipshod work and wasted hours into the fabric of today. Ambition, courage, industry, vim, energy, initiative, thoroughness poured into your day's work, and perseverance in self-improvement in your spare time, these are the ingredients warranted to make a golden future, to bring you wealth, knowledge, wisdom, power, fame .. whatever you set your heart on.

"Believe me," said England's great statesman, William E. Gladstone, "when I tell you that thrift of time will repay you in after life with a usury of profit beyond your most sanguine dreams, and that waste of it will make you dwindle alike in intellectual and moral stature beyond your darkest reckoning." The way in which they spent their spare time has made all the difference between mediocrity and grand achievement to tens of thousands of men and women, who were intelligent enough in youth to know the value of the priceless odds and ends of time which others were recklessly wasting.

If someone offered to purchase a large percentage of your life power you would not think of selling it, even for a fabulous sum. It is what gives you your chance to make good, to make your life a masterpiece, and naturally you would not part with it.

You would say that you could not afford to sell your birthright of power in which is wrapped up your whole destiny, . . your enthusiasm, your zest, your career, your ambition. But do you realize that you are practically doing the same thing when you allow your most precious success asset, your time, to run away from you in all sorts of leaks; in sheer idleness, in dissipation, in superficial, silly pleasures, or worse, in pleasures which kill your self-respect and make you hate yourself the next day? If you would succeed in any adequate way, in a way at all commensurate with your possibilities, you must not only shut off all time leaks, but you must also repair every leak in your mental and physical system, and stop every output of energy that does not tell in rendering you more fit to make your life the great success it is possible for you to make it.

How often we are reminded of the value of time by the expression, "Time is money." But time is more than money; it is life itself; for every separate moment as it flies takes with it a part of our life span. Time is opportunity. Time represents our success capital, our achievement possibilities. Everything we hope for, everything we dream of accomplishing is dependent on it.

"Short as life is," said Victor Hugo, "we make it still shorter by the careless waste of time." I would advise every youth starting out in life to put that sentence up on the wall in his sleeping room, and over his desk or work bench, where it would constantly remind him of the immense possibilities stored in the minutes and hours of every single day. If at the outset of your career you resolve to make good every day, and live up to your resolution, nothing can keep you from being a successful man or woman, a superb character. You are the architect of your fate, the master of your destiny, and right now you are shaping your future. Every day is a step nearer to, or farther from, the goal of your ambition. The precious hours of youth are invaluable.

The realization of all your dreams lives in them. Letters come to me from time to time from young people deploring the fact that it is impossible for them to attend school or college.

They say they have to work for a living, and therefore have no opportunity to acquire an education. They never stop to think that many of the most prominent men and women of the world have been self-educated. I do not mean that they have worked their way through school or college, but that they have actually gained an education in its widest and best sense, by their own efforts, with little or no actual schooling. You who complain that you have no opportunity to get an education, and therefore no opportunity to do anything worthwhile, read the lives of men and women who have lifted themselves into places of power by self-education, biographies like that of Franklin, of Lincoln, of Greeley, of Garfield, of men of all nations who came from the direst poverty, and by sheer force of will and the wise use of every spare moment lifted themselves to the highest stations of life, to positions of honor, of great power and wealth.

As Hamilton W. Mabie said "One of the prime qualities of a man of force and ability is his clear understanding of what can be done with the time and tools at his command. Such a man wastes no time in idle dreaming of the things he would do if he could go to college, or travel, or have command of long periods of uninterrupted time. He is not guilty of a feeble evasion of 'no possibility' for his career by getting behind adverse conditions. If the conditions are adverse, he gets in front of them, and so gets away from them.

"The question for each man to settle is not what he would do if he had means, time, influence, and educational opportunities; the question is what he will do with the things he has. The moment a young man ceases to dream or to bemoan his lack of opportunities and resolutely looks his conditions in the face, and resolves to change them, he lays the corner stone of a solid and honorable success."

No matter how limited your time, or how exacting your daily work, you can so train your mind, so cultivate yourself by reading and study in your spare moments, that you can, if you will, become an educated man or woman, with a much broader outlook on life and an infinitely greater earning capacity than the uneducated man or woman.

Andrew Carnegie, the young Scotch lad, for example, had only an elementary school education at the start, but by reading and studying in his leisure moments he acquired the culture that fruited in several books and many magazine articles on topics of worldwide interest, to say nothing of his business achievements and the immense fortune he acquired.

George Stephenson, inventor of the locomotive engine, seized every leisure moment as though it were gold. He educated himself and did much of his best work during his spare time. He learned to read and write at a night school, and studied arithmetic during the night shifts when he was assistant fireman in a colliery.

The lives and work of multitudes of the world's benefactors prove that no matter what investment a man may make in life, there is none so satisfactory as self investment, . . coining bits of leisure into knowledge and power.

The bigger the man the greater value he puts upon time. He regards it as a great asset, as the most precious capital, which can enrich life. Whether his ambition be to acquire a fortune or to achieve success in some other direction, he knows that everything depends on what he does with his spare time. Weak natures, on the other hand, never regard time as a precious asset, they never want to pay the price which strong natures are willing to pay, to make their dreams come true. They cannot resist the lure of pleasure for the sake of their ambition. They practice no more thrift in the use of their time than they do in the use of their money. They kill a lot of time without realizing that in doing this they are killing their prospects, killing their future, killing themselves.

"I will make this day worthwhile!" would be a splendid daily motto for all of us to adopt. When you awake in the morning; when you start to work; and many times during the day, say to yourself: "I will make this day worthwhile. It shall not pass into the story of my life as time half wasted, or not utilized to the best advantage. No matter whether I feel like it or not, I am going to make this day count. I am going to make it stand out in my life as a red-letter day, one in which my work was effective, efficient." If you do this every day you will be surprised at the wonderful effect it will have upon your whole life. It will lift it to the highest point of your possible efficiency and effectiveness. It will mean everything to you both in character and financial returns.

Someone says: "All that time is lost which might be better employed." If all of us realized the truth of that, there would be more success and fewer failures in life. Each of us has the same number of hours in his day, the same number of days in his year, and the chief difference between the success and the failure lies in the use to which the hours' and the days are put. Given the very same environment, the same chances to succeed, and one youth will rise to fame and fortune by the right use of the time that another recklessly wastes. It is what we put into the passing moment, just that and nothing more, that makes up all of life, all of character, all of success.

The harvest of our tomorrows will be like the seed we sow today. If we do not put that quality into the present moment that we expect in our success, in our character, in our life as a whole, it will not be there. If there is not energy, vim, courage, initiative, industry, a high quality of work in today the results of these cannot appear in your future. It is the daily ambition which starts out every morning with the firm resolution not to let the hours slip through one's fingers until one has wrung from them their utmost possibility that makes the successful day; and it is the accumulation of daily successes that makes the big life success, that enables the man to realize the ambitious dream of the boy.

Chapter XIX

The Positive Versus The Negative Man

- The negative mind never gets anywhere; it can only destroy, tear down.

- It is very easy to develop a negative state of mind, and it is very fatal to success. We must get rid of it before we can attract prosperity or develop efficiency.

- We cannot act negatively without getting negative results.

- The vacillating man, however strong in other respects, is always pushed aside in the race of life by the determined, positive, decisive man who knows what he wants to do, and does it. Even brains must give way to decision.

- Even if sometimes wrong, it is better to decide positively and carry out your decision with energy than to be forever hanging in the balance, contemplating, and procrastinating.

- Every important decision involves the letting go of something, and the more one tries to get away from the difficulty, the more he thinks over the thing to be decided, the more he entangles the whole situation.

- It is not only necessary to keep your mind positive, but to be immune from all the enemies of prosperity and happiness, it must be vigorously positive.

- It is the positive, vigorous mentality that does things, that makes things move. The negative character is always a weakling, a nobody, who follows in the beaten path.

IF WE could only learn always to talk and think decisively, constructively, what a wonderful civilization this would be! It is the strong, optimistic, expectant-of-good-things mind, the mind of faith, and of hope and confidence, belief in the good, that attracts the good. The mind of the pessimist attracts pessimistic products.

If you do not learn to decide firmly and finally and then act on. your decision; if you waver and dilly-dally, allow yourself to be carried this way and that by conflicting circumstances, your life ship will always be adrift; you will never be anchored. You will always be at the mercy of storms and tempests, and will never make the port of prosperity.

When a young man asks my opinion of his chances for success in life, I try to find out something about his ability to decide things. If he can do this quickly, firmly, and finally, I am very sure he will win out. There is no other one quality which plays such an important part in business careers especially as the ability to decide things wisely, quickly, firmly, and finally.

The. man who is made of winning material does not hesitate and dawdle and waver and balance on the fence. He jumps right in and tackles the hardest thing first, and goes through with it. Voltaire tells us that vacillation is the most prominent feature of weakness of character.

What we get out of life we do not get by-physical force, but by the subtle power of mental attraction. We bring it to ourselves by making our minds magnets to attract it out of the great cosmic storehouse of intelligence. Gut of the great ocean of supply that surrounds us we attract the things for which our mental attitude has an affinity.

Some attract success, some failure; some attract opulence, plenty; others, poverty and lack. It all depends upon the difference in thought whether it is positive or negative, constructive or destructive, Negative thoughts demagnetize the mind so that it attracts just the opposite of what we want.

People who plod along in mediocrity, or who fail in life, might make a very creditable life record if they could only keep the things out of their minds which make them negative. It is their discouraging moods and all of their enemy thoughts, . . their doubts, fears, worries, uncertainties, and their lack of confidence in themselves that kill the creative power of the mind and make it negative.

The negative mind never gets anywhere. It is the positive mind that radiates force and pushes its way in the world. A negative mind can only destroy, tear down. Many people dwell so much upon their failure to get on in the world, their poverty, their misfortunes, that they develop a real failure atmosphere; they surround themselves with destructive, tearing-down thoughts, disintegrating suggestions, until they make impossible that mental condition, that positive mental attitude which creates, produces.

We are just beginning to learn that we can not only control our moods and all of our thoughts, but that we can also control our environment, because our environment is largely our objectified thought, feeling, emotion, and mental attitude. We make our own world by our thoughts, our motives.

As long as you keep your mind positive and creative you will have courage, initiative, and sound judgment, you will be a producer. But the moment you become discouraged and blue, your ability, your mind, becomes demagnetized, negative, and you are no longer a creator or a producer. Your decision wobbles, your judgment is weak and uncertain, your whole mental kingdom is demoralized. Keep your mind positive by refusing to admit to it such traitors as doubt, discouragement, fear or worry. They are your fatal enemies. You can never succeed while you entertain them.

Drive them out. Don't leave the doors of your mind open to them. Be known as a man of great faith regarding everything in the world; believe that everything is right in the world because God made it, God ordered it. Believe only in the best. Live success; walk about among your fellows as though you were successful, with a triumphant, victorious air; show that you are victory organized.

Never fear failure; don't visualize it; don't picture poverty or have a horror of it, for this tends to make it a reality and keeps away from you the very things you desire.

"What is the use of dreaming about the wonderful things I am going to do in the future? There is no such achievement in store for me. I am not a genius. I must content myself with an ordinary career." These negative thoughts and assertions permeate the atmosphere of most homes and chill the youthful ardor of the children with the result that their ambition sags, their ideals shrivel, and, having no great life incentive, they drop into a humdrum routine and fall far below the level they might have attained.

It is criminal not to correct the tendency to negatives in a child's mind. It is not very difficult to cultivate a positive habit of thinking and acting if undertaken when a child is young. With the adult it is not so easy, but it is possible.

When you long for something that it is perfectly legitimate for you to have, sow your affirmation seed in perfect confidence that it will bloom in reality. Say to yourself, "God is no respecter of persons. He is not partial in his treatment of His children.

They all have the same rights, the same privileges. He will give me through my own effort what I need, what I ask for. The poorest, most ragged wretch that crawls has just as many hours in his day as has the richest and most powerful magnate. I can and I will do what I long to do. I will be what I desire to be."

Whatever you do, don't set up in your mind and in that of others, a picture of yourself as a weak, ineffective, negative personality.

If you are constantly depreciating yourself, other people will think there is a reason for it, that you are not worthy, that there is something about you that they do not know about as a basis of your own judgment. Why should not others think meanly of you if you do yourself?

If you carry about with you a negative mental attitude yours will be a negative life. You cannot act negatively without getting negative results.

Negative people do not start vigorous, positive vibrations; they are so passive and so susceptible to the influences about them that their negative minds take off all of the negative vibrations from all the cross currents from other negative minds.

It is perfectly possible to make our mentality so vigorously positive that, no matter what conflicting currents or vibrations from other negative, discordant minds strike us, they find no response. Then we are immune to all negative thoughts; we can walk through all sorts of adverse conditions about us without responding, because we do not vibrate to the negative thought and the negative condition, and we can still keep our robust, positive poise. Living in the stronger thought makes us stronger. People with a vigorous, positive mental attitude, people with a strong, firm decision, people with great faith, have a much stronger mentality than do negative minds, because they habitually live in a more vigorous mental attitude, and a positive mental attitude makes for growth, for mental enlargement. We all know the negative man, the man who never has any opinion of his own, who is always asking other people's advice and depending upon others. The negative character is always a weakling.

The negative man in any community is the nobody. It is the positive, vigorous mentality that does things, that makes things move, which puts things through. It is the positive man who does his own thinking; who dares to step out of the beaten path and blaze his own way; who dares to have opinions of his own and dares to express them.

This is the sort of man who gains the respect and confidence of mankind. A lot of people go through life doing little things, because their negative thought paralyzes their initiative; they do not dare undertake anything important. The negative mind, the man who is afraid to act, who is always deliberating or hesitating, never accomplishes much.

The leader is always characterized by positive qualities. He rules by his vigorous affirmatives. There is nothing negative or minus about him. The positive man, the natural leader, is always assertive, while the negative man shrinks, and effaces himself, waits for someone else to take the initiative.

One of the most pathetic sights in the world is the man who never has any opinion of his own, . . the backboneless, shiftless, slovenly, negative man, who never differs from you, whose only opinion is assent to the one you express. We instinctively despise such a weakling, a man who never opposes us, who always says "yes, yes," to everything we say.

We want leaders and originators more than we want followers or imitators. We have enough, and to spare, of those who are willing to lean on others. We want our young people to depend on themselves. We want them to be so educated and trained that their qualities of leadership, their originality and their individuality, will be emphasized and strengthened instead of obliterated.

All negative thinking, all negative mental attitudes, such as doubting one's ability, hesitating to undertake things, the habit of putting off, waiting for more favorable conditions, and of reconsidering one's decisions, are deadly enemies of initiative. If one does not cultivate a positive mental attitude he will have a weak, wishy-washy initiative, and initiative is the executive officer of the other faculties. It is the brain leader.

Do not forget that the force that is going to project you to the success and prosperity goal is actually inside of you. Do not look to others to push you, to give you a pull or to use their influence. Your resources, your assets, are right inside of you; they are nowhere else.

If you feel paralyzed by the very responsibility of deciding things, beginning things of your own accord, make up your mind that if you ever are to amount to anything in the world you must strangle this habit. The only way to do this is to form the counter habit of starting out every morning with the grim resolution not to allow yourself, during the day, to waver, to wait for somebody to show you the way. Resolve that during the entire day you are going to be a pusher, a leader; that you are not going to be a trailer, not going to wait for somebody to tell you what to do and how to do it; that you are going to take the initiative, start things yourself, put them through without advice. Determine to carry a positive mental attitude. This will sharpen the faculties, put a keen edge upon them, and make the mind alert and eager for opportunities.

It is not only necessary to keep your mind positive, but to be immune from all the enemies of your success and happiness it must be vigorously positive. When the mind is saturated with all sorts of negation, with the thoughts of sickness, of failure and poverty, it becomes chronically discordant, and gradually deteriorates. Form the habit of talking up, not down, of talking optimism instead of pessimism. Cut criticism, fault-finding and blame out of your vocabulary. One of the first signs of deterioration in many minds is a tendency to be negative; to hold the discordant, belligerent, envious, jealous mental attitude. This is just as abnormal as is chronic melancholy, gloom, and despondency. These indicate an abnormal or diseased condition of the mind. Try to see things from a large, generous standpoint; hold a large consciousness. Show everybody that you have a great faith in humanity, in your calling, and in yourself. Resolve to keep the negatives out of your life. You are too large for jealousy or envy, too big for worry, or to be anxious about your career, or about your future.

Making yourself positive to everybody and everything you contact with in life is what counts. This is the key to mastership, to success and prosperity.

Chapter XX

Thrift And Prosperity

- If you would be sure that you are beginning right, begin to save. The habit of saving money, while it stiffens the will, also brightens the energies. - Theodore Roosevelt.

- Enter into a compact with yourself to save a certain amount every week out of your salary.

- The little difference between what we earn and what we spend is capital.

- Thrift is the friend of man, a civilization builder.

- The practice of thrift gives an upward tendency to the life of the individual, and to the life of the nation; it sustains and preserves the highest welfare of the race.

- Nothing makes a businessman so absolutely independent as ready cash.

- It is the "man with the savings bank habit who seldom gets laid off; he's the one who can get along without you, but you cannot get along without him."

- Thrift means wise management of what you have . . money, time, energies, opportunities.

BENJAMIN FRANKLIN is one of the most inspiring examples of what the practice of thrift can do for the poorest boy or girl in this land of opportunities. Son of a poor tallow chandler and soap boiler, the fifteenth child in a family of seventeen, he began at the age of ten to earn his living by working in his father's shop. From these humble beginnings he succeeded, entirely by his own efforts, in becoming one of the world's greatest men . . a distinguished patriot, scientist, statesman, inventor, diplomat, philosopher, author, and, last but not least, a noted humorist.

All this he accomplished by the practice of thrift. That does not mean merely economy in financial matters, the wisest expenditure of his income, but the wisest expenditure of his time and efforts in all the business of life. For to him thrift meant not only prudence in business and money spending, but the conservation of health, of energy, of life capital, and the utmost development of all his natural resources. As well as being the thriftiest, Franklin was the most generous of men, and would share his last cent with one who needed it.

One of Franklin's favorite maxims . . one that he literally lived by himself . . was "God helps those who help themselves." And the first lesson for those who would help themselves to learn is the one that he constantly taught . . Thrift. Headed with a picture of Benjamin Franklin, the great apostle of thrift, a calendar, issued by the Y. M. C. A. in New York, has this slogan . . "Make Your Money Mean More." Then, it gives the "Ten Commandments for a Young Man's Financial Life."

1. . . Work and Earn.

2. . . Make a Budget.

3. . . Record Your Expenditures.

4. . . Have a Bank Account.

5. . . Carry Life Insurance.

6. . . Own Your Own Home.

7. . . Make a Will.

8. . . Pay Your Bills Promptly.

9. . . Invest in Reliable Securities.

10. . . Share With Others.

If you "forge these links of success into your character," as the calendar suggests, you will not only develop a self-reliant, vigorous type of manhood or womanhood, but you will also be laying the foundation of enduring prosperity, contentment, and happiness.

Every man knows that it is easier to earn money than to save it; so if there is any one link in the "Ten Commandments" the wage earner, the man or woman of limited means, should pay special attention to, it is the second, "Make a Budget." And here again the Y.M. C.A. is meeting a great need in supplying "A Budget Book With a Conscience," which shows the best way to plan the expenditure of your income, and how to keep an accurate account of your income and outlay.

From Benjamin Franklin to Sir Thomas Lipton, thousands of successful men in every field have given testimony to the value of thrift, or economy, as a wealth and happiness maker. Lipton says it is "the first great principle of all success. It creates independence, it gives a young man standing, fills him with vigor, it stimulates him with the proper energy; in fact, it brings to him the best part of any success . . happiness and contentment."

Unless you make it a cast-iron rule to lay aside a certain percentage of your earnings each week, each month, you will never succeed in becoming a really independent man or woman. You will always be at the mercy of circumstances. No matter how small it may be, or if you have to go without a great many things you think you need, put a portion of your earnings away every year where it will be absolutely safe. You don't know what this will mean to you in case of illness, accident, or some unlooked for emergency when a little ready money may save you great suffering or financial ruin.

The wise expenditure of one's income, however small it may be, involves the same principles as the investment and handling of the business man's capital. And the successful businessman carries these principles into the conduct of all his affairs, his personal and household expenditures as well as those relating directly to his business. Even multimillionaires have to be thrifty or their millions would take wings. In his little book "Succeeding With What You Have," Charles M. Schwab says: "Not long ago the expenses of running my New York home got exorbitant. I called in the steward and said to him: 'George, I want to strike a bargain with you. I will give you ten per cent of the first thousand dollars you save in house expenses, twenty-five per cent of the second thousand, and one-half of the third thousand.' The expense of operating the house was cut in two."

I once sent an interviewer to Marshall Field to ask him, among other things, what he considered the turning-point in his career, and his answer was: "Saving the first five thousand dollars I ever had, when I might just as well have spent the modest salary I made. Possession of that sum, once I had it, gave me the ability to meet opportunities. That I consider the turning-point." John Jacob Astor, the founder of the Astor fortune, said that if it had not been for the saving of his first thousand he might have died in the almshouse.

What a pathetic thing it is to see, as we do on every hand, well-educated, well-bred men and women, people with a great deal of ability, but with no money sense, going about with practically nothing ahead of them, between themselves and want, spending everything as they go! What a pathetic story the charity organizations could tell about people who have been in better circumstances, but who have lost their money, of people who have never been able to lay up anything; to put by anything, for a "rainy day."

What an assurance and sense of protection we get from the consciousness of a little "nest egg," a little money laid up for the future, something to stand between us and possible emergency or want, no matter what might happen to us.

No one can feel easy or safe who is living from hand to mouth. How many poor people in our great cities are constantly dispossessed, put out on the sidewalk, oftentimes when a parent or some other member of the family is ill, because they can't pay the rent, and this is often due to the lack of early training in thrift and wise economy; no provision made for an emergency; nothing laid up for a rainy day.

I have no sympathy for the rainy-day philosophy of many people; the rainy-day fear and terror, that cheeseparing saving, pinching, stingy policy. Such people make the very rainy day they are trying to guard against. It is the good sense, the wise precaution, which gives a reasonable provision for future needs, or for accidents, or for emergency, or for anything which may impair one's earning capacity, or any loss which may result from fire or flood, that wins our approval.

The saving habit, the bank-book habit, is an indication of the ambition to get on and up in the world. It is also an indication of many other good success qualities. The bank-book habit is seldom found in bad company.

The habit of thrift not only opens the door to opportunity, but is a safeguard against our own weaknesses, our gullibility, the tendency to scatter our earnings and make fools of ourselves. The saving of money so often means the saving of a man. It means cutting out indulgences or avoiding vicious habits. It often means health in the place of dissipation. It means a clear instead of a cloudy and muddy brain. It means that a man has vision, foresight, intelligence in planning and providing for his future. In fact, the thrift habit, the habit of saving, is not only one of the foundation-stones of a fortune, but also of character.

Theodore Roosevelt once wisely said, "If you would be sure that you are beginning right, begin to save. The habit of saving money, while it stiffens the will also brightens the energies."

The moment a young man begins to put aside money, systematically, and to make wise investments, he becomes a larger man. He begins to have a broader view of life. He begins to have more confidence in himself, in his ability, in his power to shoulder responsibility, to make his own program, to be his own boss. In early learning the lesson of thrift, he has taken the first step in the development of a sturdy character, the sort of character that distinguishes the best type of self-made man . . the Benjamin Franklins of the race.

Nothing will do more to help a young man to get credit and gain for him the assistance of successful people than the reputation for thrift, of having the saving habit, . . of having something ahead, something laid by, whether in government bonds, or in a life insurance policy, or in some other investment. Such thrift gives him standing.

A prominent businessman says: "Give me the youth who saves to make the man worthwhile." If you want to make your dreams of a prosperous future come true you will enter into a compact with yourself to save a certain amount every week out of your salary.

No matter how small this may be, or if you have to go without a great many things that you think you need; put this certain percentage of your earnings where it will be absolutely safe. This may mean riches to you in the future. A little ready money attracts opportunities. I have known of young men to get a splendid opportunity to start in business for themselves on five hundred dollars, some on less. Many a fortune has been started on less than a thousand dollars. The head of five big stores in New York told me he began business with three hundred dollars. Frank Woolworth, who built up the mammoth five and ten cent store business, started with something like three hundred dollars of his own, borrowing enough to bring it up to five hundred. Several of his first stores were failures, but he was not a failure. He had an idea and his small earnings helped him to back up his idea and to make his Dreams come true.

The power of money is usually not half appreciated by young men and young women. This is a land of opportunity, and good chances are constantly coming to those who have the ready cash. How often we hear people plead as an excuse for not seizing a rare opportunity for investment, that they hadn't the money! Multitudes of men have been obliged to let splendid opportunities pass because of this same lack. Great bargains for cash everywhere have been offered and only comparatively few men have had the reserve funds or the" ready cash to avail themselves of these splendid chances.

Some of the shrewdest business men I know tell me that there is nothing that pays the business man so well, in the long run, as to keep money in the bank, ready for an emergency, ready for an unexpected opportunity or a great bargain. It gives one a great sense of security to know that he is prepared for any ordinary emergency, that he has ready cash to help him. We can never tell when illness or accident may impair our earning capacity, or when some unforeseen emergency may make an unexpected call upon us. The thrifty man is never caught unprepared.

There are opportunities to save all around us. The facilities for saving are unparalleled and the rewards are certain. When we get a little money ahead it arouses enthusiasm to add to it. It is a perpetual suggestion, when we are tempted to spend, that we try to save. It is a little easier to say "No" when inclined to spend foolishly or for things which are really not worthwhile. Our savings are a constant encouragement, a tonic, a stimulant. His small savings have kept many a young man from falling into temptations which might have crippled or ruined him.

The little difference between what we earn and what we spend is capital. A little ready money suggests to young people just establishing a home wonderful possibilities in the way of comforts, the means of self-culture and growth. It means a little better reading matter, better books and periodicals. It means a possible college course later on for the children, and did age protection. It means less worry and less anxiety about the future, exemption from the fear of coming to want, or that those dear to us may suffer. It may mean a good physician, a skillful surgeon, instead of a bungler when sickness enters our home.

"I have been asked," says a great businessman, "to define the true secret of success. It is thrift in all its phases, and especially, thrift as applied to savings. Saving is the first great principle of success. It creates independence, it gives a young man standing, fills him with vigor, it stimulates him with the proper energy; in fact, it brings to him the best part of any success . . happiness and contentment." Can you desire anything better in your future than these?

I AM — ?

I AM stored-up happiness.

I lead the way to peace, power, and plenty. I bring you freedom from anxiety and worry over the living problem.

I AM a friend alike of the rich and the poor.

I AM common sense applied to life in all sorts of ways.

I AM a tower of strength in youth and a staff in old age.

I increase hope, confidence, assurance, certainty as to the future.

I was one of the chief factors in the winning of the World War.

I AM the best form of insurance against poverty and failure. I remove the shadow of the poorhouse.

I make for health, for efficiency, for the highest possible welfare of the individual.

I kill that "rainy day" dread; in fact, I do away with the "rainy day" altogether.

I put hope into the heart of man, a light into human eyes that was never there before.

I put people in a position to take advantage of all sorts of opportunities for investment, for advancement, to take advantage of chances that, but for me, would be lost.

I mean the best physicians, the most skilled surgeons, the best hospitals in case of need, as well as the best health resorts.

I make possible a needed vacation, rest, recreation and travel. I mean leisure, more living with natural art and with the beautiful things in the world.

I mean better opportunities for your children, better schools, better clothing, a more refining environment, greater security for their future.

I show you how to make the most of your income; how to expend the margin to the best advantage; how to make the wisest investments of your time, your strength and your ability as well as your money.

I AM the friend of man, a civilization builder. I not only give an upward tendency to the life of the individual, but also to the life of a nation.

I sustain and preserve the highest welfare of the race.

I safeguard the future; I enable you to work with confidence, to look up and not down, to rise superior to your surroundings.

I keep thousands of people out of the penitentiary; prevent them from committing theft and other crimes.

I increase the confidence of others in struggling young men and add tremendously to their credit.

I AM an employee's best recommendation, for I belong to a large and most excellent family. Every employer knows that the employee who cultivates me has many other sterling qualities, such as honesty, thoroughness, ambition, reliability, foresight, prudence.

I AM a symbol of character, of stability, of self-control; a proof that a man is not a victim of his appetites and weaknesses, but their master.

I AM often the savoir of a man, cutting off indulgences and vicious habits, putting health in the place of dissipation and insuring a clear brain instead of a cloudy, befuddled one.

I AM the enemy of that great curse of mankind . . debt . . which wrecks multitudes of homes, causes divorce, blasts love, and destroys all peace of mind.

I AM that which helps a man to lift his head above the crowd; to be independent, self-reliant, and to stand for something in the world.

Multitudes of families are homeless, moneyless, and are enduring all sorts of hardship, privation, and humiliation because the husbands and fathers never took me into partnership.

The failure army, today, is largely recruited by people who never learned to know me, who ridiculed the suggestion of needing me, who rather despised and looked down on me as standing for meanness and penuriousness and as being an enemy of their enjoyment.

I AM the best friend of woman. I make her a better businesswoman, a better housekeeper, a better wife and mother, a better citizen. I help her to make herself independent, self-reliant, and teach her how to finance herself.

However you make your living, whether by the work of your hand or of your brain, in a trade or in a profession, at home or in the shop, whether your income be small or large, you will always be placed at a disadvantage, will always be taking chances with your future security and happiness, unless you have me as a working partner.

I AM an incentive to high living, the simple life and high thinking. I urge spending upward, living upward, dwelling in honesty, in simplicity, living the life that is worthwhile, the genuine life, the life that will give enduring satisfaction.

I AM the beginning of real success; that which puts a foundation under your air castles, that which makes your dreams come true, which builds that "home of my own" to which every healthy, ambitious young person looks forward as the culmination of his hopes.

I AM THRIFT

Chapter XXI

As A Man Expecteth So Is He

- We never can get more out of ourselves than we expect. If we expect large things, if we hold the large mental attitude toward our work, toward our life, we shall get much greater results than if we depreciate ourselves, and only look for little things.

- The habit of expecting great things of ourselves calls out the best that is in us.

- No one can become prosperous while he really expects, or half expects, to remain poor. We tend to get what we expect, and to expect little is to get little.

- We ask little things, we expect little things, and thus we limit our supply.

- There is a tremendous power in the habit of anticipating good things, of believing that we shall realize our ambition; that out dreams will come true.

Multitudes queer their success at the very outset by anticipating bad things, expecting that they are going to fail, that their dreams will never be realized.

WHEN I was graduated from a New Hampshire academy my greatest stimulus to further endeavor was my favorite teacher's belief in me. Taking me by the hand at parting, as he bade me goodbye, he said: "My boy, I expect to hear from you, . . that the world will hear from you, . . in the future. Don't disappoint me. I believe in you, and can see something in you that you do not see in yourself."

There is only one thing more stimulating, more helpful, in the struggle for success, than the knowledge that others . . our teachers, our parents, our friends and relatives . . believe in us and expect great things of us; that is, to expect great things of ourselves. The difference between what two people get out of life, what they accomplish, and what they represent to others, depends upon the difference in what they expect of themselves.

A general who goes into a battle expecting to be beaten will be beaten. His expectation of defeat communicates itself to his army, demoralizes it at the start, and makes it impossible for the men to do their best. It is the same in the battle of life. To enter it with the expectation of defeat, is to be defeated before you begin. If you desire to succeed you must show your confident expectancy of success in your very presence. You must also live day by day in the very soul of expectancy of splendid things which are coming to you.

Working for one thing and expecting the opposite can bring only one result . . failure. Every time you say you don't expect ever to be anything, or to get anything, or to accomplish anything worthwhile, you are neutralizing the efforts you are making to be or to get or to do what you want. Our expectations must correspond with our endeavor. If we are convinced that we are never going to be really happy, that we are destined to plod along in discontent and wretchedness, to suffer all our lives, we shall tend to get what we expect. To be ambitious for happiness and yet always expect to be miserable, to continually doubt our ability to get what we long for, whatever it may be, is like getting on a train which is headed east when we wish to go west. We must expect to go in the direction of our desire, of our longing and effort. If you would succeed in what you are trying to do or to be, you must turn your back upon failure, blot out of your mind every thought, every picture, every suggestion of failure, and head toward success.

When, through a series of reverses and disappointments, a man has lost his grip upon himself, and feels convinced that he cannot possibly get on his feet; when he expects nothing but failure, there is only one thing you can do for him, . . try to arouse his hope; to restore his lost faith; to show him that, being divine, there is something in him which can never fail; that he and his Maker are one, and that, working together, they are a majority in any situation.

I have just received some manuscripts accompanied by a letter, in which the writer says: "I know the enclosed are nothing like your articles, for I couldn't write like you no matter how hard I might try. I don't expect you will want to publish these, but thought I would send them along because of the possibility that you might."

Now, at the very outset, this writer prejudiced me against his articles by his self-expressed inferiority and the suggestion that they were not worth publishing, and would probably be returned. It was as though a young man should start out in a disheartened mood to look for a job, discouragement in his face and in his every action, and should say to a prospective employer: "I don't think you will hire me; I didn't expect any luck when I came in, but thought I would try. I haven't much confidence in myself, and don't know that I can do work along this line. I doubt very much if I should suit you. Still I will try my best if you want to give me a chance, though I don't believe you will, for I never have any luck in hunting jobs."

This may sound ridiculous, but it expresses the mental attitude which multitudes of people hold toward the thing they long for and are striving to attain. They never expect to succeed in anything they undertake; never expect to be comfortable, to say nothing of having the luxuries and refinements of life. They expect only failure and poverty, and do not understand that this very expectancy increases the power of their mental magnet to attract these things, even though they are trying to get away from them.

I was recently talking with a man who is a good illustration of what this mental attitude does for us. He told me that for many years he had been working very hard, with no vacations, no let up in his efforts; that he worked holidays and most of his Sundays, and yet had never gotten anywhere and never expected to; that, in fact, things seemed to be in a conspiracy to disappoint and defeat him. "Of course you haven't succeeded, my friend, because you never expected to," I said to myself. "Moreover, you never gave yourself a chance. Holding your nose to the grindstone all this time, fearing and expecting poverty, failure, disappointment, limitation, defeat in everything, has made you a magnet for these things and drawn you into a failure rut."

We don't necessarily get what we work for; it is what we expect that comes to us. What you fear, as well as what you long for, is headed your way. All your fears, all your doubts, all your failure thoughts are taking shape in your life, molding conditions to their likeness; and no matter how hard you work for the thing you want, if you hold constantly in mind negative, discouraged thoughts; if you expect failure instead of success, evil instead of good, it is what you expect that will come to you. In other words, your thought is the creative force that molds and determines the conditions of your life.

"You must have birds in your heart, Madam, before you can find them in the bushes," said John Burroughs, the great naturalist, to a woman who complained that no birds ever came to her orchard, while he counted a score or more there, even while she uttered her plaint. It is what you hold in your heart, what you believe will manifest itself to you, that comes into your life. No one can accomplish anything great in this world who is confident that he was made to do little things, and is satisfied with an inferior position, hopeless of being anything but an underling all his life. On the other hand, a man who expects great things of himself is constantly trying to open a little wider the doors of his narrow life, to extend his limited knowledge, to reach a little higher, to get a little farther on than those around him. He has enough of the divine disposition to spur him on to nobler endeavors; he has a quenchless ambition to make the most of himself.

No matter what the conditions of your birth, it is you who shape your career, fashion your life for happiness or unhappiness, success or failure. It is true of all men and women that . . "They themselves are makers of themselves."

If you want to live the larger life, the happy, useful life, you must think the larger life; you must enlarge your model of yourself and of your possibilities; you must expect to realize your ideal of yourself and of the thing you long to do; for, as a man expecteth, so will his happiness, so will his life be.

It doesn't matter what we are trying to do, it is the hope and expectancy of success that nerves us to put forth our greatest effort; arms us with the assurance that compels success. The greatest difference, for instance, between the Al salesman and the mediocre one is the difference in their mental attitude.

"Beaten before he began"; "Didn't believe he was going to get the order," is written all over some salesmen. In trying to get orders they lack the hope, the expectation of success, the assurance and self-confidence that presage victory. They don't know the psychology of salesmanship; that it consists in holding the conviction of success always in mind, and so they fall down before the slightest opposition.

There are thousands of second-rate salesmen who have enough ability to make cracker-jacks, but who fail to get results because of their doubts and fears. At every little objection made by a prospect, they keep thinking and saying to themselves: "There, I am going to lose that man; I just feel it in my bones. I wish I could get an order from him, but it's no use; he's not going to sign." They do not realize that they are communicating their own doubts and fears to their prospect. It doesn't take a very sensitively organized person to feel the negative, failure atmosphere, and when he first lays his eyes upon one of those timid, doubting salesmen, the prospect knows that he is not a winner. Instead of victory, he sees defeat in his face; and if defeat is in a man's face he can't win no matter how much ability he has. His failure atmosphere repels everyone he contacts with.

Negative minds never make great salesmen or great anything else, because they don't build; they tear down. They are not creative, but destructive. They go through life closing the very doors ahead of them which they long to open; pulling with one hand, so to speak, on the door-knob, while at the same time holding a foot of doubt against that very door which they are trying to open. If they affirm their belief that there are good things for them, almost before they leave their lips they neutralize their affirmations by their secret doubts. They say one thing, but expect the opposite, just like the woman who prayed to the Lord to remove the sand heap from her yard, and when she got through praying looked out and said, "There it is, just as I expected! Of course the Lord didn't remove it!" That is the trouble with most of us. We pray and we work hard for things, and when we don't get them it is, "just as we expected." We couldn't get what we wanted and longed for because there was no faith, no belief, back of our efforts and our prayers. You know what St. James says of the man who doubts and fears and has no faith: "Let not that man think that he shall receive anything of the Lord."

Some people cannot understand how it is that bad men, cruel, brutal, conscienceless men, often succeed so well in their business. They succeed by the exercise of the mental law that like thoughts produce like results. This law works as unerringly as any physical law. It is neither ethical nor unethical. It is scientific. It is an inexorable principle, a changeless fact, that what we hold persistently in the mind is ultimately objectified in the body, in the life, whether it relates to our health, to our success or to our happiness. Ignorance of the law does not save us from the consequences of its violation, just as ignorance of our State or Federal laws does not condone an offense against them.

This is why it is so important that children should be trained in right thinking from the start. Every child should be reared to expect big things of himself: to understand that the Creator sent him here on an important mission, and that he must prepare himself for a life of achievement. Being a child of Omnipotence, of the All-Supply, man is the heir of all that is; health, success and happiness are his divine birthright, and every child should grow up with the conviction that good things instead of evil are waiting for him; that the longings of his heart, the yearnings of his soul, are prophecies of what he may become if he does his part in making a thorough preparation for his life work.

Do you realize that your environment today, your achievement, and your poverty or prosperity are really made up of your expectations of the past; what you expected of yourself years ago, when you started out in life? If you have been true to your vision of a successful future, and have backed up your faith, your ability, with hard work and intelligent endeavor, you have worked in harmony with the law and are reaping the harvest of your thought and endeavor. If, on the other hand, you find yourself poverty stricken and wretched, you have violated the law, and your only hope of bettering your condition is to turn about face and go the other way. Work with the law, not against it. Work for what you want, but work with confidence, with the hope, the belief, that you will get it.

Expecting to be happy; expecting to be successful; expecting to win out in our undertakings; expecting health instead of disease; ' expecting good luck instead of ill luck; expecting harmony instead of discord and trouble; expecting to make friends wherever we go; expecting to be thought well of, to stand for something in our community, . . this is to establish relations with the things we want and are working for; it is to attract them to us: for as a man expecteth so is he; so has he.

Chapter XXII

I Can't Afford It . . The Habit Of Going Without

- People who are always fearing the future, who always see rocks, shoals, and all sorts of snags and dangers ahead, who are forever preparing for a "rainy day," not only attract the very things they fear, but also lose all the joy and happiness of living.

- You will never be anything but a beggar while you think beggarly thoughts, but a poor man while you think poverty, a failure while you think failure thoughts.

- Train yourself persistently away from the thought of limitation, away from the thought of lack, of want, of pinched supply. Thinking abundance, and defying limitation, will open up your mind and set your thought currents toward a greatly increased supply.

- When we learn the art of seeing opulently, instead of stingily; when we learn to think without limits, how not to cramp ourselves by our limiting thought, we shall find that the thing we are seeking is seeking us, and that tomorrow it will meet us half way.

- You do not inherit poverty, squalor, and humiliating limitations. Lack and want have nothing whatever to do with God's children. Your inheritance is rich, sublime beyond description.

Do you know that every time you say "I can't afford it, such things are for others, but not for me," or, "I have been poor and had to deny myself things all my life, and I expect it will always be so," you are closing the doors to prosperity? If you want to realize prosperity and plenty you must dismiss forever from your mind the can't-afford-it thought, the thought that you can't afford anything which is good for you, anything which will contribute to the growth or highest possible development of the man or woman. It is your birthright to have these things. They belong to you by divine heritage, and you should claim them. The Creator intended that His children should have plenty, and the best of everything that is good for them, that will contribute to growth, enlargement of character, and happiness.

The idea that riches are possible only to those who have superior advantages, more ability, or those who have been favored by fate, is false and demoralizing. The Creator has given man dominion over a world teeming with riches for all, not for a favored few. If we claim our inheritance and work in harmony with His laws we will have the abundance and happiness He meant we should have. We will be glorious successes. It is not in our nature that we are paupers, but in our mean, stingy estimate of ourselves and our powers.

To me, one of the most pitiable things in the world is a family where the parents, through mistaken ideas of economy, fail to bring up their children generously, who refuse to furnish them with the mental food, the change, the variety, the amusement, that are so necessary to their largest possible development.

How many parents, fearing future want, hoard their money and starve their children's minds, stunt their growth, so that they become dwarfed human beings instead of the superb personalities they might have been if the parents had made a generous effort in their education, in the development of their mental growth!

People are often obliged to go through life exhibiting deplorable ignorance, and are many times blamed for this when their parents were really at fault. They never gave them as children the nourishment, the mental food necessary to develop their larger qualities, their greater possibilities. They are compelled to plod along in mediocrity, so far as mentality and personality are concerned, because they never have had a fair chance. Their ability, their brains, were never backed up with the proper preparation for the larger possible life.

Many of these parents, perhaps most of them, fully intended to be generous to their children, but the habit of saving, the fear of coming to want, which in time develops into a strangling, dwarfing, blighting greed, kept them putting off from year to year a present privilege and duty. They did not put the emphasis on the right thing, to the lifelong detriment of those they loved more than anything else in the world.

True economy is not parsimony, miserliness. It is neither extravagance nor meanness. It means a wise expenditure, an expenditure which brings the largest results. It is being good to ourselves in as large and scientific a way as possible. It means that we should always have the best we can possibly afford when the thing has any reference to our physical and mental health, to our growth in efficiency and power. It often means very liberal spending. It is a perpetual protest against putting the emphasis on the wrong thing.

"Extravagance leads to insubordination and parsimony to meanness," we are told. Don't deceive yourself by going through life patronizing cheap things, wearing cheap clothes, looking seedy, with the belief that you are doing the wisest thing. Remember that your appearance will largely determine your status in society. The world accepts or rejects us by the evidence of our personality, the impression we make. The feeling that you can't afford this and you can't afford that; always dwelling upon something cheap, cheapens your life, cheapens your mentality, limits and narrows it, dwarfs your personality and makes anything but a favorable impression.

Wise, thrifty, and often generous expenditure in the thing which helps us along the line of our ambition, which will make a good impression, secure us quick recognition, and help our promotion, is often an infinitely better investment than putting money in a savings-bank.

The secret of health, of success and happiness, is largely in being good to one's self, in putting one's self in a superb condition, so that one is always able to do the biggest thing possible to him, always ready to take advantage of whatever opportunities come his way. Anything which prevents a person from attaining this high-water mark of efficiency is a sin against true economy. Every young man should have an understanding with himself at the outset that he will have nothing to do with the false economy that results in lowered vitality or efficiency, that anything which tends to cut down his power, even by a small fraction, is poor economy and very unscientific.

What is good policy in this respect for the individual is equally good for the home and for business. Many a business concern has gone on the rocks because the proprietor was too much occupied with picayune economies, turning down gas and saving and pinching on petty things, to give his attention to the important things.

While saving a trifle here and there, he was losing trade and falling behind in the race, by not putting enough money into his business to keep up with his competitors. While the shortsighted proprietor is hugging pet theories about economy and trying to save on little things, the big things will suffer for a little expenditure which would bring in infinitely greater returns. Liberal expenditure is often the best kind of business economy. Spending precious time and energy in petty savings is often the worst kind of business policy. In order to bring money in one must put out money.

Some people never get out of the world of pennies into the world of dollars. They work so hard to save the cents that they lose the dollars and also the larger growth, the richer experience and the better opportunity.

"The superior man," says Confucius, "is anxious lest he should not get truth; he is not anxious lest poverty should come upon him." Multitudes of people think too much about poverty and economizing. They dwell upon the "can't-afford-it" philosophy, and continually feel the pressure of the rainy-day idea, which has been dinned into their ears from infancy, until it stunts and dwarfs the whole life.

Those who haven't the money cannot, of course, always do that which will contribute to their highest comfort and efficiency; but many people overestimate the advantage of saving a dollar in comparison with their physical well-being. Power is the goal of the highest ambition. Anything which will add to one's power, to one's growth, no matter how much it costs, if it is within possible reach, is worth its price.

We have all met the "can't afford it" men and women who go through life pinching and cheeseparing. We see them stopping at cheap hotels or boarding houses, traveling long distances in the day coach, carrying their lunch with them; seldom or ever buying a newspaper, a magazine, or a book, investing in nothing which will enlarge the mentality or enrich the life; putting every penny they can Squeeze out of a very poor living into the bank or in other investments. They may think that what they thus save is going to help their children; but, nevertheless, from every point of view it is very short-sighted economy. I have scarcely ever known an instance where money squeezed out of the real necessities of life was appreciated by the children who inherited it, to say nothing of the dwarfing, impoverishing, aging effect upon those who accumulated it by such self-sacrifice. Oftentimes the hard-earned, sweat-of-the brow savings have really been a detriment to youthful inheritors, because it has prevented them from using their ability and developing their powers of self-reliance and vigor.

Many families live constantly under the shriveling influence of the stinginess consciousness, the lack and want consciousness, the conviction that the good things of the world were intended for others but not for them. As a result they have never been able to demonstrate anything else but lack, want and limitation. Multitudes of children are reared in this poverty atmosphere, and in time become so convinced that they can't afford things that others have that they never do have them. Their poverty conviction shuts off the supply. They think the little thought and they demonstrate littleness.

Getting along with little and being half-satisfied to continue doing this, generally means that we shall have to get along with less, for it is not a creative mental attitude, not an attitude which attracts plenty and builds success. The "can't afford it" consciousness, the "going without" consciousness, brings you nearer and nearer to the point where you can't afford it, just as the "can afford it" consciousness tends to bring you nearer to the point where you can afford it, for he can who thinks he can, and he can't who thinks he can't. We can't do what we think "we can't do; we can't get what we think we can't get.

If you are hard up, you have had a hard-up mind, that is, a hard-up mental attitude, a hard-up conviction, and that has cut off your supply.

The poverty thought, the poverty conviction, is a colossal giant wrestling with human beings and overcoming multitudes of them. It is only those who know the secret hold of the wrestling match, as Dr. W. John Murray says, who can hope to escape the fatal blow of this giant.

I know people in fair circumstances who live so completely in the poverty conviction that they are always hunting for bargains, are always buying cheap things, . . cheap food, cheap clothing, cheap furniture, cheap everything. The result is that nothing they have wears or lasts any length of time. While they pinch and screw on prices and think they are saving, they really spend more in the end for poor cheap stuff which is always coming to pieces than they would need to spend on good things, because these would last so much longer than the inferior articles, to say nothing of the infinitely greater satisfaction they would give.

Getting into the current of cheapness not only narrows and pinches the life, but it deteriorates the taste for and appreciation of quality, just as a cheap piano in a home, a piano which is always out of tune, tends to deteriorate the musical taste of the members of the family.

Bargain hunters are nearly always victims of false economy; and women are special offenders in this respect. They will waste hours of precious time, sometimes most of a day, and suffer much discomfort in chasing around from one store to another, looking for bargains and trying to save a few cents on some small purchase they wish to make. Then they will buy wearing apparel and all sorts of articles of inferior material because the price is low, although they know the articles will not wear well. They actually buy, because they are cheap, a great many things they do not need, and then they will probably tell you how much they have saved. If these women would only reckon up what they have expended in this way in one year, they would generally find that, apart altogether from the loss of time and the wear and tear on themselves, they have lost rather than gained on their transactions. They would find that they had spent more than if they had only bought what they really needed, when they needed it, and had paid the regular price for it.

There are many ambitious people with mistaken ideas of economy who very seldom get the kind and quality of food which is capable of building the best blood and the best brain. This going without what would reinforce physical power, create mental force and virility, keeps multitudes of people plodding along in mediocrity who are really capable of doing infinitely better things. This is wretched economy. The ambitious farmer selects the finest ears of corn and the finest grain, fruits and vegetables for seed. He cannot afford to cumber his precious soil with poor seed.

Can the man who is ambitious to make the most of himself afford to eat cheap, stale foods, which' lack, or have lost, great energizing elements? Can he afford to injure his health by trying to save a little money at the cost of letting the fire of his energy languish or die?

No one who hopes to accomplish anything, in life can afford to feed his brain with poor fuel. To do so would be as foolhardy as for a great factory to burn bad coal on the ground that good coal was too expensive. Whatever you do, however poor you may be, don't stint or try to economize in food fuel, which is the very foundation and secret of your success in life. To make a high class man you must have first class food, and this is not extravagance. You can't build a superior brain out of cheap, inferior, adulterated foods, gulped down at a cheap lunch counter.

It is wholly a question of what you get out of your expenditure, not its amount, which makes it a wise expenditure or a foolish one. For instance, it will sometimes pay the biggest kind of returns to pay five or even ten dollars for a dinner where you can hear great men with worldwide reputations speak. In other words, it always pays to get into the most ambition-arousing and helpful atmosphere possible. It is a great thing to learn about the experiences of men who have won out in the very lines in which we are struggling; even if they do not happen to be in our particular line, the principles by which they have succeeded are much the same as those that bring success in any line, and it is extremely valuable to know how they have been applied in any particular instance.

Success attracts success. Money attracts money. Prosperity attracts prosperity, and it pays you to get with people who are prosperous, who have honorably won out in what they attempted. There is a perpetual success suggestion radiating from them which no ambitious young man can afford to lose.

A miserable pinching economy was never intended for God's children. There is a larger and fuller life for them. Man was made for good things, for grand things, to have everything which can minister to his complete growth and development. If he condemns himself to a narrow, unfruitful life of cheeseparing, pinching economies he has no one to blame but himself. Our condition is what our words, our thoughts, our convictions, as well as the result of our efforts, make it. If you are thinking and constantly saying, "I can't afford to do this," or "I can't afford that," "We must make this do," "Money is so scarce," you are sowing the seed which will give you the same kind of a harvest. Your poverty thought will make your future as narrow and limited and poverty stricken as your present.

Chapter XXIII

How To Bring Out The Man You Can Be

• We should judge ourselves by what we feel capable of doing, not by what we have done. Nothing else will so nerve you to accomplish greatly as a belief in your own inherent greatness, your godlike possibilities.

• There is a potency inside of you which, if you would unlock it, would make of you everything you ever dreamed or imagined you could become.

• Don't be afraid to think too highly of yourself. If the Creator made you and is not ashamed of the job, certainly you should not be. He pronounced His work good, and you should respect it.

• Persistently hold the thought that you are eternally progressing towards something higher in every atom of your being. This will make you grow, will enrich your life.

• The constant struggle to measure up to a high ideal is the only force in heaven or on earth that can make a life great.

• That vision which grips your heart, that longing of your soul to do something significant, that dream of high achievement which haunts your imagination, is not a mere fantasy, a whimsical unreality, it is a prophecy of the big things you will do if you get your higher self to work for you.

SAID the great psychologist, William James, "The average individual develops less than ten per cent of his brain cells and less than thirty per cent of his possible physical efficiency. We all live below our maximum of accomplishment."

Suppose a human being, because of lack of proper nourishment, or of some accident in childhood, should attain only ten per cent of his possible physical height and only thirty per cent of his normal weight, what a pitiable object he would present!

What a wretched apology for the well-proportioned, perfectly developed being the Creator had planned the unfortunate dwarf would be!

Yet, so far as the man of the God-plan is concerned, most of us are self-made dwarfs, falling short not ten, twenty, or thirty, but a hundred per cent of our possible development. Even those who climbed to the mountain peaks of human achievement, . . the Michael Angelos, the Beethovens, the Shakespeares, the Miltons, the Dantes, the great men and women in every field of creative work, . . never reached the maximum of their possible accomplishment.

During a visit to California, I one day stood in awe before a giant tree, in the hollow of which General John C. Fremont, "Pathfinder of the Rockies," with his staff, lived for months when on a government survey expedition. More than a hundred soldiers had been in the trunk of this tree at one time. Nearby was another, over three hundred feet in height, estimated to contain about two hundred thousand feet of lumber, . . enough to build all the houses of a small village. As my eye wandered over their huge trunks and limbs, the thought came, that had the same seeds which produced these giants of the forest been planted in a cold northern country, in soil which contained but little nourishment, then, even with the greatest care, they would have been dwarfs instead of giants. Instead of being capable of housing a detachment of soldiers, or of producing enough timber to make houses for a whole village, they would have been mere scrubs of trees, pigmies instead of the giants they might have been under the right conditions for development.

Just as unfavorable conditions in the vegetable kingdom dwarf a possible giant tree and make it a pigmy, so do unfavorable conditions in the animal kingdom dwarf a possible giant in a man and make him a pigmy. But while the tree has no power of itself to change conditions, to alter or improve its environment, man is made to dominate his environment; to bend conditions to his will; to overcome all obstacles that may hinder or delay his highest possible development. In other words, every acorn, if conditions are just right, may become a grand oak, but every human acorn, in spite of conditions, no matter how bad they may be, can become, if he will, a grand man.

Man's development depends on his ideal of himself, the mental picture of his appearance and environment which he constantly visualizes. So long as we think that we are merely human, sons of Adam, inheriting only his weaknesses, his limitations; so long as we are convinced that we are helpless victims of heredity, of circumstances and environment, we can never express, anything but mediocrity, weakness, inferiority.

A great artist who put his whole soul in his work would never look at inferior pictures, because he said, if he did, he would become familiar with false artistic ideals, and his own pencil would soon catch the taint of inferiority. It is familiarity with a weak, inferior ideal of ourselves that dwarfs and stunts our development. As long as we think we are poor ineffectual nobodies no power in the world can make us anything else. Our mental attitude fixes the limit of our development. Nothing can save us from our own conviction of inferiority, and inability to rise above the things that hold us down.

"We actually have powers of many kinds which we habitually fail to use," says Dr. James J. Walsh. "We have acquired the habit of not being equal to ourselves." This habit of not being equal to ourselves is what causes a great majority of human beings to underestimate what they are capable of doing. They measure their capacity by what they have done in the past or by what others think they can do, and so they plod along in a narrow groove of inferiority, in which their real power is never exercised.

Unless some fortunate accident intervenes, the larger man remains undiscovered, and they go to their graves without ever having gone below the surface of their almost limitless hidden powers.

I recently met a man who had plodded along in a very ordinary way through what is commonly regarded as the most productive years of life without showing any special ability. In fact he failed in several things he had attempted. But, although he was not strong on self-confidence, he kept hammering away and happened to make a business hit. His success aroused a new man in him, gave him a new sense of power. He was never quite the same afterwards. He carried himself more confidently, with more assurance. The vision of new power he had glimpsed in the great within of himself opened his eyes to his possibilities, and he rapidly developed a marvelous business capacity which he never before realized he possessed. His whole outlook and his entire methods of business changed. Timidity, hesitation, diffidence, a wobbly uncertain policy of life gave place to boldness, self-confidence, quickness and firmness of decision, and he went up by leaps and bounds until he became a great financial power, and a leader in his community. He had found the hidden spring which opened up the gate of his life and gave him a glimpse of his divine resources.

Not what you have done, or have failed to do, but what you are capable of doing now; not what you are, but what you are capable of becoming, . . these are the important facts in your life. It doesn't matter so much what others think of you; what they believe is possible to you; it is what you think of yourself; what you believe you have the ability to do that counts. This is of immense importance to you, because you will not begin to touch your possibilities until you make the acquaintance of your real self, the bigger possible "me" in you.

After his seventy-five years of marvelous individual accomplishment, Thomas A. Edison says that man is yet in the chimpanzee stage of development, and that he has gained but a mere glimpse of his environment.

The unfolding of man's hidden powers has progressed more rapidly during the past twenty-five years than in any other fifty years of the world's history. But the advance in individual progress is nothing compared with the developments this century will witness. There is no name so secure in the Hall of Fame, there is no leader in any line of endeavor today, who is not likely to be superseded by someone who is yet entirely unknown to fame. There may be at this moment, on this continent, some youth who will break all previous records in music, in art or literature. There may be working for some American merchant today a clerk who will eclipse the records of the greatest merchant princes of the world. A greater than Shakespeare may now be in swaddling clothes.

When every human being awakens his sleeping genius, brings out the giant in the great within of him, we will have a world of supermen, a race of gods.

John Drinkwater, author of the great play, "Abraham Lincoln," says: "He who most completely realizes himself is he who most fitly assumes leadership of men, not only in the days of his life on earth, but in the story that he becomes thereafter. And for nearly two thousand years there has been no man of whom we have record who has so supremely realized himself to the very recesses of his being as this American, Lincoln."

There is no man, however humble his birth or environment, who brings out the best that is in him, realizes himself "to the very recesses of his being," who will not be a great man. But it is only at long intervals that anyone does this; that a man arises whose full power has been given anything like complete expression as in a Lincoln.

Many of the richest mines in the world were abandoned time and again before their hidden wealth was discovered by the more gritty and persevering prospectors. These men were not satisfied with superficial digging, but went down into the very bowels of the earth until they found the treasure they were after. They became fabulously rich, while the fellows who quit, or wandered from claim to claim, never giving time or energy enough to one; never having enough faith in its possibilities to dig deeper, died in poverty. In one instance I know of a man who mortgaged everything he had in the world, borrowed all he could, and even sold his clothing, to raise enough money to enable him to sink a shaft below the point at which a former prospector had quit, and, going only a few yards deeper, he struck one of the richest silver mines on this continent.

The men who never amount to much, the failures and ne'er-do-wells, are like the prospectors who dug only a little way down into their claims and then quit, dying in poverty and wretchedness when they might have been rich beyond their wildest dreams. There are thousands of down-and-outs in the great failure army today who had possibilities that would have made them captains in the ranks of industry, leaders in different vocations; there are multitudes of employees, much abler men and women than their employers, plodding hopelessly in inferior positions, who have enough undiscovered ability hidden away in them to make them supreme in their line, but they have never had the grit, the courage and the perseverance to dig down to the treasure-house of their hidden wealth. They prospected a little along the surface of their being and then quit.

There is just as much success material; there are just as many success potencies in many of those who fail as there are in those who succeed. The trouble with most of the failures is that they never dig deep enough into themselves to bring out the bigger man that is hidden in them. Multitudes of men and women never discover their real selves, because their investigations are so superficial. They don't think deeply or work in the right way; they don't focus their efforts with sufficient intensity to open the door to their locked-up possibilities.

Are you willing to go through life as a pigmy when there is something in you which Even now is telling you that you can be a giant? Are you going to put forth a giant's efforts to bring out the biggest thing in you, or are you going to sit around waiting for luck or something outside of yourself to come to your assistance, . . . for outside capital, for somebody to give you a lift?

You will never unfold the bigger man God has wrapped up in you in this way, my friend. The only power that will develop the giant in you is right inside of you. God himself can't develop the human acorn that chooses to remain a dwarf, a scrub oak instead of the grand human oak of the Creator's plan.

How to Have Abundance

by

Lillian DeWaters

Originally Published in the August 1916
Christian Science Journal

WHEN Christian Science was first presented to me about fifteen years ago, I was in excellent health, and therefore began to study it merely to understand its spiritual teachings; but it was only after faithfully continuing to do so for over two years that I began to grasp them. The light came all at once. While reading Science and Health one afternoon, suddenly it came as though a veil had been lifted from my eyes. Every page I turned to was full of meaning, whereas the same words had formerly been meaningless to me. At that hour the basic teachings of Christian Science were made entirely clear to me. I would say to those discouraged because of lack of comprehension, do not be intense in thought and yearning, for it takes time to understand the fundamentals of mathematics, and generally takes time for one to comprehend the Science of Mind.

When the Principle of Christian Science was revealed to me I was teaching school, and began at once to put my understanding into practice. I was called upon by the head master to take charge of the music, play the piano, and so on. Several years before this I had gained some knowledge of music, but at this time both fingers and knowledge were inactive from disuse; however, I was told that unless the music was undertaken I could not retain my position. After an earnest study of passages in the Bible and Science and Health, I felt that I could do what my duty required of me. It was therefore with the utmost confidence in God that I seated myself at the piano in the assembly hall in the school.

With no nervousness, nor fear, I placed a march before me, and although my fingers touched the keys, it was as though someone else played; something within me compelled the music to flow regularly and correctly from my fingers, though humanly speaking I had not the musical education to enable me to read the sheet of music before me. Jesus had knowledge without need of books or study, so all knowledge is within man as God's idea, and we are sure to find it when in critical moments, like mine, we are compelled to depend entirely upon the divine resources, look only to Truth for help.

Later, I gave up my work and was married, and when our babies were born I depended upon Christian Science treatment for strength, and courage to face the ordeal. I was up doing light work about the house the morning following the birth of one baby, and the second morning after the birth of the other. In both cases I was strong and in a normal condition. During the past year I have realized more than ever the sin of criticism, . . that one cannot be lovable or loving while speaking words of condemnation or unkindness against another. The less one judges or criticizes others the healthier and happier he becomes, and one learns through Christian Science how to overcome sin and wrong thinking.

I am grateful for the many blessings that have come to me because of Christian Science, grateful to those who have helped me and for the help which I in turn have been able to give others.

Lillian De Waters,

Stamford, Conn.

How to Have Abundance

The only satisfying search for all people is to find God, understanding, for as understanding unfolds in the mind (the invisible), all good things (the visible) will be manifested as result.

There are certain laws that govern music, certain laws that govern mathematics, still other laws that govern art. So, also there are certain laws which govern health, happiness and prosperity. These laws are mental laws and pertain to the thinking and feeling of the individual.

The very first step for one to take, who is bound by sickness, sin, or poverty, is to know that he is bound by fear and ignorant beliefs. Nature, God, is not responsible for your sickness or poverty and there is a way for you to put off these erring beliefs and their manifestations and reveal the real nature and character of your being.

The first step to take in order to fulfill your desire is to seek a simple, intelligent and satisfying understanding of Life.

The desire for health, happiness and prosperity, you must build upon goodness; that is, you must not expect to hold to sinful thoughts and habits with one hand, while you grasp God, understanding, with the other.

"Seek ye first the Kingdom," the realm of Mind . . right thought, and herein you will solve your problems, and as a result health, wealth, and happiness will follow.

"Ye shall find me when ye shall search for me with all your heart."

The desire for good, that is, the desire to be good, must be uppermost in consciousness. Selfish aims, erring thoughts and expressions, must be put aside, and the heart (feeling) must palpitate for good alone.

Each individual has the nature and character of God, is a God-being, and has the power to create and bring forth all good. Many would like the "added" things without having or using the thoughts and feelings that cause or create these "things."

You cannot and should not expect to be well if you are constantly thinking sick or sinful thoughts, neither can you achieve success and prosperity if you are thinking thoughts of poverty, stinginess or inactivity. There are many who strive religiously to avoid expressing the word money in their conversation. They will speak of "supply" and "abundance," and although what they really need is money, they nevertheless hold to the mistaken mental position that money is material and they believe it wrong to desire money, yet never refuse it when offered them.

This is unreasonable. The right way to think about money is that money is good and right to have and that it is not material but entirely mental as is all else.

If you need money, think money. When you think poverty thoughts you are thinking "no money."

Money of itself is good; it is the erring sense about money that is at fault. Pure water is good and right to drink, but it would work ill to the individual who drank too much of it at one time.

To have money in abundance and to spend it freely, yet wisely, is not a wrong. By this I do not mean that it is right to want money for the mere sake of accumulating wealth.

One must have the right desire back of the thought of money if he desires to make a success of his life. To use the Mind for any other purpose than the working out of goodness, honesty and service, is to defraud oneself of the true nature of universal good.

Let us learn of the law of prosperity, and be obedient to this law.

It requires us to be good, to be trustful, to be active, to be courageous, to be patient.

Faith is a mental quality to be acquired and cultivated. Without a live faith, which is the feeling of conviction, confidence and courage, creation cannot take place. We must have faith in Science, God, the same as we have faith in mathematics. Faith looks into the Kingdom, the invisible world, and there beholds Reality.

Faith believes in the invisible perfection rather than outward appearances. There is no way to prove your faith other than by acting upon it. When we say to the mountain (discord) "be thou removed," do we then act as though it were out of our way? Faith is bold and fearless. It is divided faith that fails. I might tell here of how simple faith in the Right and Good and absolute single-mindedness won for me a success which otherwise would never have come into my experience.

It was some years ago while I was a public school teacher that, finishing my term in a suburb, I applied in person for a position in a large city. The Superintendent of the City

Schools met me kindly, listened to my oral application, and then said; "We could not possibly give you a position to teach in our city. Firstly, we accept only College Graduates. This is absolute. Your certificate is Normal, and you would receive no consideration whatsoever. Secondly, every room in every school in this city has a teacher engaged for the coming term."

I listened in silence, thanked him for his time, left my name and address upon his desk, and walked out of his office.

The first thought that came to me was exhilarating. It was this: "There is no reason for you to feel disappointed. His decision is not final. He does not give you your place nor position in this world. God gives you your place."

I did not understand then that my own right Mind was God, but my faith in Right and Might was omnipotent and I saw nothing at all in the way or in the path that I desired.

It was the end of June that I made this application and not a word did I hear in furtherance during July and August of the vacation period. However, a doubt never entered my mind but what I would be given the position that I asked. Never once did my mind waver, worry nor fear.

I knew it would come and simply I rested upon this fact. I felt it would come because it would be right. My parents were then living in that city and I wished with all my heart to live with them, for we had been separated for several years. The feeling that there was a place here for me because it would be good for us all was what gave me the supreme confidence and mental conviction of success. The first week of September was nearly passed, and but two days were left before the opening of the school term; still I can truly say that never a doubt nor anxiety entered my mind. I was calm, poised, at perfect rest in the feeling that I would have that place that I desired. That day a telegram was sent to me, by the very Superintendent whom I had interviewed, and the message told me that I had been appointed a position as teacher in his schools and he would expect me on the opening day.

I can distinctly recall how I stood reading that telegram without a quiver of surprise, only gladness and joy.

I soon discovered that the school in which I was placed was in the best residential section, the most desirable school in the whole city, the teacher appointed for that room being unable to accept the position.

I obeyed the law of single-mindedness. I had supreme faith and loving feeling, and, of course, this fixed right sense and feeling manifested itself in the thing that I desired.

The law of Mind says that with God nothing is impossible. Think of it. That is, everything right that it is possible for you to think and feel you can do or have, You CAN DO AND CAN HAVE.

Do not see God afar off or without you, sometimes giving and sometimes not giving. Make Nature, God, Life, Mind, (or whatever name you choose to use) as near and as certain to you as the law of mathematics. You never doubt in your heart but what if you make right use of the rules in mathematics you will obtain the correct answer. Look at the demonstrations of Jesus. For him to speak or command was for him to expect a certain result. Thus, if it is a home you wish, or a position, or money, or love, expect to have it and expect it "with all your heart," and, "never doubting."

You know that the rules in mathematics are already established, certain, fixed, inevitable, so you do not worry about this end of it; you merely endeavor to gain an understanding of these rules and their application, and, as certain as night follows day, you will obtain the correct results if you correctly apply the rules.

So also there are rules and laws governing health, happiness, prosperity, and if we learn what these laws are, and apply them correctly, we must obtain the correct results.

Be good. Live the good thoughts that you think. Learn what right thoughts to think for the particular problem at hand. If you wish prosperity, then consciously and actually think thoughts of plenty, abundance, freedom. Know that Mind has infinite and supreme power to externalize for you that which you desire. If you are filling a certain position and wish a more lucrative one, yet believe in your heart that you really are not worth more than you are at present receiving, do not grumble nor wonder if you remain where you are. No one will value you in excess of what you value yourself. Those who place high value upon their services are they who believe in their own worth and who see no obstacles in the way of obtaining their right desires.

Suppose the universal belief is poor times, etc., do not let this wrong belief about Life enter your consciousness as true. You must see infinite abundance, the spiritual laws of Life as fixed, changeless and as governing you and your experiences in spite of "times," "friends," 'business operations," etc. "A thousand shall fall at thy side and ten thousand at thy right hand but it shall NOT come nigh THEE." Who? You who know and obey the true law of the Universe.

The power that gives you your health and happiness is also the source of your so-called material supply. Since God is one and God is all and God is Mind, this is therefore a mental universe and all therein is the result of Mind or thought from the head of a pin to a palace and from a penny to a gold mine. Everything that you see, hear, or understand through your senses is mental or is the result of thought and feeling.

At one time I wanted a new home. My desire was to sell the house in which I lived and buy something larger and better. The first step that I took in this problem was to go out and find the house of my desire.

I pictured in my mind what kind of a house I desired, and just what street I wished to live upon, and then I acted. I went right out, motored down the avenue of my desire and found the house. The moment my eyes rested upon it there was nothing else for to see.

I knew that it was the house of my desire. Size, style, location, environment, everything accorded with my thought.

I stepped from my car, walked up the steps and rang the bell. I asked my question and this was the answer . . "This house is not for sale at any price."

I continued my search through the city for several days, but found nothing at all that appealed to my thought, and so gave up the search and settled down to find out what kept this house of my desire from me. I inquired from real estate men and they advised me that the owner of the house built it himself and for himself, and that many besides myself had wished to purchase it, but it was useless, etc., etc.

But I was not daunted, for I knew the spiritual law and that if it were right for me to have this house that Mind, God would make a way for me to possess it without injury to the present owner or anyone else.

This was my mental foundation and the rock upon which I worked (thought). I again called upon the owner and asked him if he would allow me to see the rooms as it might be that they would not suit me and then I would no longer trouble him. This time he willingly took me through the house, and I found everything to my delighted satisfaction. We sat and chatted a while and all the time that the owner was affirming that he would never sell the house to anyone, my mind was searching for something. What was it that was holding this house from me? I had a distinct sense that something would be unfolded. And it was. Presently he said to me, . . "Where do you expect my daughter and myself to live if I sold you this house? We cannot go into the street, and we will never live on any avenue but this one, and in no other house but a house that I myself built."

I smiled to myself, knowing that the way was then open and free. Before I left he confided to me that really his daughter wished for a smaller home, but knew not how to acquire it. He would be glad to buy the vacant lot next door, and would build a house of their present desire if I would wait. So we were all happy and satisfied, and at the end of five months' patient waiting, I sold the house that I then owned and took possession of the new house of my desire.

This taught me the lesson to give. We must not alone want to take, to have our desires granted or fulfilled, but we must always be considerate of the feelings of those with whom we are in business relation and be willing to give as well as to take.

Success and prosperity come then not from outside sources as Cause but from within you. You are the Cause primarily of your success or of your failure. Nature unfolds from within out. Be positive and firm in your convictions and feelings and above all be certain that your desires are right desires, and injure no one and nothing, and then nothing can stop your success or advancement. It is our nature to be able to have everything good. You should praise God, so praise the good in yourself, and let your thoughts and feeling be rich in quality. It is not merely the quantity of your thinking and feeling, but both quantity and quality of your thinking and feeling that count.

Called suddenly to give my help upon a problem that must be met at once, if at all, I have many times succeeded in bringing about the desired change in a few moments of time, whereas, days and weeks may have elapsed in other cases not so urgent before such changes have taken place, therefore be sure that you put the necessary quality in your mental work. The quality of a thought is that substance of which the thought consists. To have the right quality, a thought must have richness of feeling, confidence, power, courage, conviction, faith. To think thoughts of good with power, strength, life, activity, understanding back of them, will result in greater externalization of good than to think the very same thoughts all day long, yet think them in a doubting half-hearted, wondering mental attitude.

Take right thought into all of your affairs. You can start with one right thought and let it expand in consciousness until more right thoughts are formed and more understanding, which is true substance, takes possession of your consciousness. You cannot demonstrate things until you demonstrate thoughts, for thoughts precede things. The financier has faith and courage in himself, in his own ideas, and he believes his own ideas are money-making, money-producing. He is using the mental law of prosperity, although he may be ignorant of this fact. Ignorance of the mental law in no way interferes with the fulfillment of that law.

If obstacles seem in your way, endeavor to think of them as gone, or as not present, for infinite perfection holds no obstacle in its way. If you have faith and confidence in the power of right thinking, which is divine Mind in operation, there will be the right adjustment in your affairs. If we had no temptations and no trials, we would not prove our strength and power.

Know that the good that is yours cannot be withheld from you and it is wrong for you to suffer because of the sins of others. Think of all good as flowing unto you as the mighty river pours ceaselessly its stream of living waters.

In many cases it seems as though the life experiences of those near and dear to us cross our path, retard our progress and cause us suffering. We are each individual and we each therefore have individual life problems and we each have a work to do for ourself that no other one can do for us.

To attempt therefore to carry the burdens of others or to grieve because of the seeming failures of others is wrong.

Preserve yourself respect or your respect for your own mind, which is as great in quality as is the quality in the mentality of any other individual.

Do not become a mental door mat nor allow others to make you a rendezvous for their tales of self pity and discord. Do not be continually sorry for people, . . . sorry for the laundress, who tells you about her five children that she has left alone at home; sorry for the neighbor who lost his position, seemingly through no fault of his own; sorry for the friend or relative, who simply will not listen to your heedings and pleadings, has no use for Truth, but continues in his erring thoughts and habits. It is hard not to feel sorry for people when we see them steeped in sickness and poverty, which we can plainly see is the result of their false education and living.

Talking along these lines with a friend metaphysician one day, he told me the following story (which is a true story). This was helpful to me at the time and will no doubt prove helpful to others: "We camped one night, in the Ozark Hills, in Missouri. Some 20 or 30 outfits camped the same night at the same place. In the morning we started about sunrise in a long procession. We drove about a mile when the procession came to a standstill. We all got out and surrounded the saddest sight I had ever seen. A horse was lying dead while hitched to the wagon and his mate was standing by his side.

A woman and two children were weeping while the husband was sitting on the wagon with his face in his hands. They were on their way to Kansas, but the dead horse put an end to their journey as they had no money to buy another horse. More than 50 people gathered around them. Some wept, and some said, 'We pity you'; but with all the tears, and all the pity, the dead horse never moved a muscle, and the man did not lift his head, and the children did not stop crying. After a few minutes of sobbing and groaning by the crowd, a young fellow in the background pressed his way to the front, and, reaching over the heads of some of the mourners, said: Here, old man, I pity you just $10.00 worth,' and handed him a ten dollar bill.

The act was contagious. The crowd began to shed dollars instead of tears. A man in the crowd had an extra horse and in less time than it takes me to tell it, the horse was bought, hitched to the wagon, and the thankful family made a new start for Kansas. How many groans and tears would have been required to start that poor family on their way? The people that wept and groaned were willing to help but they did not think the right way."

Those of us who learn how to help should not weep because others weep, nor should we bear the burdens of others except to help where our help is wanted and will be received.

God's supply is mental. That is, that which can be thought can also be externalized. Jesus through a mental process produced loaves of bread. Ordinarily it would cover a period of weeks from the time the grains of wheat were planted in the field to the time that the bread made from this wheat appeared upon the table. Jesus eliminated this period of time and through right thought (Mind) produced the bread and fish at the very moment they were needed.

Because we cannot now do likewise is no reason why we should not start with simpler problems of supply. We have every right to every good thing and also the right to enjoy it. I have often marveled at the lavishness that would almost appear like wanton extravagance in Nature. In the spring time of the year we can find hillsides and valleys covered with flowers of exquisite patterns, colors, and fragrance and in vicinities where scarcely there is a soul to see them or enjoy them. We might wonder why Nature manifests itself so lavishly in these isolated spots. The goodness of Nature is universal. As the sun shines upon all alike, so also we each are entitled to have and enjoy the richness and fullness of every good thing.

There is a mental law or reason back of every effect. Grapes come from grapevines and apples come from apple trees, sickness from the seed of ignorance and abundance from the tree of Understanding. That like produces like is a mental law, self-acting, self-sustaining and self-existing. There may appear obstacles in your path which can easily be set aside as you come into mental touch with Life, Understanding.

Without thought nothing has ever been or ever will be made to appear. So look unflinchingly over your visible external horizon and know that you have power within your own consciousness to bring about your desired good in your affairs. Trials are stepping stones very often and as we rise and overcome them we make our character stronger and more enduring.

The outer abundance is dependent upon our inner riches of thought. Believe in plenty, in infinite abundance. In the beginning was God-Mind, and God, Mind, is the same in quality today as yesterday and is self-sustained and self-operating. This Mind in activity is right thinking and feeling and each individual can himself put this creative Mind to work through the right thinking and right feeling and bring about the creation that he knows is right and good to have.

The more we know about Truth (true thinking) the more successful we shall be in all our affairs. As all outward success and prosperity depends upon mental laws and obedience thereto, it is quite necessary that we gain an understanding of these laws, and think and live in harmony with them if we wish happiness and success. The poverty belief is delusion; it is founded upon wrong belief.

As the sun shines upon all without partiality so in the fitness and fairness of Nature we all have the same right to prosperity and abundance. But it takes effort upon our part. We should not sit still and expect money to fall into our laps.

We do not sit still and let the blackboard solve the mathematical problems for us. The answers to the problems already exist in the invisible even before we take the chalk in our hands, but we are not conscious of them, and we have to think and act before these answers become known to us. Thus, in working out our life problems of harmony and prosperity. Everything good and right is ours in the mental world of Reality, but if we wish to bring this all good into our experience or wish to externalize or to bring into visible manifestation some particularly desired good thing, we must work mentally toward that end and mentally see and understand that what we need is already in our possession.

"He that soweth sparingly shall reap also sparingly and he which soweth bountifully shall reap also bountifully." Sow your seeds, good thoughts, bountifully, and expect to reap from them abundance. No one can rise higher than his own thought. We must plant the bulb before we obtain the lily, and thus we must plant the seeds or thoughts of success and plenty in order to have abundance manifested in our outer life.

What seeds are you sowing in your mental garden?

Sow thoughts of wisdom and reason and reap Understanding.

Sow thoughts of health and harmony and reap health and harmony.

Sow thoughts of success and activity and reap prosperity and abundance.

Sow thoughts of love, faith, courage, poise, and reap that which is right and good, the fullness of your desires.

Plant your desires in all earnestness and expectancy, guard them with love and care, prune them with increasing wisdom and they will become for you the tree of life whose seed is in itself.

Anyone can prove that the Word (thought) is seed, by planting it in consciousness.

Do not be faltering, wavering, doubtful, nor uncertain, but strive in all your mental progress to achieve courage and patience.

We should not hoard outward riches, neither should we hoard the mental or invisible thought riches. Give the goodness and wealth of your Mind (thought) and heart (feeling) and this good shall return to you or be turned back or externalized unto you. Let us teach and preach the Wisdom that we know even though we have not yet "overcome" in all ways that we desire nor yet have fully demonstrated the complete Truth in our experiences. The magnet for all good is to be good, be loving, be forgiving, be active, and be joyous. Take these thoughts and feelings for your mental companions if you wish to demonstrate or bring into the mental world your supply of abundance and success. There are no bargain counters in Nature, no sales days, nothing marked down. The price (Law) is established and reigns inviolate from everlasting to everlasting. Be willing to pay the price, for, as you give up the false sense or ignorant beliefs are you ready to gain heaven and harmony.

There are those who believe that Jesus was poor because he had no house nor lands, and the Bible says that he had nowhere to lay his head. Jesus was capable of speaking the Word into being, and so how could it ever be thought that he was poor? For him to think was for him to have. What he desired to externalize came into visibility not through manual effort, but through Understanding. We are all justified in having what we need for our comfort and joy. We should not have to slave for a living. We should labor for Understanding for this alone will plant our feet upon a higher plane and make our experiences easier and happier. Daniel was master of the lions because he had enough understanding to be master of himself (of his own thoughts and feeling) at that time. We need not be afraid of the lions in our path if we have understanding, for with the understanding of Life the lions will not harm us, but will be chained, as far as we are concerned.

Have you ever read the story about the men who started out through a dense forest to find the home of the King who lived in a wonderful palace far on the other side of the forest?

It seems that the King had written to these three men and invited them to come to him and had even sent them a paper upon which was an outline of the forest and the very path they were to follow in order to reach his home. The path they were to follow was in the middle of the forest and was very narrow, while wide bypaths branched off from it all the way along. He warned them against these tempting by-paths and promised them if they would faithfully follow his directions they would reach his palace and live with him forever in all joy and happiness. So these three men started on the journey with the King's script before them. Very soon one man fell back because people on the way told him how utterly foolish he was in such an attempt; that many had tried it and had failed because huge lions lay in the path before them.

So now the two went on. Presently a great noise was heard. It was the roar of a lion. The sound echoed throughout the great forest, and it seemed that the lion must be directly in their path. Another of the men was now afraid and hastening from the straight path took a road that led him into another direction. But one man was now left and with sinking heart and quivering breath he continued in the straight and narrow path. The lions continued to roar until the very earth upon which he was standing trembled beneath him. Then was he terrified, indeed. Again he looked long and earnestly at the sketch the King had sent him to follow. There was no mistake; he was following right in the very path that the King had outlined and which he said if he followed would bring him safely to his wonderful home. Could the King be wrong? Would the King deceive him? A thousand times, No! But the lions in his path? What did they mean? He could not answer. All he could do was to trust, to have faith and confidence in the King's promises, and to continue regardless of the lions.

So now he walked on and soon the roars were so loud and so close to him that he could not move another inch, his trembling was so great. And then, right before him, right in the very path, it seemed, were two great lions whose cries shook the earth.

But, having come so far the man would not now turn back. All he could think was this; "the King would not deceive me." Shaking and trembling he moved forward right toward the lions, when behold! . . what did he see? . . Why, the lions were chained! One on each side of the path, yet neither could reach him. Oh, what joy was his! With happy heart he walked along the path right between the hungry roaring lions and there, right before him, was the King's palace and the King himself coming to greet him and give him the joys that he had promised.

Oh troubled hearts, ponder this lesson well and, when fearful and worried over evil appearances strive to understand the reality and certainty of the promise of

Nature, Life. Strive to live in harmony with the laws of Life and thus eradicate the sense of fear. These laws are fixed, certain, absolute, and unfailing. What if we are terrified! What if the lions do seem real and true to us! We know that Life's promises are truer than all the seeming lions in our path. And, if we do our mental work faithfully and well, we will soon discover to our great joy that the lions we so feared are indeed chained, that is, powerless to harm us.

If you seem to be in a state of poverty or lack, realize that it is but a temporary seeming and strive to make mental connection with Life in all its abundance. This connection is a process in mind, a process of thinking, knowing and feeling; 'I AM Life Itself, and so I can desire and expect every good thing for as I think I will be and will have. The selfhood which is Life, God, cannot lack for any good thing, and it is my right to demand and command that which is actually mine by Nature."

See your desire as already fulfilled; that is, as thought is the one and only Creator, then, it is by seeing (thinking) your desire as realized now that the objectification takes place or the Word (thought) becomes manifested. In plain words, see and feel yourself in possession of that good which you desire.

This universe is One (uni) and God is One, hence all Life or being is the One-Life, One-God. As God possesses all and is all so you in your very nature must have and must be that which God is.

Practice thinking of your real nature or thinking of yourself as you really are, having abundance of life, health, happiness, and supply. Electricity does not come into your house without some means or channel of connection with the powerhouse, so even though the Powerhouse of abundance of all good is within you or is actually your own

Mind and Spirit, yet you need to make a conscious connection with the Power before it manifests itself or externalizes itself to you. This connection can be made and is made in thinking and in feeling only.

Try your understanding with what seems like a small demonstration and then as confidence and clearer understanding come to you, you will be able to do greater things.

You do not lack a thing in your real being, . . it is only a sense or a belief of lack that is felt and this wrong sense must be and will be destroyed as you gain and hold the right and real sense of Life and Self.

We read in the Bible that God (Mind) giveth to every seed (thought) his (its) own body (external embodiment). Thoughts (seeds) of anxiety and doubt and fear should be courageously forced aside while the mind holds clearly and firmly to its true position. Affirm your desire as already fulfilled in the invisible realm and hence no obstruction to its visible form or manifestation.

Wisdom is your nature and in order that this wisdom become known to you, you must claim it and put your mind in conscious touch with it. Realize that the mentality that you have is all knowing and, so, if there is some particular thing or problem that you desire to understand, declare "I know all things. I do know now all there is to know about this problem and its harmonious solution."

To illustrate. One day I suddenly became aware that my wedding ring was missing from my finger. I never remove it voluntarily so I knew I had not mislaid it. Its disappearance was certainly a mystery to me. However, I silently thought, "Mind knows just where that ring is and this fact will be made known to me." Every time I thought of the ring I just knew this truth and then dismissed the subject from my mind. I felt certain that Mind would reveal to me the location of the ring and I made no search whatever. The next day, suddenly a thought came to me so clearly that it sounded like spoken words, "Look in the ice box for your ring." Now, I was surprised as if someone had spoken to me, for at that time I had not been thinking of the ring at all.

I walked directly towards the ice box and felt impelled to open the top of the box and lift up the piece of ice, and, there embodied in the bottom of the piece of ice laid my ring. I recalled then that I had rearranged the ice after the man had left it and it could be easily understood how the ring was caught and held. I have had many similar experiences in locating lost articles and have also had wonderfully happy results in shopping excursions. To sit silently at home and know just what you want in the way of a gown or a coat and later to walk into a shop and find your mental pictures externalized before you eliminates hours of travel, worriment and inconvenience.

Within you is the Kingdom or Source of all-knowing or Understanding, and within you is also the ability and power to bring this wisdom into conscious activity. Claim God, Understanding, as the reality of your being and aim to bring peace and joy into your daily living, knowing that the One-Life of abundance is "above all and through all and in you all."

The new heaven and new earth will come to us by degrees through renewed thinking and feeling until we are "changed from glory to glory" and become a new creature, born of God, Understanding; fearless, confident and pure, until we come "unto a perfect man . . . unto the fullness of Christ."

REMEMBER

Remember that thinking lack manifests itself in the outer as the absence of that which you should have. Thinking abundance manifests itself in abundant supply.

Remember to have a live faith in divine Substance (thinking) from which all good proceeds.

Remember, if you want good to come to you, you must also give good unto others, for love is the fulfilling of the law.

Remember, in order to experience abundance of all good, you must gain understanding.

Remember, that the one and only purpose of Life in you is that you acquire the right and true understanding of God and Self.

Remember, that every day is filled with possibilities. Are you thinking of your blessings and are you establishing in consciousness the activity that promotes growth, harmony and abundance?

Remember to keep away the belief that you are but effect and know that you are Cause Itself.

Remember to think: I possess unlimited supply of all good things, for infinite Mind is my resource and I have and manifest that which I desire.

Remember, that Understanding is priceless. When you have enough understanding you will not experience lack of any kind.

Remember, that all good belongs to you; claim it; think it; feel it; believe in it now, and your Word shall not return unto you void but shall externalize itself in the very thing that you desire.

Riches Manifest

By

Maude Rockwell

Originally Published in 1933

Contents

Chapter 1 - God
Chapter 2 - The Wealth Consciousness
Chapter 3 - Consciousness, Subconscious and Superconscious
Chapter 4 - Necessity as a Creating Agent
Chapter 5 - Opportunity
Chapter 6 - Visualization
Chapter 7 - Acceleration
Chapter 8 - Non-Resistance
Chapter 9 - Positiveness
Chapter 10 - The Habit of Shifting Blame
Chapter 11 - Love
Chapter 12 - Tithing
Chapter 13 - Judgment and Discrimination

Chapter 1

GOD

Desire made manifest through the knowledge of God; this is the story of human life.

The desire for success creates a bright, powerful aura that envelopes you with a wave of dominant optimism and assurance, and a steady consciousness of success and prosperity that cannot be broken through. This desire will in time bring to you all things that you have visualized, for the desire is the underlying quality back of all human activity. Desire is an inward motive that works outward, and so it is not hampered by the outer.

Desire sets in motion the attractive forces. There is no limit to your possibilities through this ardent fiery desire which like an unquenchable hunger will be fed.

Wishing alone does nothing. There must be the energy that makes one reach out for the thing desired. We are told a story of a sage, who was asked by a student: "Sir, what must I do to become wise?" At length the sage took him down to the river, and held him under the water, in spite of his struggles. After releasing him, the sage asked: "Son, when you were under the water, what did you desire most?" Regaining his breath, the student replied: "Air, air, air! Sir, I wanted only and thought only of air!" Then said the sage: "To become wise, you must desire Wisdom with as great intensity as you just now desired Air."

Yes, you must struggle to the exclusion of everything else for the desire of your heart to manifest.

There is no desire without the possibility of its satisfaction and attainment, providing you follow the law. God, as Substance, is molded to your desire by this concentration on an idea. For all there is, is God.

Omnipotence: All Power, means that nothing can alter God. Use this in producing your desire, by willing yourself to accomplish that to which you give thought. God is as much concerned with you as a producing principle, or a personal individual, as He was and is in Christ Jesus. He is just as much in sympathy with New York as He was with Jerusalem, New or Old, for God is everywhere present and has always been. Without beginning and without end.

As you take this thought for the production of your prosperity through the vision or channel you have named for yourself, everything that develops points to the bringing forth of the desire, providing you allow nothing else to cross the vision. Make anything opposite your desire an impossibility through the perfect visioning of the God Mind. Connect up God with what you have need of, in order to produce your desire.

If you need health, when you think of God, think of health, and all the joy there is in perfect health and its radiation, and keep on with this thought. If you need prosperity, think of God as Power, unlimited, boundless, and transferable at all times to the channel you wish to produce through.

The moment you realize the power of the word spoken, in and through your knowledge of God, and what that word is symbolic of, you are at once in the aura or vibration of the thing you want, and the concentrated Mind Power draws this to you in material form. It just can't help it!

You must remember that the world is ruled by God through Law. Prayer sets in action the vibrations in the ether, and these are caught up by the Spirit . . the Mind of God. By the very intensity of the prayer the thought formation is drawn towards you and you receive the outer substance.

Now, in every atom God is the ruling power. And you, as the individualized idea of God are the ruling power for yourself, but not for the other fellow. This is why Jesus stressed the answer: "What is that to thee? Follow thou Me!" Turn your back on the idea the other fellow may want you to use, and use the one God gave you; it is the only one that belongs to you. And turn your back also on the idea that you have to force your idea on the other fellow; he has his own God, or God-idea, to follow.

In this way you will find you make greater progress and a bigger manifestation in everything for you and yours; and an easier and more open channel through which to express. Make your God Mind work with you, not letting any other minds have power to say "Yea" or "Nay" to the God Mind with which you are bringing forth health or prosperity.

Chapter 2

The Wealth Consciousnesses

How to Live in it

How to make it produce

We have read the story of the fig tree that was withered by the Word of God because it was barren. In the same way, a consciousness not productive becomes barren, and in course of time withers and dries up.

To acquire the wealth consciousness you must be very sure to view all things through this Law of producing. A half-filled consciousness is like a half-baked loaf of bread. Only part of it is usable, and in the using of the perfect part you are forced to sacrifice the good to do away with the half-baked.

The wealth consciousness never carries a thought of "I have not," or "I cannot." Instead it carries: "I Have" . . "I AM." This continual carrying of constructive thinking makes the thought become, as it were, second nature, and you find no time for the opposite.

The first idea that came to me in reading books such as "Life and Teachings of The Masters of The Far East" was the absolute certainty of everything written being an accepted fact in the mind of the writer, and every circumstance being a realization of God's Law and not a "miracle" or an unusual instance. It just was.

Notice the way an expressman carries a trunk. Try and do it yourself. What makes it so easy for him? Two things: the knowledge of how, and the fact that he is using his knowledge. What, then, makes for success in any individual? The knowledge that he is a success, and that he is applying the principle he knows.

Wealth is Spirit, and Spirit is Wealth. This is the God definition. It does not make any difference how many added names there are in the family; the Eternal Name is Wealth. The little kittens in the basket may be male or female, but they are kittens!

Wealth expresses through whatever idea you are harboring in consciousness. I have a wealth consciousness: then I must be thinking of wealth in the words and pictures that represent in the outer the vision I receive when I think or speak them while thinking wealth. Thus I attract wealth in my surroundings, my friends, my ideas.

Wealthy people, whether recognized as such or not, will not take up residence with poverty-thought people, no matter how much they may love them personally. The poor, contracted thought hampers them from the free expression of their own greater consciousness.

The greater the consciousness, the greater will you become, and the more able to create in the outer. To hold this creative consciousness there must be no adulteration of the first perfect seed of greatness. No substitute for the perfect article is accepted in the Spirit consciousness or Mind consciousness wherein God is actively at work. The gardener is never ready to receive diseased plants in his perfect garden. Better wait until the perfect can be brought forth. Haste has brought forth many an inferior article. "I must do something," says the anxious one, "I must have some return on this or that." So they produce that often-quoted "Half-baked Bread."

Write down what you consider the greatest thing in the way of wealth. Many will say, the wealth of a healthy body; some will only see wealth in money; others again, riches of harmony or Love.

Let us take the thought of a wealthy consciousness for perfect health. How shall you plant, or make ready to plant the first seed for health; by making null and void, by the power of the spoken word; the old records of lack of ease.

Affirm: I make null and void, by the power of my spoken word . . God speaking in and through me . . every old record of disease and separation from God-health.

Use this affirmation for the erasing of everything that keeps you from expressing perfection to yourself; use it for health, harmony, success, or whatever you are working to bring forth into the outer.

The wealth consciousness never sees a thing as it is in the outer, but as it is in the spirit mind or perfect Christ picture.

The great worker in the wealth consciousness is like a service station. It is a never-failing energy that improves with use. The more service is given, the more the wealth consciousness increases and desires to give forth. Suppression of service through fear of letting go, creates the proverbial poverty consciousness! On the other hand, the continual desire to serve, freely expressed, becomes in time a Christ condition of mind; and the constant thinking of the desire attracts to you the wealth with which to serve, whether in love, harmony, health or money. Like creates like, and multiplies and increases it. But, in order to get the second and third crops, we must plant the first seed.

The Thought Consciousness is magnified by concentration; by picturing the thing desired and nothing else; by not seeing the opposite under any circumstances.

There are three rules necessary to abide by in seeking the Wealth Consciousness.

First: Do not seek from the outer vision. Spirit Mind governs, and not Man Mind. Spirit creates through the thought placed in your mind. You do not create; you are the user.

Second: Use the thought that the creative Spirit gives you. Nothing happens by chance. Your own laws are set in motion by your own thinking and using. "As a man thinketh in his heart, so is he," in his heart-mind.

Last, and most important believe in yourself. Your belief starts the Spirit Power working for you. All is within yourself. Remember the spider and his spinning; the endless thread that comes from Within out. Never forget. Obstacles Without are from Obstacles Within. You cannot have an overflow of water from an empty bucket!

Clear the Within. "Make clean first the inside of the platter!"

Chapter 3

Conscious, Subconscious & Superconscious Mind

I AM going to give you the definition that will most clearly express to you the inner idea in relationship to the practical working out of the principle.

The conscious mind: the mind that receives from without.

The subconscious mind: the intuitive soul mind, or memory mind, that works on suggestion of the conscious mind, and draws all like things from the memory part to support the outer production.

The superconscious mind: the mind that involves knowledge and insight or experience of a kind transcending the possibilities of human consciousness.

These definitions if thoroughly studied will produce a talisman; a mode for the expressing, or pressing out, of everything for your advancement into the realization that all things are possible.

The conscious mind is the acting mind; and what is active is also reactive. You speak your word. It returns to you, in the same way as the echo comes back from the valley between mountains.

There are two facts to be held in mind at all times. One is that every subconscious action is the reaction of or from the conscious mind, and this produces an expression on the individual or thing set in vibration to it.

The other fact is, that the deeper the thought or conviction of a thing is, through the conscious mind, the deeper will be the print on the subconscious mind, for that is rich in mentality.

The subconscious mind has been called "The Great Within." There are more riches buried there than could be unearthed through untold reincarnations! The sooner, therefore, you get to work to draw on these riches by implanting your desires or ambitions on the conscious mind, the better off you will be.

The poverty idea is an outward expression of thoughts planted there by fear of ability to produce, or by allowing limitation in vision and thought.

The first law for success is to learn to think constructively, not only for and about yourself, but also for and about others. So long as you know the power of registration through conscious thinking, you are able to call up what you want, and not what you do not want.

But you must stick to what you call for, and not make provision to open other doors or channels. By so doing, you give a counter order; and as the subconscious mind has all things needed to complete your production from within itself, your production will suffer according to your change of thought.

No matter what your present environment or circumstances may be, you are able, in fact it is your duty, to change it for the better by allowing your subconscious to work on the changed plans, and by the absolute letting go of all other ideas that held for you before.

Don't bother with denials. Take the affirmative of what you want. It wants you!

Use all the depth of feeling possible, in a firm, steady way. Don't shock your vibration by voicing fear.

When things are going seemingly wrong, impress upon the subconscious in the most vital manner of which you are capable, the idea as you want it to come forth.

Use mental joy and sunshine, and keep it going! This will draw to you every force from the Soul or Memory Mind that is needed, and soon you will see the perfect produced, instead of the imperfect.

When you are about to do something that seems to demand more power than you have before used, call on this subconscious mind for greater, higher power. Call for the best and better still! There is always more than we know of. Wait a few moments, and then start forth fearlessly.

This power will at once begin to work for you in such a way that nothing can stop you from coming into your own! Keep impressing and reimpressing upon the subconscious this added power. The increase will continue until there is a wonder in your heart at the super-abundance of power and strength that you are expressing.

As a noted teacher says: "Begin to live in the Great Within!" And see how the Great Within will begin to pour its manifestation on the Without. Begin, and desire, and desire, and desire! Every one develops according to his desire, for this is the key to the subconscious. The greater the desire, and the more you impress the mind with that desire, the greater will be your unfoldment in the outer. Call continually for production, and call all the time!

Don't be afraid to name the time for your subconscious mind to produce. Don't be uncertain. God rules the Universe through Divine Order, and the subconscious mind, being a part of this great Universe, and a big part, is able to live up to principle. Don't begin to slip in a substitute. There are no such things in God's kingdom. Always let the mind know how much power is needed, and what the power is for. This is very essential.

Make the conscious hold the very highest conception of the idea that is being impressed, and the clearer the picture on the conscious mind, the greater and surer the production. Remember, whatever the impression calls for, the subconscious will supply. The superconscious mind has it waiting, and through the power of the thinking it is brought into active vibration for you. Don't let anything else cross the vision. This is very necessary, in fact, indispensable for success.

The greatest work is done by the subconscious mind when the conscious mind is off duty. The conscious mind must clear all channels, and give the subconscious the thought that it wishes carried out. The more perfect the detail given, and the more complete the plan laid out for working, the easier and more quickly the subconscious will produce.

Charge the subconscious mind, always in Love, and in the knowledge that you are working for the Father, not only to give you the very best material in ideas and plans, but also to give you the very best ways and means of expressing these ideas in the outer. This mind will give you power and ability to create through your work and in your work that magnetic something that will make people seek you and appreciate all you do.

Remember, the subconscious is unlimited! You, therefore, if in the right vibration, can make yourself a channel of unlimited expression, whether of wealth, health, happiness, or whatever may be your ideal.

Direct the subconscious to express what may be necessary in order to take the next step forward. Concentrate all the forces of mind on that step, and do not go beyond until you have made the vision plain and perfect. Then, hold it! One step at a time, holding the perfect, completed image in mind, and then taking the next step as the former one is finished.

But have the perfect blue print before you to direct from!

God is power.

Power lies in the mind.

Power is generated and called forth by concentration and the realization of oneness.

Chapter 4

Necessity as a Creating agent Opening the Door

So many people never come into the greatness of Life, nor do they realize what they are capable of until necessity has pushed them forth.

So many make the plea: "I have never had to do anything," or: "I have never had any training." This state is brought about by laziness of mind. As long as you feel you will not do this or that because there is no particular motive to do so, or you are not forced to tackle it, you will not go very far.

Remember the man with the ten talents; the truest story that was ever written. These talents were given out to several men. The one who was ambitious made the most of what was given him, letting go of all fear that it would be lost. The other wrapped his talent in a napkin; kept it out of sight. There was no thought of praise or love or joy, or anything constructive, in the hiding away of what had been given him. So the vibrant quality within the gift died.

Necessity makes us very keen to call on the unexplored parts of the mentality. Nine times out of ten, inventions and other works of genius are brought forth by sheer necessity. You hear one say: "I just must put this over!" This declares the law through his material vision, and he is driven to action by fear. But there is no must in God's Kingdom. "I AM" or "I will" would release the tenseness, and start the idea towards you in a gentle manner.

When you have a need that must be met, it is because you have not used that which was given you at the right time, or else you have used it wrongly. Applying the law of

God at all times releases you from a need for any certain thing, and keeps you in a state of receptivity to make the contact. It is because you do not keep yourself in a keen, vibrant state, that the things you need do not become connected with you. Therein necessity makes you look out, and look up!

Remember: it was the loss of the setting hen that brought forth the idea of the incubator, and brought unlimited wealth to the woman whose necessity drove her to use her "unexplored mentality."

Back of every seeming loss or letting go is the Divine Mind, with its gold mine of unopened ideas. When you refuse to sit down and hold the empty cup, you don't get filled with new ideas. But when you do hold the empty cup to Divine Mind in the Silence, you receive a new, fresh, vital knowledge from the new-filled cup that replaces the seemingly empty one. The contents have only been withdrawn by the power of the all-present Divine Mind, in order that a better and more perfect measure may be given to God's ideas.

As long as a door is open, and all things flowing easily to you through it, you do not notice the door. But when it shuts, you realize that it has been open. So it is with Divine Supply. As long as it comes, you do not seek to trace the channel; but when the channel closes, you get busy. This is because the necessity arises for you to do something. The sooner you start, the sooner shall you receive, and the less time is allowed for the congealing of the God idea through inaction.

Why do you eat? You are taught that it is necessary to do so, in order to keep alive. How many stop to think of cause and effect? Not many, unless it becomes necessary to them. If you continually hold in mind the necessity for activity' in

God's Kingdom, you cannot be stopped when the need for instant decision or action presents itself. This opens the door for necessity to stir the unknown depths, and unfold from within what has always been waiting for you. The greater the necessity in the outer, the more you will strive to produce through this man-made Law of Supply. When you fail to get the result from outer contacts that you expect, you turn to the within, and then God opens the door to the Right Idea for you. Not until the need has been made known, will the Door of Divine Mind open!

We are told over and over again this truth: "Ask and ye shall receive." If you will look over the situation as it is today in all branches, you will find the truth of the law: necessity is the mother of invention. Mother means producer. "Mother" the word, may be applied to all generative power, for through birth all things become usable in the outer for man.

There is the birth of children, to replenish the earth, and carry on the work of past incarnations. There is also the birth of ideas, so that the work may be carried on in a bigger way. A spirit of desire is necessary, just as in human birth, before the birth of any idea can take place. Mothering an idea gives it power. This is true of either a good or a bad idea. For instance, the man who dwells on revenge, does not at first think of killing, but by his continual dwelling on, or "mothering" the idea, the picture of revenge touches the visioning faculty, and this becomes productive to help him attain his desire; the means to an end. Man always gets what he wants deep in his heart, even if he cannot see it manifest as he has pictured. Within the wrappings is the original seed, and he nurtures it by his thought.

There was once a woman who hated home and housekeeping. She got what she wanted, release from both, but not as she imagined she would. She was forced to work for her living, and to live in one room, because she had pushed from her by her constant affirming of hatred her home and her husband.

Spite also works that way. Undertaking anything for spite will make you do the thing of necessity before you are through with it. All the five, or seven, physical senses are keenly awaiting a chance to become active, and it is up to the Indwelling Mind to make of them a working force for Good. Thus, when necessity arises, the need will be met by a force working in perfect harmony and order, because it is in training, and therefore open to receive the word of God for the new, necessary idea.

Alertness is a God Power: the power to see behind and around a situation by putting every faculty to work. Never get panicky when things are happening.

God does not work in a panic. Peace, poise will show you the way out.

Remember the great Iroquois fire. One person saved many thousands of lives by alertness and poise. Be alert; be poised. Practice these. Then you will be ready for necessity when it comes, and necessity will be to you what God meant it to be: A great producer in all walks of life.

Chapter 5

Opportunity

God himself is your source of supply

Does God give occasionally? Or is His gift always there for you to call upon? This is the question you yourself must now decide in your own mind. Upon your decision rests the entire fabric of your life, and your output in this life.

All is Substance, you have been taught. All is One with You. You make it in the different parts and molds that you want, by your thinking and accepting. If you want air, you open windows. If you are wise, you open the windows before you feel the real need of the air.

In the same way, if you are wise, you will start in molding your substance before the dire need and the pinch of the so-called poverty hits you. Get ready for what you want, not for what you will have to work to get rid of.

If you let other outside interests interfere with the Oneness of yourself and your desire, you must not expect to receive as rapidly and as perfectly as if you were looking and planning for the One and Only.

Don't try to cultivate two or three things at once.

Don't try to have the other fellow do your cultivating or your garnering. You will find that you always open the channel for the other fellow, and that you yourself are left, as it were, in the discard.

I have seen more wonderful demonstrations go wrong in the outer by one student sending another for the bucket of water, than by any other mistake. Go yourself! Ask yourself for what you want! You can get it as well as the next one. What difference does it make whether there is a personal friendship or not to reckon with, or a so-called string on the gift?

Don't change your mind about a thing you are working on, as this changes your vibration and your consciousness with regard to it.

Remember: you have never failed. You have gone as far as you really want to! Whenever you want to pick up your idea, you will do so; you will go forward and carry it on. You have not failed; you have only suspended your production faculty by "laying down on the job."

Your mind is the use you make of the Mind of God. Imelda Shanklin tells us, and you know God cannot fail. So you use the Mind of God, and the fullest concept you can have of your own ability is just your God Power speaking to you.

Opportunity knocks at every door, so we have been told.

I will tell you more than that. Opportunity is an electric switch, always waiting to be turned on. By you only for yourself. Don't try to get the other fellow's switch to work, for you: it will only use your channel, and flow out to the other fellow!

Look yourself in the face during the following days, and see what you can do with opportunity when it comes to you, and what you are naming this opportunity. How many of you can recognize the instant an opportunity is yours? Are you only seeing through one window, or are you looking in all directions?

Your brain is the register of your opportunity. You were born with it. It was born with you. No one else can use it for you. It is like the man using his hands to work with, while, you stand in front of him. He'll surely get stuck sometime.

Think, and then think some more! Don't be so satisfied with yourself that you feel you have all the knowledge available on the particular idea you want to develop. The opportunity is present for you to learn more of every subject, no matter what, than you already know. That is why you are here.

Stop wailing and whining what a poor success you are, or what has jumped away from you! It was because you never learned the rules governing the grasping of opportunity. You took too much for granted. Look you well to the details. Therein lies success!

The issue at stake can be met by anyone. The right-thinking student will follow up the issue with the idea of learning how to capture it and tie it up for himself.

Don't be loose in your understanding! Get acquainted with your own Soul, your Subconscious Mind; that wonderful part of you that never becomes poorer, but richer in substance as you use and draw upon it.

Prosperity is a state of consciousness. Consciousness is an acceptance of all things as opportunities for greater prosperity, no matter through what channel or in what way it may express. You must see the thing, as you want the opportunity to produce it.

Cultivate all possible confidence in yourself! This gives opportunity a chance to work. Confidence begets opportunity; and opportunity begets confidence. Be willing to try. Put forth the very best you are capable of. That brain of yours will start into new activity, and in this way you will have a wider vision of new opportunities, as well as more richly varied means to acquire knowledge and power of all kinds.

Chapter 6

Visualization

"WHERE there is no vision, the people perish."

These words are written in our Bible. Back of the written words is more than we can conceive at first sight, for without this Vision we have no power to produce.

First the seed, then the bloom; but remember, the seed carries the bloom within it, for within the seed is the power that brings forth the bloom.

Vision is always backed by the little seed of Faith, which grows with use. So the vision grows with our claiming and acknowledging its power.

If I want to produce, I know instantly that God wants me to produce, and the two become one in vision.

The different stages of visualizing are imaging, visioning, and visualization. Visualization is the idea made concrete. Vision is the Universal idea. Imaging is the seed, or the man-made plan. Your imaginative faculty is capable of producing greater or lesser things, for it is in the control of Mind that it rests. It is a part of God, indivisible, yet, reckoned through the material man-made law, it can be limited in output by ourselves.

What are Dreams? All dreams are ideals of the Great Universal Mind, and productive of race service. Consider Columbus. His ideal was first visioned; then it was idealized into concrete form by his visualization. His consciousness carried such a perfect, complete visualization of this land beyond the horizon, that the uncharted seas had no terrors for him. Wonders un-thought of follow the first visioning into fuller visualization. This is the way God manifests or expresses through all.

The one that has brought forth has then greater faith in his own powers, which are really God Powers, whether he is conscious of this or not. The perfect Visualization sees and senses the goal in every vision and image, and allows no man-made law to say "Nay!" or "Yea!"

You must never be afraid to speak forth into the outer the picture you have visualized by daily application of the principle; nor should you seek to know the outcome except so far as you have visioned it for your working plan. Not even to this day is the finish of the visioning and the visualization of Columbus. Yet he did only what he conceived in his first mind-plan; others following him are still carrying on in our Country.

Every successful bringing forth through this visualization is the Birth of a Child of God.

Mary visualized the Christ Child in her pure praise and love of God Good. Man's visualization is the "bringing forth" method of the Universal Plan for man as God Manifest, whether in business, or the patenting of an invention, or the molding of a perfect work of art, or as the Birth of God's Highest Ideal . . Man.

"And she brought forth a man child."

In preparation for this Birth, whatever form it may take, hourly inner perfection is attained by developing our vision inwardly, concentrating on idea, and closing out all other ideas.

Realize that you are dealing with a powerful energy that as yet has no form. Now, let your mind dwell on the mental picture of that which you want, thereby centralizing the creative action or force on one center spiritually, and in the Spirit Substance making your mental picture a definite mold that is pushed out (by the creative energy that began the action) into the outer.

Visualization is easy in vibration, and contains no strenuous effort to defeat its purpose. Know that there is no negative side to anything! This knowledge lets the perfect harmony flow in and through every potent part of your picture.

Easy, instant, perfect! Keep your picture with you intact through joy and happiness. A happy state of mind unencumbered by any adverse thought is necessary at all times. Know what you want to produce, by all means, at all times. Visualize what you want, and not how you want. Never make your channel of visualization the only channel. Your business is to hold your picture; Nature and God Mind will take care of the rest!

Be consciously one with the Universal Whole, and this will prevent a half-way success.

The thought you dwell upon becomes the thing you will possess. Thought is Creative Action. Take this thought to dwell upon:

Everything I want, wants me.

It cannot be one with me unless I rest in and on that vision of what I want.

Chapter 7

Acceleration

Its Working in the Universe

It has been proven by scientists that anything called for by the right name will answer the call. This proves the use to be made of the Spoken Word, and the vibration that can be set in motion by this law. It coincides with the Word: "Ask," or call, "and it shall be given you."

Acceleration: This mighty word has very little use in this day and age; yet within it lies the outcome of your Spoken Word. Speeding up thought, speeding up the vibration, speeding up the vision. Being so enwrapped in it that the Law of Jhvh, which is instant power to bring forth your answer, becomes the center of the thought, and all radiations come from this central pivot, and as such must come forth in dynamic force.

Power . . power . . power! What is Power? Jhvh . . God. How much of this power are you using to accelerate your thought and action? Mayhap you Have never thought of this? When you begin to concentrate on the idea, and reach into the hidden depths of your Christ Mind, do you do this in a half-minded or half-interested way? Or do you put forth all the power you possibly can, and start an acceleration through mind and body that reacts into the Universe, and begins its working there?

Accelerate your speed; bring more force to bear on your thinking mind. This is what is meant by "keen, vital, alert!" Alertness means acceleration, pushing on the motor. This is what makes the high-powered salesman, but the average high-powered salesman becomes a menace to himself and everyone else, because he steps on the accelerator in a material sense, and rides over the rights and judgments of the buyer.

Power misused becomes a vicious thing. Have you ever seen an engine running away, without a guiding hand on the brakes or levers? In the same way, an idea of God's let loose without guidance, and permitted to run wild, accelerated as it were, seems to realize with an uncanny knowledge that there is no hand at the helm.

If guided rightly, this acceleration of speed will become a dynamo that nothing on earth will be able to stop, hinder or destroy. The thought currents with which you surround yourself are attracting from the Invisible Universe a like set of currents, which are strengthened and accelerated by your intensity of thought and vision.

As you vision the idea you are seeking to bring forth, you set in motion in the ethers the picture of it; and every like vibration or picture is taken into this molding process and brought forth.

There is never separation in thought. It does not divide. It is the seed; and no seed is divided before it has produced and brought forth the perfect product as was originally planned. There is no deviation from this Law of God. We may cut or change by material means; but it becomes like the pants of the boy that so many had a hand in trying to rebuild.

The brain is a receiving station. Thought is not generated there; it is only received. Scientists will tell you this, and all metaphysical books bear witness to this truth. It stands to reason that if some of these cells in the brain are "laying down on the job," your receiving set is not perfect, and you do not get the full return of that which you have tuned in for. The transmutor, or thought, must be in perfect tune to be able to send the message across. The most perfect state of consciousness, and the most perfect vitality and energy must have their place in this sending, or you will be working, or as we call it, running on one cylinder. Where can you get on one cylinder?

The generator and the receiver must be in perfect harmony to get through a message on this line. Then you need not bother about how many messages, or desires, are being broadcast! That would have no effect on you. You would then be working in a perfect Christ-Radio, and everything in a like vibration would be attracted to you.

The short wave of perfect sending is wonderful as a starter. Continue to increase your wave length; then you are increasing your vibration, and drawing from greater distances in the Universal ether. As you do this, you must accelerate the inner motion, or visioning, and also the outer.

Have you ever taken a bucket of water and swung it very fast? Nothing is spilled from it; but all things are dashed from its path as it swings around in a circle. The very momentum keeps the contents from scattering.

Acceleration intensifies and protects; carries all before it. The moment you begin to let the energy die down, just that moment you lose the attracting power that is carrying you out of the ordinary manifestations and demonstrations. You go back to the "Also-rans!" Don't! You can stop it. It means turning on the steam a little earlier in the day, and sensing the need and the way to meet it a little more vitally. Believe me, it is well worth the price.

The joy one gets from the perfect realization of God as a working power in him, more than repays him for the energy expended in stretching forth for the thing. It is far more than the thing he attains.

So when you feel like "laying down," or letting go, remember, that is the very time to put the new battery in. Get busy; don't wait; for sooner or later the demand will be made on you for speed, and then you will have no reserve force to draw from, if you have not used that which you had the opportunity to use.

In this everyday life, it is the fellow who works the accelerator that gets past you! However, you must use it right, not getting the idea that you are the only one who has a right to a thing. Use it in the God consciousness of perfect thinking and perfect visioning', of doing as you want to be done by.

Concentrate your efforts on your God-given power to succeed. Accelerate every God-given idea that comes to you, and there can be nothing for you but Success. Everything in the Universe will be working for you, and with you, and through you. Amen.

Chapter 8

Non-Resistance

THE Law of non-resistance is the law operative for the bringing forth of the perfect product. This law is unalterable, and, like all of God's laws, never fails.

As one noted teacher asked: "What is there to resist?"

This is the answer. Nothing apart from God really has existence. Consequently you are wasting God's time in resisting a circumstance that has no reality. Why not get busy and see what is creating this condition? Why not remove the cause instead of resisting the effect?

The people who marched round the walls of Jericho were making nothing of the obstruction, ignoring the wall, by praising the law of God as the only working Power, and lo! the walls were down! This is seeing the Perfect back of the outer condition or manifestation of Imperfect. Any time you ignore a person or a situation it loses its power against you. Any time you meet a circumstance with an acknowledgment of a power apart from that which you wish to have manifested, you are welcoming an imperfect condition. Thus again, you prove out the law of attraction by thinking.

The one who is able to look into the future, and know God's Law is operative, is the one who will always find the Divine Law working for him, whether he is able to see it or not. It works continually, because we are working with it, and making it possible and absolute by seeing nothing but the one outcome. See it? See it.

The only Law that will operate is the Law of Expectancy; expecting that which you ask for and nothing else. Don't accept "Just as good" articles; they will not fill the need. They may be "Just as good," but not for you.

When we believe we are able to do a certain thing, we set in vibration a law to bring forth this thing. Don't get busy and make a law as to time. Time is of Man and not of God. God can so speed up the dynamos that are working in you, if you concentrate and keep a clear mind, that the Invisible Activity will make a new record for you, and will produce, in its own time, that which would have taken much longer through the Man Mind.

Never set your time limit as a thing unalterable, for God knows no limit in the process of production. When you mentally conceive a thing, it is born already in the Unseen; and the strength to bring it forth into the tangible world depends on how much faith you have in your own power, your own Word, not the power of the other fellow, whoever or whatever you may think you have to resist.

You hinder your demonstrations by needless resistance to some outer condition, or by holding in mind the idea that you have to work hard to gain your object. The biggest demonstrations are brought forth by holding the perfect picture and releasing everything outside of it.

Nothing but what I want can come to me. This is an affirmation that tears down all resistance. Don't peddle your work. Don't vision hurdles. Don't jump at conclusions. Remember, it is concentrated thinking that brings forth; but not for a few moments . . at all times; never allowing another contrary thought to enter your consciousness. Hold the perfect thought in regard to all things, at all times.

I have seen the way so dark that there was no light anywhere. Then, in less than no time, I have known the light to show forth from all angles at once, and when it once starts pouring, it does not stop the perfect thought going on working and creating.

Man, God's Divine Idea in its highest conception, becomes creative as we see God creative, and in no other way. Of all the manifestations that have been created through the power of the Spoken Word, Man is the only one that shows resistance to the law of Divine Perfection. Man-made beliefs and intellectual ideas have caused this separation. The seed is planted on the left side of the house; it cannot refuse to grow because it is not on the right side of the house! It grows because it is the law for it to grow when planted; and through this law of unfoldment, environment has no power to stop the growth. It gives forth all it has to give where it is, and is perfect in that manifestation.

The tree cannot say it will not grow: it has no choice. This passive subjection to the life-principle within is the reason why, when all things earthly fail, so many seeming "miracles" are performed. God is all power, when you let Him be so. But not until you let go! When earthly limitations are lifted through failure or breakdown, then, and not until then, the Law of God steps in!

To further the Law of God means to hold oneself in a non-resistant vibration, affirming: "None of these things move me: I AM centered in Christ." This will clear everything of a resistant nature from you and bring you into the vibration of production in a harmonious way.

As you come more and more under this law, you will see the result of ignoring the opposite appearance, and making the Law of God your own law.

Affirmations:

I AM poised and centered in Christ.

I have no vision except for the seeing of God's perfect plan, no matter what shows forth in the outer at the time.

I know, and know that I know, easily, instantly, perfectly, and in a sustained manner that no outer condition can change or affect.

Chapter 9

Positiveness

The Subconscious Mind Production

THE Subconscious Mind has been called the Soul Mind. It is the "Mind that was in Christ Jesus." Subconsciously, Jesus was tuned in with this mind at all times, and the hours which He constantly used for meditation were for the charging of this subconscious mind, to take in only the things of God for unfoldment and release.

What is positive thinking? One metaphysical teacher has defined the difference between positive and negative states of consciousness as the difference between backward and forward movement, between action up and down the line, between success and failure. I think this is a wonderful conception of the conditions we bring to ourselves by right or wrong thinking.

Fear attracts like to itself, the same as Faith, but it attracts the thing you fear. Just as in the case of the rich boy who had so many anxious thoughts turned on him, to insure his safety and ward off disaster, he inevitably attracted an accident. The fear for his safety that was set in vibration materialized into a thing of like kind! Fear thoughts are great materializers.

Have you ever noticed the atmosphere of repulsion around a fear person, and the attractive quality that surrounds a positive or faith person? Instant registration is made in the mentality. If you couple the idea of the Lesson on Acceleration with the new thought you are taking, that of Positiveness, you make a mighty team of workers for your production. This, if directed by the Subconscious Mind in a creative manner, will bring forth a perfect manifestation, charged or accelerated as it is, and handled with a positive thought of what is wanted, and why. A clear-cut picture is needed, for you limit yourself many times by letting down before the picture has made a clear imprint on the subconsciousness.

You see, then, that the accumulating forces of all that is set in vibration by our thinking, makes a mighty instrument, or set of instruments with which to work. You use these forces in directing toward you the return of the idea you sent forth. For instance, the person who continually dwells on the thought of suicide will be able to think of more ways in which to do the deed, and more opportunities will unfold for him to do it, as he broods and concentrates on this desire.

The best way to stop a person from continuing in this vibration is to help him get what he wants, so to speak. Hit him quickly by telling him you think it would be a good idea for him to do it, as long as he insists, then get busy making the way for him easy and instant. As soon as he begins to realize that there is no sympathy in store for him, but a desire to be rid of him, he will reverse the thought, and desire to live. Remember the story of the Mouse.

Negative people are always talking about what they cannot do, and how unlucky they are. Let them stop and think for once how unlucky other people are in having to deal with them, and listen to them. Let them begin to help themselves by their own right thinking.

Don't ever think you will get anywhere by claiming that someone else put you where you are. You yourself are alone responsible for what you are and where you are, and no one else. And no one else can take you out of there until you realize that it all lies in yourself, and get busy!

The idea that anything is "too good to be true," builds a stone wall around or in front of anything you •want. Nothing is too good to be true. It is too good NOT to be true! This saying will open every door to you, and give you the good, true, perfect thing that belongs to you, and comes forth at your call.

Words are a veritable dynamo for you, you, to work with. Work, then, realizing the Law back of them. Work accordingly, letting go of every thought but the one of success. A successful man never uses "buts," "ifs," "maybe" or "I wonder." He knows "it is!"

How did that man we all know about find the Pot of Gold? By burying the horse that cultivated the bit of land where he made his meager living, he found the gold; always there, never unearthed until he dug for it! So it is in Life. There are no chance accidents, but many times there must be a taking away, as in the case of the horse, before we can look beneath the surface.

Be mighty careful about generating poisons by wrong thinking when you are in a positive state of mind. Enough poison can be sent forth by positive affirmations of wrong thoughts to poison many negative souls who lack resistance. Remember how often you have said or heard: "I felt fine until he or she said this or that!" or, "I was wonderful until I got that letter!" Nothing real has changed, only the mortal mind has begun to register on the subconscious mind, and it is busy drawing like to it. Now is the very time to hold steadfast, putting in more and more of this acceleration of speed and power, this positiveness that makes for production.

God is, and if He is, He is; and that's all there is! There just isn't any more to it!

Be positive of good. Hold the thought that only good is. Put your power behind the thought, and see it come forth in a big, beautiful manner. Get the soul of this big, positive idea you are working on. Make a clear picture, and don't bother about what the other fellow is doing or thinking. You can't ride a bicycle or a bucking horse and at the same time watch the other fellow ride! You will find yourself down in the dirt, or up against the lamp post.

One thing at a time, and all the punch possible, back of the thought, will bring it out. Keep accelerating and pouring in positiveness until it moves. It will move. It just has to!

Sooner will the Heavens fall than that My word shall pass away. Think of the power back of that idea!

Wonders will never cease for you, if you work in this attitude.

Try it; get into it deeper and deeper, and see the richness of the output. Amen.

Chapter 10

The Habit of Shifting Blame

How It Operates

WE HAVE been taught the Law of God in operation through vision and affirmation. Now, let us see wherein we sometimes let down on this God power.

How many of us are in the habit of blaming someone else for our disappointments and failures! Be true to yourself, and admit the weakness that has never been absent from your own mind. God cannot be fooled. The Bible tells us: "God is not mocked."

So many people want others to make up their minds for them, and then, when things go wrong, they blame the other one. Do you not know that if you had used the Law rightly, you would have been making your own decision, and you would have had no one to blame? And the chances are, you would have been very successful.

It is a true expression, that though we are all one, yet each is separate and apart. This is what makes the perfect adjustment and the continual pushing forth of all God's ideas. Don't be afraid to push forward into your right place by using your own ability, your own power of choice. So often I have to remind you that you are sufficient unto yourself. God working in and through the Christ Mind was always sufficient unto Himself.

Remember the story of the disciple whom Jesus asked: "Who do men say that I AM?" He did not accept the quoted opinion of anyone. He wanted this certain disciple's opinion, and none other. And when this disciple gave his reply, letting go of all other people's ideas, Jesus glorified and blessed him.

This is what happens when you go forth certain of yourself. Whenever you look to the law of appraisement from outside, you are wavering and uncertain. Uncertain vibration will accomplish nothing!

"He that wavereth is like a wave of the sea, driven with the wind, and tossed."

Have you ever noticed the man who is running away from something that might injure him? He never runs straight; he always zig-zags! This is so that he may not make himself a target for the bullet. And this is what you do, when you waver. Mentally, you zig-zag. A person who drinks, or uses any pleasure to excess, is a Zig-zag person. No stability is possible for him until this is overcome.

When you once realize the Power within yourselves you will become ashamed to admit that anyone could influence you. Learning to stand on your own feet mentally, is the same as learning to stand on your feet when you first begin to walk. As long as you are carried, you never learn. As long as someone makes up your mind for you, you will never grow!

This is the reason we use the affirmation: "Make me know, and know that I know." Can you imagine anyone trying to influence you, or make your decision for you, if this truth was ingrained in your mind?

Never reprove the other fellow who advised you; or the outer condition that decided you. You only are the one that is interested, and consequently you are answerable for the outcome. Jesus blamed no man for anything. He spoke His

Word, and stood upon His understanding that this was sufficient.

If you want success, and happiness, and love, and all the gifts of God, stop reading the news of disaster, murder, failure, disease, dishonesty. If fewer people read these things, there would be more wonderful demonstrations brought forth. If we are made from the plastic ether, and take on conditions according to the vibration of our thinking, just picture what a sewer your mind can become by filling it with these items, records of imperfection! Watch the faces of the people who read these things. Your story is there; what can you expect?

You blame someone else for your failure, when it was because you did not do your work of preparation. Jesus was always prepared, for He continually held to the Ideal: "I and My Father are one, and all that He hath is Mine." This does not apply to money or material demonstration alone, but also to the right thinking and the right visioning. It made Him always sending forth in vibration the same law of power within Himself from the Head Source, Divine Mind.

Don't blame the other fellow that you made a poor investment, because you really were talked into it. You must have thought you would get something big by going ahead; and when things turned out unfavorably you felt injured. Your thought was not honest to begin with. You have used the outer material law of "what can I get out of it," not the Christ law: "what good can I do with this proposition?"

Any time you look at the outer for the picturing of the God Idea, you are liable to be bitterly disappointed in a material way; but when you look at the perfect idea from God's hand, you will find a more perfect production than you could conceive of.

Learn to know yourself, and learn to stand on your own understanding. I have seen more failures than you can count, by lack of faith in oneself, and listening to the other man.

Do not give way to the feeling that anyone owes you anything. If you helped them, you did it because you wanted to. Don't be like the men whom Jesus speaks of as praying aloud with many words. Back of your doing this, was the pleasure you wanted.

Don't expect people to help you, when you not only refuse to accept what comes, but also will not help yourself. No one can push on you mentally, unless you let them. Keep constantly in mind the thought:

I AM a law unto myself, and I blame no one, and let no one blame me.

I stand pat on God's law: my own comes to we when I use the right effort.

Use it: use your own decision, your own effort, not the other fellow's.

Chapter 11

LOVE

Love is the Fulfilling of the law

Having the will faculty placed in your consciousness, you now want to know under what power it works best and in the most perfect way. This is the reason why I have made so forceful the idea of knowing what you want, and why you want it, and that you do want it more than anything else.

The greatest moving power in the world is Love. It is a vibrant thought, and once put into circulation never dies even in the material way.

There was never a condition so bad that Love could not change it, if we worked long enough and hard enough on it. The definition of Love carries more constructive words than any other word in the dictionary. Love, real Love, is never destructive. It is the misuse of the word, or of its application, that makes for destruction.

Prosperity is God's Love for you. It is always there, whether you receive it or not, but its development depends on you yourself, and none other.

The word Love in its working embraces a key to every situation you may enter into. I want you each and every one to concentrate on the different mental pictures you receive when Love is spoken of. This will give you the just and firmly-balanced thought to begin your work on.

If the Love that vibrates through you by your thought is a selfish one, or one that will carry no lasting effect, you will need to go to work and clear out of your mind all this, and replace it with such Love as Jesus had. This means getting down to the real perfect incentive of your desire.

Love opens the door of your mind, and gives you a vision of the beauty of the finished building, when you see with the eyes of God, or Love. God is Power, but that Power is Love, not hatred or envy or malice, Love! God is good, and Love is Good (God). Do you see how you turn back each time to God for the estimate or measurement? This is not the man-made measurement; it is the God-measurement. The Will of God being the Will for Good, is naturally the Will of Love and Loving.

Now, begin to use this God Love in this way:

Make yourself subject to Love vibrations only. Turn on these vibrations as you turn on a current of air. Get where you can feel the current; that is, away from thoughts or ideas that prevent the current from circulating freely.

As what you recognize comes forth, Emma Curtis Hopkins writes, so if you let Love vision your project for you, you get the vision of God in it, and this becomes your picture brought into manifestation. This perfect manifestation can only come through Love.

Many writers have called Love "God Power." It is. Through Love you get the vision perfectly of what you want. For you will not love an object that is not perfect, nor will you be satisfied with it. This dissatisfaction with imperfection is your salvation. It is a true sign of advancement. God will not help the man who is satisfied. It was Love that created the Son of God. It was Love that made Him open the door for you by His life. It is Love that makes you open the door for others by proving His Word in your demonstrations.

The first essential is to love what you are doing. If you can't love it, let go quickly. You'll never make the grade.

Begin to radiate Love, broadcast it. Eat it; sleep it; be it! Get the name of Love written in your mind as the one weapon you will use to give more power and push to what you are doing. Love it till it hurts! And then love it some more! I have myself loved a demonstration that came forth, so much that to material sense my heart ached; but it was a joy ache!

This urge of Love will push you over the top in your work. For prosperity, learn to love money. Get rid of false pride and deceit about your feeling for money. Many people say they do not love it. You might just as well say you do not love God. Love it; and love it some more! Money is God in manifestation, just as much so as the Sun and the Moon and every other manifestation of Nature.

You love God. You love food. You love that which symbolizes the product, food. Money is the idea of God that gives you the food; an article of exchange. Love it. As you love money with a just appreciation of its source, it comes to you naturally, and with it you do our work of further production. You cannot mix the material for your house if you have not all the ingredients, and you need money to procure the ingredients. Why separate God in any way from your building?

Now, take your desire. How much will you love it when it comes forth? Will you feel as happy as you do in anticipation? Yes. Then you are loving it to its fulfillment. Any time you begin to get discouraged, you are letting down on the Love Power. Stoke up! Find some new, vital point that you have not been loving. This puts a new vibration, a new battery in at once. See yourself as your highest vision glimpses you in this manifestation, and know that God Love is working through you to place you there.

Affirmations:

I have no fear of using Love in too big a way. Love is inexhaustible because it is God in me.

As my capacity to use Love increases, I see more places for its use. I recognize constantly Love as God in me; and I know it will prove God in manifestation as my desire shows forth.

I baptize myself daily in Love by using the words Love, Love, Love, Love, Love, Love, Love.

Love!

Love . . Love . . Love . . Love . . Love . . Love . . Love . . Love . . Love.

"God Is Love"

God Is Law.

And therefore Love is the Fulfilling of the Law.

Chapter 12

Tithing for Prosperity and Unfoldment

THE first thing in coming into the real truth is a clear, open mind, and a letting go of all but the thing desired.

The first thing to do in tithing is to let go of your tithe when you give it. Let go completely. Don't begin to think what a great thing you are doing, or have done, or how much you are helping someone, or some order, and what it is going to give you in return. This is bargaining with God, which is altogether different from giving. Each has its place in the student's mind.

The bargain-making is all right if you live up to it, and know that back of the bargain is the thought that you are using the God law in a God way, and making God a coworker with you.

Tithing is rendering unto God that which is God's, and giving it back to the Kingdom of God by letting go of what is not rightfully yours.

The Mosaic Law required a tenth as the Lord's portion, and with many students this still holds. Never tithe for the sake of receiving back something, or for the sake of reward. You will find quotations all through the Bible about this law of giving and receiving.

Many people want to give to God's work, and do not know how to go about it. This is where the law of tithing helps one. A tithe is a tenth of all supply, whether from farm produce, gifts or wages for service. It should be the first to be sent forth in the service of the One who gave all to you in the first place. It is merely the recognition that you receive from Him, and in receiving are able to realize the law enough to let go of the amount freely, in order that it may do its work without thought of return. This would limit God in His giving to you.

If you have money in your pocket-book, and you let some out, then you have space for more. The vibration and the freedom with which you make the place vacant for more, attracts more and more. This is so, because the right relation of things to one another is: God first!

Tithing is putting God first in finances, and is one of the practical ways of seeking the Kingdom of Heaven first.

Tithing produces system, which is Divine Order, providing you do not stop tithing when you happen to want something else.

Continual systematic tithing is more valuable to the student than a large gift now and then, although the large gift may amount to more in money and outer manifestation. It is the Divine Order you establish in your affairs when you let go of a part of your income to God, each and every time the income flows in, that really counts. Thus you are always tuning in with God, Divine Supply, and releasing instead of clogging the mind. By the exercise of the orderliness of giving instead of continual receiving, you keep the mind open.

The whole process is like that of the rain falling on the earth. The rain must fall gently and regularly, at the right times. If it falls all at once after a period of withholding, the earth has become dry and does not produce.

By tithing you are helping to establish the Kingdom of God on earth, and you become a part of that kingdom.

Tithing gives you a faith in God to supply your needs, and God abides in you according to your faith.

If you say you are a Child of the King, and believe what you say, there is no reason to be fearful of letting go. The swimmer does not hold onto the material life-line. He knows and goes forth to breast the waves, knowing his security. This, too, is what the tither does. By letting go of Fear, he goes forth into the Kingdom of God.

You must not expect God to fulfill the law for you, if you do not fulfill the law for God. By putting God first in all things, thought and finances, your faith is being shown in the outer. Promises do not show this faith.

A real loving tithe of one penny as the tenth of one dime is greater than a gift of an unlimited amount that you are just giving because you may receive something through it, or because you think you ought to.

Don't do it until you see the Christ behind the Idea. When man begins to give his one-tenth to God first, before anything else, begins to love his neighbor as himself, and to do to others as he would have them do to him, then the end of his troubles will be here. He will become healthy, wealthy and wise, in Prosperity. Think of your tithe as the farmer planting his seed. The farmer selects the best seed; he is thankful to have it good. We should bless and give praise that we can acknowledge God in this way, and this makes the seed doubly precious in vibration and substance. In this way it releases into the atmospheric ether the vibration which returns to the giver.

Never give unless you are able to bless and let go, either your service or your money. The increase lies in the thought that goes with it, that it is God's own. Therefore it is your joyous privilege to be one with God, as He is with us, present in all we have."

The words of Truth remove every limitation man's thought may have placed upon it or upon you, when you utter them with the full power of attraction and joy. The smaller the income, the more necessary to tithe in order to prove the law of letting go of the outer. Never feel that you have to wait until you have made more, or until your demonstration has come through. Learn the lesson of the "Widow's Mite," and remember that "the least among you shall be the greatest."

Let me repeat again: it is Divine Order in all things that brings success; not the uncertain using of the law at irregular times. The singer, for instance, who practices all day long for one day, and then not again for a week, gets nowhere, but the one who devotes his mind to it for five minutes every day is the one who will win out.

Again it isn't the amount you give; it is the letting go of that which is yours in the outer, to prove the law of refilling the vessel. The bigger the idea behind the gift, the bigger the increase. Never apologize for the amount of a tithe, or of a love gift. See it as you want to give, and watch it come up to that amount!

An accurate account should be kept with God, as in all other business transactions. The money must be put into circulation at once, as holding on until it increases causes a decreased inflow.

This applies to all other tithes as well as to actual money. If you feel you are not receiving enough Love, get busy and tithe more Love out to all those whom you can remember.

If you are not receiving service, begin and tithe service to God's ideas. Do it freely, not for what you will get in return. If you are not getting enough joy out of life, begin and give your tithe of joy by being happy and making it known, and watch the joy increase for you!

In conclusion, tithe the whole way through, not only in the tenth, but in the Spirit of God; the spirit of Christ who said: "All that the Father hath is mine." I give back that I may realize my Oneness with Him in all ways, and that He may give the increase, that I may be more to Him as the never-failing prover of His Divine Law. Tithing is not giving a love gift. These are given for your own pleasure, or for the help received, or for the joy of adding to another's store. Tithing is giving back to God and God's work the part that belongs to Him, freely and fully, and for the purpose of obeying in spirit and in all ways the Law of God.

I have faith in the Law of God, and in this faith I give of what God has given me, joyously and freely.

"Bring ye one tenth into the storehouse of the lord, into the place of God's work, and see if I will not give you measure overflowing, pressed down and running over."

Chapter 13

Judgment and Discrimination

"Judgment is Mine, saith the Lord"

THIS quotation has a double value in that it gives God all power, and by conforming to this rule we afford an opening for God's judgment to show forth.

Why should not God give Judgment, when He gives you all other things or is a part of all things you partake of? As the owner, He has a perfect right to judge and use this discrimination in judgment that can be naught else but perfect. Many a time we are fearful of making judgments of our own, but God's judgment in us is perfect.

Justice is first cousin to judgment, for where God is, judgment is ruler, and justice is the outcome. In your work for prosperity you will take the thought of justice for prosperity in finances; Wealth, Plenty, Riches being the names given to the different forms of prosperity. The first idea that must be firmly planted in the conscious mind is that you are only accepting that which is yours. This gives you a more perfect idea of abundance. Where God is, there is no lack, consequently you must see more of God before you are able to bring forth more of prosperity.

The Satan for man is not money, but greed for money. I told you in the last lesson, "Love is the Fulfilling of the Law"; to love money as an article of God. That which we love we treat kindly and in a loving manner. Never be careless in throwing money around. Don't toss money! If money could speak, it would toss itself back to you and refuse to give you that which you were seeking to acquire through this money. Fold it; bless it continually, wherever you are. Make it look neat and inviting. Don't carry money that has become soiled in a material sense. Get it exchanged at a bank. The outer dirt will not really hurt you, but you will miss a great deal of the joy in handling it. You like clean clothes, don't you? So does God desire a clean outer manifestation as He manifests to you in money.

These are little things, but they mean much. Learn how to fold money. Be a good displayer. Justice and discrimination in money matters will increase all that you have, many times. Remember the man with the dime.

Let go of money when you want anything in reason. Always remember that the money in your hand is for the present desire, and more will be brought forth for the next desire as soon as you learn to let go.

Do not let the greed of money become a part of you. It stops your growth. Even though you give and give and give, if you still hold on with greed to that which you have given out, this will stop the increase. There is no increase where a personal law is working. God is impersonal.

One may have unlimited wealth and possessions, and think so little of them because they are only a part of his inheritance. This is being impersonal in his inheritance. If you find fault with having to spend or let go of money, you will find there is a separation from money for you, and in a way you have not expected.

You must be careful not to tempt the God within yourself with wealth and money; not to try to fool the Christ that you are doing this for some higher good. There is one you can never fool . . God . . Divine mind.

The power to control wealth is only gained through loving the one who has the wealth. This is loving your neighbor as yourself. In other words, it is loving another part of God-in-manifestation. God is all, and you are all, inasmuch as we let God be all!

Discrimination is a mighty weapon, in that it helps you to keep silence on the man-made subjects. One who discriminates does not use useless words or discuss his problem. Many wonderful demonstrations are killed at the birth by the student talking of what he is doing, of what he is going to do, of how and when and where he is going to do it! If you know God's law, you do not need to deal with How and When and Where.

You are the vehicle that God operates through, and are only for that purpose. God is at the helm. It is in His hand your demonstration lies, even if His hand is your hand in the outer. You are the vase holding the flowers.

"No man knoweth except the Father." This is true. You are to do, and then stand still and receive the fulfilled word, letting go of the tomorrows and using today in its course toward your plan. You know you will receive in the increase.

The increase does not depend on what you plant, but on how you plant it. The penny will increase faster than the dollar if planted in Love, for it opens new channels that flow wherever Love is.

The Rich Mentality

By

Harriet Hale Rix

Originally Published 1916 From a Lecture in 1914 at a Hotel Brighton, Washington, D. C.

Foreword

WORDS of Truth written or spoken from a consciousness of the absolute reality of the substance in them, do more than satisfy the intellect or the senses. They are God's means of bringing to pass the very Good about which they are uttered. Therefore, Reader, read slowly and ponder these words in your heart. They will uncover the Rich Mentality, with which God has endowed you and open the Way to your perpetual Prosperity.

The author, herself, is a living demonstration of the Truth that she declares, and she knows that what has come to her is a free gift of God to all.

May this message be a fulfillment of the decree of the Author of all wealth "for it is He that giveth thee power to get wealth" . . respecting every word of Truth that He has sent forth through his consecrated Messengers: "For as the rain cometh down, and the snow from heaven, and returneth not thither, but watereth the earth, and maketh it bring forth and bud, that it may give seed to the sower, and bread to eater: So shall my word be that goeth forth from out of my mouth: it shall not return unto me void, but it shall accomplish that which I please, and prosper in the thing where to I sent it." Isaiah 55:10, 11.

Annie Rix Militz

The Rich Mentality

Thou shalt Remember the Lord, thy God, for it is He that giveth thee Power to Get Wealth.

I WILL take up tonight the second subject of my course, The Rich Mentality. The world is being educated, as never before, to recognize the truth, the whole truth, about prosperity. The world is demanding more today of the noble and ideal, of honesty in all financial dealings, than ever before. We are going through a very critical time and those who know most about the truth in connection with prosperity, success and kindred subjects will pass through this crisis with the least proportion of unrest and sense of loss. The more materialistic, those of the commercial world who must have money in order to feel rich, will suffer most from panic, the disturbance and pressure. But as we go through these critical times, we are purified and cleansed, especially if we try to think correctly of that which appears to our disadvantage. I would like to make a statement here at the very beginning and have you entertain it tonight in the silence, and plant this statement, this idea, in your heart as you would a seed, to grow. It is this: That the more difficult the situation is, the higher you will rise if you think correctly about it. Let us make a familiar and close communication with the heart of it, so that in the future when we may need to be strong under great pressure or temptation we may through this correct thinking about it be blessed and comforted.

SILENCE

This is an excellent rule and true of all our activities and especially of prosperity, that as you think correctly about a thing, you are master of the situation and no evil in it nor loss nor limitation can hold or bind you. But also you will have need to philosophize about what is the correct, the right thinking, or what the highest consciousness is about a subject. I believe that the only answer here must be to think as God thinks about it. We cannot go beyond this and to think about an experience as God thinks about it is victory.

Right thinking is health, joy, freedom, prosperity. Prosperity, as I said last night, does not consist in the things you possess in the money you have in bank. In fact, we might say from a very free standpoint, that if you absolutely understand prosperity you have no need of any bank account. Prosperity is a way, a mode, of thinking. So is poverty. You are poor if you class yourself this way, and you are rich if you can think rich thoughts, thoughts that are constructive, optimistic, unlimited these instantly crown you successful. The mentality must first be rich towards God rich in God-knowledge and consciousness.

I cannot think of wealth and prosperity and success as a lasting possession to those who are callous regarding the spiritual life. Dr. Bucke, who studied cosmic consciousness for over thirty years, states that in all his examinations of men and women he has never come across a single case of cosmic consciousness where the individual was bent on making money; whose whole conception of life was accumulation. This is a law. You cannot love God and love money. You cannot both work for a great ideal and work for selfish ends, for money or a living. It is a mistake to work for a living. To work this way is to be a slave under dominion to the laws of slavery. Never work for a living.

How can you gain a life? Life is! You cannot pay for it. You have no price to give in exchange for life, for your breath and your being. You are not here to work by strenuous effort to make life. You are here under the blessing of God to live a life of wholesome, loving kindness, of success and good will towards each other and the bringing out of your own nature, the divine self. God lives you every moment. If you are conscious that God is your very life and being you will not work to express it in the terms of mortal consciousness, in dollars and cents and salary.

You will no longer serve the old world conception of prosperity. What you do you will do with your might in the service of Principle, like Brother Lawrence he did not work for a living, he worked to express God by living in so attractive a way as to draw other men to the Divine Life? The kitchen of that monastery where he cooked was more magnetic than any other part of the whole concern. He was rich towards God and man, not like an ox driven by the duties demanded of him. He was a man serving a great Principle and he lived in security.

You are useful to God as you are emptied of self and keep from worrying, fearing and fretting about today, tomorrow or yesterday. Your life is inspired and inspiring all about you. Whoever comes in contact with an inspired soul realizes the beauty of it The Rich Mentality is the inspiration of life. I will say something about that presently, but for the moment I will affirm this, that the rich mentality is so full of awakened consciousness, so absolutely certain of the Truth, the Ideal and the Real, that it never fears poverty. It is not being hindered by any effort to fight poverty, or lack, or want. It is all love, all peace, because it is the love of recognized good.

Now the old life of poverty may be described as it is in Genesis, the curse, the old Adamic curse on man, that he shall work by the sweat of his brow, and the race has considered this law as springing from the great mind of God, the great Mind of Wisdom. But we recognize that this is not the design of the Most-High; it is an idea brought about through the mind of man, under the belief that he has fallen into sin and must be punished and, after utterly paying the price, enter into paradise. This is not the attitude as we find it in the quickened character. If you are realizing inwardly that you are the Son of God you will take the stand of Jesus Christ and throw off the yoke of the old curse and refuse to work by the sweat of your brow.

You know that the lesser laws are fulfilled in the great law that sets man in tune with the Infinite. Because he loves God first, his Divinity, he is set free from every law that limits." It Is the only law that sets man really free to love with all one's mind and soul and strength, and to exercise this love toward one's fellow beings to love your neighbor as your God, or as your Divine Self. Thus is man introduced to himself as he finds the Man who is really rich. He begins to realize that he is not poor in spirit but rich in wisdom, God being his mind, his intelligence, his thinking power, arid he is governed and guided and controlled by the Rich Mentality. He does not groan and moan, and fear poverty. Nor does he prepare for a future that will lack anything good so long as he knows but one Provider, One Inexhaustible Presence. For that faith closely allies heart with this Great Spirit, active and living within him.

Therefore he goes not prepare for old age with its sorrow and lack so unattractive. He intends to become more attractive, for the older he grows the nearer he should be to the Great Center, and the Great White Light of Being. The rich mentality fears nothing, and he is free from the" burden and care that the world groans under. He is not under the law of wear and tear and exhaustion because this rich subconsciousness of him causes him to know that his good is inexhaustible! He is not serving a good "that is liable to cease, but his good is so manifold and widely spread that it might be accused of wastefulness. Think of all that the hills and mountains contain that has never been revealed or opened up to this age! The wonderful gems and jewels, gold and silver, that await future ages, already stored underground, and this is but the symbol of the greater storehouse of God.

The man of this vision exercises faith and he wants to exercise faith. In the rich mentality he never thinks that he can be lazy and never work anymore. He knows that he can convert Divine energy and force every moment and so he is active with great dynamic power. He uses faith every moment. It is his joy and incentive, and life is thoroughly interesting to the one who practically enters into an alignment with the rich mentality.

The rich mentality is supreme in this, that it believes absolutely in the good. You cannot persuade it that evil is a reality; it does not ask down to meditate on evil; it has no moments of malice or jealousy or Hate; it has no time for these, for its whole time is taken up on lines that are strong, powerful witnesses of the good. And it pays the one who exercises his mind in this direction, and he never consents to talk about evil as a reality. He knows that thinking about good is the rule and the standard which is his unfailing resource. He entertains it for his business life, for his social life; in his relations with men; with his own family and children.

Every relationship must be maintained in the recognition of the good and the good only. Thus he is educating himself, training himself as God desires him to live and to be happy.

Now we are all after that, are we not? If we could find one word to cover our aspirations tonight, could we find a larger word, or that is more inclusive than joy or happiness? I do not mean that happiness which the world so defines to us a limitation that fritters away and is liable to be lost. I mean the lasting happiness the happiness that is secured to the individual by fidelity to principle. Infinite Mind made you for happiness; it made you capable of a supreme bliss, able to enjoy as you little dream today you can enjoy life. You will begin to smile the moment you actually believe this and do away with the wrinkled thoughts, the troubled thoughts. You will grow perpetually young through the inspiration of the Almighty penetrating to the innermost realm of your heart, and you can keep it there and it is bound to make you strong and beautiful.

The rich mentality maintains a cheerful attitude which can smile pain down, and sorrow away, and seeming trouble into nothingness. It minimizes instantly that which the world feels to be oppression and loss and in harmony, and feels the mastery over it. It is a wonderful capital!

A man once came to my door in Alameda and wanted to sell me some shoestrings. You know the kind of a man who sells shoestrings. He is a man who does not smile very much. If he smiled very much he would be selling something else than shoestrings. He does not have the rich mentality towards life and well being; he does not have the right attitude towards the law of success. And he came all bent over, although a young man in years, and begged me to buy a shoestring. He looked so lugubrious, complaining of every resident of my town, declaring that nobody was kind and nobody would buy. So he had to get a lesson and this was the lesson: He was told to go away and instead of looking so mournful that nobody wanted to open the door, he should go forth with a smile and with faith in himself and in the kindness of those with whom he should come in contact. He said: "Will that pay? And will it sell my needles and shoestrings?" He was assured that it would, far better than the attitude he had taken. In a few days he came back and told me he had taken my advice and that he had sold more in that afternoon than in a month, and his business had picked up and was growing. That is what the smile does. And the world needs your smile; it is the smile that heals the world. It is the smile, not the groan, that makes for a spiritual life and for success. Then it should be your part to contribute these to the world and help others who are bestowing smiles upon the world to redeem it.

The rich mentality can smile because it knows. It is sure of some things, because it is absolutely certain of others worthwhile. It knows God as tenderness and Love; as the All-Providing Presence and therefore it smiles with an inner smile of good cheer and certainty and strength.

The rich mentality does not love money, it loves God. How could it love God supremely and love money? It does not divide its forces foolishly, for it sees readily that those who love money become metallic, their eyes are metallic, their souls are metallic, and the strength of muscle and brain lessens daily, being sold in one who serves money. The rich mentality is master of money, does not serve money, and, being its master, money feels attracted towards that one.

In here is a certain intelligence in money. It wants to be used by those who are able intelligently to keep it in circulation, for circulation is the very spirit of money. If it is hoarded or put away, it corrodes and dies, but as it is kept in motion, it is kept in life. Therefore it is not the accumulation and the grabbing of money that constitute wealth, but the giving and letting it go forth freely. To the rich mentality money is a blessing. But to the poor mentality it is a curse. It is not that money is the source of evil, but the love of money. Pain and sickness and sorrow would vanish if we would renounce the love of money, and love God as our Provider, Success and Life. "The earth is the Lord's and The fullness thereof."

As you decide to stand by the principles of Truth in your success and prosperity, you no longer work under the false idea of economy, because many people are only economical through a belief in poverty, not from the standpoint of prosperity. Their prosperity is only beggaring them. You have seen people that deny themselves the luxuries and comforts of life, the things that make life beautiful, although they have much property and money aplenty but not the right thought. It is then a matter of thinking, of contacting this great white Truth. Ignorance or knowledge? Moses is an example. His great riches were inexhaustible; so magnificent were they that after he had taken the children of Israel out of slavery in Egypt, he fed them by a self-conscious, working miracle-law for forty years with a strange bread known as "the manna in the wilderness."

Did you think that an interfering God had given this blessing to the Israelites? It was the direct work of the mind of Moses, the God in Moses. He knew how to produce and reproduce and to keep it up indefinitely. He knew how to strike a flint rock by which it would spring forth a refreshing stream. Repeatedly he did this and it was but the forerunner of great things to come, the symbol of a consciousness-of-providing, that is close at hand, so close" to you and to me as to be "nearer than our breath" and yet we may pass through this incarnation without recognizing or receiving any benefit from it if we close our eyes to its Presence, or our hearts to its reception. It needs that we understand that God is Prosperity, and every blessing proceeds from the infinite, inexhaustible Resource, the Mind of God. We want to know more and more of this wonderful law and how to apply it in life so that it shall quickly bring to us our own inheritance.

The rich mentality is always original. You are original because God made you so. I say you are original, but do you insist upon it? Are you even willing to be original? I question whether you are willing to be as God made you. How splendid and royal and kingly, if everyone would be willing to be original! To be original is to be a God-man It is to be well and to be at home. When you do not feel at home it is because there is too much pretense. I mean that we are too willing to go with the crowd, that we would rather be a counterfeit than the genuine self that God made us.

There would be a great transformation if you would take the stand that God never made two exactly alike. We are all independent, and yet beautifully interdependent independent in one way, and from another standpoint, interdependent. If we realized this there would never be selfishness and discord. It would be the Bellamy plan come to fruition. Every man would find his work, his place, and we would all be doing what we enjoy doing. That would indeed be the Golden Age. Insist upon originality and resources will come to you when you are pushed or cornered. You will be the resourceful one that God made you. God will impress upon you the new way and means to take.

I have a cousin in the West who is an original thinker, who never insists on doing things as other people do. He has ideas of his own because he dares to think with God and to let God think through him. He believes that if he should lose all that he has he could easily regain it through this consciousness. In talking to some club friends one day he affirmed that, if given a nucleus, even though it appeared useless, that he would make it produce something without the use of capital. The friends took him up and he promised to try it out. Looking about for some nucleus they saw a pile of scrap tin which was about to go into the garbage wagon. It certainly looked useless and impossible. But the friends said, "There it is" and they left the shop laughing.

He felt almost vanquished by his nucleus, but he looked at it and concentrated his mind upon this tin and he said: "This tin will tell me what it can do, what is can shape and form and what can come out of it." Presently there came into his mind the picture of a little matchbox. And so he began to cut and bend and pretty soon he had shaped a little matchbox. He called a boy passing along and asked him to take the matchbox out and try to sell it for twenty-five cents; that, if he did, he would give him ten cents of it for selling it. The boy came back delighted a little while later, having sold the matchbox for twenty-five cents, and receiving the ten cents promised. So with this capital of fifteen cents my cousin invested in some paint with which to decorate the match boxes.

The boy being so happy with his sale, soon brought several other boys, who also wanted to sell matchboxes, and so in the course of several weeks he had quite a capital as a result of that scrap tin. And he proved there is a law within us that we need never remain cast down or crushed if we will not believe that we are crushed or cornered, but keep our eye on the original way out.

We have had such false teaching about prosperity from the pulpit. Yet the Churches and Cathedrals stand as monuments of prosperity, though the ministers have declared that Christ was poor and that in some strange way his followers should also be poor. Jesus Christ was not poor. How can you think that he was poor, or is poor? Why, we are all poor compared to him, as we are manifesting today. If you know not of what wealth consists, are you not poor as a Vanderbilt who on his deathbed cried out, "Poor and needy indeed," because his wealth consisted of things which he could not take with him, and his mind an empty void. Jesus Christ was the wealthiest man who ever trod this earth. He needed not to exercise any effort to maintain himself. He sent his disciples forth, telling them not to provide two coats, or shoes, or to take scrip with them, for, he said, "The man I send forth is worthy of his hire," that is, he will be maintained by a Divine Law. After a time he said to them, u When I sent you without purse and scrip, lacked ye anything?" and they said, "Nay, Lord, we lacked nothing."

Jesus Christ was not poor. Would you be poor if you could heal every disease that came to you? Would you be poor? Would you be poor if you could raise a dead man from the tomb? Would you be poor if you could turn weak water into rich wine? Would you be poor or would you be rich? Would you be poor if you could take two loaves and five fishes and feed five thousand Belgians today with all they want and have much left over? Would you be poor or would you be rich? Be sensible! Was Jesus Christ poor? Why he had the miracle working Mind . . the Mind that increases through rich thinking, rich knowledge. And so my Christ is not a poor Christ. I wish I were as wealthy. What were a million dollars in your hand to that power he possessed? Which would you take? Not one of you would hesitate a second if you are sensible. You would be wealthy with that knowledge. Paul says that whereas Christ was rich, he took upon himself poverty that we might be rich. That is, he took upon himself the appearance of poverty and he proved that having is not prosperity, but if one thinks richly he is indeed the wealthiest of men.

If you are working consciously with the great law of God, you are inspired. Ask yourself, "Am I inspired in the work I am doing?"

Do I put enthusiasm into my work? Or am I working as a slave man, driven and bound?" If the latter, heal yourself of these thoughts and become enthusiastic. The rich mentality does not scorn to work or scorn any character of work. It loves to work because inspired in all that it does. I said that no man could work for money only. A man demonstrated this once by hiring a man for three dollars a day just to take a brick up from a spot on one side of the street and place it in another spot across the street and vice versa all day long. At first the man entered into the job with clarity, but he soon grew weary, and the outcome was that he threw up the job, refused to work at it and said he would rather starve than to work one more day at such a terrible job as that. We are not here to work for anything less than to unfold our God nature, our Divine Self, and this is not possible when we concentrate on money alone. What is money? Why, you are the creator and maker of money. You put into it all that makes it of value and you can withdraw that and it is not worth any more than sand. God did not make money valuable; to him there is no difference between a pebble and a diamond.

You must give if you would get; the man who forgets to give, forgets how to receive. He closes the door of receptivity; he closes the door of life and is like a lake which, unless opened at both ends, becomes stagnant. Many people are planting disease, physical poverty and misery of all kinds through not maintaining the other half of the law of Prosperity. They want to receive only but the law is not a hemisphere, it is a sphere. It is only as you bring the two parts together and recognize that giving and receiving should be equal, that you can weld them into a unit and have the law work for you. "With what measure you give, it shall be measured back to you."

This mind that is the Rich Mentality never takes offense nor receives an insult. Think about that . . it never receives an insult. It never feels hurt and is never discouraged; it is never jealous. It is never angry because anger is poverty of consciousness; no one gets angry until he thinks he is inefficient or is conscious of a sense of weakness. The rich mentality never knows malice; resentment never suggests itself to it. It is never doubtful of the Good and its possibilities. It never listens to words of ill report and therefore never repeats them. It does not gossip nor love iniquitous things because the rich mentality is LOVE. It has always words of praise for all who come within its presence. It has no enemies, is not self-seeking and knows no pride. "Let this mind be in you" and your body will become perfect, enduring, strong and beautiful, and your affairs full of delight and plenty.

The rich mentality does not look for flaws, is not complaining; never worries, frets nor fears; never anxious nor overcome; it never fights, resists, nor in cowardice turns its back. Hate is unknown to it and death has no terrors, while sickness is completely under its control. It is never sad nor gloomy; it never dwells upon evil for five minutes; it has no doubt of the power of good: does not condemn or judge, all because it is the Mind of God, the richest Mind in all Being.

Let us be silent for a moment and entertain these statements. Let us relax and open our hearts to the Greater Self, to the Self more abundant, to the One Self of us which is not duality nor multiplicity nor division, but One Self, radiantly beautiful and divine, the Self that is described only in deific terms.

SILENCE

I AM rich in God's love.

I give my best to the world and the best the world has comes back to me.

I AM Prosperity. I AM Success. God made me so.

I claim my own freely and fearlessly.

My Prosperity is based upon the true foundation, therefore is changeless, is GOD, and the Spirit, overshadowing and indwelling, my one and everlasting good. Amen!

The Science of Getting Rich

By

Wallace Wattles

Originally Published 1910

Contents

Preface

Chapter 1 - The Right To Be Rich
Chapter 2 - There is A Science of Getting Rich
Chapter 3 - Is Opportunity Monopolized?
Chapter 4 - The First Principle in The Science of Getting Rich
Chapter 5 - Increasing Life
Chapter 6 - How Riches Come to You
Chapter 7 - Gratitude
Chapter 8 - Thinking in the Certain Way
Chapter 9 - How to Use the Will
Chapter 10 - Further Use of the Will
Chapter 11 - Acting in the Certain Way
Chapter 12 - Efficient Action
Chapter 13 - Getting into the Right Business
Chapter 14 - The Impression of Increase
Chapter 15 - The Advancing Man
Chapter 16 - Some Cautions, and Concluding Observations
Chapter 17 - Summary of the Science of Getting Rich

Preface

THIS book is pragmatical, not philosophical; a practical manual, not a treatise upon theories. It is intended for the men and women whose most pressing need is for money; who wish to get rich first, and philosophize afterward. It is for those who have, so far, found neither the time, the means, nor the opportunity to go deeply into the study of metaphysics, but who want results and who are willing to take the conclusions of science as a basis for action, without going into all the processes by which those conclusions were reached.

It is expected that the reader will take the fundamental statements upon faith, just as he would take statements concerning a law of electrical action if they were promulgated by a Marconi or an Edison; and, taking the statements upon faith, that he will prove their truth by acting upon them without fear or hesitation. Every man or woman who does this will certainly get rich; for the science herein applied is an exact science, and failure is impossible. For the benefit, however, of those who wish to investigate philosophical theories and so secure a logical basis for faith, I will here cite certain authorities.

The monistic theory of the universe the theory that One is All, and that All is One; That one Substance manifests itself as the seeming many elements of the material world . . is of Hindu origin, and has been gradually winning its way into the thought of the western world for two hundred years. It is the foundation of all the Oriental philosophies, and of those of Descartes, Spinoza, Leibnitz, Schopenhauer, Hegel, and Emerson.

The reader who would dig to the philosophical foundations of this is advised to read Hegel and Emerson for himself.

In writing this book I have sacrificed all other considerations to plainness and simplicity of style, so that all might understand. The plan of action laid down herein was deduced from the conclusions of philosophy; it has been thoroughly tested, and bears the supreme test of practical experiment; it works. If you wish to know how the conclusions were arrived at, read the writings of the authors mentioned above; and if you wish to reap the fruits of their philosophies in actual practice, read this book and do exactly as it tells you to do.

Wallace Wattles

Chapter 1

The Right To Be Rich

WHATEVER may be said in praise of poverty, the fact remains that it is not possible to live a really complete or successful life unless one is rich. No man can rise to his greatest possible height in talent or soul development unless he has plenty of money; for to unfold the soul and to develop talent he must have many things to use, and he cannot have these things unless he has money to buy them with.

A man develops in mind, soul, and body by making use of things, and society is so organized that man must have money in order to become the possessor of things; therefore, the basis of all advancement for man must be the science of getting rich.

The object of all life is development; and everything that lives has an inalienable right to all the development it is capable of attaining.

Man's right to life means his right to have the free and unrestricted use of all the things which may be necessary to his fullest mental, spiritual, and physical unfoldment; or, in other words, his right to be rich.

In this book, I shall not speak of riches in a figurative way; to be really rich does not mean to be satisfied or contented with a little. No man ought to be satisfied with a little if he is capable of using and enjoying more. The purpose of Nature is the advancement and unfoldment of life; and every man should have all that can contribute to the power; elegance, beauty, and richness of life; to be content with less is sinful.

The man who owns all he wants for the living of all the life he is capable of living is rich; and no man who has not plenty of money can have all he wants. Life has advanced so far, and become so complex, that even the most ordinary man or woman requires a great amount of wealth in order to live in a manner that even approaches completeness. Every person naturally wants to become all that they are capable of becoming; this desire to realize innate possibilities is inherent in human nature; we cannot help wanting to be all that we can be. Success in life is becoming what you want to be; you can become what you want to be only by making use of things, and you can have the free use of things only as you become rich enough to buy them. To understand the science of getting rich is therefore the most essential of all knowledge.

There is nothing wrong in wanting to get rich. The desire for riches is really the desire for a richer, fuller, and more abundant life; and that desire is praiseworthy. The man who does not desire to live more abundantly is abnormal, and so the man who does not desire to have money enough to buy all he wants is abnormal.

There are three motives for which we live; we live for the body, we live for the mind, we live for the soul. No one of these is better or holier than the other; all are alike desirable, and no one of the three . . body, mind, or soul . . can live fully if either of the others is cut short of full life and expression. It is not right or noble to live only for the soul and deny mind or body; and it is wrong to live for the intellect and deny body or soul.

We are all acquainted with the loathsome consequences of living for the body and denying both mind and soul; and we see that real life means the complete expression of all that man can give forth through body, mind, and soul. Whatever he can say, no man can be really happy or satisfied unless his body is living fully in every function, and unless the same is true of his mind and his soul. Wherever there is unexpressed possibility, or function not performed, there is unsatisfied desire. Desire is possibility seeking expression, or function seeking performance.

Man cannot live fully in body without good food, comfortable clothing, and warm shelter; and without freedom from excessive toil. Rest and recreation are also necessary to his physical life.

He cannot live fully in mind without books and time to study them, without opportunity for travel and observation, or without intellectual companionship.

To live fully in mind he must have intellectual recreations, and must surround himself with all the objects of art and beauty he is capable of using and appreciating.

To live fully in soul, man must have love; and love is denied expression by poverty.

A man's highest happiness is found in the bestowal of benefits on those he loves; love finds its most natural and spontaneous expression in giving. The man who has nothing to give cannot fill his place as a husband or father, as a citizen, or as a man. It is in the use of material things that a man finds full life for his body, develops his mind, and unfolds his soul. It is therefore of supreme importance to him that he should be rich.

It is perfectly right that you should desire to be rich; if you are a normal man or woman you cannot help doing so. It is perfectly right that you should give your best attention to the Science of Getting Rich, for it is the noblest and most necessary of all studies. If you neglect this study, you are derelict in your duty to yourself, to God and humanity; for you can render to God and humanity no greater service than to make the most of yourself.

Chapter 2

There is a Science of Getting Rich

THERE is a Science of getting rich, and it is an exact science, like algebra or arithmetic. There are certain laws which govern the process of acquiring riches; once these laws are learned and obeyed by any man, he will get rich with mathematical certainty.

The ownership of money and property comes as a result of doing things in a certain way; those who do things in this Certain Way, whether on purpose or accidentally, get rich; while those who do not do things in this Certain Way, no matter how hard they work or how able they are, remain poor.

It is a natural law that like causes always produce like effects; and, therefore, any man or woman who learns to do things in this certain way will infallibly get rich. That the above statement is true is shown by the following facts:

Getting rich is not a matter of environment, for, if it were, all the people in certain neighborhoods would become wealthy; the people of one city would all be rich, while those of other towns would all be poor; or the inhabitants of one state would roll in wealth, while those of an adjoining state would be in poverty.

But everywhere we see rich and poor living side by side, in the same environment, and often engaged in the same vocations. When two men are in the same locality, and in the same business, and one gets rich while the other remains poor, it shows that getting rich is not, primarily, a matter of environment. Some environments may be more favorable than others, but when two men in the same business are in the same neighborhood, and one gets rich while the other fails, it indicates that getting rich is the result of doing things in a Certain Way.

And further, the ability to do things in this certain way is not due solely to the possession of talent, for many people who have great talent remain poor, while other who have very little talent get rich.

Studying the people who have got rich, we find that they are an average lot in all respects, having no greater talents and abilities than other men. It is evident that they do not get rich because they possess talents and abilities that other men have not, but because they happen to do things in a Certain Way.

Getting rich is not the result of saving, or "thrift"; many very penurious people are poor, while free spenders often get rich.

Nor is getting rich due to doing things which others fail to do; for two men in the same business often do almost exactly the same things, and one gets rich while the other remains poor or becomes bankrupt.

From all these things, we must come to the conclusion that getting rich is the result of doing things in a Certain Way.

If getting rich is the result of doing things in a Certain Way, and if like causes always produce like effects, then any man or woman who can do things in that way can become rich, and the whole matter is brought within the domain of exact science.

The question arises here, whether this Certain Way may not be so difficult that only a few may follow it. This cannot be true, as we have seen, so far as natural ability is concerned. Talented people get rich, and blockheads get rich; intellectually brilliant people get rich, and very stupid people get rich; physically strong people get rich, and weak and sickly people get rich.

Some degree of ability to think and understand is, of course, essential; but in so far natural ability is concerned, any man or woman who has sense enough to read and understand these words can certainly get rich.

Also, we have seen that it is not a matter of environment. Location counts for something; one would not go to the heart of the Sahara and expect to do successful business.

Getting rich involves the necessity of dealing with men, and of being where there are people to deal with; and if these people are inclined to deal in the way you want to deal, so much the better. But that is about as far as environment goes.

If anybody else in your town can get rich, so can you; and if anybody else in your state can get rich, so can you.

Again, it is not a matter of choosing some particular business or profession. People get rich in every business, and in every profession; while their next-door neighbors in the same vocation remain in poverty.

It is true that you will do best in a business which you like, and which is congenial to you; and if you have certain talents which are well developed, you will do best in a business which calls for the exercise of those talents.

Also, you will do best in a business which is suited to your locality; an ice-cream parlor would do better in a warm climate than in Greenland, and a salmon fishery will succeed better in the Northwest than in Florida, where there are no salmon.

But, aside from these general limitations, getting rich is not dependent upon your engaging in some particular business, but upon your learning to do things in a Certain Way. If you are now in business, and anybody else in your locality is getting rich in the same business, while you are not getting rich, it is because you are not doing things in the same Way that the other person is doing them.

No one is prevented from getting rich by lack of capital. True, as you get capital the increase becomes more easy and rapid; but one who has capital is already rich, and does not need to consider how to become so. No matter how poor you may be, if you begin to do things in the Certain Way you will begin to get rich; and you will begin to have capital. The getting of capital is a part of the process of getting rich; and it is a part of the result which invariably follows the doing of things in the Certain Way. You may be the poorest man on the continent, and be deeply in debt; you may have neither friends, influence, nor resources; but if you begin to do things in this way, you must infallibly begin to get rich, for like causes must produce like effects. If you have no capital, you can get capital; if you are in the wrong business, you can get into the right business; if you are in the wrong location, you can go to the right location; and you can do so by beginning in your present business and in your present location to do things in the Certain Way which causes success.

Chapter 3

Is Opportunity Monopolized?

NO man is kept poor because opportunity has been taken away from him; because other people have monopolized the wealth, and have put a fence around it. You may be shut off from engaging in business in certain lines, but there are other channels open to you. Probably it would be hard for you to get control of any of the great railroad systems; that field is pretty well monopolized. But the electric railway business is still in its infancy, and offers plenty of scope for enterprise; and it will be but a very few years until traffic and transportation through the air will become a great industry, and in all its branches will give employment to hundreds of thousands, and perhaps to millions, of people. Why not turn your attention to the development of aerial transportation, instead of competing with J.J. Hill and others for a chance in the steam railway world?

It is quite true that if you are a workman in the employ of the steel trust you have very little chance of becoming the owner of the plant in which you work; but it is also true that if you will commence to act in a Certain Way, you can soon leave the employ of the steel trust; you can buy a farm of from ten to forty acres, and engage in business as a producer of foodstuffs. There is great opportunity at this time for men who will live upon small tracts of land and cultivate the same intensively; such men will certainly get rich. You may say that it is impossible for you to get the land, but I am going to prove to you that it is not impossible, and that you can certainly get a farm if you will go to work in a Certain Way.

At different periods the tide of opportunity sets in different directions, according to the needs of the whole, and the particular stage of social evolution which has been reached. At present, in America, it is setting toward agriculture and the allied industries and professions. Today, opportunity is open before the factory worker in his line. It is open before the business man who supplies the farmer more than before the one who supplies the factory worker; and before the professional man who waits upon the farmer more than before the one who serves the working class.

There is abundance of opportunity for the man who will go with the tide, instead of trying to swim against it.

So the factory workers, either as individuals or as a class, are not deprived of opportunity. The workers are not being "kept down" by their masters; they are not being "ground" by the trusts and combinations of capital. As a class, they are where they are because they do not do things in a Certain Way. If the workers of America chose to do so, they could follow the example of their brothers in Belgium and other countries, and establish great department stores and cooperative industries; they could elect men of their own class to office, and pass laws favoring the development of such cooperative industries; and in a few years they could take peaceable possession of the industrial field.

The working class may become the master class whenever they will begin to do things in a Certain Way; the law of wealth is the same for them as it is for all others. This they must learn; and they will remain where they are as long as they continue to do as they do. The individual worker, however, is not held down by the ignorance or the mental slothfulness of his class; he can follow the tide of opportunity to riches, and this book will tell him how.

No one is kept in poverty by a shortness in the supply of riches; there is more than enough for all. A palace as large as the capitol at Washington might be built for every family on earth from the building material in the United States alone; and under intensive cultivation, this country would produce wool, cotton, linen, and silk enough to cloth each person in the world finer than Solomon was arrayed in all his glory; together with food enough to feed them all luxuriously.

The visible supply is practically inexhaustible; and the invisible supply really IS inexhaustible.

Everything you see on earth is made from one original substance, out of which all things proceed.

New Forms are constantly being made, and older ones are dissolving; but all are shapes assumed by One Thing.

There is no limit to the supply of Formless Stuff, or Original Substance. The universe is made out of it; but it was not all used in making the universe. The spaces in, through, and between the forms of the visible universe are permeated and filled with the Original Substance; with the formless Stuff; with the raw material of all things. Ten thousand times as much as has been made might still be made, and even then we should not have exhausted the supply of universal raw material.

No man, therefore, is poor because nature is poor, or because there is not enough to go around.

Nature is an inexhaustible storehouse of riches; the supply will never run short. Original Substance is alive with creative energy, and is constantly producing more forms. When the supply of building material is exhausted, more will be produced; when the soil is exhausted so that foodstuffs and materials for clothing will no longer grow upon it, it will be renewed or more soil will be made. When all the gold and silver has been dug from the earth, if man is still in such a stage of social development that he needs gold and silver, more will produced from the Formless. The Formless Stuff responds to the needs of man; it will not let him be without any good thing.

This is true of man collectively; the race as a whole is always abundantly rich, and if individuals are poor, it is because they do not follow the Certain Way of doing things which makes the individual man rich.

The Formless Stuff is intelligent; it is stuff which thinks. It is alive, and is always impelled toward more life.

It is the natural and inherent impulse of life to seek to live more; it is the nature of intelligence to enlarge itself, and of consciousness to seek to extend its boundaries and find fuller expression. The universe of forms has been made by Formless Living Substance, throwing itself into form in order to express itself more fully.

The universe is a great Living Presence, always moving inherently toward more life and fuller functioning.

Nature is formed for the advancement of life; its impelling motive is the increase of life. For this cause, everything which can possibly minister to life is bountifully provided; there can be no lack unless God is to contradict himself and nullify his own works.

You are not kept poor by lack in the supply of riches; it is a fact which I shall demonstrate a little farther on that even the resources of the Formless Supply are at the command of the man or woman will act and think in a Certain Way.

Chapter 4

The First Principle in the Science of Getting Rich

THOUGHT is the only power which can produce tangible riches from the Formless Substance. The stuff from which all things are made is a substance which thinks, and a thought of form in this substance produces the form.

Original Substance moves according to its thoughts; every form and process you see in nature is the visible expression of a thought in Original Substance. As the Formless Stuff thinks of a form, it takes that form; as it thinks of a motion, it makes that motion. That is the way all things were created. We live in a thought world, which is part of a thought universe. The thought of a moving universe extended throughout Formless Substance, and the Thinking Stuff moving according to that thought, took the form of systems of planets, and maintains that form. Thinking Substance takes the form of its thought, and moves according to the thought. Holding the idea of a circling system of suns and worlds, it takes the form of these bodies, and moves them as it thinks. Thinking the form of a slow-growing oak tree, it moves accordingly, and produces the tree, though centuries may be required to do the work. In creating, the Formless seems to move according to the lines of motion it has established; the thought of an oak tree does not cause the instant formation of a full grown tree, but it does start in motion the forces which will produce the tree, along established lines of growth.

Every thought of form, held in thinking Substance, causes the creation of the form, but always, or at least generally, along lines of growth and action already established.

The thought of a house of a certain construction, if it were impressed upon Formless Substance, might not cause the instant formation, of the house; but it would cause the turning of creative energies already working in trade and commerce into such channels as to result in the speedy building of the house. And if there were no existing channels through which the creative energy could work, then the house would be formed directly from primal substance, without waiting for the slow processes of the organic and inorganic world.

No thought of form can be impressed upon Original Substance without causing the creation of the form.

Man is a thinking center, and can originate thought. All the forms that man fashions with his hands must first exist in his thought; he cannot shape a thing until he has thought that thing.

And so far man has confined his efforts wholly to the work of his hands; he has applied manual labor to the world of forms, seeking to change or modify those already existing. He has never thought of trying to cause the creation of new forms by impressing his thoughts upon Formless Substance.

When man has a thought-form, he takes material from the forms of nature, and makes an image of the form which is in his mind. He has, so far, made little or no effort to cooperate with Formless Intelligence; to work "with the Father." He has not dreamed that he can "do what he seeth the Father doing." Man reshapes and modifies existing forms by manual labor; he has given no attention to the question whether he may not produce things from Formless Substance by communicating his thoughts to it. We propose to prove that he may do so; to prove that any man or woman may do so, and to show how. As our first step, we must lay down three fundamental propositions.

First, we assert that there is one original formless stuff, or substance, from which all things are made. All the seemingly many elements are but different presentations of one element; all the many forms found in organic and inorganic nature are but different shapes, made from the same stuff. And this stuff is thinking stuff; a thought held in it produces the form of the thought. Thought, in thinking substance, produces shapes. Man is a thinking center, capable of original thought; if man can communicate his thought to original thinking substance, he can cause the creation, or formation, of the thing he thinks about. To summarize this:

There is a thinking stuff from which all things are made, and which, in its original state, permeates, penetrates, and fills the interspaces of the universe. A thought, in this substance, produces the thing that is imaged by the thought. Man can form things in his thought, and, by impressing his thought upon formless substance, can cause the thing he thinks about to be created.

It may be asked if I can prove these statements; and without going into details, I answer that I can do so, both by logic and experience.

Reasoning back from the phenomena of form and thought, I come to one original thinking substance; and reasoning forward from this thinking substance, I come to man's power to cause the formation of the thing he thinks about.

And by experiment, I find the reasoning true; and this is my strongest proof.

If one man who reads this book gets rich by doing what it tells him to do, that is evidence in support of my claim; but if every man who does what it tells him to do gets rich, that is positive proof until someone goes through the process and fails. The theory is true until the process fails; and this process will not fail, for every man who does exactly what this book tells him to do will get rich.

I have said that men get rich by doing things in a Certain Way; and in order to do so, men must become able to think in a certain way.

A man's way of doing things is the direct result of the way he thinks about things.

To do things in a way you want to do them, you will have to acquire the ability to think the way you want to think; this is the first step toward getting rich.

To think what you want to think is to think TRUTH, regardless of appearances.

Every man has the natural and inherent power to think what he wants to think, but it requires far more effort to do so than it does to think the thoughts which are suggested by appearances. To think according to appearance is easy; to think truth regardless of appearances is laborious, and requires the expenditure of more power than any other work man is called upon to perform.

There is no labor from which most people shrink as they do from that of sustained and consecutive thought; it is the hardest work in the world. This is especially true when truth is contrary to appearances. Every appearance in the visible world tends to produce a corresponding form in the mind which observes it; and this can only be prevented by holding the thought of the TRUTH.

To look upon the appearance of disease will produce the form of disease in your own mind, and ultimately in your body, unless you hold the thought of the truth, which is that there is no disease; it is only an appearance, and the reality is health. To look upon the appearances of poverty will produce corresponding forms in your own mind, unless you hold to the truth that there is no poverty; there is only abundance.

To think health when surrounded by the appearances of disease, or to think riches when in the midst of appearances of poverty, requires power; but he who acquires this power becomes a MASTER MIND. He can conquer fate; he can have what he wants.

This power can only be acquired by getting hold of the basic fact which is behind all appearances; and that fact is that there is one Thinking Substance, from which and by which all things are made.

Then we must grasp the truth that every thought held in this substance becomes a form, and that man can so impress his thoughts upon it as to cause them to take form and become visible things.

When we realize this, we lose all doubt and fear, for we know that we can create what we want to create; we can get what we want to have, and can become what we want to be. As a first step toward getting rich, you must believe the three fundamental statements given previously in this chapter; and in order to emphasize them. I repeat them here:

There is a thinking stuff from which all things are made, and which, in its original state, permeates, penetrates, and fills the interspaces of the universe. A thought, in this substance, produces the thing that is imaged by the thought. Man can form things in his thought, and, by impressing his thought upon formless substance, can cause the thing he thinks about to be created.

You must lay aside all other concepts of the universe than this monistic one; and you must dwell upon this until it is fixed in your mind, and has become your habitual thought. Read these creed statements over and over again; fix every word upon your memory, and meditate upon them until you firmly believe what they say. If a doubt comes to you, cast it aside as a sin. Do not listen to arguments against this idea; do not go to churches or lectures where a contrary concept of things is taught or preached. Do not read magazines or books which teach a different idea; if you get mixed up in your faith, all your efforts will be in vain.

Do not ask why these things are true, nor speculate as to how they can be true; simply take them on trust.

The science of getting rich begins with the absolute acceptance of this faith.

Chapter 5

Increasing Life

YOU must get rid of the last vestige of the old idea that there is a Deity whose will it is that you should be poor, or whose purposes may be served by keeping you in poverty.

The Intelligent Substance which is All, and in All, and which lives in All and lives in you, is a consciously Living Substance. Being a consciously living substance, it must have the nature and inherent desire of every living intelligence for increase of life. Every living thing must continually seek for the enlargement of its life, because life, in the mere act of living, must increase itself.

A seed, dropped into the ground, springs into activity, and in the act of living produces a hundred more seeds; life, by living, multiplies itself. It is forever Becoming More; it must do so, if it continues to be at all.

Intelligence is under this same necessity for continuous increase. Every thought we think makes it necessary for us to think another thought; consciousness is continually expanding. Every fact we learn leads us to the learning of another fact; knowledge is continually increasing. Every talent we cultivate brings to the mind the desire to cultivate another talent; we are subject to the urge of life, seeking expression, which ever drives us on to know more, to do more, and to be more.

In order to know more, do more, and be more we must have more; we must have things to use, for we learn, and do, and become, only by using things. We must get rich, so that we can live more.

The desire for riches is simply the capacity for larger life seeking fulfillment; every desire is the effort of an unexpressed possibility to come into action. It is power seeking to manifest which causes desire. That which makes you want more money is the same as that which makes the plant grow; it is Life, seeking fuller expression.

The One Living Substance must be subject to this inherent law of all life; it is permeated with the desire to live more; that is why it is under the necessity of creating things.

The One Substance desires to live more in you; hence it wants you to have all the things you can use.

It is the desire of God that you should get rich. He wants you to get rich because he can express himself better through you if you have plenty of things to use in giving him expression. He can live more in you if you have unlimited command of the means of life.

The universe desires you to have everything you want to have.

Nature is friendly to your plans.

Everything is naturally for you.

Make up your mind that this is true.

It is essential, however that your purpose should harmonize with the purpose that is in All.

You must want real life, not mere pleasure of sensual gratification. Life is the performance of function; and the individual really lives only when he performs every function, physical, mental, and spiritual, of which he is capable, without excess in any.

You do not want to get rich in order to live swinishly, for the gratification of animal desires; that is not life. But the performance of every physical function is a part of life, and no one lives completely who denies the impulses of the body a normal and healthful expression.

You do not want to get rich solely to enjoy mental pleasures, to get knowledge, to gratify ambition, to outshine others, to be famous. All these are a legitimate part of life, but the man who lives for the pleasures of the intellect alone will only have a partial life, and he will never be satisfied with his lot.

You do not want to get rich solely for the good of others, to lose yourself for the salvation of mankind, to experience the joys of philanthropy and sacrifice. The joys of the soul are only a part of life; and they are no better or nobler than any other part.

You want to get rich in order that you may eat, drink, and be merry when it is time to do these things; in order that you may surround yourself with beautiful things, see distant lands, feed your mind, and develop your intellect; in order that you may love men and do kind things, and be able to play a good part in helping the world to find truth.

But remember that extreme altruism is no better and no nobler than extreme selfishness; both are mistakes.

Get rid of the idea that God wants you to sacrifice yourself for others, and that you can secure his favor by doing so; God requires nothing of the kind.

What he wants is that you should make the most of yourself, for yourself, and for others; and you can help others more by making the most of yourself than in any other way.

You can make the most of yourself only by getting rich; so it is right and praiseworthy that you should give your first and best thought to the work of acquiring wealth.

Remember, however, that the desire of Substance is for all, and its movements must be for more life to all; it cannot be made to work for less life to any, because it is equally in all, seeking riches and life.

Intelligent Substance will make things for you, but it will not take things away from someone else and give them to you.

You must get rid of the thought of competition. You are to create, not to compete for what is already created.

You do not have to take anything away from anyone.

You do not have to drive sharp bargains.

You do not have to cheat, or to take advantage. You do not need to let any man work for you for less than he earns.

You do not have to covet the property of others, or to look at it with wishful eyes; no man has anything of which you cannot have the like, and that without taking what he has away from him.

You are to become a creator, not a competitor; you are going to get what you want, but in such a way that when you get it every other man will have more than he has now.

I am aware that there are men who get a vast amount of money by proceeding in direct opposition to the statements in the paragraph above, and may add a word of explanation here. Men of the plutocratic type, who become very rich, do so sometimes purely by their extraordinary ability on the plane of competition; and sometimes they unconsciously relate themselves to Substance in its great purposes and movements for the general racial upbuilding through industrial evolution. Rockefeller, Carnegie, Morgan, et al., have been the unconscious agents of the Supreme in the necessary work of systematizing and organizing productive industry; and in the end, their work will contribute immensely toward increased life for all. Their day is nearly over; they have organized production, and will soon be succeeded by the agents of the multitude, who will organize the machinery of distribution.

The multi-millionaires are like the monster reptiles of the prehistoric eras; they play a necessary part in the evolutionary process, but the same Power which produced them will dispose of them. And it is well to bear in mind that they have never been really rich; a record of the private lives of most of this class will show that they have really been the most abject and wretched of the poor.

Riches secured on the competitive plane are never satisfactory and permanent; they are yours today, and another's tomorrow. Remember, if you are to become rich in a scientific and certain way, you must rise entirely out of the competitive thought. You must never think for a moment that the supply is limited. Just as soon as you begin to think that all the money is being "cornered" and controlled by bankers and others, and that you must exert yourself to get laws passed to stop this process, and so on; in that moment you drop into the competitive mind, and your power to cause creation is gone for the time being; and what is worse, you will probably arrest the creative movements you have already instituted.

KNOW that there are countless millions of dollars' worth of gold in the mountains of the earth, not yet brought to light; and know that if there were not, more would be created from Thinking Substance to supply your needs.

KNOW that the money you need will come, even if it is necessary for a thousand men to be led to the discovery of new gold mines tomorrow.

Never look at the visible supply; look always at the limitless riches in Formless Substance, and KNOW that they are coming to you as fast as you can receive and use them. Nobody, by cornering the visible supply, can prevent you from getting what is yours.

So never allow yourself to think for an instant that all the best building spots will be taken before you get ready to build your house, unless you hurry. Never worry about the trusts and combines, and get anxious for fear they will soon come to own the whole earth. Never get afraid that you will lose what you want because some other person "beats you to it." That cannot possibly happen; you are not seeking any thing that is possessed by anybody else; you are causing what you want to be created from formless Substance, and the supply is without limits. Stick to the formulated statement:

There is a thinking stuff from which all things are made, and which, in its original state, permeates, penetrates, and fills the interspaces of the universe. A thought, in this substance, produces the thing that is imaged by the thought. Man can form things in his thought, and, by impressing his thought upon formless substance, can cause the thing he thinks about to be created.

Chapter 6

How Riches Come to You

WHEN I say that you do not have to drive sharp bargains, I do not mean that you do not have to drive any bargains at all, or that you are above the necessity for having any dealings with your fellow men. I mean that you will not need to deal with them unfairly; you do not have to get something for nothing, but can give to every man more than you take from him.

You cannot give every man more in cash market value than you take from him, but you can give him more in use value than the cash value of the thing you take from him. The paper, ink, and other material in this book may not be worth the money you pay for it; but if the ideas suggested by it bring you thousands of dollars, you have not been wronged by those who sold it to you; they have given you a great use value for a small cash value.

Let us suppose that I own a picture by one of the great artists, which, in any civilized community, is worth thousands of dollars. I take it to Baffin Ray, and by "salesmanship" induce an Eskimo to give a bundle of furs worth $500 for it. I have really wronged him, for he has no use for the picture; it has no use value to him; it will not add to his life.

But suppose I give him a gun worth $50 for his furs; then he has made a good bargain. He has use for the gun; it will get him many more furs and much food; it will add to his life in every way; it will make him rich.

When you rise from the competitive to the creative plane, you can scan your business transactions very strictly, and if you are selling any man anything which does not add more to his life than the thing he gave you in exchange, you can afford to stop it. You do not have to beat anybody in business. And if you are in a business which does beat people, get out of it at once.

Give every man more in use value than you take from him in cash value; then you are adding to the life of the world by every business transaction.

If you have people working for you, you must take from them more in cash value than you pay them in wages; but you can so organize your business that it will be filled with the principle of advancement, and so that each employee who wishes to do so may advance a little every day.

You can make your business do for your employees what this book is doing for you. You can so conduct your business that it will be a sort of ladder, by which every employee who will take the trouble may climb to riches himself; and given the opportunity, if he will not do so it is not your fault.

And finally, because you are to cause the creation of your riches from Formless Substance which permeates all your environment, it does not follow that they are to take shape from the atmosphere and come into being before your eyes.

If you want a sewing machine, for instance, I do not mean to tell you that you are to impress the thought of a sewing machine on Thinking Substance until the machine is formed without hands, in the room where you sit, or elsewhere. But if you want a sewing machine, hold the mental image of it with the most positive certainty that it is being made, or is on its way to you. After once forming the thought, have the most absolute and unquestioning faith that the sewing machine is coming; never think of it, or speak, of it, in any other way than as being sure to arrive. Claim it as already yours.

It will be brought to you by the power of the Supreme Intelligence, acting upon the minds of men. If you live in Maine, it may be that a man will be brought from Texas or Japan to engage in some transaction which will result in your getting what you want.

If so, the whole matter will be as much to that man's advantage as it is to yours.

Do not forget for a moment that the Thinking Substance is through all, in all, communicating with all, and can influence all. The desire of Thinking Substance for fuller life and better living has caused the creation of all the sewing machines already made; and it can cause the creation of millions more, and will, whenever men set it in motion by desire and faith, and by acting in a Certain Way.

You can certainly have a sewing machine in your house; and it is just as certain that you can have any other thing or things which you want, and which you will use for the advancement of your own life and the lives of others.

You need not hesitate about asking largely; "it is your Father's pleasure to give you the kingdom," said Jesus.

Original Substance wants to live all that is possible in you, and wants you to have all that you can or will use for the living of the most abundant life.

If you fix upon your consciousness the fact that the desire you feel for the possession of riches is one with the desire of Omnipotence for more complete expression, your faith becomes invincible.

Once I saw a little boy sitting at a piano, and vainly trying to bring harmony out of the keys; and I saw that he was grieved and provoked by his inability to play real music. I asked him the cause of his vexation, and he answered, "I can feel the music in me, but I can't make my hands go right." The music in him was the URGE of Original Substance, containing all the possibilities of all life; all that there is of music was seeking expression through the child.

God, the One Substance, is trying to live and do and enjoy things through humanity. He is saying "I want hands to build wonderful structures, to play divine harmonies, to paint glorious pictures; I want feet to run my errands, eyes to see my beauties, tongues to tell mighty truths and to sing marvelous songs," and so on.

All that there is of possibility is seeking expression through men. God wants those who can play music to have pianos and every other instrument, and to have the means to cultivate their talents to the fullest extent; He wants those who can appreciate beauty to be able to surround themselves with beautiful things; He wants those who can discern truth to have every opportunity to travel and observe; He wants those who can appreciate dress to be beautifully clothed, and those who can appreciate good food to be luxuriously fed.

He wants all these things because it is Himself that enjoys and appreciates them; it is God who wants to play, and sing, and enjoy beauty, and proclaim truth and wear fine clothes, and eat good foods. "It is God that worketh in you to will and to do," said Paul.

The desire you feel for riches is the infinite, seeking to express Himself in you as He sought to find expression in the little boy at the piano.

So you need not hesitate to ask largely.

Your part is to focalize and express the desire to God.

This is a difficult point with most people; they retain something of the old idea that poverty and self-sacrifice are pleasing to God. They look upon poverty as a part of the plan, a necessity of nature. They have the idea that God has finished His work, and made all that He can make, and that the majority of men must stay poor because there is not enough to go around. They hold to so much of this erroneous thought that they feel ashamed to ask for wealth; they try not to want more than a very modest competence, just enough to make them fairly comfortable.

I recall now the case of one student who was told that he must get in mind a clear picture of the things he desired, so that the creative thought of them might be impressed on Formless Substance. He was a very poor man, living in a rented house, and having only what he earned from day to day; and he could not grasp the fact that all wealth was his. So, after thinking the matter over, he decided that he might reasonably ask for a new rug for the floor of his best room, and an anthracite coal stove to heat the house during the cold weather. Following the instructions given in this book, he obtained these things in a few months; and then it dawned upon him that he had not asked enough. He went through the house in which he lived, and planned all the improvements he would like to make in it; he mentally added a bay window here and a room there, until it was complete in his mind as his ideal home; and then he planned its furnishings.

Holding the whole picture in his mind, he began living in the Certain Way, and moving toward what he wanted; and he owns the house now, and is rebuilding it after the form of his mental image. And now, with still larger faith, he is going on to get greater things. It has been unto him according to his faith, and it is so with you and with all of us.

Chapter 7

Gratitude

THE illustrations given in the last chapter will have conveyed to the reader the fact that the first step toward getting rich is to convey the idea of your wants to the Formless Substance.

This is true, and you will see that in order to do so it becomes necessary to relate yourself to the Formless Intelligence in a harmonious way.

To secure this harmonious relation is a matter of such primary and vital importance that I shall give some space to its discussion here, and give you instructions which, if you will follow them, will be certain to bring you into perfect unity of mind with God.

The whole process of mental adjustment and atonement can be summed up in one word, gratitude.

First, you believe that there is one Intelligent Substance, from which all things proceed; second, you believe that this Substance gives you everything you desire; and third, you relate yourself to it by a feeling of deep and profound gratitude.

Many people who order their lives rightly in all other ways are kept in poverty by their lack of gratitude. Having received one gift from God, they cut the wires which connect them with Him by failing to make acknowledgment.

It is easy to understand that the nearer we live to the source of wealth, the more wealth we shall receive; and it is easy also to understand that the soul that is always grateful lives in closer touch with God than the one which never looks to Him in thankful acknowledgment.

The more gratefully we fix our minds on the Supreme when good things come to us, the more good things we will receive, and the more rapidly they will come; and the reason simply is that the mental attitude of gratitude draws the mind into closer touch with the source from which the blessings come.

If it is a new thought to you that gratitude brings your whole mind into closer harmony with the creative energies of the universe, consider it well, and you will see that it is true. The good things you already have, have come to you along the line of obedience to certain laws. Gratitude will lead your mind out along the ways by which things come; and it will keep you in close harmony with creative thought and prevent you from falling into competitive thought.

Gratitude alone can keep you looking toward the All, and prevent you from falling into the error of thinking of the supply as limited; and to do that would be fatal to your hopes.

There is a Law of Gratitude, and it is absolutely necessary that you should observe the law, if you are to get the results you seek.

The law of gratitude is the natural principle that action and reaction are always equal, and in opposite directions.

The grateful outreaching of your mind in thankful praise to the Supreme is a liberation or expenditure of force; it cannot fail to reach that to which it addressed, and the reaction is an instantaneous movement towards you.

"Draw nigh unto God, and He will draw nigh unto you." That is a statement of psychological truth.

And if your gratitude is strong and constant, the reaction in Formless Substance will be strong and continuous; the movement of the things you want will be always toward you. Notice the grateful attitude that Jesus took; how He always seems to be saying, "I thank Thee, Father, that Thou hearest me." You cannot exercise much power without gratitude; for it is gratitude that keeps you connected with Power.

But the value of gratitude does not consist solely in getting you more blessings in the future. Without gratitude you cannot long keep from dissatisfied thought regarding things as they are.

The moment you permit your mind to dwell with dissatisfaction upon things as they are, you begin to lose ground. You fix attention upon the common, the ordinary, the poor, and the squalid and mean; and your mind takes the form of these things. Then you will transmit these forms or mental images to the Formless, and the common, the poor, the squalid, and mean will come to you.

To permit your mind to dwell upon the inferior is to become inferior and to surround yourself with inferior things.

On the other hand, to fix your attention on the best is to surround yourself with the best, and to become the best.

The Creative Power within us makes us into the image of that to which we give our attention.

We are Thinking Substance, and thinking substance always takes the form of that which it thinks about.

The grateful mind is constantly fixed upon the best; therefore it tends to become the best; it takes the form or character of the best, and will receive the best.

Also, faith is born of gratitude. The grateful mind continually expects good things, and expectation becomes faith. The reaction of gratitude upon one's own mind produces faith; and every outgoing wave of grateful thanksgiving increases faith. He who has no feeling of gratitude cannot long retain a living faith; and without a living faith you cannot get rich by the creative method, as we shall see in the following chapters.

It is necessary, then, to cultivate the habit of being grateful for every good thing that comes to you; and to give thanks continuously.

And because all things have contributed to your advancement, you should include all things in your gratitude.

Do not waste time thinking or talking about the shortcomings or wrong actions of plutocrats or trust magnates. Their organization of the world has made your opportunity; all you get really comes to you because of them.

Do not rage against, corrupt politicians; if it were not for politicians we should fall into anarchy, and your opportunity would be greatly lessened.

God has worked a long time and very patiently to bring us up to where we are in industry and government, and He is going right on with His work. There is not the least doubt that He will do away with plutocrats, trust magnates, captains of industry, and politicians as soon as they can be spared; but in the meantime, behold they are all very good.

Remember that they are all helping to arrange the lines of transmission along which your riches will come to you, and be grateful to them all. This will bring you into harmonious relations with the good in everything, and the good in everything will move toward you.

Chapter 8

Thinking in the Certain Way

TURN back to chapter 6 and read again the story of the man who formed a mental image of his house, and you will get a fair idea of the initial step toward getting rich. You must form a clear and definite mental picture of what you want; you cannot transmit an idea unless you have it yourself.

You must have it before you can give it; and many people fail to impress Thinking Substance because they have themselves only a vague and misty concept of the things they want to do, to have, or to become.

It is not enough that you should have a general desire for wealth "to do good with"; everybody has that desire.

It is not enough that you should have a wish to travel, see things, live more, etc. Everybody has those desires also. If you were going to send a wireless message to a friend, you would not send the letters of the alphabet in their order, and let him construct the message for himself; nor would you take words at random from the dictionary. You would send a coherent sentence; one which meant something. When you try to impress your wants upon Substance, remember that it must be done by a coherent statement; you must know what you want, and be definite. You can never get rich, or start the creative power into action, by sending out unformed longings and vague desires.

Go over your desires just as the man I have described went over his house; see just what you want, and get a clear mental picture of it as you wish it to look when you get it.

That clear mental picture you must have continually in mind, as the sailor has in mind the port toward which he is sailing the ship; you must keep your face toward it all the time. You must no more lose sight of it than the steersman loses sight of the compass.

It is not necessary to take exercises in concentration, nor to set apart special times for prayer and affirmation, nor to "go into the silence," nor to do occult stunts of any kind. There things are well enough, but all you need is to know what you want, and to want it badly enough so that it will stay in your thoughts.

Spend as much of your leisure time as you can in contemplating your picture, but no one needs to take exercises to concentrate his mind on a thing which he really wants; it is the things you do not really care about which require effort to fix your attention upon them.

And unless you really want to get rich, so that the desire is strong enough to hold your thoughts directed to the purpose as the magnetic pole holds the needle of the compass, it will hardly be worthwhile for you to try to carry out the instructions given in this book.

The methods herein set forth are for people whose desire for riches is strong enough to overcome mental laziness and the love of ease, and make them work.

The more clear and definite you make your picture then, and the more you dwell upon it, bringing out all its delightful details, the stronger your desire will be; and the stronger your desire, the easier it will be to hold your mind fixed upon the picture of what you want.

Something more is necessary, however, than merely to see the picture clearly. If that is all you do, you are only a dreamer, and will have little or no power for accomplishment.

Behind your clear vision must be the purpose to realize it; to bring it out in tangible expression.

And behind this purpose must be an invincible and unwavering FAITH that the thing is already yours; that it is "at hand" and you have only to take possession of it.

Live in the new house, mentally, until it takes form around you physically. In the mental realm, enter at once into full enjoyment of the things you want.

"Whatsoever things ye ask for when ye pray, believe that ye receive them, and ye shall have them," said Jesus.

See the things you want as if they were actually around you all the time; see yourself as owning and using them. Make use of them in imagination just as you will use them when they are your tangible possessions. Dwell upon your mental picture until it is clear and distinct, and then take the Mental Attitude of Ownership toward everything in that picture. Take possession of it, in mind, in the full faith that it is actually yours. Hold to this mental ownership; do not waiver for an instant in the faith that it is real.

And remember what was said in a proceeding chapter about gratitude; be as thankful for it all the time as you expect to be when it has taken form. The man who can sincerely thank God for the things which as yet he owns only in imagination, has real faith. He will get rich; he will cause the creation of whatsoever he wants.

You do not need to pray repeatedly for things you want; it is not necessary to tell God about it every day.

"Use not vain repetitions as the heathen do," said Jesus said to his pupils, "for your Father knoweth the ye have need of these things before ye ask Him."

Your part is to intelligently formulate your desire for the things which make for a larger life, and to get these desire arranged into a coherent whole; and then to impress this Whole Desire upon the Formless Substance, which has the power and the will to bring you what you want.

You do not make this impression by repeating strings of words; you make it by holding the vision with unshakable PURPOSE to attain it, and with steadfast FAITH that you do attain it.

The answer to prayer is not according to your faith while you are talking, but according to your faith while you are working.

You cannot impress the mind of God by having a special Sabbath day set apart to tell Him what you want, and the forgetting Him during the rest of the week. You cannot impress Him by having special hours to go into your closet and pray, if you then dismiss the matter from your mind until the hour of prayer comes again.

Oral prayer is well enough, and has its effect, especially upon yourself, in clarifying your vision and strengthening your faith; but it is not your oral petitions which get you what you want. In order to get rich you do not need a "sweet hour of prayer"; you need to "pray without ceasing." And by prayer I mean holding steadily to your vision, with the purpose to cause its creation into solid form, and the faith that you are doing so.

"Believe that ye receive them."

The whole matter turns on receiving, once you have clearly formed your vision. When you have formed it, it is well to make an oral statement, addressing the Supreme in reverent prayer; and from that moment you must, in mind, receive what you ask for. Live in the new house; wear the fine clothes; ride in the automobile; go on the journey, and confidently plan for greater journeys. Think and speak of all the things you have asked for in terms of actual present ownership. Imagine an environment, and a financial condition exactly as you want them, and live all the time in that imaginary environment and financial condition. Mind, however, that you do not do this as a mere dreamer and castle builder; hold to the FAITH that the imaginary is being realized, and to the PURPOSE to realize it.

Remember that it is faith and purpose in the use of the imagination which make the difference between the scientist and the dreamer. And having learned this fact, it is here that you must learn the proper use of the Will.

Chapter 9

How to Use the Will

TO set about getting rich in a scientific way, you do not try to apply your will power to anything outside of yourself.

You have no right to do so, anyway.

It is wrong to apply your will to other men and women, in order to get them to do what you wish done.

It is as flagrantly wrong to coerce people by mental power as it is to coerce them by physical power. If compelling people by physical force to do things for you reduces them to slavery, compelling them by mental means accomplishes exactly the same thing; the only difference is in methods. If taking things from people by physical force is robbery, then taking things by mental force is robbery also; there is no difference in principle.

You have no right to use your will power upon another person, even "for his own good"; for you do not know what is for his good. The science of getting rich does not require you to apply power or force to any other person, in any way whatsoever. There is not the slightest necessity for doing so; indeed, any attempt to use your will upon others will only tend to defeat your purpose.

You do not need to apply your will to things, in order to compel them to come to you.

That would simply be trying to coerce God, and would be foolish and useless, as well as irreverent.

You do not have to compel God to give you good things, any more than you have to use your will power to make the sun rise.

You do not have to use your will power to conquer an unfriendly deity, or to make stubborn and rebellious forces do your bidding.

Substance is friendly to you, and is more anxious to give you what you want than you are to get it.

To get rich, you need only to use your will power upon yourself.

When you know what to think and do, then you must use your will to compel yourself to think and do the right things. That is the legitimate use of the will in getting what you want . . to use it in holding yourself to the right course. Use your will to keep yourself thinking and acting in the Certain Way.

Do not try to project your will, or your thoughts, or your mind out into space, to "act" on things or people.

Keep your mind at home; it can accomplish more there than elsewhere.

Use your mind to form a mental image of what you want, and to hold that vision with faith and purpose; and use your will to keep your mind working in the Right Way.

The more steady and continuous your faith and purpose, the more rapidly you will get rich, because you will make only POSITIVE impressions upon Substance; and you will not neutralize or offset them by negative impressions.

The picture of your desires, held with faith and purpose, is taken up by the Formless, and permeates it to great distances throughout the universe, for all I know.

As this impression spreads, all things are set moving toward its realization; every living thing, every inanimate thing, and the things yet uncreated, are stirred toward bringing into being that which you want. All force begins to be exerted in that direction; all things begin to move toward you. The minds of people, everywhere, are influenced toward doing the things necessary to the fulfilling of your desires; and they work for you, unconsciously.

But you can check all this by starting a negative impression in the Formless Substance. Doubt or unbelief is as certain to start a movement away from you as faith and purpose are to start one toward you. It is by not understanding this that most people who try to make use of "mental science" in getting rich make their failure. Every hour and moment you spend in giving heed to doubts and fears, every hour you spend in worry, every hour in which your soul is possessed by unbelief, sets a current away from you in the whole domain of intelligent Substance. All the promises are unto them that believe, and unto them only. Notice how insistent Jesus was upon this point of belief; and now you know the reason why.

Since belief is all important, it behooves you to guard your thoughts; and as your beliefs will be shaped to a very great extent by the things you observe and think about, it is important that you should command your attention.

And here the will comes into use; for it is by your will that you determine upon what things your attention shall be fixed.

If you want to become rich, you must not make a study of poverty.

Things are not brought into being by thinking about their opposites. Health is never to be attained by studying disease and thinking about disease; righteousness is not to be promoted by studying sin and thinking about sin; and no one ever got rich by studying poverty and thinking about poverty.

Medicine as a science of disease has increased disease; religion as a science of sin has promoted sin, and economics as a study of poverty will fill the world with wretchedness and want.

Do not talk about poverty; do not investigate it, or concern yourself with it. Never mind what its causes are; you have nothing to do with them.

What concerns you is the cure.

Do not spend your time in charitable work, or charity movements; all charity only tends to perpetuate the wretchedness it aims to eradicate.

I do not say that you should be hard hearted or unkind, and refuse to hear the cry of need; but you must not try to eradicate poverty in any of the conventional ways. Put poverty behind you, and put all that pertains to it behind you, and "make good."

Get rich; that is the best way you can help the poor.

And you cannot hold the mental image which is to make you rich if you fill your mind with pictures of poverty. Do not read books or papers which give circumstantial accounts of the wretchedness of the tenement dwellers, of the horrors of child labor, and so on. Do not read anything which fills your mind with gloomy images of want and suffering.

You cannot help the poor in the least by knowing about these things; and the widespread knowledge of them does not tend at all to do away with poverty.

What tends to do away with poverty is not the getting of pictures of poverty into your mind, but getting pictures of wealth into the minds of the poor. You are not deserting the poor in their misery when you refuse to allow your mind to be filled with pictures of that misery.

Poverty can be done away with, not by increasing the number of well to do people who think about poverty, but by increasing the number of poor people who purpose with faith to get rich.

The poor do not need charity; they need inspiration. Charity only sends them a loaf of bread to keep them alive in their wretchedness, or gives them an entertainment to make them forget for an hour or two; but inspiration will cause them to rise out of their misery. If you want to help the poor, demonstrate to them that they can become rich; prove it by getting rich yourself.

The only way in which poverty will ever be banished from this world is by getting a large and constantly increasing number of people to practice the teachings of this book.

People must be taught to become rich by creation, not by competition.

Every man who becomes rich by competition throws down behind him the ladder by which he rises, and keeps others down; but every man who gets rich by creation opens a way for thousands to follow him, and inspires them to do so.

You are not showing hardness of heart or an unfeeling disposition when you refuse to pity poverty, see poverty, read about poverty, or think or talk about it, or to listen to those who do talk about it. Use your will power to keep your mind OFF the subject of poverty, and to keep it fixed with faith and purpose ON the vision of what you want.

Chapter 10

Further Use of the Will

YOU cannot retain a true and clear vision of wealth if you are constantly turning your attention to opposing pictures, whether they be external or imaginary.

Do not tell of your past troubles of a financial nature, if you have had them, do not think of them at all. Do no tell of the poverty of your parents, or the hardships of your early life; to do any of these things is to mentally class yourself with the poor for the time being, and it will certainly check the movement of things in your direction.

"Let the dead bury their dead," as Jesus said.

Put poverty and all things that pertain to poverty completely behind you.

You have accepted a certain theory of the universe as being correct, and are resting all your hopes of happiness on its being correct; and what can you gain by giving heed to conflicting theories?

Do not read religious books which tell you that the world is soon coming to an end; and do not read the writing of muckrakers and pessimistic philosophers who tell you that it is going to the devil.

The world is not going to the devil; it is going to God.

It is wonderful Becoming.

True, there may be a good many things in existing conditions which are disagreeable; but what is the use of studying them when they are certainly passing away, and when the study of them only tends to check their passing and keep them with us? Why give time and attention to things which are being removed by evolutionary growth, when you can hasten their removal only by promoting the evolutionary growth as far as your part of it goes?

No matter how horrible in seeming may be the conditions in certain countries, sections, or places, you waste your time and destroy your own chances by considering them.

You should interest yourself in the world's becoming rich.

Think of the riches the world is coming into, instead of the poverty it is growing out of; and bear in mind that the only way in which you can assist the world in growing rich is by growing rich yourself through the creative method . . not the competitive one.

Give your attention wholly to riches; ignore poverty.

Whenever you think or speak of those who are poor, think and speak of them as those who are becoming rich; as those who are to be congratulated rather than pitied. Then they and others will catch the inspiration, and begin to search for the way out.

Because I say that you are to give your whole time and mind and thought to riches, it does not follow that you are to be sordid or mean.

To become really rich is the noblest aim you can have in life, for it includes everything else.

On the competitive plane, the struggle to get rich is a Godless scramble for power over other men; but when we come into the creative mind, all this is changed.

All that is possible in the way of greatness and soul unfoldment, of service and lofty endeavor, comes by way of getting rich; all is made possible by the use of things.

If you lack for physical health, you will find that the attainment of it is conditional on your getting rich.

Only those who are emancipated from financial worry, and who have the means to live a care-free existence and follow hygienic practices, can have and retain health.

Moral and spiritual greatness is possible only to those who are above the competitive battle for existence; and only those who are becoming rich on the plane of creative thought are free from the degrading influences of competition. If your heart is set on domestic happiness, remember that love flourishes best where there is refinement, a high level of thought, and freedom from corrupting influences; and these are to be found only where riches are attained by the exercise of creative thought, without strife or rivalry.

You can aim at nothing so great or noble, I repeat, as to become rich; and you must fix your attention upon your mental picture of riches, to the exclusion of all that may tend to dim or obscure the vision.

You must learn to see the underlying TRUTH in all things; you must see beneath all seemingly wrong conditions the Great One Life ever moving forward toward fuller expression and more complete happiness.

It is the truth that there is no such thing as poverty; that there is only wealth.

Some people remain in poverty because they are ignorant of the fact that there is wealth for them; and these can best be taught by showing them the way to affluence in your own person and practice.

Others are poor because, while they feel that there is a way out, they are too intellectually indolent to put forth the mental effort necessary to find that way and by travel it; and for these the very best thing you can do is to arouse their desire by showing them the happiness that comes from being rightly rich.

Others still are poor because, while they have some notion of science, they have become so swamped and lost in the maze of metaphysical and occult theories that they do not know which road to take. They try a mixture of many systems and fail in all. For these, again, the very best thing, to do is to show the right way in your own person and practice; an ounce of doing things is worth a pound of theorizing.

The very best thing you can do for the whole world is to make the most of yourself.

You can serve God and man in no more effective way than by getting rich; that is, if you get rich by the creative method and not by the competitive one.

Another thing. We assert that this book gives in detail the principles of the science of getting rich; and if that is true, you do not need to read any other book upon the subject. This may sound narrow and egotistical, but consider: there is no more scientific method of computation in mathematics than by addition, subtraction, multiplication, and division; no other method is possible. There can be but one shortest distance between two points. There is only one way to think scientifically, and that is to think in the way that leads by the most direct and simple route to the goal. No man has yet formulated a briefer or less complex "system" than the one set forth herein; it has been stripped of all non-essentials. When you commence on this, lay all others aside; put them out of your mind altogether.

Read this book every day; keep it with you; commit it to memory, and do not think about other "systems" and theories. If you do, you will begin to have doubts, and to be uncertain and wavering in your thought; and then you will begin to make failures.

After you have made good and become rich, you may study other systems as much as you please; but until you are quite sure that you have gained what you want, do not read anything on this line but this book, unless it be the authors mentioned in the Preface.

And read only the most optimistic comments on the world's news; those in harmony with your picture.

Also, postpone your investigations into the occult. Do not dabble in theosophy, Spiritualism, or kindred studies. It is very likely that the dead still live, and are near; but if they are, let them alone; mind your own business.

Wherever the spirits of the dead may be, they have their own work to do, and their own problems to solve; and we have no right to interfere with them. We cannot help them, and it is very doubtful whether they can help us, or whether we have any right to trespass upon their time if they can. Let the dead and the hereafter alone, and solve your own problem; get rich. If you begin to mix with the occult, you will start mental crosscurrents which will surely bring your hopes to shipwreck. Now, this and the preceding chapters have brought us to the following statement of basic facts:

There is a thinking stuff from which all things are made, and which, in its original state, permeates, penetrates, and fills the interspaces of the universe.

A thought, in this substance, Produces the thing that is imaged by the thought.

Man can form things in his thought, and, by impressing his thought upon formless substance, can cause the thing he thinks about to be created.

In order to do this, man must pass from the competitive to the creative mind; he must form a clear mental picture of the things he wants, and hold this picture in his thoughts with the fixed PURPOSE to get what he wants, and the unwavering FAITH that he does get what he wants, closing his mind against all that may tend to shake his purpose, dim his vision, or quench his faith.

And in addition to all this, we shall now see that he must live and act in a Certain Way.

Chapter 11

Acting in a Certain Way

THOUGHT is the creative power, or the impelling force which causes the creative power to act; thinking in a Certain Way will bring riches to you, but you must not rely upon thought alone, paying no attention to personal action. That is the rock upon which many otherwise scientific metaphysical thinkers meet shipwreck . . the failure to connect thought with personal action.

We have not yet reached the stage of development, even supposing such a stage to be possible, in which man can create directly from Formless Substance without nature's processes or the work of human hands; man must not only think, but his personal action must supplement his thought.

By thought you can cause the gold in the hearts of the mountains to be impelled toward you; but it will not mine itself, refine itself, coin itself into double eagles, and come rolling along the roads seeking its way into your pocket.

Under the impelling power of the Supreme Spirit, men's affairs will be so ordered that someone will be led to mine the gold for you; other men's business transactions will be so directed that the gold will be brought toward you, and you must so arrange your own business affairs that you may be able to receive it when it comes to you. Your thought makes all things, animate and inanimate, work to bring you what you want; but your personal activity must be such that you can rightly receive what you want when it reaches you. You are not to take it as charity, nor to steal it; you must give every man more in use value than he gives you in cash value.

The scientific use of thought consists in forming a clear and distinct mental image of what you want; in holding fast to the purpose to get what you want; and in realizing with grateful faith that you do get what you want.

Do not try to 'project' your thought in any mysterious or occult way, with the idea of having it go out and do things for you; that is wasted effort, and will weaken your power to think with sanity.

The action of thought in getting rich is fully explained in the preceding chapters; your faith and purpose positively impress your vision upon Formless Substance, which has THE SAME DESIRE FOR MORE LIFE THAT YOU HAVE; and this vision, received from you, sets all the creative forces at work IN AND THROUGH THEIR REGULAR CHANNELS OF ACTION, but directed toward you.

It is not your part to guide or supervise the creative process; all you have to do with that is to retain your vision, stick to your purpose, and maintain your faith and gratitude.

But you must act in a Certain Way, so that you can appropriate what is yours when it comes to you; so that you can meet the things you have in your picture, and put them in their proper places as they arrive.

You can really see the truth of this. When things reach you, they will be in the hands of other men, who will ask an equivalent for them.

And you can only get what is yours by giving the other man what is his.

Your pocketbook is not going to be transformed into a Fortunata's purse, which shall be always full of money without effort on your part.

This is the crucial point in the science of getting rich; right here, where thought and personal action must be combined. There are very many people who, consciously or unconsciously, set the creative forces in action by the strength and persistence of their desires, but who remain poor because they do not provide for the reception of the thing they want when it comes.

By thought, the thing you want is brought to you; by action you receive it.

Whatever your action is to be, it is evident that you must act NOW. You cannot act in the past, and it is essential to the clearness of your mental vision that you dismiss the past from your mind. You cannot act in the future, for the future is not here yet. And you cannot tell how you will want to act in any future contingency until that contingency has arrived.

Because you are not in the right business, or the right environment now, do not think that you must postpone action until you get into the right business or environment. And do not spend time in the present taking thought as to the best course in possible future emergencies; have faith in your ability to meet any emergency when it arrives.

If you act in the present with your mind on the future, your present action will be with a divided mind, and will not be effective.

Put your whole mind into present action.

Do not give your creative impulse to Original Substance, and then sit down and wait for results; if you do, you will never get them. Act now. There is never any time but now, and there never will be any time but now. If you are ever to begin to make ready for the reception of what you want, you must begin now.

And your action, whatever it is, must most likely be in your present business or employment, and must be upon the persons and things in your present environment.

You cannot act where you are not; you cannot act where you have been, and you cannot act where you are going to be; you can act only where you are.

Do not bother as to whether yesterday's work was well done or ill done; do today's work well.

Do not try to do tomorrow's work now; there will be plenty of time to do that when you get to it.

Do not try, by occult or mystical means, to act on people or things that are out of your reach.

Do not wait for a change of environment, before you act; get a change of environment by action.

You can so act upon the environment in which you are now, as to cause yourself to be transferred to a better environment.

Hold with faith and purpose the vision of yourself in the better environment, but act upon your present environment with all your heart, and with all your strength, and with all your mind.

Do not spend any time in day dreaming or castle building; hold to the one vision of what you want, and act NOW.

Do not cast about seeking some new thing to do, or some strange, unusual, or remarkable action to perform as a first step toward getting rich. It is probable that your actions, at least for some time to come, will be those you have been performing for some time past; but you are to begin now to perform these actions in the Certain Way, which will surely make you rich.

If you are engaged in some business, and feel that it is not the right one for you, do not wait until you get into the right business before you begin to act.

Do not feel discouraged, or sit down and lament because you are misplaced. No man was ever so misplaced but that he could not find the right place, and no man ever became so involved in the wrong business but that he could get into the right business.

Hold the vision of yourself in the right business, with the purpose to get into it, and the faith that you will get into it, and are getting into it; but ACT in your present business. Use your present business as the means of getting a better one, and use your present environment as the means of getting into a better one. Your vision of the right business, if held with faith and purpose, will cause the Supreme to move the right business toward you; and your action, if performed in the Certain Way, will cause you to move toward the business.

If you are an employee, or wage earner, and feel that you must change places in order to get what you want, do not 'project" your thought into space and rely upon it to get you another job. It will probably fail to do so.

Hold the vision of yourself in the job you want, while you ACT with faith and purpose on the job you have, and you will certainly get the job you want.

Your vision and faith will set the creative force in motion to bring it toward you, and your action will cause the forces in your own environment to move you toward the place you want. In closing this chapter, we will add another statement to our syllabus:

There is a thinking stuff from which all things are made, and which, in its original state, permeates, penetrates, and fills the interspaces of the universe. A thought, in this substance, produces the thing that is imaged by the thought. Man can form things in his thought, and, by impressing his thought upon formless substance, can cause the thing he thinks about to be created. In order to do this, man must pass from the competitive to the creative mind; he must form a clear mental picture of the things he wants, and hold this picture in his thoughts with the fixed PURPOSE to get what he wants, and the unwavering FAITH that he does get what he wants, closing his mind to all that may tend to shake his purpose, dim his vision, or quench his faith.

That he may receive what he wants when it comes, man must act NOW upon the people and things in his present environment.

Chapter 12

Efficient Action

YOU must use your thought as directed in previous chapters, and begin to do what you can do where you are; and you must do ALL that you can do where you are.

You can advance only be being larger than your present place; and no man is larger than his present place who leaves undone any of the work pertaining to that place.

The world is advanced only by those who more than fill their present places.

If no man quite filled his present place, you can see that there must be a going backward in everything. Those who do not quite fill their present places are dead weight upon society, government, commerce, and industry; they must be carried along by others at a great expense. The progress of the world is retarded only by those who do not fill the places they are holding; they belong to a former age and a lower stage or plane of life, and their tendency is toward degeneration. No society could advance if every man was smaller than his place; social evolution is guided by the law of physical and mental evolution. In the animal world, evolution is caused by excess of life.

When an organism has more life than can be expressed in the functions of its own plane, it develops the organs of a higher plane, and a new species is originated.

There never would have been new species had there not been organisms which more than filled their places. The law is exactly the same for you; your getting rich depends upon your applying this principle to your own affairs.

Every day is either a successful day or a day of failure; and it is the successful days which get you what you want. If every day is a failure, you can never get rich; while if every day is a success, you cannot fail to get rich.

If there is something that may be done today, and you do not do it, you have failed in so far as that thing is concerned; and the consequences may be more disastrous than you imagine.

You cannot foresee the results of even the most trivial act; you do not know the workings of all the forces that have been set moving in your behalf. Much may be depending on your doing some simple act; it may be the very thing which is to open the door of opportunity to very great possibilities. You can never know all the combinations which Supreme Intelligence is making for you in the world of things and of things and of human affairs; your neglect or failure to do some small thing may cause a long delay in getting what you want.

Do, every day, ALL that can be done that day. There is, however, a limitation or qualification of the above that you must take into account. You are not to overwork, nor to rush blindly into your business in the effort to do the greatest possible number of things in the shortest possible time. You are not to try to do tomorrow's work today, nor to do a week's work in a day.

It is really not the number of things you do, but the EFFICIENCY of each separate action that counts.

Every act is, in itself, either a success or a failure.

Every act is, in itself, either effective or inefficient.

Every inefficient act is a failure, and if you spend your life in doing inefficient acts, your whole life will be a failure.

The more things you do, the worse for you, if all your acts are inefficient ones.

On the other hand, every efficient act is a success in itself, and if every act of your life is an efficient one, your whole life MUST be a success.

The cause of failure is doing too many things in an inefficient manner, and not doing enough things in an efficient manner.

You will see that it is a self-evident proposition that if you do not do any inefficient acts, and if you do a sufficient number of efficient acts, you will become rich. If, now, it is possible for you to make each act an efficient one, you see again that the getting of riches is reduced to an exact science, like mathematics.

The matter turns, then, on the questions whether you can make each separate act a success in itself. And this you can certainly do.

You can make each act a success, because ALL Power is working with you; and ALL Power cannot fail.

Power is at your service; and to make each act efficient you have only to put power into it.

Every action is either strong or weak; and when everyone is strong, you are acting in the Certain Way which will make you rich.

Every act can be made strong and efficient by holding your vision while you are doing it, and putting the whole power of your FAITH and PURPOSE into it.

It is at this point that the people fail who separate mental power from personal action. They use the power of mind in one place and at one time, and they act in another pace and at another time. So their acts are not successful in themselves; too many of them are inefficient. But if ALL Power goes into every act, no matter how commonplace, every act will be a success in itself; and as in the nature of things every success opens the way to other successes, your progress toward what you want, and the progress of what you want toward you, will become increasingly rapid.

Remember that successful action is cumulative in its results. Since the desire for more life is inherent in all things, when a man begins to move toward larger life more things attach themselves to him, and the influence of his desire is multiplied.

Do, every day, all that you can do that day, and do each act in an efficient manner.

In saying that you must hold your vision while you are doing each act, however trivial or commonplace, I do not mean to say that it is necessary at all times to see the vision distinctly to its smallest details. It should be the work of your leisure hours to use your imagination on the details of your vision, and to contemplate them until they are firmly fixed upon memory. If you wish speedy results, spend practically all your spare time in this practice.

By continuous contemplation you will get the picture of what you want, even to the smallest details, so firmly fixed upon your mind, and so completely transferred to the mind of Formless Substance, that in your working hours you need only to mentally refer to the picture to stimulate your faith and purpose, and cause your best effort to be put forth. Contemplate your picture in your leisure hours until your consciousness is so full of it that you can grasp it instantly. You will become so enthused with its bright promises that the mere thought of it will call forth the strongest energies of your whole being.

Let us again repeat our syllabus, and by slightly changing the closing statements bring it to the point we have now reached.

There is a thinking stuff from which all things are made, and which, in its original state, permeates, penetrates, and fills the interspaces of the universe.

A thought, in this substance, produces the thing that is imaged by the thought.

Man can form things in his thought, and, by impressing his thought upon formless substance, can cause the thing he thinks about to be created.

In order to do this, man must pass from the competitive to the creative mind; he must form a clear mental picture of the things he wants, and do, with faith and purpose, all that can be done each day, doing each separate thing in an efficient manner.

Chapter 13

Getting into the Right Business

SUCCESS, in any particular business, depends for one thing upon your possessing in a well-developed state the faculties required in that business.

Without good musical faculty no one can succeed as a teacher of music; without well-developed mechanical faculties no one can achieve great success in any of the mechanical trades; without tact and the commercial faculties no one can succeed in mercantile pursuits. But to possess in a well-developed state the faculties required in your particular vocation does not insure getting rich. There are musicians who have remarkable talent, and who yet remain poor; there are blacksmiths, carpenters, and so on who have excellent mechanical ability, but who do not get rich; and there are merchants with good faculties for dealing with men who nevertheless fail.

The different faculties are tools; it is essential to have good tools, but it is also essential that the tools should be used in the Right Way. One man can take a sharp saw, a square, a good plane, and so on, and build a handsome article of furniture; another man can take the same tools and set to work to duplicate the article, but his production will be a botch. He does not know how to use good tools in a successful way.

The various faculties of your mind are the tools with which you must do the work which is to make you rich; it will be easier for you to succeed if you get into a business for which you are well equipped with mental tools.

Generally speaking, you will do best in that business which will use your strongest faculties; the one for which you are naturally "best fitted." But there are limitations to this statement, also. No man should regard his vocation as being irrevocably fixed by the tendencies with which he was born.

You can get rich in ANY business, for if you have not the right talent for you can develop that talent; it merely means that you will have to make your tools as you go along, instead of confining yourself to the use of those with which you were born. It will be EASIER for you to succeed in a vocation for which you already have the talents in a well-developed state; but you CAN succeed in any vocation, for you can develop any rudimentary talent, and there is no talent of which you have not at least the rudiment.

You will get rich most easily in point of effort, if you do that for which you are best fitted; but you will get rich most satisfactorily if you do that which you WANT to do.

Doing what you want to do is life; and there is no real satisfaction in living if we are compelled to be forever doing something which we do not like to do, and can never do what we want to do. And it is certain that you can do what you want to do; the desire to do it is proof that you have within you the power which can do it.

Desire is a manifestation of power.

The desire to play music is the power which can play music seeking expression and development; the desire to invent mechanical devices is the mechanical talent seeking expression and development.

Where there is no power, either developed or undeveloped, to do a thing, there is never any desire to do that thing; and where there is strong desire to do a thing, it is certain proof that the power to do it is strong, and only requires to be developed and applied in the Right Way.

All things else being equal, it is best to select the business for which you have the best developed talent; but if you have a strong desire to engage in any particular line of work, you should select that work as the ultimate end at which you aim.

You can do what you want to do, and it is your right and privilege to follow the business or vocation which will be most congenial and pleasant.

You are not obliged to do what you do not like to do, and should not do it except as a means to bring you to the doing of the thing you want to do.

If there are past mistakes whose consequences have placed you in an undesirable business or environment, you may be obliged for some time to do what you do not like to do; but you can make the doing of it pleasant by knowing that it is making it possible for you to come to the doing of what you want to do.

If you feel that you are not in the right vocation, do not act too hastily in trying to get into another one. The best way, generally, to change business or environment is by growth.

Do not be afraid to make a sudden and radical change if the opportunity is presented, and you feel after careful consideration that it is the right opportunity; but never take sudden or radical action when you are in doubt as to the wisdom of doing so.

There is never any hurry on the creative plane; and there is no lack of opportunity.

When you get out of the competitive mind you will understand that you never need to act hastily. No one else is going to beat you to the thing you want to do; there is enough for all. If one space is taken, another and a better one will be opened for you a little farther on; there is plenty of time. When you are in doubt, wait. Fall back on the contemplation of your vision, and increase your faith and purpose; and by all means, in times of doubt and indecision, cultivate gratitude.

A day or two spent in contemplating the vision of what you want, and in earnest thanksgiving that you are getting it, will bring your mind into such close relationship with the Supreme that you will make no mistake when you do act.

There is a mind which knows all there is to know; and you can come into close unity with this mind by faith and the purpose to advance in life, if you have deep gratitude.

Mistakes come from acting hastily, or from acting in fear or doubt, or in forgetfulness of the Right Motive, which is more life to all, and less to none.

As you go on in the Certain Way, opportunities will come to you in increasing number; and you will need to be very steady in your faith and purpose, and to keep in close touch with the All Mind by reverent gratitude.

Do all that you can do in a perfect manner every day, but do it without haste, worry, or fear. Go as fast as you can, but never hurry.

Remember that in the moment you begin to hurry you cease to be a creator and become a competitor; you drop back upon the old plane again.

Whenever you find yourself hurrying, call a halt; fix your attention on the mental image of the thing you want, and begin to give thanks that you are getting it. The exercise of GRATITUDE will never fail to strengthen your faith and renew your purpose.

Chapter 14

The Impression of Increase

WHETHER you change your vocation or not, your actions for the present must be those pertaining to the business in which you are now engaged.

You can get into the business you want by making constructive use of the business you are already established in; by doing your daily work in a Certain Way.

And in so far as your business consists in dealing with other men, whether personally or by letter, the key-thought of all your efforts must be to convey to their minds the impression of increase.

Increase is what all men and all women are seeking; it is the urge of the Formless Intelligence within them, seeking fuller expression.

The desire for increase is inherent in all nature; it is the fundamental impulse of the universe. All human activities are based on the desire for increase; people are seeking more food, more clothes, better shelter, more luxury, more beauty, more knowledge, more pleasure . . increase in something, more life.

Every living thing is under this necessity for continuous advancement; where increase of life ceases, dissolution and death set in at once.

Man instinctively knows this, and hence he is forever seeking more. This law of perpetual increase is set forth by Jesus in the parable of the talents; only those who gain more retain any; from him who hath not shall be taken away even that which he hath.

The normal desire for increased wealth is not an evil or a reprehensible thing; it is simply the desire for more abundant life; it is aspiration.

And because it is the deepest instinct of their natures, all men and women are attracted to him who can give them more of the means of life.

In following the Certain Way as described in the foregoing pages, you are getting continuous increase for yourself, and you are giving it to all with whom you deal.

You are a creative center, from which increase is given off to all.

Be sure of this, and convey assurance of the fact to every man, woman, and child with whom you come in contact. No matter how small the transaction, even if it be only the selling of a stick of candy to a little child, put into it the thought of increase, and make sure that the customer is impressed with the thought.

Convey the impression of advancement with everything you do, so that all people shall receive the impression that you are an Advancing Man, and that you advance all who deal with you. Even to the people whom you meet in a social way, without any thought of business, and to whom you do not try to sell anything, give the thought of increase.

You can convey this impression by holding the unshakable faith that you, yourself, are in the Way of Increase; and by letting this faith inspire, fill, and permeate every action.

Do everything that you do in the firm conviction that you are an advancing personality, and that you are giving advancement to everybody.

Feel that you are getting rich, and that in so doing you are making others rich, and conferring benefits on all.

Do not boast or brag of your success, or talk about it unnecessarily; true faith is never boastful.

Wherever you find a boastful person, you find one who is secretly doubtful and afraid. Simply feel the faith, and let it work out in every transaction; let every act and tone and look express the quiet assurance that you are getting rich; that you are already rich. Words will not be necessary to communicate this feeling to others; they will feel the sense of increase when in your presence, and will be attracted to you again.

You must so impress others that they will feel that in associating with you they will get increase for themselves. See that you give them a use value greater than the cash value you are taking from them.

Take an honest pride in doing this, and let everybody know it; and you will have no lack of customers. People will go where they are given increase; and the Supreme, which desires increase in all, and which knows all, will move toward you men and women who have never heard of you. Your business will increase rapidly, and you will be surprised at the unexpected benefits which will come to you. You will be able from day to day to make larger combinations, secure greater advantages, and to go on into a more congenial vocation if you desire to do so.

But doing thing all this, you must never lose sight of your vision of what you want, or your faith and purpose to get what you want.

Let me here give you another word of caution in regard to motives.

Beware of the insidious temptation to seek for power over other men.

Nothing is so pleasant to the unformed or partially developed mind as the exercise of power or dominion over others. The desire to rule for selfish gratification has been the curse of the world. For countless ages kings and lords have drenched the earth with blood in their battles to extend their dominions; this not to seek more life for all, but to get more power for themselves.

Today, the main motive in the business and industrial world is the same; men marshal their armies of dollars, and lay waste the lives and hearts of millions in the same mad scramble for power over others. Commercial kings, like political kings, are inspired by the lust for power.

Jesus saw in this desire for mastery the moving impulse of that evil world He sought to overthrow. Read the twenty-third chapter of Matthew, and see how He pictures the lust of the Pharisees to be called "Master," to sit in the high places, to domineer over others, and to lay burdens on the backs of the less fortunate; and note how He compares this lust for dominion with the brotherly seeking for the Common Good to which He calls His disciples.

Look out for the temptation to seek for authority, to become a "master," to be considered as one who is above the common herd, to impress others by lavish display, and so on.

The mind that seeks for mastery over others is the competitive mind; and the competitive mind is not the creative one. In order to master your environment and your destiny, it is not at all necessary that you should rule over your fellow men and indeed, when you fall into the world's struggle for the high places, you begin to be conquered by fate and environment, and your getting rich becomes a matter of chance and speculation.

Beware of the competitive mind!! No better statement of the principle of creative action can be formulated than the favorite declaration of the late "Golden Rule" Jones of Toledo: "What I want for myself, I want for everybody."

Chapter 15

The Advancing Man

WHAT I have said in the last chapter applies as well to the professional man and the wage-earner as to the man who is engaged in mercantile business.

No matter whether you are a physician, a teacher, or a clergyman, if you can give increase of life to others and make them sensible of the fact, they will be attracted to you, and you will get rich. The physician who holds the vision of himself as a great and successful healer, and who works toward the complete realization of that vision with faith and purpose, as described in former chapters, will come into such close touch with the Source of Life that he will be phenomenally successful; patients will come to him in throngs.

No one has a greater opportunity to carry into effect the teaching of this book than the practitioner of medicine; it does not matter to which of the various schools he may belong, for the principle of healing is common to all of them, and may be reached by all alike. The Advancing Man in medicine, who holds to a clear mental image of himself as successful, and who obeys the laws of faith, purpose, and gratitude, will cure every curable case he undertakes, no matter what remedies he may use.

In the field of religion, the world cries out for the clergyman who can teach his hearers the true science of abundant life. He who masters the details of the science of getting rich, together with the allied sciences of being well, of being great, and of winning love, and who teaches these details from the pulpit, will never lack for a congregation. This is the gospel that the world needs; it will give increase of life, and men will hear it gladly, and will give liberal support to the man who brings it to them.

What is now needed is a demonstration of the science of life from the pulpit. We want preachers who can not only tell us how, but who in their own persons will show us how. We need the preacher who will himself be rich, healthy, great, and beloved, to teach us how to attain to these things; and when he comes he will find a numerous and loyal following.

The same is true of the teacher who can inspire the children with the faith and purpose of the advancing life. He will never be "out of a job." And any teacher who has this faith and purpose can give it to his pupils; he cannot help giving it to them if it is part of his own life and practice.

What is true of the teacher, preacher, and physician is true of the lawyer, dentist, real estate man, insurance agent . . of everybody.

The combined mental and personal action I have described is infallible; it cannot fail. Every man and woman who follows these instructions steadily, perseveringly, and to the letter, will get rich. The law of the Increase of Life is as mathematically certain in its operation as the law of gravitation; getting rich is an exact science.

The wage-earner will find this as true of his case as of any of the others mentioned. Do not feel that you have no chance to get rich because you are working where there is no visible opportunity for advancement, where wages are small and the cost of living high. Form your clear mental vision of what you want, and begin to act with faith and purpose.

Do all the work you can do, every day, and do each piece of work in a perfectly successful manner; put the power of success, and the purpose to get rich, into everything that you do.

But do not do this merely with the idea of currying favor with your employer, in the hope that he, or those above you, will see your good work and advance you; it is not likely that they will do so.

The man who is merely a "good" workman, filling his place to the very best of his ability, and satisfied with that, is valuable to his employer; and it is not to the employer's interest to promote him; he is worth more where he is.

To secure advancement, something more is necessary than to be too large for your place.

The man who is certain to advance is the one who is too big for his place, and who has a clear concept of what he wants to be; who knows that he can become what he wants to be and who is determined to BE what he wants to be.

Do not try to more than fill your present place with a view to pleasing your employer; do it with the idea of advancing yourself. Hold the faith and purpose of increase during work hours, after work hours, and before work hours. Hold it in such a way that every person who comes in contact with you, whether foreman, fellow workman, or social acquaintance, will feel the power of purpose radiating from you; so that everyone will get the sense of advancement and increase from you. Men will be attracted to you, and if there is no possibility for advancement in your present job, you will very soon see an opportunity to take another job. There is a Power which never fails to present opportunity to the Advancing Man who is moving in obedience to law.

God cannot help helping you, if you act in a Certain Way; He must do so in order to help Himself.

There is nothing in your circumstances or in the industrial situation that can keep you down. If you cannot get rich working for the steel trust, you can get rich on a ten-acre farm; and if you begin to move in the Certain Way, you will certainly escape from the "clutches" of the steel trust and get on to the farm or wherever else you wish to be.

If a few thousands of its employees would enter upon the Certain Way, the steel trust would soon be in a bad plight; it would have to give its workingmen more opportunity, or go out of business. Nobody has to work for a trust; the trusts can keep men in so called hopeless conditions only so long as there are men who are too ignorant to know of the science of getting rich, or too intellectually slothful to practice it.

Begin this way of thinking and acting, and your faith and purpose will make you quick to see any opportunity to better your condition.

Such opportunities will speedily come, for the Supreme, working in All, and working for you, will bring them before you.

Do not wait for an opportunity to be all that you want to be; when an opportunity to be more than you are now is presented and you feel impelled toward it, take it. It will be the first step toward a greater opportunity.

There is no such thing possible in this universe as a lack of opportunities for the man who is living the advancing life.

It is inherent in the constitution of the cosmos that all things shall be for him and work together for his good; and he must certainly get rich if he acts and thinks in the Certain Way. So let wage-earning men and women study this book with great care, and enter with confidence upon the course of action it prescribes; it will not fail.

Chapter 16

Some Cautions and Concluding Observations

MANY people will scoff at the idea that there is an exact science of getting rich; holding the impression that the supply of wealth is limited, they will insist that social and governmental institutions must be changed before even any considerable number of people can acquire a competence.

But this is not true.

It is true that existing governments keep the masses in poverty, but this is because the masses do not think and act in the Certain Way.

If the masses begin to move forward as suggested in this book, neither governments nor industrial systems can check them; all systems must be modified to accommodate the forward movement.

If the people have the Advancing Mind, have the Faith that they can become rich, and move forward with the fixed purpose to become rich, nothing can possibly keep them in poverty.

Individuals may enter upon the Certain Way at any time, and under any government, and make themselves rich; and when any considerable number of individuals do so under any government, they will cause the system to be so modified as to open the way for others.

The more men who get rich on the competitive plane, the worse for others; the more who get rich on the creative plane, the better for others.

The economic salvation of the masses can only be accomplished by getting a large number of people to practice the scientific method set down in this book, and become rich. These will show others the way, and inspire them with a desire for real life, with the faith that it can be attained, and with the purpose to attain it.

For the present, however, it is enough to know that neither the government under which you live nor the capitalistic or competitive system of industry can keep you from getting rich. When you enter upon the creative plane of thought you will rise above all these things and become a citizen of another kingdom.

But remember that your thought must be held upon the creative plane; you are never for an instant to be betrayed into regarding the supply as limited, or into acting on the moral level of competition.

Whenever you do fall into old ways of thought, correct yourself instantly; for when you are in the competitive mind, you have lost the cooperation of the Mind of the Whole.

Do not spend any time in planning as to how you will meet possible emergencies in the future, except as the necessary policies may affect your actions today. You are concerned with doing today's work in a perfectly successful manner, and not with emergencies which may arise tomorrow; you can attend to them as they come.

Do not concern yourself with questions as to how you shall surmount obstacles which may loom upon your business horizon, unless you can see plainly that your course must be altered today in order to avoid them.

No matter how tremendous an obstruction may appear at a distance, you will find that if you go on in the Certain Way it will disappear as you approach it, or that a way over, though, or around it will appear.

No possible combination of circumstances can defeat a man or woman who is proceeding to get rich along strictly scientific lines. No man or woman who obeys the law can fail to get rich, any more than one can multiply two by two and fail to get four.

Give no anxious thought to possible disasters, obstacles, panics, or unfavorable combinations of circumstances; it is time enough to meet such things when they present themselves before you in the immediate present, and you will find that every difficulty carries with it the wherewithal for its overcoming.

Guard your speech. Never speak of yourself, your affairs, or of anything else in a discouraged or discouraging way.

Never admit the possibility of failure, or speak in a way that infers failure as a possibility.

Never speak of the times as being hard, or of business conditions as being doubtful. Times may be hard and business doubtful for those who are on the competitive plane, but they can never be so for you; you can create what you want, and you are above fear.

When others are having hard times and poor business, you will find your greatest opportunities.

Train yourself to think of and to look upon the world as a something which is Becoming, which is growing; and to regard seeming evil as being only that which is undeveloped.

Always speak in terms of advancement; to do otherwise is to deny your faith, and to deny your faith is to lose it.

Never allow yourself to feel disappointed. You may expect to have a certain thing at a certain time, and not get it at that time; and this will appear to you like failure.

But if you hold to your faith you will find that the failure is only apparent.

Go on in the certain way, and if you do not receive that thing, you will receive something so much better that you will see that the seeming failure was really a great success.

A student of this science had set his mind on making a certain business combination which seemed to him at the time to be very desirable, and he worked for some, weeks to bring it about. When the crucial time came, the thing failed in a perfectly inexplicable way; it was as if some unseen influence had been working secretly against him. He was not disappointed; on the contrary, he thanked God that his desire had been overruled, and went steadily on with a grateful mind. In a few weeks an opportunity so much better came his way that he would not have made the first deal on any account; and he saw that a Mind which knew more than he knew had prevented him from losing the greater good by entangling himself with the lesser.

That is the way every seeming failure will work out for you, if you keep your faith, hold to your purpose, have gratitude, and do, every day, all that can be done that day, doing each separate act in a successful manner.

When you make a failure, it is because you have not asked for enough; keep on, and a larger thing then you were seeking will certainly come to you. Remember this.

You will not fail because you lack the necessary talent to do what you wish to do. If you go on as I have directed, you will develop all the talent that is necessary to the doing of your work.

It is not within the scope of this book to deal with the science of cultivating talent; but it is as certain and simple as the process of getting rich.

However, do not hesitate or waver for fear that when you come to any certain place you will fail for lack of ability; keep right on, and when you come to that place, the ability will be furnished to you. The same source of Ability which enabled the untaught Lincoln to do the greatest work in government ever accomplished by a single man is open to you; you may draw upon all the mind there is for wisdom to use in meeting the responsibilities which are laid upon you. Go on in full faith.

Study this book. Make it your constant companion until you have mastered all the ideas contained in it. While you are getting firmly established in this faith, you will do well to give up most recreations and pleasure; and to stay away from places where ideas conflicting with these are advanced in lectures or sermons. Do not read pessimistic or conflicting literature, or get into arguments upon the matter. Do very little reading, outside of the writers mentioned in the Preface. Spend most of your leisure time in contemplating your vision, and in cultivating gratitude, and in reading this book. It contains all you need to know of the science of getting rich; and you will find all the essentials summed up in the following chapter.

Chapter 17

Summary of the Science of Getting Rich

THERE is a thinking stuff from which all things are made, and which, in its original state, permeates, penetrates, and fills the interspaces of the universe.

A thought in this substance produces the thing that is imaged by the thought.

Man can form things in his thought, and by impressing his thought upon formless substance can cause the thing he thinks about to be created.

In order to do this, man must pass from the competitive to the creative mind; otherwise he cannot be in harmony with the Formless Intelligence, which is always creative and never competitive in spirit.

Man may come into full harmony with the Formless Substance by entertaining a lively and sincere gratitude for the blessings it bestows upon him. Gratitude unifies the mind of man with the intelligence of Substance, so that man's thoughts are received by the Formless. Man can remain upon the creative plane only by uniting himself with the Formless Intelligence through a deep and continuous feeling of gratitude.

Man must form a clear and definite mental image of the things he wishes to have, to do, or to become; and he must hold this mental image in his thoughts, while being deeply grateful to the Supreme that all his desires are granted to him. The man who wishes to get rich must spend his leisure hours in contemplating his Vision, and in earnest thanksgiving that the reality is being given to him. Too much stress cannot be laid on the importance of frequent contemplation of the mental image, coupled with unwavering faith and devout gratitude. This is the process by which the impression is given to the Formless, and the creative forces set in motion.

The creative energy works through the established channels of natural growth, and of the industrial and social order. All that is included in his mental image will surely be brought to the man who follows the instructions given above, and whose faith does not waver. What he wants will come to him through the ways of established trade and commerce.

In order to receive his own when it shall come to him, man must be active; and this activity can only consist in more than filling his present place. He must keep in mind the Purpose to get rich through the realization of his mental image. And he must do, every day, all that can be done that day, taking care to do each act in a successful manner. He must give to every man a use value in excess of the cash value he receives, so that each transaction makes for more life; and he must so hold the Advancing Thought that the impression of increase will be communicated to all with whom he comes in contact.

The men and women who practice the foregoing instructions will certainly get rich; and the riches they receive will be in exact proportion to the definiteness of their vision, the fixity of their purpose, the steadiness of their faith, and the depth of their gratitude.

Suggested Reading

Robert Collier - "The Secret of the Ages"

Robert Collier - "The Secret of Gold"

Napoleon Hill - "Think and Grow Rich"

Annie Rix Militz - Prosperity Through the Knowledge and Power of Mind

Joseph Murphy - Your Infinite Power to Be Rich

Anthony Norvell - Money Magnetism - How to Grow Rich Beyond Your Wildest Dreams

Franklyn Hobbs - The Secret of Wealth

Benjamin Franklin - The Way to Wealth

Julia Seton Sears M.D. - The Key to Health, Wealth and Love

Charles Fillmore - Prosperity

John Seaman Garns - Prosperity Plus

Franklin Fillmore Farrington - Realizing Prosperity

Florence Barnard - The Prosperity Book

James Allen - Eight Pillars of Prosperity

Bernard C. Ruggles - Creative Abundance; The Psychology of Ability and Plenty

David Allen - The Power of I AM (2014), The Power of I AM - Volume 2 (2015) , The Power of I AM - Volume 3 (2017)

David Allen - The Creative Power of Thought, Man's Greatest Discovery (2017)

David Allen - The Secrets, Mysteries & Powers of The Subconscious Mind (2017)

David Allen - The Money Bible - The Secrets of Attracting Prosperity (2017)

David Allen - Your Faith Is Your Fortune, Your Unlimited Power

The Neville Goddard Collection (All 10 of his books plus 2 Lecture series) (2016)

Neville Goddard - Assumptions Harden Into Facts: The Book (2016)

Neville Goddard - Imagination: The Redemptive Power in Man (2016)

Neville Goddard - The World is At Your Command - The Very Best of Neville Goddard (2017)

Neville Goddard - Imagining Creates Reality - 365 Mystical Daily Quotes (2017)

Neville Goddard's Interpretation of Scripture (2018)

The Definitive Christian D. Larson Collection (6 Volumes, 30 books) (2014)

www.ingramcontent.com/pod-product-compliance
Lightning Source LLC
Chambersburg PA
CBHW021111300426
44113CB00006B/115